Islamic Banking

Islamic Banking

Mervyn K. Lewis

National Australia Bank Professor
School of International Business
University of South Australia, Adelaide, Australia

Latifa M. Algaoud

Chief of Training and Development
Ministry of Finance and National Economy
State of Bahrain

Edward Elgar
Cheltenham, UK • Northampton MA, USA

Published by
Edward Elgar Publishing Limited
Glensanda House
Montpellier Parade
Cheltenham
Glos GL50 1UA
UK

Edward Elgar Publishing, Inc.
136 West Street
Suite 202
Northampton
Massachusetts 01060
USA

A catalogue record for this book
is available from the British Library

Library of Congress Cataloguing in Publication Data

Lewis, Mervyn.
    Islamic Banking / Mervyn Lewis, Latifa M. Algaoud.
        p. cm.
    Includes bibliographical references and index.
        1. Banks and banking — Islamic countries. 2. Banks and banking — Religious aspects — Islam. 3. Banking law (Islamic law) I. Algaoud, Latifa M., 1956- II. Title

HG3368.A6 L49 2001
332.1'0917'671 — dc21

2001023004

ISBN 1 85898 808 X (cased)
Printed and bound in Great Britain by MPG Books Ltd, Bodmin, Cornwall

Contents

List of figures   vi
List of tables   vii
Foreword   viii
Glossary   x

1   An introduction to Islamic banking   1
2   Islamic law   16
3   The basis of Islamic banking   34
4   Islamic banking and financial intermediation   62
5   Islamic financial systems   88
6   Islamic banking in mixed systems   119
7   Corporate governance in Islamic banking   158
8   Islamic and Christian attitudes to usury   185
9   Directions in Islamic finance   211
10   Conclusion   240

References   247
Index   267

Figures

3.1	*Musharaka* long-term financing	50
3.2	Trade finance through *Murabaha*	54
5.1	Sudanese Islamic Bank, Rural Development Department Agricultural Financing Model	106
6.1	Corporate structure of the Dar Al-Maal Al-Islami Trust Group	136
7.1	A taxonomy of corporate governance	161
7.2	Key stakeholders in an Islamic bank	164
7.3	Corporate governance in an Islamic bank	169
7.4	*Shari'a* supervision in three banks	180
9.1	Structure of an individual *Takaful* life policy	218

Tables

1.1 Islamic financial institutions   8
1.2 Profile of Islamic banks, 1997   12
5.1 Islamic Republic of Iran: modes of permissible transactions
    corresponding to types of economic activity   101
5.2 Islamic financing modes employed by banks in the Islamic
    Republic of Iran, 1995–98 (per cent of total credit facilities)   102
5.3 Possible modes of financing for various transactions in Pakistan   112
6.1 Establishment of Islamic banks and financial institutions, 1963–99   122
6.2 A comparison of the deposit structure of FIBE and BIMB, 1985–86   129
6.3 A comparison of the lending operations of FIBE and BIMB,
    1985–86   130
6.4 Term structure of investments by 20 Islamic banks, 1988   131
6.5 Financing instruments of Islamic banks, by region, 1997   134
6.6 Financing instruments of DMI group institutions, 1997   137
6.7 Deposit structure of Bank Islam Malaysia Berhad, 1994–96   139
6.8 Financing operations of Bank Islam Malaysia Berhad, 1994–96   140
6.9 Financing modes of Islamic banks in Bangladesh, 1997   143
6.10 Financing operations of Jordan Islamic Bank, 1994–95   144
6.11 Balance sheet of Muslim Community Cooperative (Australia) Ltd,
     1998–99   145
7.1 Comparison of financial position of Faisal Islamic Bank, Bahrain
    Islamic Bank and Al-Baraka Investment Bank, 1997   173
7.2 Geographic distribution and industry distribution of assets and
    liabilities of Faisal Islamic Bank and Bahrain Islamic Bank 1997   174
7.3 Return on equity (ROE) of selected banks   176
9.1 *Takaful* (Islamic insurance) institutions in operation, 1999   212
9.2 Range of investment banking activities   225

Foreword

It is usual to begin a book by explaining how it came to be written and, in the case of jointly authored works, how the authors came to form a team. The latter seems particularly pertinent, since one is an academic in Australia and the other a government official in Bahrain. In fact, the common ground was provided by the MBA programme at the University of Nottingham in 1996, although it soon became apparent that for this particular topic the roles of teacher and student might have to be reversed. It also seemed when we began to work together that we could bring a distinctive Arabic–Western perspective to a subject that is usually approached from one viewpoint alone.

In keeping with this East–West approach, we have adopted a number of stylistic conventions. First, while we have for the most part preferred to use Arabic terms, for example, '*ijara*' rather than 'leasing', we have adopted a minimalist form when transliterating the Arabic words, doing away with most of the diacritical marks that seem baffling to most Western eyes. A glossary of Arabic words is provided. Second, we have followed Common Era datings, rather than giving dates from the Muslim calendar (AH *anno Hegirae*, 'from the year of the *hijra*' in 622 CE, when the Muslim calendar begins). Third, when Muslims mention the Prophet Muhammad in speech or print, they usually follow the name with an expression in Arabic which can be translated, 'May the peace and blessings of Allah be upon him', sometimes written as 'pbuh', short for 'peace be upon him'. We use the full salutation whenever the Prophet is first mentioned in any chapter and the abbreviation 'pbuh' thereafter.

A word of explanation is needed about the title we have chosen. When the subject matter first began to be written about, it was common to use the terms 'Islamic banks' and 'Islamic banking'. Nowadays, it has become fashionable to talk of Islamic finance and Islamic financial institutions, reflecting in part the shift - evident in Western markets as well as Islamic ones - away from what used to be banking activities to financing activities more generally previously carried out by investment banks and assorted non-banking inter-mediaries. Nevertheless, so long as this wider agenda is recognised, we prefer the simplicity of the original terms.

In the course of preparing this volume, we have been assisted in a number of ways. In the State of Bahrain, the Bahrain Islamic Bank, Faisal Islamic Bank of Bahrain (now operating under the name Shamil Bank of Bahrain) and

Al-Baraka Islamic Investment Bank are thanked for their generous cooperation and assistance with this study. The authors are particularly grateful to Mr Abdullrahman Muhammed of the Ministry of Finance and National Economy for his help with the first set of structured interviews with Bahraini banks. Special thanks go to Sheikh Nizam Yaquby, Shari'a Adviser, Takaful International, Bahrain who very kindly read a number of chapters and suggested some important improvements.

In Australia, a number of people have lent assistance. The Muslim Community Cooperative (Australia) Ltd willingly provided details of their operations. Mrs Judy Melbourne has cheerfully borne the brunt of preparing the manuscript. Zafar Iqbal has kindly commented in detail on the manuscript and provided valuable guidance on a number of issues. Staff at the Inter-Library Loans Section of the University of South Australia have diligently tracked down a number of difficult-to-obtain references. Karlos Knapp kept us informed about developments in Indonesia.

Finally, we thank our publishers, Edward Elgar Publishing, for their wholehearted support for the project.

Mervyn Lewis
Latifa Algaoud

Glossary

This section explains some Arabic words and terms occurring in the study.

Allah is Arabic for God.

Al-wadiah is safe keeping (see *Wadia*).

Amana is trust; the contract of *amana* gives rise to fiduciary relationships and duties.

Bai bi-thamin ajil is deferred payment sale by instalments.

Bai'muajjal is deferred-payment sale.

Bai'salam is pre-paid purchase.

Bay (*bai*) is a comprehensive term that applies to sale transactions, exchange.

Bayt al-mal means house of wealth. It is a medieval financial institution aimed at managing the monetary activities of the 'Islamic state' and can be regarded as a public treasury.

Bida refers to innovation, deviation from Islamic tradition.

Fatawa (sing. *fatwa*) are legal decisions or opinions rendered by a qualified religious leader (*mufti*).

Fiqh is Islamic jurisprudence, the science of religious law, which is the interpretation of the Sacred Law, *shari'a*.

Fuqaha (sing. *faqih*) are Muslim jurisprudents who have religious authority.

Gharar is uncertainty, speculation.

Hadîth (plural *ahadith*) is the technical term for the source related to the *Sunna*; the sayings – and doings – of the Prophet (pbuh), his traditions.

Hajj is pilgrimage to Mecca.

Halal means permitted according to the *shari'a*.

Haram means forbidden according to the *shari'a*.

Hiyal (plural of *hila*) are 'permissions' or legal manipulations, evasions.

Ijara contract is a leasing contract.

Ijara wa iqtina is a lease-purchase contract, whereby the client has the option of purchasing the item.

Ijma means consensus among jurists based on the Holy Qur'an and *sunna*, and one of the four sources of law in Sunni Islam.

Ijtihad means the act of independent reasoning by a qualified jurist in order to reach new legal rules.

Islam is submission or surrender to the will of God.

Iman means faith, and is commonly used as a title for significant religious leaders.

Istisnaa is a contract to manufacture.

Ju'alah is the stipulated price (commission) for performing any service.

Maysir means gambling, from a pre-Islamic game of hazard.

Mudaraba contract is a trustee financing contract, where one party, the financier, entrusts funds to the other party, the entrepreneur, for undertaking an activity.

Mudaraba al-muqayada refers to limited trustee financing.

Mudaraba al-mutlaqa refers to absolute trustee financing.

Mudarib means an entrepreneur or a manager of a *mudaraba* project.

Mufti is a jurist who is authorised to issue a *fatwa* or legal decision on a religious matter.

Murabaha is resale with a stated profit, for example the bank purchases a certain asset and sells it to the client on the basis of a cost plus mark-up profit principle.

Musaqah is a contract for the lease of agricultural land with profit-sharing.

Musharaka contract is an equity participation contract, whereby two or more partners contribute with funds to carry out an investment.

Muslim is one who professes the faith of Islam or is born to a Muslim family.

Muzarah is an agricultural contract where the landlord provides seed, land and plants, and the worker provides labour.

Nisab is the minimum acceptable standard of living.

Qard hasan is a benevolent loan (interest free).

Qiyas means analogical deduction.

Qur'an is the Holy Book, the revealed word of God, followed by all Muslims.

Rabb al-mal refers to the owner of capital or financier in a *mudaraba* partnership agreement (also *sahib al-mal*).

Riba is literally 'excess' or 'increase', and covers both interest and usury.

Shari'a is Islamic religious law derived from the Holy Qur'an and the *sunna*.

Shirkah (or *sharika*) is a society or partnership.

Shi'ite comes from the religio-political party championing the claims of 'Ali ibn abi Talib and his heirs to the rightful leadership of the community and to their status as Imams. Since the beginning of the sixteenth century, Shi'ism has been the official state religion of Iran and most of its followers live there. They comprise about 10 per cent of the world population of Muslims.

Sunna is a source of information concerning the practices of the Prophet Muhammad (pbuh) and his Companions, and is the second most authoritative source of Islamic law.

Sunnis constitute the majority form of Islam, those who follow the *sunna* (thus being called the *ahl al-sunna*), who do not recognise the authority of the Shi'ite Imams.

Sura (pl. *surat)* is a chapter of the Holy Qur'an. There are 114 *suras* of varying length and in all references to the Holy Qur'an (for example 30:39) the first number refers to the *sura* and the second to the *aya* or verse.

Takaful refers to mutual support which is the basis of the concept of insurance or solidarity among Muslims.

'Ulama' are the learned class, especially those learned in religious matters.

Umma means the community; the body of Muslims.

Wadia means safe custody or deposit.

Waqf is a trust or pious foundation.

Zakat is a religious levy or almsgiving as required in the Holy Qur'an and is one of Islam's five pillars.

1.   An introduction to Islamic banking

OUTLINE OF THIS BOOK

Twenty-five years ago Islamic banking was virtually unknown. Now 55 developing and emerging market countries have some involvement with Islamic banking and finance.[1] In addition, there are Islamic financial institutions operating in 13 other locations: Australia, Bahamas, Canada, Cayman Islands, Denmark, Guernsey, Jersey, Ireland, Luxembourg, Switzerland, United Kingdom, United States and the Virgin Islands. In Pakistan, Iran and Sudan, all banks need to operate under Islamic financing principles. Elsewhere, in the mixed systems, the Islamic banks are in a minority and operate alongside conventional banks. Despite this expansion, Islamic banking remains poorly understood in many parts of the Muslim world and still continues to be almost an enigma in much of the West. Our objective is to provide a succinct analysis of the nature of Islamic banking and finance, accessible to a wide range of readers.

In fact, the basic idea of Islamic banking can be stated simply. The operations of Islamic financial institutions primarily are based on a profit-and-loss-sharing (PLS) principle. An Islamic bank does not charge interest but rather participates in the yield resulting from the use of funds. The depositors also share in the profits of the bank according to a predetermined ratio. There is thus a partnership between the Islamic bank and its depositors, on one side, and between the bank and its investment clients, on the other side, as a manager of depositors' resources in productive uses. This is in contrast with a conventional bank which mainly borrows funds at interest on one side of the balance sheet and lends funds at interest on the other. The complexity of Islamic banking comes from the variety (and nomenclature) of the instruments employed, and in understanding the underpinnings of Islamic law.

In conducting this examination of the subject, the volume seeks to bring a different perspective on a number of aspects. First, in the analytical part of this study, there is an outline of the prohibition of interest (*riba*) according to the doctrines of Islamic economics, along with an analysis of the implications which follow from this ban for the character of financial intermediation and governance structures in Islamic financing. This analysis is undertaken against the backdrop of modern theories of financial intermediation which are concerned with transactions costs, information problems and the design of

1

incentive-compatible contracts. There is thus an attempt to integrate the Western-based literature with that developed in the Islamic tradition.

Second, the empirical aspect of the study deals with the workings of Islamic banks in both complete and mixed systems. Consideration is given to both the legal and institutional structure needed to support Islamic banking operations and the problems which have been encountered in putting the theory of Islamic banking into practice. The latter are often overlooked in criticisms of actual operations by Islamic scholars, while the former shape the special systems of corporate governance followed by Islamic banks.

Third, the book brings an historical dimension to the topic, for Islam is not the only (or indeed the first) religion to ban interest. In particular, Christianity maintained a prohibition (or severe restriction) for over 1400 years. What were the origins of the Christian stand and how was it enforced? Why has Islam succeeded where Christianity failed? The answers we provide to these questions shed an important new light on the achievements of Islamic banking methods, while at the same time revealing a number of interesting parallels with present day Islamic financing techniques.

WHAT IS ISLAMIC BANKING?

Islamic banking provides services to its customers free from interest, and the giving and taking of interest is prohibited in all transactions. Islam bans Muslims from taking or giving interest (the Arabic term for which is *riba*), and this prohibition makes an Islamic banking system differ fundamentally from a conventional banking system. Technically, *riba* refers to the addition in the amount of the principal of a loan according to the time for which it is loaned and the amount of the loan. While earlier there was a debate as to whether *riba* relates to interest or usury, there now appears to be consensus of opinion among Islamic scholars that the term extends to all forms of interest.

Later chapters explore in more detail the origins of the terms 'interest' and 'usury', and the way in which in Western usage the meanings have been transposed over time, so that the former meaning of usury and the present meaning of interest are practically identical (Divine, 1967). Usury (from the Latin *usura* meaning enjoyment, interest or money paid for the use of money) was a term originally used to describe interest generally, but in modern times has come to mean excessive interest, particularly that in excess of maximum rates fixed by law (Munn, Garcia and Woelfel, 1991). Some Islamic modernist views have contended that *riba* refers to usury practised by petty moneylenders and not to interest charged by modern banks and that no *riba* is involved when interest is imposed on productive loans. But these arguments have not won general acceptance amongst Muslim writers.

In any case, it is doubtful if the distinction between interest and usury matters to the orthodox Muslim. The term *riba*, in Islamic law (the *shari'a*), means an addition, however slight, over and above the principal. According to the Federal Shariat Court of Pakistan, this means that the concept covers both usury and interest; that it is not restricted to doubled and redoubled interest; that it applies to all forms of interest, whether large or small, simple or compound, doubled or redoubled; and that the Islamic injunction is not only against exorbitant or excessive interest, but also against a minimal rate of interest (Hamid, 1992; M.S. Khan and Mirakhor, 1992). Financial systems based on Islamic tenets are therefore dedicated to the elimination of the payment and receipt of interest in all forms. It is this taboo that makes Islamic banks and other financial institutions different in principle from their Western counterparts.

Some scholars have put forward economic reasons to explain why interest is banned in Islam. It has been argued, for instance, that interest, being a predetermined cost of production, tends to prevent full employment (M.A. Khan, 1968; Ahmad, 1952; Mannan, [1970]1986). In the same vein, it has been contended that international monetary crises are largely due to the institution of interest (M.A. Khan, 1968), and that business cycles can in some measure be attributed to the phenomenon of interest (Ahmad, 1952; Su'ud, 1980). Others have taken a somewhat different tack by arguing that modern economic theory has not provided a justification for the existence of, or the need for, interest (Khan and Mirakhor, 1992).

But these arguments are strictly secondary to the religious underpinnings. The fundamental sources of Islam are the Holy Qur'an and the *sunna*, a term which in Ancient Arabia meant 'ancestral precedent' or the 'custom of the tribe', but which is now synonymous with the teachings and traditions of the Prophet Muhammad (may God bless him and grant him salvation) as transmitted by the relators of authentic tradition. Both of these sources treat interest as an act of exploitation and injustice and as such it is inconsistent with Islamic notions of fairness and property rights. While it is often claimed that there is more to Islamic banking, such as it contributing towards economic development and a more equitable distribution of income and wealth, and increased equity participation in the economy (Chapra, 1982), Islamic banking nevertheless derives its specific *raison d'être* from the fact that there is no place for the institution of interest in the Islamic order.

This rejection of interest poses the question of what replaces the interest rate mechanism in an Islamic framework. If the paying and receiving of interest is prohibited, how do Islamic banks operate? Here PLS comes in, substituting profit-and-loss-sharing for interest as a method of resource allocation. Although a large number of different contracts feature in Islamic financing, certain types of transaction are central: trustee finance (*mudaraba*); equity participation (*musharaka*); and 'mark-up' methods. *Mudaraba*[2] is a profit- and risk-sharing contract where one party entrusts funds to an investor in return for a predetermined share in the profit/loss outcome of the project concerned. This principle lies at the heart of the system of Islamic banking since most funds are provided to an Islamic bank under such arrangements. Under *musharaka,* on the other hand, there is usually more than one single contributor of funds; all of the parties invest in varying proportions and the profits or the losses are shared according to their contributions in the project. The *musharaka* involves a more active partnership between entities who pool their capital and manage and control the enterprise together, with profits and losses divided amongst them according to a prearranged ratio. When we add to these two the idea of 'mark-up', for which there are a great number of variants, where assets and other items are acquired for later resale or lease with a mark-up on purchase price, we have the main ingredients of the Islamic alternatives to having banks borrow and lend at interest.

A BRIEF HISTORY

Profit-sharing arrangements such as *mudaraba* and *musharaka* almost certainly pre-date the genesis of Islam. Business partnerships based on what was in essence the *mudaraba* concept co-existed in the pre-Islamic Middle East along with interest loans as a means of financing economic activities (Crone, 1987; Kazarian, 1991; Cizaka, 1995). Following the birth of Islam, interest-based financial transactions were forbidden and all finance had to be conducted on a profit-sharing basis. The business partnership technique, utilizing the *mudaraba* principle, was employed by the Prophet Muhammad (pbuh) himself when acting as agent (*mudarib*) for his wife Khadija, while his second successor Umar ibn al-Khattab invested the money of orphans with merchants engaged in trade between Medina and Iraq. Simple profit-sharing business partnerships of this type continued in virtually unchanged form over the centuries, but they did not develop into vehicles for large-scale investment involving the collection of large amounts of funds from large numbers of individual savers – notwithstanding that it was usually legally possible under the law of partnership developed by the Hanefite legal school to expand *mudaraba* partnerships along such lines. This development did not happen until the growth of Islamic financial institutions.

The first known financial institution established by a Muslim community was created about ten years after the death in 632 CE of the Prophet Muhammad (pbuh) by the second Calipha (prince) Umar.[3] The expansion of the Arab nation that began shortly after the Prophet Muhammad's (pbuh) death under Calipha Abu Bakr (the Prophet's (pbuh) father-in-law) was fuelled by the sense of unity, common purpose and self-confidence produced by Islam. Nevertheless, the Bedouin warriors' love of war and booty had not been entirely transcended and something had to be done about the distribution of the prizes of battle. Despite his armies' triumphal defeat of the established empires of Byzantium and Persia, the two principal powers of the region, Umar retained the austerity and simplicity of his early life and had a strong moral purpose. All needy members of the Islamic state were to be allocated (according to specified criteria) an annual pension from the spoils of conquest and imperial revenue. The institution established, *diwan*, was inspired and adopted from the Persian bureaucracy, and aimed at registering all members of the community in order to facilitate the distribution of the acquired wealth (*ata*). The common funds acquired from the conquered territories were kept in a so-called house of wealth, *bayt al-mal*, which is a combination of the institution of *ata* and the institution of *diwan* (Kazarian, 1991). It was the duty of the leader of the new community to ensure that every individual should be guaranteed a 'fair share' of the wealth. Both Arab and non-Arab Muslims immediately were granted a share in the wealth on an equal basis.

In more recent times, early experiments with Islamic banking took place in Malaya in the mid 1940s, in Pakistan in the late 1950s, via the Indian *Jamā 'at Islāmi* in 1969, Egypt's Mit Ghamr Savings Banks (1963–67), and the Nasser Social Bank (1971). Most institutions had a rural orientation and most were unsuccessful (although not necessarily for that reason). For example, the aim of the Pakistani institution was to extend interest-free credit to the poorer landowners for agricultural purposes and improvements. The bank charged no interest on its lending and its moneyed landowner backers deposited money in this bank and received no interest (*riba*) on their deposits. It can be assumed that a higher standard of agricultural husbandry then led to an expansion of profits for all concerned since the bank's landowner depositors had some say about the way in which loans and advances were extended and to whom. Nevertheless, the bank was disbanded after only a few years, although the debts were mostly cleared by the early 1960s as this bank's debtors gradually met their obligations to the bank (Wilson, 1983, p. 75).

In the Arab world, the first modern experience with Islamic banking was undertaken in Mit Ghamr in Egypt in 1963. The experiment combined the idea of German savings banks with the principles of rural, cooperative banking within the general framework of Islamic financing precepts to cater for those unwilling on religious grounds to use conventional banks. However, the bank was formed under cover, without projecting an Islamic image, for fear of being seen as a manifestation of Islamic fundamentalism, which was anathema to the political regime. The project was closed for political reasons in the second half of 1967 and the operations taken over by the National Bank of Egypt and made interest-based. Nine such banks in the country were taken over. These banks, which neither charged nor paid interest, invested mostly by engaging in trade and industry, directly or in partnership with others, and shared the profits with their depositors, yet were functioning essentially as saving investment institutions rather than as full commercial banks.

It may be noted that similar political antagonism to Islamic banking like that in Egypt has occurred elsewhere in the Muslim world, where Islamic banking sometimes has been distrusted because of presumed associations with Islamic political opposition movements. At various times, Syria, Iraq, Oman and Saudi Arabia have 'discouraged' the formation of new Islamic financial institutions (Henry, 1999b), while populous Muslim countries such as Turkey and Indonesia have been slow to promote the idea. Pakistan has advanced only slowly towards its goal of an interest-free economy.

The only Islamic institutions to survive this early period are the Nasser Social Bank (Egypt) and *Tabung Haji* (Malaysia). The former was created as an interest-free commercial bank in 1971, under the Presidency of Mr Anwar Sadat, operating as a public authority with an autonomous status, but without a specific reference to Islam in its charter. It still exists as a social lending agency to the poor unable to meet unexpected debts, to provide loans to students and for small projects, and functions under the Ministry of Social Affairs and Insurance. The Muslim Pilgrims Savings Corporation was set up in 1963 to help Malaysians save for performing *hajj* (pilgrimage to Mecca and Medina). In 1969, this body evolved into the Pilgrims Management and Fund Board or the *Tabung Haji* as it is now popularly known. The *Tabung Haji* has been acting as a finance company that invests the savings of would-be pilgrims in accordance with Islamic law, but its role is rather limited, as a non-bank financial institution. The success of the *Tabung Haji*, however, provided the main impetus for establishing Bank Islam Malaysia Berhad (BIMB) which is a fully-fledged Islamic commercial bank in Malaysia.

A number of lessons would seem to be suggested by this experience. First, if the concept of Islamic banking was to take hold in a significant way, the institutions needed to provide a full range of commercial banking services, while conforming to Islamic rules and norms, rather than operate as specialised, limited savings institutions. Second, the activities of the banks had to be commercial as opposed to predominantly socio-economic. Some Muslim scholars have sought to force a distinction between an Islamic bank (one which has a socio-economic responsibility) and a *halal* bank, or interest-free bank (the activities of which are strictly commercial but based on interest-free financial products). However, this distinction has not gained support among Islamic jurists. Third, it seemed clear that Islamic financial institutions could not prosper in the face of hostility from government authorities (irrespective of whether this derived from fear of fundamentalism or from catering to the entrenched interests of conventional banks).

As it turned out, an extraneous event intervened to bring about these pre-conditions. Arab oil wealth in the wake of the 1973–74 energy price rises provided the financial capital base needed to support large-scale commercial banking while creating a target market from amongst its recipients broad enough to support an expansion of conventional and Islamic banks alike. Oil resources enabled a wide range of institutions to participate in the social and economic development of Muslim countries, while facilitating a resurgence in self-confidence in the Middle East. The result was a change in the political climate in many Muslim countries so that there was no longer the need to establish Islamic financial institutions under cover. Almost all of the major Islamic banks and banking groups formed in the 1970s were funded to a large extent from oil-linked wealth.

GROWTH IN RECENT DECADES

Since the mid 1970s, Islamic banking has expanded so that at present there are nearly 70 countries encompassing most of the Muslim world, which have some form of Islamic financial institutions operating. Table 1.1 shows some of these countries and the institutions involved.

How many Islamic financial institutions are there in operation? Justice Mufti Usmani in 1998 estimated there to be 200 Islamic banks and financial institutions in 43 countries of the world, controlling a financial pool of US$100 billion.[4] All of these figures are in fact considerable underestimates for reasons given below.

An obvious starting point is Table 1.2. This is based on the 176 banks which report financial data to the International Association of Islamic Banks (IAIB).[5] The table sets out the number of banks, paid up capital, total deposits and total assets of these Islamic banks, classified by region. It shows that the total assets of these reporting banks amounted to US$148 billion in 1997, with principal operations in terms of the value of deposits and assets in the Middle East, Gulf countries and South Asia.

However, there are some significant omissions from Table 1.2. In terms of assets, the major omissions are the Islamic Development Bank (IDB) and the business groups associated with the two large Islamic groups, DMI and Al-Baraka. The IDB, based in Jeddah, was the first Islamic financial institution to benefit from the inflow of oil-related wealth. Established in 1974 with the support of the Saudi Arabian government and the Organization of Islamic Countries (OIC) it is primarily an intergovernmental bank aimed at providing funds for development projects in member countries. The IDB provides fee-based financial services and profit-sharing financial assistance to member countries. Operations are free of interest and are explicitly based on

Table 1.1.   Islamic financial institutions[1] excluding Iran, Pakistan and Sudan[2] (date of establishment where known)

Country	Islamic Financial Institutions
Albania	Arab Albanian Bank (1992)
Algeria	Banque Al Baraka D'Algerie (1991)
Australia	Muslim Community Cooperative (Aust) (MCCA), Melbourne (1989)
Bahamas	Dar al Mal al Islami Trust, Nassau (1981)
	Islamic Investment Company of the Gulf (1978)
	Masraf Faisal Islamic Bank & Trust, Bahamas Ltd (1982)
Bahrain	ABC Islamic Bank (1985)
	Al-Amin Co. for Securities and Inv. Funds (1987)
	Albaraka Islamic Investment Bank (1984)
	Al Tawfeek Company for Investment Funds (1987)
	Arab Islamic Bank (1990)[3]
	Bahrain Islamic Bank (1979)
	Bahrain Islamic Investment Co. (1981)
	Citi Islamic Investment Bank (1996)
	Faysal Investment Bank of Bahrain (1984)[3]
	Faysal Islamic Bank of Bahrain (1982)
	First Islamic Investment Bank (1996)
	Gulf Finance House (1999)
	Islamic Investment Co. of the Gulf (1983)[3]
	Islamic Leasing Company
Bangladesh	Al-Arafah Islami Bank (1995)
	Albaraka Bank Bangladesh (1987)
	Islamic Bank Bangladesh (1983)
	Prime Bank (1995)
	Social Investment Bank (1995)
Brunei	Perbadanan Tabung Amanah Islam (1991)
	Islamic Bank of Brunei Berhad (1998)
Canada	Islamic Cooperative Housing Corporation, Toronto (1980)
	Qurtaba Housing Society, Montreal
Cayman Islands	Ibn Majid Emerging Marketing Fund (1992)
Côte D'Ivoire	International Trading Company of Africa
Denmark	Islamic Bank International of Denmark, Copenhagen (1983)
Djibouti	Banque Albaraka Djibouti (1989)
Egypt	Alwatany Bank of Egypt (1980), Cairo (One Islamic Branch)

Country	Islamic Financial Institutions
	Arab Investment Bank (Islamic Banking Operations), Cairo
	Bank Misr (Islamic Branches), Cairo (window opened in 1980)
	Faisal Islamic Bank of Egypt, Cairo (1977)
	International Islamic Bank for Investment and Development, Cairo (1980)
	Islamic Investment and Development Company, Cairo (1983)
	Nasir Social Bank, Cairo (1971)
	Egyptian Saudi Finance Bank (1980)
Gambia	Arab Gambian Islamic Bank (1994)
Guernsey	Al-Fahah Investment Company
Guinea	Islamic Investment Company of Guinea, Conakry (1984)
	Masraf Faisal al Islami de Guinea, Conakry (1983)
	Banque Islamique de Guinee (1983)
India	Al-Ameen Financial and Investment Corporation, Bangalore (1985)
	Baitun Nasr Urban Cooperative Society, Bombay
	Albaraka Finance House (1989)
Indonesia	Bank Muamalat Indonesia (1992)
	Bank IFI (*syariah* unit, 1999)
	Bank Syariah Mandiri (1999)
Iraq	Iraqi Islamic Bank for Investment and Development (1993)
Ireland	Al Meezan Commodity Fund, IES, Dublin (1996)
Jersey	The Islamic Investment Company, St Helier
	Masraf Faisal al-Islami (Jersey), St Helier
	Faisal Finance Jersey (1996)
Jordan	Beit El-Mal Saving and Investment Co. (1983)
	Jordan Islamic Bank for Finance and Investment (1978)
	Islamic International Arab Bank (1998)
Kazakhstan	Lariba Bank, Alma Ata (1995)
Kibris (Turkish Cyprus)	Faisal Islamic Bank of Kibris, Lefkosa (1982)
Kuwait	International Investment Group (1993)
	Kuwait Finance House, Safat (1977)
	The International Investor (1992)
Lebanon	Al Baraka Bank Lebanon (1992)

Country	Islamic Financial Institutions
Liberia	African Arabian Islamic Bank, Monrovia
Liechtenstein	Arinco Arab Investment Company, Vaduz
	Islamic Banking System Finance SA, Vaduz
Luxembourg	Islamic Finance House Universal Holding SA (1979)
	Faisal Holding, Luxembourg (1990)
Malaysia	Bank Islam Malaysia Berhad, Kuala Lumpur (1983)
	Tabung Haji (Pilgrims Management and Fund Board), Kuala Lumpur (1963)
	Bank Bumi-Muamalat Malaysia Bhd (1999)
	Malayan Banking Berhad, KL (window 1993)
	United Malayan Banking Corporation Berhad, KL (window 1993)
	Dallah Al Baraka (Malaysia) Holding (1991)
	Adil Islamic Growth Fund, Labuan (1996)
	Arab-Malaysian Merchant Bank Berhad, KL
Mauritania	Al-Baraka Islamic Bank, Mauritania (1985)
Niger	Banque Islamique du Niger (1983)
Nigeria	Habib Nigeria Bank, Kaduna (Islamic windows 1999)
Philippines	Amanah Islamic Investment Bank, Manila (1990)
Qatar	Al-Jazeera Investment Company, Doha (1989)
	Qatar Islamic Bank (SAQ) (1983)
	Qatar International Islamic Bank (1990)
Russia	Badr Bank, Moscow (1998)
Saudi Arabia	Al-Baraka Investment and Development Company, Jeddah (1982)
	Islamic Development Bank, Jeddah (1975)
	Al Rajhi Banking and Investment Corporation (1988)
Senegal	Banque Islamique du Senegal (1983)
South Africa	Albaraka Bank, Durban (1989)
Switzerland	Dar al Mal al Islami Trust, Geneva (1984)
	Faisal Finance (Switzerland) SA (1990)
	Islamic Investment Fund (1985)
	Pan Islamic Consultancy Services Istishara (1991)
Thailand	Arabian Thai Investment Company Ltd, Bangkok
	Bank for Agriculture and Agricultural Cooperatives (30 Islamic branches, 1999)
Tunisia	Bank al Tamwil al Saudi al Tunisi (1983)
Turkey	Al-Baraka Turkish Finance House, Istanbul (1985)
	Faisal Finance Institution, Istanbul (1985)

Country	Islamic Financial Institutions
	Turkish–Kuwaiti Finance House, Istanbul (1989)
	Andalu Finance Kurumu As, Ankara
UAE	Dubai Islamic Bank, Dubai (1975)
	Islamic Investment Company of the Gulf, Sharjah (1977)
	Abu Dhabi Islamic Bank (1977)
UK	Al-Baraka Investment Co., London (1983)
	Al Rajhi Company for Islamic Investment Ltd, London
	ANZ Global Islamic Finance (1989)
	Dallah Albaraka Europe, London (1993)
	Islamic Investment Company, London (1982)
	The International Investor Advisory Group (1992)
United States	Albaraka Bancorp (Chicago) Inc. (1989)
	Albaraka Bancorp (California) Inc. (1987)
	Albaraka Bancorp (Texas) Inc. (1987)
	Al Manzil Islamic Financial Services, New York (1998)
	Amana Income Fund (1994)
Virgin Islands	Ibn Khaldoun International Equity Fund (1996)
Yemen	Saba Islamic Bank (1997)
	Tadhamon Islamic Bank (1996)
	Yemen Islamic Bank for Finance and Investment (1996)

Notes:
1. The list includes Islamic banks as well as Islamic investment companies but it does not include Islamic insurance or *Takaful* companies.
2. All banks in Iran, Pakistan and Sudan operate on a profit-and-loss-sharing basis. There are 10 banks in Iran, 45 banks in Pakistan and 26 banks in Sudan.
3. Faisal Islamic Bank of Bahrain and the Islamic Investment Company of the Gulf (Bahrain), two sister companies of the DMI group, merged in 2000 to form the Shamil Bank of Bahrain (Islamic Bankers), with authorised capital of $500 million and paid up capital of $230 million. Earlier, the Arab Islamic Bank agreed to merge with The Islamic Investment Company of the Gulf.

Sources: Directory of Islamic Banks and Financial Institutions, 1997. Encyclopedia of Islamic Banking and Insurance, 1995. Concise Directory of Islamic Financial Institutions, 1997. *New Horizon* (various issues).

shari'a principles; with capital of two billion Islamic dinárs (the dinár is on a par with the SDR), it is the largest Islamic financial institution. Its present membership comprises 50 countries, but the majority shareownership is held by Saudi Arabia, Kuwait, UAE and Libya. Despite the IDB's multilateral origins, it gave momentum to the Islamic banking movement generally, being followed soon afterwards by both private (for example, Dubai Islamic Bank,

Table 1.2   Profile of Islamic banks, 1997 (no. of institutions and US$ million)

Region	No. of banks	Paid-up capital	Total deposits	Total assets
Middle East	26	3 684	69 076	83 136
Gulf countries (GCC)	21	1 787	14 088	20 449
United States & Europe	9	617	1 139	908
South East Asia	31	149	1 887	2 332
South Asia	51	888	25 665	39 273
Central Asia	2	3	3	5
Africa	35	202	730	1 574
Australia	1	5	n.a.	6
Total	176	7 333	112 589	147 685

Source: The International Association of Islamic Banks.

1975, Faisal Islamic Bank of Egypt, 1977, Bahrain Islamic Bank, 1979) and government institutions (for example, Kuwait Finance House, 1977).

Not all banks created in the early 1970s can be traced to oil wealth. The Philippine Amanah Bank (PAB) was established in 1973 by President Marcos as a specialized banking institution without reference to its Islamic character in the bank's charter. The establishment of the PAB was a response by the Philippines Government to the Muslim rebellion in the south, ostensibly to serve the special banking needs of the Muslim community, but also to assist rehabilitation and reconstruction in Mindanao, Sulu and Palawan in the south (Mastura, 1988). The PAB, however, was not strictly an Islamic bank, since interest-based operations continued to coexist with the Islamic modes of financing and the PAB operated two 'windows' for deposit transactions, that is, conventional and Islamic. Its later failure was because it was seen as a political move rather than a genuine attempt at Islamic banking. Another Islamic bank, Amanah Islamic Investment Bank, was established in 1990.

The next important development in Islamic banking took place in the early 1980s with the formation of the two international Islamic holding companies, namely, the Dar al-Maal al-Islami (DMI) Trust (House of Islamic Funds) in 1981 and the Al-Baraka group in 1982. Founded in the Bahamas and head-quartered in Geneva, DMI operates 10 banks, 7 investment companies, 7 business companies and 3 Islamic (*Takaful*) insurance companies in 15 countries. Dallah Al-Baraka was established in Saudi Arabia, and operates 15 banks and over 2000 other companies, including insurance companies, production companies, research and training centres with activities in 43 countries. Banks associated with Al-Baraka, the larger of the two groups, hold 26 per cent of the assets and 23 per cent of the deposits of private Islamic banks.[6]

While the banks affiliated with the two groups are included in the IAIB statistics, most of the other companies are not. These include the *Takaful* and *Retakaful* (Insurance and Reinsurance) Companies, along with the business and trading companies. They are part of the network of institutions established by the groups in order to provide channels for the utilisation and investment of funds collected by the group banks. For example, DMI collects deposits from its Jeddah office or through its offshore banking unit in Bahrain, which are then funnelled into projects, trading activities and other Islamically-approved investments on a global basis. These companies also allow businessmen and other financial institutions to participate directly in agricultural, commercial, industrial, real estate, leasing and inventory management activities, all in conformity with Islamic financing precepts. Various investment funds have been set up in Bahrain, Luxembourg, Labuan and Jersey to facilitate individual investment of this type in the form of Islamic mutual funds. These developments are examined in later chapters.

In terms of the statistics of numbers of Islamic institutions (although relatively unimportant in terms of assets), IAIB data neglect the many hundreds of financial institutions operating Islamically at the local level. For example, India has no Islamic banks because the Indian Banking Act does not provide for interest-free banking operations. A number of Islamic Investment Companies are registered under the Companies Act of India, including Al-Ameen, Albaraka and Buit-un-Nas'r (for example, Barkat leasing). Nevertheless, there are over 300 Islamic financial institutions operating in India as Islamic cooperative credit societies, Islamic welfare societies, and financial associations ('Baitulmas') in the unorganised financial sector (Bagsiraj, 2000). Indonesia – the most populous Muslim country – has only one general purpose Islamic bank, Bank Muamalat. That has 30 outlets, hardly a large number for a population of 200 million with 250 distinct languages and 300 different ethnic groups scattered over an archipelago 5000 kilometres long. Some of that void is filled by the Bait Al-Maal Wa At-Tumwil (BMT) and *Shari'a* Rural Banks (BPRS). The former are cooperative organisations which focus on small business entities, such as traders and street dealers. In 1998, there were 898 BMTs in Indonesia (Arifin, 1998). Rural banks are limited in their fund-gathering activities but contribute actively in the finance of Muslim business entities in the regions. In 1999, there were 78 Islamic rural banks operating in Indonesia (Karim, 2000). Broadly equivalent types of cooperative institutions and rural-based organisations operate in other countries.

As noted at the beginning of this chapter, this expansion of Islamic banking has basically taken two forms. The first form that the development of Islamic banking has taken involves the restructuring of the whole financial system to accord with Islamic precepts. Three countries where this transformation of the system is underway are Iran, Sudan and Pakistan. In Iran all banks have operated under Islamic law since March 1984 when *riba* (interest) was abolished from banking operations, and profit-sharing techniques substituted. In Sudan, conventional banks were instructed to turn Islamic from July 1984, but the transition was not implemented fully until July 1990 when Islamic scholars were involved in the governance of the banks – an issue emphasised in Chapter 7 below. Pakistan was the first country to move towards full conversion of its financial system, but has adopted a gradualist approach. An Advisory Council of Islamic Ideology was formed under the Constitution of 1962 to advise on the legal and institutional framework for an interest-free economic system. In 1977, the President of Pakistan asked the Council to prepare a blueprint for the transition. Following its recommendations in 1980, profit-and-loss-sharing accounts were introduced in 1981. From July 1985, all commercial banking in rupees was made interest-free, and there is the objective of moving the whole system to this basis in 2001.

The second form has been an attempt to establish Islamic financial institutions side by side with traditional banks. In such mixed systems, the types of institutions which have evolved are Islamic banks created mostly in Muslim countries, and Islamic investment and holding companies operating in some Muslim countries, but mainly in non-Muslim countries. These banks, which neither charge nor pay interest, invest predominantly by engaging in trade and industry, directly or in partnership with others, and sharing the profits with their depositors. In both cases, generally, the banking operations are subject to regulations that apply to all banks.

A number of institutions have located at the international level, outside Muslim countries. DMI (including the Islamic Investment Company of the Gulf) and Al-Baraka are examples, and Al Rajhi Banking and Investment Company of Saudi Arabia is another, the latter having operations in London and Luxembourg. At the same time, banks such as Citibank (USA), ANZ (Australia), ABN Amro (Netherlands), Goldman Sachs (USA), HSBC (UK), Deutsche Bank (Germany), Saudi American Bank (USA–Saudi), Saudi British Bank (UK–Saudi), and Société Generale (France) have Islamic banking units or subsidiaries. Banks such as these have been active in Islamic finance from the beginning of the movement, assisting with the investment of interbank funds (in accordance with Islamic principles) and in arranging lease financing and other appropriate avenues of investment. Otherwise, through their 'Islamic windows' from which they offer their own products, the focus of their attention has been in providing banking services in Islamic countries, even when the windows or Islamic banking units operate in Western locations.[7]

Our examination of the workings of Islamic banking focuses on the two main types of systems, and the study proceeds as follows. Chapter 2 examines the basis of Islamic law and its rulings on financial dealings. Chapter 3 analyses the basic principles of Islamic banking, while Chapter 4 compares these principles with those of conventional banking in the light of the theories of financial intermediation. These two chapters identify the incentive problems in Islamic banking. Chapter 5 examines the legal and other conditions which must be met in order to create an entire financial system based on Islamic principles, and uses the case of Pakistan to illustrate these requirements based on a study of the evolution of Pakistani laws and rulings of the Federal Shariat Court. Chapter 6 looks at the operations of the mixed system, and assesses some of the criticisms of Islamic banks from Islamic scholars. Then the next three chapters, in different ways, consider the success factors shaping the future of the concept. Chapter 7 looks at corporate governance in Islamic banking and the distinctive features of the corporate culture. In marked contrast, Chapter 8 uses historical analogy, asking why Islam has succeeded in keeping the issue of usury alive when other religions, most notably Christianity, failed. Finally, Chapter 9 outlines new directions and innovations in Islamic banking and finance, followed by some conclusions in Chapter 10.

NOTES

1. These countries are: Afghanistan, Albania, Algeria, Azerbaijan, Bahrain, Bangladesh, Benin, Brunei Darussalam, Burkina Faso, Cameroon, Chad, Comoros, Côtc D'Ivoirc, Djibouti, Egypt, Gabon, Guinea Bissau, Guinea, Indonesia, Iraq, Islamic Republic of Iran, Jordan, Kazakhstan, Kibris (North Cyprus), Kuwait, Kyrgyz Republic, Lebanon, Malaysia, Maldives, Mali, Mauritania, Morocco, Niger, Nigeria, Oman, Pakistan, Philippines, Qatar, Republic of Yemen, Russia, Saudi Arabia, Senegal, Sierra Leone, Socialist People's Libyan Arab Jamahiriya, Somalia, Sri Lanka, Sudan, Syria Arab Republic, The Gambia, Tunisia, Turkey, Turkmenistan, Uganda, United Arab Emirates, West Bank and Gaza (WBG).
2. *Mudaraba, mudarabha, mudarabah, mudarba, and modarabah* are all different English spellings of the same Arabic word.
3. Caliph, Calipha or Khalifa from the Arabic word meaning 'successor'. Although elected temporal princes, as rulers of the Islamic state they were also spiritual heads of Islam and came to be known as 'Commanders of the Faithful'.
4. *New Horizon*, No. 82, December 1998, p. 17. He is Chairman of Centre for Islamic Economics, Pakistan, and a judge of the Islamic Shariat Court.
5. An independent body, the IAIB supervises the workings of the individual *Shari'a* boards which monitor the operations of Islamic banks to ensure conformity with religious precepts. Chapter 7 examines the role of the *Shari'a* boards.
6. Reported in the *Encyclopedia of Islamic Banking and Insurance*, p. 267.
7. For example, ABC International Bank, Arab Bank, Bank Rydah, Citibank International, Gulf International Bank, IBJ International, J Aron (Goldman Sachs), Dresdener Kleinwort Benson, United Bank of Kuwait all have Islamic units ('windows') in London, but deal with Middle Eastern and Asian clients from these offices.

2. Islamic law

THE ESSENCE OF ISLAM

It is difficult to examine the workings of Islamic banking without some knowledge of the economic and legal principles underlying an Islamic banking system. The first thing which has to be eschewed is the notion that Islamic economics is a new paradigm. Certainly, Islamic economic thought has come to the fore in recent years in a number of Muslim states. But as noted in Chapter 1, the ideas can be traced back to the message of the Holy Qur'an in the seventh century, and in this sense Islamic economics is as old if not older than the theoretical foundations of most Western economic systems, especially modern capitalism.[1]

Those who pioneered Islamic economic thought developed rules for carrying on banking and finance from Islamic law or the s*hari'a* (formally *shari'a Islami'iah* but generally abbreviated to *shari'ah* or *shari'a*). The literal meaning of the Arabic word *shari'a* is 'the way to the source of life' and, in a technical sense, it is now used to refer to a legal system in keeping with the code of behaviour called for by the Holy Qur'an and the *hadith* (the authentic tradition). Muslims cannot, in good faith, compartmentalise their behaviour into religious and secular dimensions, and their actions are always bound by the *shari'a*. Islamic law thus embodies an encompassing set of duties and practices including worship, prayer, manners and morals, marriage, inheritance, crime and commercial transactions: that is, it embraces many aspects that would not necessarily be considered as law elsewhere. It is thus entirely religious, and as sacred law contains the core of Islamic faith itself. Accordingly our starting point is the nature of Islam.[2]

Islam is numerically the second-largest religion, with 1.2 billion followers (after Christianity's 2 billion). It was promulgated by the Prophet Muhammad (peace be unto him) in Arabia early in the seventh century CE. The religion spread rapidly and barely a century after the Prophet's (pbuh) death in 632 CE, had travelled across the whole northern coast of Africa and into Spain; in the East it crossed Persia and reached the Indus. A second wave of conquest by the Ottoman dynasty from the 1300s established the dominance of Islam in South East Europe. In Asia, Pakistan was established last century as a Muslim state. India was ruled mainly by Muslims for over 700 years, and Muslims still comprise around 14 per cent of the population. The non-Chinese inhabitants of Malaysia are predominantly Muslim, Indonesia is 90 per cent Muslim, and Muslims constitute 12 per cent of the population of Thailand and the Philippines. China itself has a large Muslim population, mainly Turkic-speaking Uighurs, Kazakhs and Kirgiz. Islam holds sway in the Nile Valley, in most of what used to be called French West Africa, along with Northern Nigeria and Somalia, Tanzania and Kenya on the East Coast. In all, Muslims form a majority of the population in over 40 countries. There are sizable numbers of Muslims in the West – 6 to 8 million in both the United States and Europe. All Muslims are bound by a common faith.

Islam follows Judaism and Christianity as the third and last of the great monotheistic religions. One who professes the faith of Islam is a Muslim. The origins of the word *Islam* are in the root *s-l-m* which means 'tranquillity', 'peace' (*salâm*) or 'to remain whole'. The term *aslama* means 'to submit oneself with complete peace of mind' or 'to give oneself up to God', and it is from this that the word *Muslim* derives. Frequently *Islam* is defined simply as 'submission to God' or 'surrender to God'. Those who 'submit to' this path form the *umma*, the community of Muslims.

Belief in the sovereignty of God is at the centre-piece of the Islamic faith, in that it is focused around the worship of God (in Arabic *Allah*) and divine revelations as given in the Holy Qur'an, revealed between 610 and 632 CE to the Prophet Muhammad ibn 'Abd Allah (pbuh).[3] The Holy Qur'an is for Muslims in a most literal sense the word of God, and Islamic law flows directly from it and is wholly inspired by it.

A work roughly the same length as the New Testament, the Holy Qur'an calls on polytheists (believers in many Gods), Jews and Christians alike to commit themselves to God's final revealed message. All injustices of this world are to be redressed in the next. There is to be a resurrection and a Day of Judgement. Paradise (Heaven) awaits those who heed the call, Hell for those who ignore it – a position that fits in with the Judaeo-Christian heritage.

At this juncture we should seek to clarify the relationship of Islam with Judaism and Christianity, for this is an area around which much misunderstanding has existed. One misconception has been analogical; since Jesus Christ is the basis of Christian faith, it was sometimes assumed – quite incorrectly – that the Prophet Muhammad (pbuh) was to Islam as Christ was to Christianity. Hence the old term 'Muhammadanism' was wrongly given to Islam in the West until relatively recently. Although for Muslims the Prophet Muhammad (pbuh) is *insan-i-kamil*, the perfect person, he is not divine, and is seen not as the founder of Islam, merely as God's messenger – carrying the message of Islam, of peace. As the name of Islam is not linked to the founder of the religion (like Buddhism after Buddha), it is also not tied to a geographical area unlike Hinduism, which derives its name from Hind or the river Indus, or Judaism, which gets its name from the land of Judaea.

Islam, Christianity and Judaism are interlinked because all three are, in reality, worshipping the same One God. Thus the God of Muslims is the same God of the Jews and the Christians, although without what perhaps might be seen as the racial exclusiveness attributed to Him by Judaism, or the intricate theology woven around Him by Christianity in the form of the Trinity (Latin = three-foldness) by which God is considered to exist as Father, Son and the Holy Spirit. The beliefs of Islam are those of simple, uncompromising monotheism, building on the Judaeo-Christian tradition but rejecting anything in it that could be interpreted as tending towards polytheism, such as the divinity of Christ or the doctrine of the Trinity. Christ is accepted as a prophet, and is, throughout the Holy Qur'an, referred to as 'Jesus, son of Mary'. Jesus, revered as a messenger of God, was neither His son, nor a God himself.

In fact, Islam is the only non-Christian religion that makes it an article of faith to believe in Jesus as a prophet. The Holy Qur'an simply disapproves of the worship of Jesus and Mary besides Allah, which is seen as conflicting with true monotheism, and also exonerates Jesus from having so advised his followers. But a Muslim is not a Muslim unless he or she believes in Jesus and all the prophets of Allah.

There is a genealogical link as well as a theological relationship between Judaism and Islam; Jews claim descent from Abraham through his son Isaac while Arabs claim descent through his son Ismail. In addition, both have a well-defined system of sacred law. Both forbid the eating of pork and other meat which has not been ritually killed (*kosher* to the Jews, and *halal* to the Muslims). Both forbid statues and religious images. There are many similarities in ritual and practice. Both insist on the unity of God and reject the Christian creed of the Trinity. Muslims reject the Christian concept of original sin and the idea that there can be any intercessor between a person and God, since in Islam, each person is responsible for his or her own salvation. Muslims also revere the Old Testament prophets, Abraham (Ibrahim in Arabic), Moses (Musa), Jacob (Yacub), Joseph (Yusuf), David (Dawud), Solomon (Sulaiman) and so on.

Certainly Islam claims no monopoly on monotheism. The Holy Qur'an teaches that God sent a series of messengers and prophets culminating in the Prophet Muhammad (pbuh), the last of the prophets, reviving and completing their message. Many of the familiar stories and names of the Bible are to be found in the Holy Qur'an. Twenty-eight prophets are recorded in the Holy Qur'an and all of them, except the Prophet Muhammad (phub), are written about in the Jewish and Christian scriptures, although differences exist in the narrations and in the details. In this respect, the Holy Qur'an proclaims no originality in the sense of presenting a new religion. Rather, it revives and fulfils the same message which it maintains God has given to all the prophets throughout the ages and to every people, from Adam through to Jesus, and the

Prophet Muhammad (pbuh). Moreover, the Holy Qur'an explicitly declares: 'We make no distinction between any of them' (S2: 136). For this reason, Muslims cannot understand why Christians do not accept the Prophet Muhammad (pbuh) as a prophet, since they grant that status to Jesus. In the Holy Qur'an, Jews and Christians are called *ahl-al-kitab*, the People of the Book, and were generally allowed to practise their beliefs freely in the Islamic empire, which has played host to Christians and Jews for centuries.[4]

Despite the common roots and common bonds between the three religions, there are, of course, some significant differences. Prophet Muhammad's (pbuh) revelation was the first time God had sent a messenger to the Arabs (the Qureysh) and had revealed a scripture in their own language. Significantly, at one point, the Prophet Muhammad (pbuh) is called 'the seal of the prophets' (S.33: 40). In some eyes, this may have implied no more than that the revelations confirmed those given to previous prophets, but has come to mean that the Prophet Muhammad (pbuh) was the final, uniting Prophet of the covenant, correcting errors that had crept into previous revelations, and giving the full and most perfect version of God's revelation to humanity. While God alone is god, and the Prophet Muhammad (pbuh) is not regarded as divine, the Prophet Muhammad (pbuh) is unique in the respect and reverence afforded him by Muslims. His behaviour and words are studied by Muslims and his life is an example to be followed.

To become[5] a Muslim all that one has to do is to 'testify' by reciting the words, 'I believe that there is no god but Allah, and that Muhammad is the Messenger of Allah'. This is the first of the so-called Five Pillars of Islam, or fundamental observances, which form the basis of the Muslim faith:

1. Acceptance of the *shahada* or witness of faith which consists of reciting the sentence '*la ilaha illa llah, Muhammadu rasulu llah*' (in its alternative translation, 'There is no God but the God and Muhammad is his Prophet'). Anyone who utters the *shahada* in full faith must be regarded as a Muslim.
2. Prayer, or *salat*, is prescribed to be performed five times per day (at dawn, around midday, in the afternoon, at sunset, and at night before going to bed), preceded by self-purification through ritual washing, performed facing in the direction of the Holy Mosque in Mecca, demonstrating 'submission to God's will' by word of mouth and physical gesture.
3. Alms, or *zakat* (a term derived from the Arabic *zaka*, meaning 'pure'). The Holy Qur'an stresses that the giving of alms is one of the chief virtues of the true believer, the generally accepted amount being one-fortieth of a Muslim's accumulated personal or business wealth. Because all such revenue benefits the poor and pays for certain activities within a

community, the very act of giving shows the believer's sense of social responsibility, thus leaving acquired wealth free of disrepute.

4.   Fasting or *sawm*. All believers are required to observe the ninth lunar month of the Muslim year, Ramadan, as a period of fasting in which they abstain from eating, drinking, smoking and sexual relations from sunrise to sunset (Holy Qur'an 2:185–6). The purpose is to subjugate the body to the spirit and to fortify the will through mental discipline, thus helping the believer to come nearer to God.

5.   Pilgrimage. The *hajj*, or pilgrimage to Mecca must be performed at least once in the life of every Muslim, health and means permitting (Holy Qur'an 3.97).

Above all, however, the practising Muslim is expected to respect the teachings of the Holy Qur'an in its entirety – the basis of Islamic law.

NATURE AND SOURCES OF ISLAMIC JURISPRUDENCE[6]

Islamic law, or *shari'a*, as it developed out of the teachings and example of the Prophet Muhammad (pbuh), claimed to regulate all aspects of life, ethical and social, and to encompass criminal as well as civil matters. The *shari'a* is comprehensive, embracing all human activities, defining man's relations with God and with his fellow men; consequently it combines what in Western societies comes under the separate headings of civil and criminal law. In Islam the realms of God and Caesar become one, instead of having separate jurisdictions, as allowed by Christianity.

The unique validity of Islamic law comes from it being the manifested will of God, who at a certain point in history revealed it to mankind through his prophet Muhammad (pbuh); as such it does not rely on the authority of any earthly law-maker. Its origins in addition to the Holy Qur'an, are to be found in the judgements given by the Prophet (pbuh) himself, reflecting the application of rules, principles and injunctions already enunciated in the Holy Qur'an. As the centuries passed these rules grew into a complete system of law, both public and private, as well as prescriptions for the practice of religion.

While the Holy Qur'an produced a number of general rules, these did not delineate all possible problems, and in the century after the Prophet Muhammad (pbuh) they were supplemented by references to the *sunna* or standard practice. This was known from thousands of statements about what the Prophet (pbuh) had said or done, and found in the literature of the *hadith*. The *shari'a* grew out of the attempts made by early Muslims, as they confronted immediate social and political problems, to devise a legal system in keeping with the code of behaviour called for by the Holy Qur'an and the *hadith*.

The study of the *shari'a* is *fiqh*, 'jurisprudence', and its practitioners are *fuqaha*, 'jurists'. Another word used is *ulama*, which is properly 'those who know' but is mostly translated 'scholars' or 'scholar-jurists'. This is because in Islam the place of theology is taken by laws and jurisprudence. Those who deal with the intellectual aspects of the religion are jurists and not theologians, and at the centre of higher education is jurisprudence and not theology. After the Prophet Muhammad's (pbuh) death, there were many informal groups discussing and advising on the interpretation of the rules of the Holy Qur'an. These groups gradually developed into more organised schools, and produced the '*fuqaha*' and '*ulama*'. Eventually four slightly different schools of thought came to be recognised in Sunnism.

Thus the sources of the *shari'a* are the Holy Qur'an and the *sunna* (the primary sources) and the interpretations and opinions of the learned jurists (the secondary sources). A brief outline is given below.

Holy Qur'an

By far the most important source is the Holy Qur'an, the collection of the revelations to the Prophet Muhammad (pbuh). The Holy Qur'an is obviously not purely a legal text, nevertheless it does contain approximately 500 injunctions of a legal nature (20 of which are on economic issues). 'Abdur Rahman i Doi (1989, pp. 38–9) has classified the 500 legal verses under four headings:

(i) The concise injunctions – these are precise commandments but the Holy Qur'an does not give detailed rules about how they are to be carried out. Examples of these are prayer, fasting, and payment of *zakat*.

(ii) The concise and detailed injunctions – these are commandments about which some details are given in the Holy Qur'an, but further information may be discovered from the *hadith* and other recognised sources. Examples are the rules about relations with non-Muslims.

(iii) The detailed injunctions – the Holy Qur'an gives complete details about these commandments and nothing further is required or may be sought, for example the punishments for specific crimes and also rules about inheritance.

(iv) Fundamental principles of guidance – these principles do not have clear-cut definitions and the way to put them into effect must be determined through *ijtihad* (use of personal reasoning) in every age.

It is generally agreed that the injunctions contained in the Holy Qur'an must not be altered, but the legal consequences, if any, which attach to their disregard is often not specified, for example, ignoring the ban on usury.

The 'Hadith' and 'Sunna'

Next in importance after the Holy Qur'an as a source of guidance are the *hadith* (plural *ahadith*), the 'traditions' or 'sayings' relating to the life of the Prophet Muhammad (pbuh). In classical doctrine, *sunna* – tradition, the 'Traced Path' of the Prophet (pbuh) and his Companions – can be known only by means of the *hadith*. Over the centuries a great body of rules for correct behaviour and belief – the basis of Islamic law and theology – came into being and gained almost universal acceptance. Its guiding principle was respect for tradition – that is for the *sunna*, a term which in ancient Arabia meant 'ancestral precedent' or the 'custom of the tribe'. *Sunna* was equated with the practice and precept of the Prophet (pbuh) as transmitted by the narrators of authentic tradition (*hadith*), and is composed of three parts: *sunna qawliya* (words), *sunna fi'liya* (acts) and *sunna taqrirya* (approbation and participation).

Ijma (Consensus)

Scholars treated the Holy Qur'an as containing the general principles by which all matters should be regulated, and where the meaning of the Holy Qur'an was imprecise they sought clarification from the *hadith*. Thus the foundations of the *shari'a* were the clear and unambiguous commands and prohibitions to be found in these sources. *Ijma*, the informed consensus of the community of scholars, was established, not for matters of faith or fundamental observances – which were agreed – but on the application of *shari'a* to worldly affairs. This source is of importance for Islamic finance because models of Islamic banking are not mentioned in either the Holy Qur'an or in the *hadith*, although the basic principles which govern the system are. Consequently the development of Islamic banking has been based to a large degree on the consensus of modern Muslim scholars and jurisprudents at both national and international levels. One example is the *Handbook of Islamic Banking*, published by the International Association of Islamic Banks, which provides the framework for Islamic financial institutions.

Qiyas (Analogical Deduction)

Additional sources of law are *qiyas* (analogy from established law) and *ijtihad* (formulation of law by the individual's struggle for proper understanding). Using reason and judgement to determine a course of action in keeping with

the spirit of the Holy Qur'an and *hadith* is called *ijtihad*, and decisions made
in this manner are *ijma* – the collective judgements of learned Muslim
scholars, the *ulama*. In making decisions, account must be taken of earlier
opinions, previous discussions and the reasons for them, and a general sense
of justice. *Qiyas* means analogical reasoning, using past analogies with their
decisions as precedents in each new situation.

In application, *qiyas* involves a comparison between two things with the
view of evaluating one in the light of the other. In Islamic law it is the
extension of *shari'a* value from an original case to a new case, because the
latter has the same effective cause as the former. *Qiyas* may be resorted to
discover the law on a certain matter only if no solution can be found in the
Holy Qur'an or *hadith*, or in cases covered by *ijma*. For example, it is deduced
that it is *haram* (forbidden) to use narcotics on the same basis that alcohol is
forbidden, in that they generally alter the state of the mind for the worse.

Madhahib (Schools of Law)

Unlike Christianity, classical Islam had no priestly hierarchy and no central
religious authority to promulgate official doctrine; truth needed no
authorisation. The nearest to clergy in Islam are the jurists known as the *ulama*
(from *alim* or scholar), who differ in their roles and gradation. A mullah (also
maulvi or *maulana*) is in charge of a local mosque. A sheikh has higher status
and more learning. An Iman is a senior figure, often in charge of a large
mosque. Iman is also the title given to spiritual leaders in Shiism, while an
ayatollah is the most senior category of *alim* in Shia Islam.

The most important sectarian division in Islam is the one which separates
Sunni and Shia believers, which arose in 661 CE on the question of the rightful
leadership of the community. Shi'ism, which has various sub-sects, is
predominant in Iran, and has significant numbers of followers in Iraq, India
and many of the Gulf States. There are considerable doctrinal differences
between the Shia and the four Sunni schools of Islamic law, in terms of who
is permitted to interpret *shari'a* law. Shi'ites believe that living religious
scholars, known as *mujtahids,* have an equal right to interpret Divine Law as
eminent jurists of the past, and their judgements replace the Sunni source of
deduction by analogy, *qiyas*.[7]

Sunni legal doctrine has four main schools, each with its own system of
theory and applications of law, although each recognises the legitimacy of all
of the others. The four orthodox schools are the Hanafi (rationalist), the Maliki
(traditionalist), the Hanbali (fundamentalist) and the Shafii (moderate). The
Hanafi school is followed by the majority of Sunni Muslims in Lebanon, Iraq,
Syria, Turkey, Afghanistan, Pakistan, Bangladesh and in different places in
India. The Moors who ruled Spain were followers of the Maliki school which,

nowadays, is found mostly in Africa. The Hanbali school is predominant in Saudi Arabia. Followers of the Shafii school today are found extensively in South East Asia.

The differences of emphasis between individual scholars and schools led to some concern lest Islamic law disintegrate in a plethora of private opinions. In order to counter this risk, as-Shafii, who died in CE 820, produced a doctrine of the four 'roots' of Islamic law (cited in Zweigert and Kötz, 1998), which was to provide jurists with a fixed and common method of finding law. The first 'root' of Islamic law is naturally the Holy Qur'an. The second 'root' is the *sunna*, the sum total of inspired practice of the Prophet (pbuh), so important for interpreting and clarifying the rules of the Holy Qur'an. The third 'root' is the *ijma*, the consensus reached by the learned in the Islamic community. The fourth and last 'root' is analogy (*qiyas*), that is, the application to new and similar cases of rules established by the Holy Qur'an, the *sunna*, or *ijma*. Subsequent doctrine made only one change in this scheme, a change in the idea of *ijma*, in that a proposition was to be regarded as a rule of law if at any time the living *legal scholars* of all or even one of the schools of law agreed on it. As Zweigert and Kötz (1998, p. 308) note, this classical system of the four 'roots' of Islamic law comprises very different things, namely: two sources – the Holy Qur'an and the *sunna*; a method – the use of analogy *qiyas*; and a judgement – that of *ijma*.

In short, the four schools give different emphasis to the sources of law, but all are unanimous in requiring that Islamic law be God-given and not man-created. As such, the Holy Qur'an and the *sunna* are fully binding; the other sources of authority are in one way or another justified by reference to these two basic sources. This is important when we come to consider Islamic commercial and financial law.

DUTIES AND OBLIGATIONS

Since Islamic law reflects the will of God rather than the will of a human lawmaker, it covers all areas of life and not simply those which are of interest to a secular state or society. It is not limited to questions of belief and religious practice, but also deals with criminal and constitution matters, as well as many other fields which in other societies would be regarded as the concern of the secular authorities. In an Islamic context there is no such thing as a separate secular authority and secular law, since religion and state are one. Essentially, the Islamic state as conceived by orthodox Muslims is a religious entity established under divine law.

In practice, the position is more complex than this, as secular and sacred co-exist and to some degree always have done. When Arab conquests took place shortly after the death of the Prophet (pbuh) in lands formerly under Byzantium or Persia, it was found increasingly difficult to enforce the *shari'a* as the universal civil and criminal law of the whole Muslim community. This community now included a diversity of peoples with their own ancient laws and customs, many of which they were unwilling to relinquish despite their acceptance of Islam. The continuation of a custom of a particular place or community is allowable under Islamic law, and may in fact be assimilated into the law, as were many of the customs of the Arabs. To be permissible a custom must not be contrary to revealed injunctions, and this point remains highly controversial in some areas, for example the treatment of women.

Much later, in the last days of the Ottoman Empire and under Western colonisation, a system of secular law arose to supplement or replace *shari'a* in all criminal and civil jurisdiction save matters of marriage, divorce, and inheritance. For example, Qatar has two completely independent court structures. *Shari'a* courts have jurisdiction in personal status cases, murder and morals crimes, while the *Adliyya* courts have jurisdiction over all civil matters and those crimes not falling under the *shari'a* system. But the relationship between them is undefined and uneasy (Brown, 1997).

Consequently, although *shari'a* doctrine was all-embracing, Muslim legal practice has had to acknowledge jurisdictions other than those of the *shari'a* courts. As an expression of a religious ideal, the *shari'a* was always the focal point of legal activity. In Qatar, the state courts recognise as strong the claims to legitimacy of the *shari'a* courts, and see the *shari'a* as an essential component of any Islamic society. But the *Adliyya* judges also argue that modern governments have certain obligations to fulfil, including that of the guarantee of due process under courts of law. Politics and taxation are also matters that remain only theoretically under the guidance of the religious code.

In any case, the *shari'a* is essentially a complex of rules to which individual adherents must adhere if they are to meet the requirements of their faith, irrespective of whether the observance of these is enforced by temporal authorities. That is, the *shari'a* is a comprehensive ethic according to which Muslims ought to behave and conduct their lives, and human actions are classified, in descending order, as: obligatory, meritorious, permissible, disliked and forbidden. The distinctions between the five categories are in whether their performance or non-performance is rewarded, not-rewarded, punished or not-punished.[8]

Shari'a duties can be broadly divided into those that an individual owes to God (*ibadat*, acts of devotion and ritual) and those owed to fellow people, that is, what would constitute law in the Western sense (*muamalat*). The former we need not detail, and include prayer, ablutions, fasting, pilgrimage, the establishment of Mosques, observance of holy days, gestures and behaviour.

Strict food laws forbid pork, blood, carrion, specify the method of preparing animals and ban the drinking of any alcoholic beverages. Also prohibited is the representation of animals or the human figure in art, as a precaution against any lapse into idolatry.

The other areas covered by Islamic law are considerable, and include *inter alia,* marriage, divorce, sexual relations, care of children, adoption, maintenance, and so on. Hussain (1999) provides a recent survey, while Brown (1997) examines how traditional *shari'a* law has been adapted in a variety of ways to meet present social needs in Egypt and some of the Gulf states. Here we focus on a number of specific areas.

Inheritance

An individual's power of testamentary disposition is basically limited to one-third of the net estate (that is, the assets remaining after the payment of funeral expenses and debts) and two thirds of the estate passes to the legal heirs of the deceased under the compulsory rules of inheritance. Here *shari'a*, providing for every member of the family by allotting fixed shares not only to wives and children, but also to fathers and mothers, aimed at achieving a measure of fairness (for example, a son's share is twice that of a daughter on the grounds that the male is expected to provide as well for his own family).

Penal Law

For six specific crimes (apostasy, highway robbery, theft, extramarital sexual relations, false accusation of unchastity, and drinking alcohol), the punishment is fixed (*hadd*). Outside the *hadd* crimes, both the determination of offences and the punishment is at the discretion of the executive or the courts.

Procedure and Evidence

Traditionally, *shari'a* law was administered by the court of a single *qâdi* (judge) who was the judge of the facts as well as the law, although on difficult legal issues he might seek the advice of a professional jurist, or *mufti*. The first task of the *qâdi* was to decide which party bore the burden of proof. In the case of an alleged criminal offence, for example, the presumption is the innocence of the accused, and in a suit for debt the presumption is that the alleged debtor is free from debt. Proof required the production of two (and in some cases four) witnesses to testify orally of their direct knowledge of the truth of the contention, with judgement for plaintiff or defendant according to the required production of proof.

COMMERCIAL TRANSACTIONS

Many verses in the Holy Qur'an encourage trade and commerce, and the attitude of Islam is that there should be no impediment to honest and legitimate trade and business, so that people earn a living, support their families and give charity to those less fortunate.

Just as Islam regulates and influences all other spheres of life, so it also governs the conduct of business and commerce. Muslims ought to conduct their business activities in accordance with the requirements of their religion to be fair, honest and just towards others. A special obligation exists upon vendors as there is no doctrine of *caveat emptor*. Monopolies and price-fixing are prohibited.

The basic principles of the law are laid down in the four root transactions of (1) sales (*bay*), transfer of the ownership or corpus of property for a consideration; (2) hire (*ijâra*), transfer of the usufruct (right to use) of property for a consideration; (3) gift (*hiba*), gratuitous transfer of the corpus of property; and (4) loan (*ariyah*), gratuitous transfer of the usufruct of property. These basic principles are then applied to the various specific transactions of, for example, pledge, deposit, guarantee, agency, assignment, land tenancy, *waqf* foundations (religious or charitable bodies) and partnerships.

Partnerships play an important role in Islamic financing and the law is extremely complex (see Nyazee, 1999). In broad terms there are a number of different forms of partnership recognised by Islamic law:

Shirkah al-'inan (limited partnership). In this kind of partnership, partners contribute capital, property and/or labour. Profits and losses are shared in an agreed manner. Each partner is only the agent and so a partner is not liable for a debt contracted by his co-partners and is only able to sue someone with whom he has contracted.[9]

Musharaka. When two or more people combine their resources to invest in an enterprise, a *musharaka* partnership is formed according to Islamic law. In this category of partnership, management and participation is stipulated for all partners, whether or not all partners actually participate in the management.

Mudaraba or *Qirad* (dormant partnership). In this category of partnership, management is stipulated for one of the partners and the other partner(s) are investors who share the profits in return for the capital they have provided. Thus a *qirad* is a contract whereby one person (the dormant partner) gives funds or property to another on the basis that the financier will share in the active partner's profits in a proportion agreed upon in advance. The dormant partner remains the owner of the capital, but takes no active part in the enterprise. The trader is responsible only for negligence or breach of contract.

There are two other principal categories of business enterprise. The first is a wage–rent enterprise, based on *ijara* (hire), in which the person with capital hires labour for a specific job or time and at a fixed wage. The financier receives all profit and is responsible for all losses. Such an enterprise may be arranged by a sole proprietor, or as a partnership (*shirkah*).

The other main type of enterprise is, of course, the modern corporation. Investments can be made in the stock market providing that the companies involved trade only in *halal* commodities. This is similar to the modern Western idea of ethical investment. Under Islamic law it is lawful to own ordinary shares in companies, but it is not lawful to hold preference shares since these offer a pre-determined rate of return which amounts to *riba*. Similarly it is not lawful to invest in debenture or futures.

As the preceding paragraph indicates, there are strict rules applying to finance under Islamic law, and it is to these that we now turn.

ISLAMIC FINANCING PRINCIPLES[10]

In order to conform with Islamic rules and norms, five religious features, which are well established in the literature, must be followed in investment behaviour. These are:

(a)   the absence of interest-based (*riba*) financial transactions;
(b)   the introduction of a religious levy or almsgiving, *zakat*;
(c)   the prohibition of the production of goods and services which contradict the value pattern of Islam (*haram*);
(d)   the avoidance of economic activities involving *maysir* (gambling) and *gharar* (uncertainty);
(e)   the provision of *Takaful* (Islamic insurance).

These five elements give Islamic banking and finance its distinctive religious identity, and we now explain each in turn.

Riba

Perhaps the most far-reaching and controversial aspect of Islamic economics, in terms of its implications from a Western perspective, is the prohibition of interest (*riba*). The payment of *riba* and the taking of interest as occurs in a conventional banking system is explicitly prohibited by the Holy Qur'an, and thus investors must be compensated by other means. It is further stated in the Holy Qur'an that those who disregard the prohibition of interest are at war with God and His Prophet Muhammad (pbuh), although the temporal punishment for an unrepentant perpetrator is not prescribed.

The prohibition of *riba* is mentioned in four different verses in the Holy

Qur'an.[11] The first of the verses emphasises that interest deprives wealth of God's blessings. The second condemns it, placing interest in juxtaposition with wrongful appropriation of property belonging to others. The third enjoins Muslims to stay clear of interest for the sake of their own welfare. The fourth establishes a clear distinction between interest and trade, urging Muslims, first, to take only the principal sum and second, to forgo even this sum if the borrower is unable to repay. The ban on interest is also cited in unequivocal terms in the *hadith* or *sunna*. Furthermore, the Islamic ban on *riba* – literally 'increase' but widely understood in this context to mean all predetermined interest payable on a loan of any kind – has parallels in similar bans on usury in medieval Christianity and (at least for loans to other Jews) in Judaism (see Chapter 8 below).

Zakat

Islam comprises a set of principles and doctrines that guide and regulate a Muslim's relationship with God and with society. In this respect Islam is not only a divine service like Judaism and Christianity, but also incorporates a code of conduct which regulates and organises mankind in both spiritual and material life. According to the Holy Qur'an, God owns all wealth, and private property is seen as a trust from God. Property has a social function in Islam, and must be used for the benefit of society. Moreover, there is a divine duty to work. Social justice is the result of organising society on Islamic social and legal precepts including employment of productive labour and equal opportunities such that everyone can use all of their abilities in work and gain just rewards from that work effort. Justice and equality in Islam means that people should have equal opportunity and does not imply that they should be equal either in poverty or in riches (Chapra, 1985). However, it is incumbent on the Islamic state to guarantee a subsistence level to its citizens, in the form of a minimum level of food, clothing, shelter, medical care and education (Holy Qur'an 58: 11). The major purpose here is to moderate social variances in Islamic society, and to enable the poor to lead a normal, spiritual and material life in dignity and contentment.

A mechanism for the redistribution of income and wealth is inherent in Islam, so that every Muslim is guaranteed a fair standard of living, *nisab*. *Zakat* is the most important instrument for the redistribution of wealth. This almsgiving is a compulsory levy, and as we saw earlier constitutes one of the five basic tenets of Islam. The generally accepted amount of the *zakat* is a one fortieth (2.5 per cent) assessment on assets held for a full year (after a small initial exclusion, *nisab*), the purpose of which is to transfer income from the wealthy to the needy. Consequently, in countries where *zakat* is not collected by the state, every Islamic bank or financial institution has to establish a *zakat* fund for collecting the funds and distributing them exclusively to the poor directly or through other religious institutions. This religious levy is applied to the initial capital of the bank, on the reserves, and on the profits as described in the Handbook of Islamic Banking (HIB, 1986, Vol. 3, pp. 19–24).

Haram

In order to ensure that the practices and activities of Islamic banks do not contradict the Islamic ethics, Islamic banks are expected to establish a Religious Supervisory Board (RSB), (HIB, 1982, Vol. 6, p. 293). This board consists of Muslim jurists, who act as independent *Shari'a* auditors and advisers to the banks. A strict code of 'ethical investments' operates. Hence Islamic banks cannot finance activities or items forbidden (that is, *haram*) in Islam, such as trade of alcoholic beverages and pork meat. Furthermore, as the fulfilment of material needs assures a religious freedom for Muslims, Islamic banks are encouraged to give priority to the production of essential goods which satisfy the needs of the majority of the Muslim community. As a guide, participation in the production and marketing of luxury activities, *israf wa traf*, is considered as unacceptable from a religious viewpoint (HIB, 1982, Vol. 6, p. 293) when Muslim societies suffer from a lack of essential goods and services such as food, clothing, shelter, health and education.

Gharar/Maysir

Prohibition of games of chance is explicit in the Holy Qur'an (S5: 90–91). It uses the word *maysir* for games of hazard, derived from *usr* (ease and convenience), implying that the gambler strives to amass wealth without effort, and the term is now applied generally to all gambling activities. Gambling in all its forms is forbidden in Islamic jurisprudence. Along with explicit forms of gambling, Islamic law also forbids any business activities which contain any element of gambling (Siddiqi, 1985). The *shari'a* determined that in the interests of fair, ethical dealing in commutative contracts, unjustified enrichment through games of pure chance should be prohibited.

Another feature condemned by Islam is economic transactions involving elements of speculation, *gharar* (literally 'hazard'). While *riba* and *maysir* are condemned in the Holy Qur'an, condemnation of *gharar* is supported by *ahadith*. In business terms, *gharar* means to undertake a venture blindly without sufficient knowledge or to undertake an excessively risky transaction, although minor uncertainties can be permitted when there is some necessity. In a general context, the unanimous view of the jurists held that in any transaction, by failing or neglecting to define any of the essential pillars of contract relating to the consideration or measure of the object, the parties undertake a risk which is not indispensable for them. This kind of risk was deemed unacceptable and tantamount to speculation due to its inherent uncertainty. Speculative transactions with these characteristics are therefore prohibited.

This prohibition applies in a number of circumstances such as when the seller is not in a position to hand over the goods to the buyer or when the subject matter of the sale is incapable of acquisition, for example the sale of fruit which is not yet ripened, or fish or birds not yet caught, that is, short-selling. Speculative business like buying goods or shares at low prices and selling them for higher prices in the future is considered to be illicit (HIB, 1982, Vol. 5, p. 427, and also Mannan, [1970]1986, p. 289).

Gharar applies also for investments such as trading in futures on the stock market; indeed, *gharar* is present in all future (*mudhaf*) sales and, according to the consensus of scholars, a *gharar* contract is null and void (*batil*). The position of jurisprudence on a future sale is explained by Sheikh Dhareer (1997):

> In this variety of sale the offer (to sell something) is shifted from the present to a future date; for instance, one person would say to another: 'I sell you this house of mine at such a price as of the beginning of next year' and the other replies: 'I accept'. The majority of jurists are of the view that the sale contract cannot accept clauses of this nature; if the sale is shifted to a future date the contract becomes invalid ...
>
> ... *gharar* in a future contract lies in the possible lapse of the interest of either party and to his consent with the contract when the time set therein comes. If someone buys something by a '*mudhaf*' contract and his circumstances change or the market changes bringing its price down at the time set for fulfilment of contract, he will undoubtedly be averse to its fulfilment and will regret entering into it. Indeed, the object in question may itself change and the two parties may dispute over it.
>
> Thus, we can say that *gharar* infiltrates the '*mudhaf*' contract from the viewpoint of uncertainty over the time, that is, when the parties conclude the contract they do not know whether they will still be in agreement and have continued interest in that contract when it falls due. (pp. 18-19)

The rejection of *gharar* has led to the condemnation of some or all types of insurance by Muslim scholars, since insurance involves an unknown risk. Further, an element of *maysir* arises as a consequence of the presence of *gharar*. This has led to the development of *Takaful* (cooperative) insurance.

Takaful

Positions taken by scholars on insurance differ according to their views about the presence of *gharar* and *maysir* in insurance contracts. It is mainly on the basis of prohibition of *maysir* and *gharar* that conventional Western-style insurance is forbidden in Islamic law, but not entirely. In addition, many forms of life insurance are merely thinly disguised investment methods, and the majority of insurance companies conduct their business by investing collected premiums and reinsuring with other insurers, thereby contravening the Islamic laws regarding *riba* along with *gharar* and *maysir*.

The basic objection is that this type of insurance is effectively a gamble upon the incidence of the contingency insured against, because the interests of both parties are diametrically opposed, and both parties do not know their respective rights and liabilities until the occurrence of the insured events. The only type of insurance that would appear to be lawful according to the *shari'a* is mutual (or 'joint-guarantee') insurance. The OIC Islamic *Fiqh* Academy, at its second session held in Jeddah on 10–16 Rabi'll, A.H. (22–28 December 1985), resolved as follows:

(1) The commercial insurance contract with the fixed premium offered by commercial insurance companies is a contract that contains excessive and, hence, contract-invalidating *gharar*. Therefore, it is *haram* (forbidden) by the *Shari'a*.

(2) An alternative contract that meets Islamic principles for transactions is a cooperative insurance contract based on voluntary contributions and cooperation. The same applies to re-insurance based on cooperative insurance.

(3) Islamic countries should be called upon to set up cooperative institutions of insurance and re-insurance .... (cited in Dhareer, 1997, p. 57).

This form of insurance, which includes both general and family (life) insurance, is examined further in Chapter 9.

NOTES

1. The interrelationship between Christianity and capitalism is explored in Tawney (1926).
2. Accounts of the elements of Islam are given in A.S. Ahmed (1999), Armstrong (1991), Chebel (1997), Clarke (1988), Cook (1996), Forward (1997), Frishman and Khan (1994) and Watt (1996). Islamic social thought is explained by Ahmad (1982), while Islamic economic thought is contained in K. Ahmad (1980), Presley and Sessions (1994) and M.F. Khan (1995). Much of the English language literature rests on the work of the so-called 'orientalists', Sir William Muir (1819–1905), D.S. Margoliouth (1858–1940) and W. Montgomery Watt (1909–). Bibliographical details, along with a critique and refutation of their work, is contained in an authoritative study by M.M. Ali (1997) published under the auspices of the King Fahd Complex for the Printing of the Holy Qur'an, Madinah.
3. In 610, the Prophet Muhammad (pbuh) was torn from sleep in his spiritual retreat on Mount Hira close to Mecca, felt himself overwhelmed by a devastating divine presence and received the command: '*iqra*' 'Recite!'. So begins the opening passage of Surat al-Alaq (96), and the Word of God had been spoken for the first time in Arabia and in Arabic. These revelations continued over a period of 23 years for the rest of His life, and constitute the Holy Qur'an: the Recitation. It should be noted that the word Allah for the name of God was

known and used before the Holy Qur'an was revealed; for example, the name of the Prophet's (pbuh) father was Abd Allah, or 'servant of God'.
4. Witness the Coptic Church in Egypt, and the Jews in Morocco.
5. Muslims believe that at birth all humans are naturally *muslim*, that is, at peace with and submissive to God. It is thus inaccurate to speak of a convert to Islam; rather one is a revert.
6. Outlines of Islamic law are given in Schacht (1964), Vogel and Hayes (1998), Zweigert and Kötz (1998), Hussain (1999) and Brown (1997). Again, the perspective of the orientalists in shaping some of the English language literature needs to be noted (see note 2 above).
7. In an attempt to make the differences understandable to Western readers, Baldick (1998) draws the following analogy:
   'The Shia, the party, bears a resemblance to the Roman Catholic Church, with its belief in papal infallibility. It is a sect of mediations, unlike the Sunni majority, which resembles Protestantism, placing the individual believer alone and immediately before his Maker' (p. 15).
8. Briefly, for personally obligatory (prescribed, mandatory, required) duties, such as *salat* and *zakat*, performance is rewarded and non-performance is punished. Recommended (preferable, meritorious, desirable) actions, such as night vigil prayers, and remembrance of Allah, are rewarded for performance but not punished for non-performance. Performance and non-performance of the permissible (allowed, indifferent) is neither rewarded nor punished. Non-performance of both the disliked (offensive, detested, reprehensible) and the forbidden (unlawful, prohibited, *haram*) is rewarded. Performance of the unlawful is punished, but that of the disliked is not punished.
9. An exception to this is the *inan sharikat a'mal (abdan)* partnership where partners contribute labour. One partner can bind the others in undertaking to perform work for an employer and each is entitled to claim the total salary due from the employer.
10. These are examined in Muslehuddin (1982), Ahmed *et al.* (1983), Rayner (1991) and Hussain (1999).
11. *Surah al-Rum* (Chapter 30), verse 39; *Surah al-Nisa* (Chapter 39), verse 161; *Surah al-Imran* (Chapter 3), verses 1302; *Surah al-Baqarah* (Chapter 2), verses 275–81.

3. The basis of Islamic banking

THE PROHIBITION ON *RIBA*

By definition, an Islamic bank abides by Islamic law, the *shari'a*. The preceding discussion makes clear that a number of elements are involved:

(i)   *riba* is prohibited in all transactions;
(ii)   business and investment are undertaken on the basis of *halal* (legal, permitted) activities;
(iii)   transactions should be free from *gharar* (speculation or unreasonable uncertainty);
(iv)   *zakat* is to be paid by the bank to benefit society;
(v)   all activities should be in line with Islamic principles, with a special *shari'a* board to supervise and advise the bank on the propriety of transactions.

Of these, the first is central. Islamic finance, like Islamic commercial law in general, is dominated by the doctrine of *riba*. Before examining the basis of Islamic banking, it is important that we understand the nature of, and reasons for, this prohibition.

Nature of *Riba*

A general principle of Islamic law, based on a number of passages in the Holy Qur'an, is that unjustified enrichment, or 'receiving a monetary advantage without giving a countervalue', is forbidden on ethical grounds. According to Schacht (1964), *riba* is simply a special case of unjustified enrichment or, in the terms of the Holy Qur'an, consuming (that is, appropriating for one's own use) the property of others for no good reason, which is prohibited. *Riba* can be defined formally as 'a monetary advantage without a countervalue which has been stipulated in favour of one of the two contracting parties in an exchange of two monetary values' (p. 145)

The literal meaning of the Arabic word *riba* is 'increase', 'excess', 'growth' or 'addition'. Saeed (1996, p. 20) notes that the root *r-b-w* from which *riba* is derived, is used in the Holy Qur'an twenty times. The root *r-b-w* has the sense in the Holy Qur'an of 'growing', 'increasing', 'rising', 'swelling', 'raising', and 'being big and great'. It is also used in the sense of 'hillock'. These usages appear to have one meaning in common, that of 'increase', in a qualitative or quantitative sense.

In one of the most quoted verses of the Holy Qur'an relating to *riba,* a distinction is made between gain through enterprise and gain through a condemned practice called *rib-a. Riba* is usually interpreted as usury, as in this translation prepared for King Fahd of Saudi Arabia by the Presidency of Islamic Researches: 'That is because they say: "Trade is like usury," But Allah hath permitted trade/And forbidden usury ....' (S2: 275).

The actual meaning of *riba* has been debated since the earliest Muslim times. Umar, the second Caliph, regretted that the Prophet (peace be upon him) died before having given a more detailed account of what constituted *riba.* Amongst Westerners, the term usury is now generally reserved for only 'exorbitant' or 'excessive' interest. But the evidence from the Holy Qur'an is that all interest is to be condemned: 'But if ye repent, ye shall have your capital sums [that is principal]' (S2: 279).

On this basis, most Islamic scholars have argued that *riba* embraces not only usury, but all interest (*riba*). This is reminiscent of arguments by medieval Western scholars that all interest is usurious. *Riba* comes from the root *rab-a* meaning to increase (or exceed), while *rib.h* comes from the root *rabi.ha* meaning to gain (or profit). Certainly the above verse makes it clear that profit is not a form of *rib-a,* and Islamic banking rests on this foundation (Ahmad, 1982, p. 478).

The concept of *riba* is not limited to interest. Two forms of *riba* are identified in Islamic law. They are *riba al-qarud* which relates to usury involving loans, and *riba al-buyu* which relates to usury involving trade. The latter can take two forms. *Riba al-fadl* involves an exchange of unequal qualities or quantities of the same commodity simultaneously, whilst *riba al-nisa* involves the non-simultaneous exchange of equal qualities and quantities of the same commodity. The prohibition applies to objects which can be measured or weighed and which, in addition, belong to the same species. Forbidden are both an excess in quantity and a delay in performance.

Riba al-qarud, the usury of loans, involves a charge on a loan arising due to the passage of time, in other words a loan at interest, and is sometimes referred to as *riba al-nasia,* the usury of waiting. It arises where a user of another's wealth, in any form, is contracted by the other to pay a specified increase in addition to the principal amount in repayment. If the increase is pre-determined as a specified amount at the outset of the transaction, however this increase occurs, then the loan becomes a usurious one. The prohibition has been extended to all loans and debts where an increase accrues to the creditor.

That all *riba* is banned absolutely by the Holy Qur'an, the central source of Islamic law, cannot be denied. Similarly, in the *ahadith,* the next most authoritative source, the Prophet Muhammad (pbuh) condemns the one who takes it, the one who pays it, the one who writes the agreement for it and the witnesses to the agreement. Nevertheless, despite these clear injunctions, some scholars have questioned the circumstances surrounding the ban in the Holy Qur'an and have wondered whether the objection to *riba* applies (or ought to apply) with equal force today.[1] Fazlur Rahman (1964), in particular, argues as a dissenting view that there has been a disregard of what *riba* was historically, why the Holy Qur'an banned it so categorically, and the function of bank interest in a modern economy.

Revisionist Views

The essence of Rahman's position is that *sunna* is not fixed, but dynamic. The prohibition on *riba* clearly does extend back to the Holy Qur'an and the Prophet (pbuh). But the particular definition given to *riba*, as formalised by earlier generations and enshrined in the *hadith* – namely that it represents any amount of interest – need not be applied. What is needed instead according to Rahman is to study *hadith* in a situational context in order to understand the true meaning and extract the real moral value. Rather than apply *ahadith* directly, they should be studied for clues to the spirit of the injunction.

On this basis, it might be argued that the interest prohibition relates only to exorbitant interest rates and not to all forms of interest. The reference in the Holy Qur'an to *riba* 'doubled and multiplied' (S3: 130) may reflect that at the rise of Islam the practice of lending money was being exploited so as to reap excessive gains from the interest charged on loans. If borrowers could not meet the due date by which to return the capital borrowed, the lenders would double and then redouble the interest rates thus reducing the debtor to penury. Such practices were deemed intimidatory, unjust and against social and economic welfare. The Islamic interdiction of *riba* therefore fell into the net of social reform instituted by the Prophet (pbuh) upon pre-Islamic practices. Certainly, the Islamic code urges leniency towards debtors, and the Holy Qur'an specifies no punishment for unpaid debts.

Similarly, the characteristics of Arab society[2] at the time should be recalled – a largely agricultural, partly nomadic, civilisation living as settled communities in walled towns (to protect themselves from marauding Bedouins), linked by caravan routes to each other and Asia Minor. In such an environment, the need for borrowing often arose, not from normal commercial expansion, but from misfortune – famine, crop failure, loss of a caravan, and so on. To charge interest to kin, under such circumstances, would violate tribal loyalty. Since crop failure and so on may occur to anyone, through no fault of their own, a system of lending freely without interest could be seen as a sort of mutual-help insurance system.

Drawing on some of these points, modernists have raised a number of issues about the definition of *riba*. Some have claimed that Islam has prohibited 'exploitative' or 'usurious' *riba* rather than interest *per se*, thereby allowing for a 'fair' return on loanable funds (Rida, 1959). Others like the Syrian Doualibi, would differentiate between 'consumption' loans and 'production' loans on the grounds that the verses in the Holy Qur'an relating to *riba* go hand-in-hand with injunctions to alleviate the condition of the poor, needy and weaker sections of the community (cited in Abu Zahra, 1970). There has also been advanced the view that the prohibition of *riba* covers only individuals, not the giving or taking of interest among corporate entities, such as companies, banks or governments. Some such as Tantawi, the Sheikh of al-Azhar in Cairo, even argue that bank interest is a sharing of the bank's commercial profit and, being a profit share, is therefore permissible. This view, like the other modernist views, has been almost unanimously rejected.

Also rejected have been those arguments that see fixed interest rates to be *haram* and variable interest rates *halal*. It is said that if the rate of interest is allowed to vary then this is permissible since the actual rate of return is not fixed in advance. While it is true that the absolute amount of interest under a floating rate contract is not fixed, the formula is specified (for example, LIBOR plus a set spread) and in this sense the payment is pre-determined. In effect, both fixed and variable loan contracts require interest to be paid and only the method of determining the amount of interest differs.

'Zeros' have also been rejected. When first introduced, some commentators argued that the zero-coupon bonds are 'Islamic' because no interest is paid during their lifetime. A bond is a 'zero coupon bond' if no coupons (that is, interest instalments) are due to the bondholder during the life of that bond. Investors therefore are only prepared to buy zero-coupon bonds at a price that is below face value so that, when the bond matures, the difference between the purchase price and the face value is realised as a gain of waiting. Again, interest is paid, it is just that it is all paid at the maturity date instead of in instalments over the life of the bond.

Thus, despite the modernist views on the meaning of *riba* and how it should justifiably be defined, the dominant position remains intact. One of the most important documents on Islamic banking, the CII (Council of Islamic Ideology) Report (1983) is explicit: 'There is complete unanimity among all schools of thought in Islam that the term *riba* stands for interest in all its types and forms' (p. 7).

Razi's Five Reasons

This leaves the question: why? Razi ([1872]1938) set forth some of the reasons as to the prohibition of *riba*:

1. That *riba* is but the exacting of another's property without any
    countervalue while according to the saying of the Prophet (pbuh) a man's
    property is unlawful to the other as his blood. It is argued that *riba* should
    be lawful to the creditor in return for the use of money and the profit
    which the debtor derives from it. Had this been in the possession of the
    creditor he would have earned profit by investing it in some business. But
    it should be noted that profit in business is uncertain while the excess
    amount which the creditor gets towards interest is certain. Hence
    insistence upon a sum certain in return for what is uncertain is but harm
    done to the debtor.
2. That *riba* is forbidden because it prevents men from taking part in active
    professions. The moneyed man, if he gets income through *riba*, depends
    upon this easy means and abandons the idea of taking pains and earning
    his livelihood by way of trade or industry which serves to retard the
    progress and prosperity of the people.
3. That the contract of *riba* leads to a strained relationship between man and
    man. If it is made illegal there will be no difficulty in lending and getting
    back what has been lent, but if it is made legal people, in order to gratify
    their desires, will borrow even at an exorbitant rate of interest which
    results in friction and strife and strips society of its goodliness.
4. That the contract of *riba* is a contrivance to enable the rich to take in
    excess of the principal which is unlawful and against justice and equity.
    As a consequence of it, the rich grow still richer and the poor still poorer.
5. That the illegality of *riba* is proved by the text of the Holy Qur'an and is
    not necessary that men should know the reasons for it. We have to discard
    it as illegal though we are unaware of the reasons (Vol. 2, p. 531).

For most scholars the last is sufficient. The meaning and scope of *riba* and
its grave nature have been brought to light in the Holy Qur'an (S2: 225). Its
prohibition cannot be questioned, as the verse 'God permitteth trading and
forbideth *riba*' is quite clear. When the text is clear on this point there is no
need for further clarification. Because the Holy Qur'an has stated that only the
principal should be taken, there is no alternative but to interpret *riba* according
to that wording. Therefore, the existence or otherwise of injustice in a loan
transaction is irrelevant. Whatever the circumstances are, the lender has no
right to receive any increase over and above the principal.

The Coverage of Islamic Law

Despite these clear rulings, Islamic law has not achieved, nor does it claim,
universality on this point. Islamic law is binding for the Muslim to its full
extent in the territory of the Islamic state, to a slightly lesser extent in enemy

territory, and for the non-Muslim only to a limited extent in Islamic territory. Also, Islamic law has been conscious of its status on this issue as a religious ideal. Most modern Islamic countries have legislated for, or tacitly approve, the role of interest within their economies, and allow enforcement of interest claims, albeit with a government-imposed ceiling upon rates (usury laws). Although this practice occurs, it remains not acceptable by *shari'a*.

Exceptions to this modern solution are Iran, Pakistan, Sudan and also Saudi Arabia. Saudi Arabia never came under British colonial rule, and the pre-existing *shari'a* court system retains general jurisdiction in the Kingdom, although a complex system of tribunals enforce commercial, labour and financial regulations (Lerrick and Mian, 1982; Brown, 1997). Islamic banking in Saudi Arabia is not mandatory, and conventional banks operate. In Pakistan, Sudan and Iran, in contrast, statutory enforcement of Islamic banking precepts does exist.

Other than in these three countries, Islamic banking has developed to fill the void between religious ideal and actual commercial practice. In all its guises, however, the concept of Islamic banking which has been practised is built on the narrow interpretation of the nature of *riba*.

PROFIT-SHARING ARRANGEMENTS: *MUDARABA* AND *MUSHARAKA*[3]

In banning *riba*, Islam seeks to establish a society based upon fairness and justice (Holy Qur'an 2: 239). A loan provides the lender with a fixed return irrespective of the outcome of the borrower's venture. It is much fairer to have a sharing of the profits and losses. Fairness in this context has two dimensions: the supplier of capital possesses a right to reward, but this reward should be commensurate with the risk and effort involved and thus be governed by the return on the individual project for which funds are supplied (Presley, 1988). Hence, what is forbidden in Islam is the predetermined return. The sharing of profit is legitimate and the acceptability of that practice has provided the foundation for the development and implementation of Islamic banking. In Islam, the owner of capital can legitimately share the profits made by the entrepreneur. What makes profit-sharing permissible in Islam, while interest is not, is that in the case of the former it is only the profit-sharing ratio, not the rate of return itself, that is predetermined.

A banking system in which interest is not allowed appears strange to those accustomed to Western banking practices. In this respect, it is necessary to distinguish between the expressions 'rate of interest' and 'rate of return'. Whereas Islam clearly forbids the former, it not only permits, but rather encourages, trade and the profit motive, as we saw in the previous section. The difference is that in trade there is always the risk of loss or low returns. What is eschewed is the guaranteed rate of interest: the pre-agreed, fixed return or amount for the use of money (Khan, 1986).

In the interest-free system sought by adherents to Muslim principles, people are able to earn a return on their money only by subjecting themselves to the risk involved in profit-sharing. According to the Hanafi school, profit can be earned in three ways. The first is to use one's capital. The second is to employ one's labour. The third is to employ one's judgement which amounts to taking a risk. Al-Kásáni, the Hanafi jurist, states: 'The rule, in our view, is that entitlement to profit is either due to wealth (*mál*) or work ('*amal*) or by bearing a liability for loss (*damán*).' ([1910]1968, vol. 7, p. 3545).

With the use of interest rates in financial transactions excluded, Islamic banks are expected to undertake operations only on the basis of profit-and-loss-sharing (PLS) arrangements or other acceptable modes of financing. Gafoor (1995) considers the concept to be of very recent origin:

> The earliest references to the reorganisation of banking on the basis of profit-sharing rather than interest are found in Anwar Qureshi ([1946]1991), Naiem Siddiqi (1948) and Ahmad (1952) in the late forties, followed by a more elaborate exposition by Mawdudi in 1950 (1961). ... They have all recognised the need for commercial banks and the evil of interest in that enterprise, and have proposed a banking system based on the concept of *Mudarabha* – profit and loss sharing (p. 37–8)

But, of course, the idea has earlier origins:

> This situation was envisaged by Islam 1400 years ago. The Islamic law asserted that there should be no pre-agreed rates of interest on loans. Uzair ([1955]1978) says that Islam emphasises on agreed ratios of profit sharing rather than fixed and predetermined percentages. Instead, the transactions should be on profit and loss sharing basis (Siddiqui, 1994, p. 28)

Under Islamic commercial law, partnerships and all other forms of business organisation are set up primarily for a single objective: the sharing of profits through joint participation. *Mudaraba* and *musharaka* are the two profit-sharing arrangements preferred under Islamic law, and of these *mudaraba* is the most commonly employed PLS method (at least in terms of the raising of funds). Note that although PLS is the generally used description for the Islamic financing arrangements, it is not strictly 'loss sharing' from an economic viewpoint, because the owner of the capital is the partner who loses the capital, the other losing his effort only. This distinction is made clear below.

Mudaraba

A *mudaraba* can be defined as a contract between at least two parties whereby one party, the financier (*sahib al-mal* or *rabb al-mal*), entrusts funds to another party, the entrepreneur (*mudarib*), to undertake an activity or venture. This type of contract is in contrast with *musharaka*. In arrangements based on *musharaka* there is also profit-sharing, but all parties have the right to participate in managerial decisions. In *mudaraba*, the financier is not allowed a role in management of the enterprise. Consequently *mudaraba* represents a PLS contract where the return to lenders is a specified share in the profit/loss outcome of the project in which they have a stake.

The *mudarib* becomes a trustee (*amín*) for the capital entrusted to him by way of *mudaraba*. The *mudarib* is to utilise the funds in an agreed manner and then return to the *rabb al-mal* the principal and the pre-agreed share of the profit. The *mudarib* keeps for himself what remains of such profits. The following are the significant characteristics:

1. The division of profits between the two parties must necessarily be on a proportional basis and cannot provide for a lump-sum or guaranteed return to the *rabb al-mal* (beneficial owner).
2. The *rabb al-mal* is not liable for losses beyond the capital he has contributed.
3. The *mudarib* (labour partner) does not share in the losses except for the loss of his time and efforts.

These contractual arrangements may be either simple or complex, and restricted or unrestricted. A simple *mudaraba* may have two parties to the contract, an investor and an entrepreneur or 'worker', or it may have more than one party on either side, that is, a number of investors and a number of workers, and the arrangements may vary. Complex *mudaraba* may take several forms; for example, the investor may be a partnership and the worker may be a partnership. The unrestricted or absolute type is one in which the capital is handed over and neither the type of work that is to be done, nor the location, nor the time, nor the quality of work, nor those with whom he is to trade is determined. The restricted type is one in which some or all of these things are determined.

Considering its origins and historical validity, the word *mudaraba* has been derived from *darb fi al-ard*, which means those 'who journey through the earth (*yadribuna fi al-ard*) seeking the bounty of Allah' (S73: 20). Because of his work and travel, the *mudarib* becomes entitled to part of the profits of the venture. In terms of the *sunna*, jurists rely on the precedent of the contract of *mudaraba*, concluded by the Prophet (pbuh) with Khadija prior to his marriage, as a result of which he travelled to Syria. Thus the legal evidence employed in support of the arrangement rest on both the Holy Qur'an and the *sunna*.

When defining a *muduraba*, jurists focused on it as a 'participation in profits' (Nyazee, 1999, p. 244). Those who wanted to distinguish *mudaraba* from the other types of partnerships, within this broad definition, added the words: 'with wealth from one side and work from the other'. Al-Quduri said: '*Mudarabah* is a contract for participation in profits with wealth from one partner and work by the other'. According to the terminology used by the jurists of Medina, *mudaraba* is also called *muqarada* or *qirad*.

A feature of a *mudaraba* comes from the dual roles of the *mudarib* as agent and partner. The *mudarib* is the agent of the *rabb al-mal* in whatever transactions he undertakes in the wealth of the *mudaraba*. The *mudarib* then becomes a partner of the *rabb al-mal* when profit emerges, because *mudaraba* is a partnership in profit, and an agent is not entitled to profit on the basis of his work after the emergence of profit, but he becomes a partner in this situation due to the contract of partnership. The wealth of the *mudaraba* becomes a joint ownership between *mudarib* and the *rabb al-mal*, and the share of the *mudarib* is now on the basis of his undivided share in co-ownership. All division of profit must be expressed as a ratio or as a part of the total profit. The profit cannot be expressed as a percentage of the capital invested. This principle is the *sine qua non* of a valid contract. Any deviation from it or condition that leads to uncertainty in this requirement will render the contract unenforceable.

Although profit-sharing and interest lending may seem alike, the differences are clearly more than semantic ones. The yield is not guaranteed in profit-sharing, while, in interest lending, the loan is not contingent on the profit or loss outcome, and is usually secured, so that the debtor has to repay the borrowed capital plus the fixed (or pre-determined) interest amount regardless of the resulting yield of the capital. Thus, with interest lending, the financial losses fall most directly upon the borrower. Under *mudaraba,* financial losses are borne completely by the lender. The entrepreneur as such loses the time and effort invested in the enterprise, and the reward for his labour. This distribution effectively treats human capital equally with financial capital.

Musharaka

Interest lending and *mudaraba* can be said to represent the two polar alternatives in terms of financing. *Musharaka*-based transactions represent something of a middle road between these two. Under a *musharaka*, the entrepreneur adds some of his own capital to that supplied by the financial investors, so exposing himself to the risk of capital loss. In this respect, the entrepreneur's own financial contribution defines the difference between the two profit-and-loss-sharing modes of financing. Because the agent also contributes to the capital, he can therefore claim a greater percentage of the profit. In most other respects, the *musharaka* bears the same characteristics as the *mudaraba*.

Formally, *musharaka* (from the Arabic *shirkah* or *shirikah*) implies partnership in a venture, and can be defined as a form of partnership where two or more persons combine either their capital or labour together, to share the profits, enjoying similar rights and liabilities. It can take the form of a *mufawada*, meaning an unlimited, unrestricted and equal partnership in which the partners enjoy complete equality in the areas of capital, management and right of disposition. Each partner is both the agent and the guarantor of the other. A more limited investment partnership is known as an *'inan* (*shirkah al-'inan*). This type of partnership occurs when two or more parties contribute to a capital fund, either with money, contributions in kind or labour. Each partner is only the agent and not the guarantor of his partner. An *'inan musharaka* is limited in scope to the specific undertaking.[4] For both the partners share profits in an agreed manner and bear losses in proportion to their capital contributions.

Such (contractual partnerships) can be considered proper because the parties concerned have willingly entered into a contractual agreement for joint investment and the sharing of profits and risks. The agreement need not necessarily be formal and written, it could be informal and oral. As in *mudaraba*, the profits can be shared in any equitably agreed proportion. The basis for entitlement to the profits of a *musharaka* are capital, active participation in the *musharaka* business and responsibility. Profits are to be distributed among the partners in business on the basis of proportions settled by them in advance. The share of every party in profit must be determined as a proportion or percentage. Losses must, however, be shared in proportion to the capital contribution. On this point all jurists are unanimous.

Banks' Role

While *musharaka* is the term used to describe partnerships that are formed for various commercial activities, the basic concept of a *musharaka* has also been used as a technique for Islamic financial institutions to provide finance to commercial enterprises. For example, the features of *musharaka* can be used to structure a working capital facility for a company, or it can be used for joint investment in activities such as real estate development. In Sudan, the *musharaka* has been utilised extensively in rural finance. In Western countries, diminishing *musharaka* has been used for residential property financing.

Islamic bankers have also adapted and refined the *mudaraba* concept to form the two-tier or triple *mudaraba* (sometimes called re-*mudaraba, mudarib yudarib*). In this arrangement, the *mudaraba* contract has been extended to include three parties: the depositors as financiers, the bank as an intermediary, and the entrepreneur who requires funds. The bank acts as an entrepreneur (*mudarib*) when it receives funds from depositors, and as a financier (*rabb al-mal*) when it provides the funds to entrepreneurs. The main conditions associated with a *mudaraba* contract are as follows:

1. The bank receives funds from the public on the basis of unrestricted *mudaraba*. There are no constraints imposed on the bank concerning the kind of activity, duration, and location of the enterprise. However, a *mudaraba* contract cannot be applied to finance *haram* activities which are forbidden by Islam. Such a contract is considered null and void.
2. The bank has the right to aggregate and pool the profit from different investments, and share the net profit (after deducting administrative costs, capital depreciation and Islamic tax) with depositors according to a specified formula.[5] In the event of losses, the depositors lose a proportional share or the entire amount of their funds. The return to the financier has to be strictly maintained as a share of profits.
3. The bank applies the restricted form of *mudaraba* when funds are provided to entrepreneurs. The bank has the right to determine the kind of activities, the duration, and the location of the projects and monitor the investments. However, these restrictions may not be formulated in a way so as to harm the performance of the entrepreneur. When a project is undertaken, the bank cannot interfere with the management of the investment and take part in the daily operation of the business. Thus loan covenants and other such constraints usual in conventional commercial bank lending are not allowed in Islamic banking.
4. Under a *mudaraba*, the *rabb al-mal* cannot demand any guarantee from the *mudarib* to return the capital or the capital with a profit, since the relationship between the investor and the *mudarib* is a fiduciary one and the *mudarib* is a trustworthy person. Accordingly, the bank cannot require any guarantee such as security and collateral from the entrepreneur in order to insure its capital against the possibility of an eventual loss. Such a condition makes the *mudaraba* contract null and void. But it is allowable for there to be a guarantee from an independent third party.
5. The *mudaraba* contract should assign a profit rate for each party. The rate should be a ratio, and not a fixed amount. Assigning a fixed amount to either party invalidates the *mudaraba* due to the possibility that the profit realised may not equal the sum so stipulated. Before arriving at a profit figure, the *mudaraba* venture should be converted to money, and the capital should be set aside. The *mudarib* is entitled to deduct all business-related expenses from the *mudaraba* capital.

6. The liability of the financier is limited exclusively to the capital provided. On the other hand, the liability of the entrepreneur is also restricted, but in this case solely to his labour and effort. Nevertheless, if negligence or mismanagement can be proven the entrepreneur may be liable for the financial loss and be obliged to remunerate the financier accordingly.
7. The entrepreneur shares the profit with the bank according to a previously agreed division. Until the investment yields a profit, the bank is able to pay a salary to the entrepreneur. This salary is determined on the basis of the ruling market salary.

Mudaraba and *musharaka* constitute, at least in principle if not always in practice, the twin pillars of Islamic banking (Ariff, 1982). The two methods conform fully with Islamic principles, in that under both arrangements lenders share in the profits and losses of the enterprises for which funds are provided. The *musharaka* principle is invoked in the equity structure of Islamic banks and is similar to the modern concepts of partnership and joint stock ownership. Insofar as the depositors are concerned, an Islamic bank acts as a *mudarib* which manages the funds of the depositors to generate profits subject to the rules of *mudaraba*. The bank may in turn use the depositors' funds on a *mudaraba* basis in addition to other lawful (but less preferable) modes of financing, including mark-up or deferred sales, leasing and beneficence loans (see below). In other words, the bank operates a two-tier *mudaraba* system in which it acts both as the *mudarib* on the saving side of the equation and as the *rabbul-mal* (owner of capital) on the investment portfolio side.

Some Incentive Questions

In summary, then, a *mudaraba* loan contract is a device for directly linking the remuneration to capital to the outcome of the project. A *riba* contract, by contrast, creates an explicit relationship between the input and remuneration of capital. This is the formal position. But the differences between the two might go beyond this formal distinction, and may extend to economic incentives and managerial performance. Under a standard incentive compatible *riba* contract, the manager is left free to choose the individually optimal level of effort contingent on the specified level of investment. *Mudaraba*, on the other hand, allows there to be a relationship between capital investment and the outcome of the project. Lowering the specified return from the project in the bad state (and therefore the associated level of effort) below that which may be desirable given the level of investment, provides an inducement for the manager in the good state truthfully to report the investment prospects. With this second instrument for achieving incentive compatibility, *mudaraba* might act to reduce inefficiently large fluctuations in capital investment (Presley and Sessions, 1994). These possible incentive differences are examined further when we compare governance structures in Islamic banking with those in traditional Western banking.

At this juncture, we should also note that Islamic banking and the *mudaraba* contract have been criticised on political and ideological grounds (Haque, 1985, p. 213). It is argued that Islamic banks, established by Muslim capitalists, will exploit small savers by using a medievally-derived religious financial instrument as a legal device. The shareholders of Islamic banks would put the funds of small depositors at risk in order to make an exorbitant profit without exposing their own wealth (Haque, 1985, pp. 214–6). Again, we take up this issue later, when examining the performance of Islamic banks. For the moment, we consider how these Islamic contracting principles are put into operation in Islamic banking.

FUNDING OPERATIONS

Besides their own capital and equity, Islamic banks rely on two main sources of funds: transaction deposits, which are risk free but yield no return; and investment deposits, which carry the risks of capital loss for the promise of variable return (Khan and Mirakhor, 1989). In all, there are four main types of accounts:

(a) Current accounts
(b) Savings accounts
(c) Investment accounts
(d) Special investment accounts

These accounts constitute the principal source of funds for Islamic banks, as outlined in the *Handbook of Islamic Banking* (HIB).   Except for the requirement that the return to the depositors is not fixed in advance for some but rather based on profit-and-loss-sharing principles, these accounts are similar to those of traditional banks (HIB, 1982, Vol. 5, pp. 122–85). The main characteristics of the various accounts are outlined below.

Current Account

Islamic banks offer the usual chequing, savings and investment accounts as depositing options. An Islamic bank has the possibility of requiring a fixed minimum amount as a condition for opening an account. The banks provide a broad range of payment facilities, clearing mechanisms, bank drafts, bills of exchange, travellers' cheques, and so on (but not all offer credit cards or bankcards). Usually, no charges are made by the banks for these services.

From the viewpoint of Islamic law, there are some differences between *fiqh* and banks on the treatment of current deposits. In general, *fiqh* consider deposits in current accounts as guaranteed loans. Full repayment of these funds is guaranteed at any time on demand and they are seen as loans from depositors to the banks. As viewed by banks, the Islamic basis of current accounts derives from the principle of *al-wadiah* (trust or safekeeping). *Wadia* can be defined as 'setting up an agency contract for the purpose of protecting one's wealth' (Jaziri, of the Maliki school, p. 248). Some scholars see demand deposits as a trust, funds handed to the bank for protection or for safekeeping.

As a corollary, the depositor does not receive remuneration for depositing funds in a current account, because the guaranteed funds will not be used for PLS ventures. The Islamic banks' argument is that since the bank is in fact 'borrowing' money from the depositor, it is only obliged to return the amount loaned, the depositor not being entitled to any return, on the basis of the rule in Islamic law that 'any loan which begets any advantage is *riba*' even though the bank has utilised the deposit.[6] For this reason, the funds accumulating in these accounts can only be used to balance liquidity needs of the bank and for short-term transactions on the bank's responsibility, not for other investments.

Savings Accounts

An Islamic savings account is similar to any usual savings deposit in a traditional commercial bank, except that they do not earn any fixed return. A number of different methods of operating them have emerged (Ahmed, 1995). One is to accept savings deposits on the *al-wadiah* principle, described above, but in this case requesting the depositors to grant the bank permission to employ the funds at its own risk, while guaranteeing full return of the deposits and sharing any profits voluntarily. A second method is to treat savings deposits as *qard hasan* deposits (benevolent loans) from the depositors to the bank, giving them pecuniary or non-pecuniary benefits. The third method involves integrating savings deposits in various ways with investment accounts. Balances or the required minimum balance may, with appropriate authorisation, be invested or incorporated into an investment pool, with profits shared in an agreed manner on the basis of *mudaraba*. According to *shari'a* scholars, holders of savings deposits should receive a return which varies with the profits of the bank, provided that they agree also to share in any losses of the bank. However, in some cases, such as Bank Islam Malaysia Bethad, for example, a share of profits may be paid, though the return of the nominal value of deposit is guaranteed. In other cases, in order to encourage deposits in savings accounts, depositors may be given the special privilege of drawing funds for financing a small project or the purchase of productive or durable consumer goods, and this will be on either a *mudaraba* or interest-free basis.

Investment Accounts

Depositors in this category of deposits primarily are concerned with earning profits, rather using the account for safekeeping their money or for using it for transaction purposes. An investment account operates under the *mudaraba al-mutlaqa* principle, described above. The conditions of this account differ from those of the savings accounts by virtue of (a) a higher fixed minimum amount, (b) a longer duration of deposits, and (c) most importantly, the depositor may lose some of or all of his funds in the event of the bank making losses. The *mudarib* (active partner) must have absolute freedom in the management of the investment of the subscribed capital. In this type of account the bank acts as an entrepreneur and the depositors provide the capital. The funds may be placed for terms ranging from one month upwards and can be withdrawn if advance notice is given to the bank.

Special Investment Accounts

Special investment accounts also operate under the *mudaraba* principle, and usually are directed towards larger investors and institutions. The difference between these accounts and the investment account is that the special investment account is related to a specified project, and the investor has the choice to invest directly in a preferred project carried out by the bank. The maturity and the distribution of profits are negotiated separately for each special investment account, with the yield directly related to the success of the particular investment project.

FINANCING ACTIVITIES

Mudaraba al-Mugayada (Trustee)

The bank provides 100 per cent financing for the project in question. An investor such as a bank or group of investors entrusts capital to an entrepreneur who ploughs this capital into production or trade and then returns to the investor(s) a prespecified share of his revenue. The remaining share is kept by the entrepreneur as a reward for his time and effort. The bank may not interfere with the management of the project but has the right to undertake follow-up and monitoring tasks. If the business fails, the capital loss is borne exclusively by the bank(s). The entrepreneur loses only the yield of his labour unless negligence or mismanagement can be proven. The difference between this contract and the deposit contract *mudaraba al-mutlaqa* described earlier is thus that the *al-muqayada* contract is limited to a particular project.

Musharaka (Equity Participation)

Musharaka is used in long-term investment projects, whereas *mudaraba* have traditionally been employed in investment projects with short horizons and in trade and commerce. In the *musharaka* type of participation, the bank engages in projects and enterprises under a PLS contract. Since the entrepreneur has added some of his own capital to that supplied by the banks, the entrepreneur bears some of the capital loss. Profits and losses are shared according to pre-fixed proportions, but for profits these proportions need not coincide with the ratio of financing input. The bank often participates in the execution of the projects in which it has subscribed, sometimes by providing managerial expertise. Figure 3.1 illustrates the elements of a *musharaka* arrangement.

Norhashimah Mohd Yasin (1997) has summarised the rules governing *musharaka* as follows:

- *Musharaka* can be for a general or specific transaction for a specified period of time, which may be extended if the partners agree.
- All partners should receive regular information concerning the operation of the business and its finances.
- Partners must agree in advance before entering a new *musharaka* contract with others.
- The proportion of profit to be shared must be agreed at the time of making the contract.[7]
- The ratio of sharing the loss must be strictly in accordance with the proportion of investment.
- Ideally the capital should be in money, rather than commodities. If the latter, the monetary value must be estimated.
- The *musharaka* contract is terminated on death or the giving of notice.

Buckmaster (1996), for the Institute of Islamic Banking and Finance, gives an example of how *musharaka* can be used to finance a working capital facility for a company with a history of profitability. The Islamic financial institution would provide the funds to its customer, usually by the deposit of the funds to the customer's account with the financial institution. The customer would then make use of those funds in the ordinary course of its business. The difference, however, in comparison with a conventional working capital facility, is that instead of debiting the customer's account with a predetermined rate of interest, the Islamic bank would periodically debit the

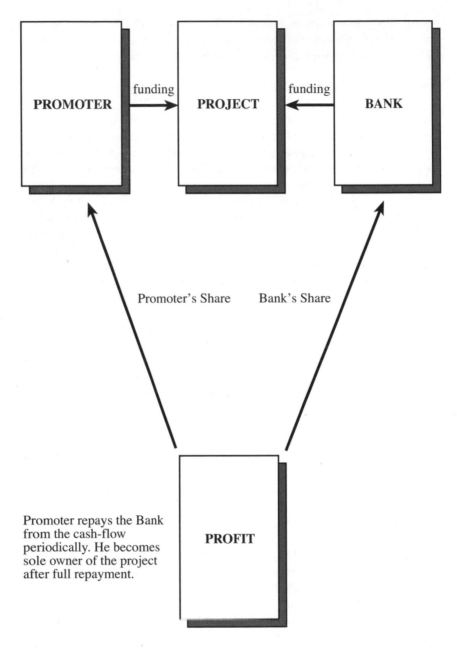

Promoter repays the Bank from the cash-flow periodically. He becomes sole owner of the project after full repayment.

Source: Dresdner Bank (1996).

Figure 3.1   Musharaka long term financing

customer's account for an amount equal to a pre-determined rate of profit, subject to adjustment on a regular basis, usually quarterly.

At the end of the financial year, the profits are calculated. If the amount due to the Islamic bank exceeds the provisional profit already debited from the account, the amount not paid to it will be credited to a special reserve account which the company will create in its books. Conversely, if the amount due to the bank is less than the provisional profit already collected by the Islamic institution, the special reserve account will be reduced by the amount of the excess payment to the Islamic bank. Upon the termination of the *musharaka* financing, a final profit and loss account is prepared and at that time any balance in the special reserve account is shared by the financing institution and the customer in accordance with the ratio they have agreed upon on their contract.

A central feature of a *musharaka* financing is the joint determination of the customer's investment in the business, which in turn dictates the ratio used to allocate profits and losses between the customer and the financial institution. If, for example, during a financial year, the company generates losses, the special reserve account is reduced by the amount of those losses. If the balance of the special reserve account is insufficient to make good such losses, the customer may ask the Islamic bank for a refund (in whole or in part) of the provisional profits previously paid to it.

There are two main types of *musharaka* contracts: (i) constant (permanent) and (ii) decreasing (diminishing) participation. In the first case, the bank participates in the equity and receives a share of the profit on a pro-rata basis annually, and period of termination of the contract is not specified. So the contract may continue as long as the parties concerned agree to it. By contrast, the diminishing partnership of *musharaka* is getting more popular in Islamic banks than permanent *musharaka* because of its potential to bankers (Ahmed, 1997). In permanent *musharaka*, funds are committed for a long period, but this is not so in the case of diminishing *musharaka*. Decreasing *musharaka* allows equity participation in the first place and shared profit on a pro-rata basis. This system also provides further payment of money over and above the bank's share in the profit as a repayment of the part of equity held by the bank. In this manner, the equity held by the bank is reduced progressively with the passage of time. After the lapse of a certain period of time, the bank will have zero equity and will cease to be a partner.

Muzarah/Musaqah

These are traditional financing methods employing *mudaraba* and *musharaka* principles. *Muzarah* is the traditional counterpart of *mudaraba* in farming in which the farmer takes agricultural land on a share-cropping basis. Banks hand over to farmers land which they own or which is otherwise in their possession. The plot of land has to be completely specified in the contract and must be given for a specified period. The output from the land is shared by the bank and farmers in an agreed proportion. *Musaqah* is the counterpart of *musharaka* in orchard keeping, and an arrangement is made for planting and tending fruit trees. The harvest of the orchard or garden is divided among the contracted parties (bank and farmer) in a specified ratio, normally according to their respective contributions.

Other Financing Modes

Musharaka and *mudaraba* and their traditional counterparts are all Islamic investments based on the principle of profit-and-loss-sharing. These are supposedly the main conduits for the outflow of funds from the banks. But not all uses of funds are amenable to PLS, and certain alternative financing modes are available, and in practice, Islamic banks have often shown a strong preference for these other less risky modes. These alternative methods, which are meant to be applied by Islamic banks when the PLS principles cannot be utilised, include mark-up (*murabaha*), instalments (*bai bi-thamin ajil*), deferred payment (*bai'muajjal*), pre-paid purchase (*bai'salam*), manufacturing (*istisnaa*), leasing (*ijara*) and lease-purchase (*ijara wa iqtina*), and beneficence (*qard hasan*). In some cases these overlap, in others (such as for housing finance) they are combined with PLS techniques. Almost all are based on the charging of a fixed cost rather than an allocation of profit and loss.

Murabaha (cost plus mark-up)

The most commonly used mode of financing seems to be the 'mark-up' device which is termed *murabaha*. In a *murabaha* transaction, the bank finances the purchase of a good or asset by buying the item on behalf of its client and adding a mark-up before reselling the item to the client on a 'cost plus' basis profit contract (HIB, Vol. 5, pp. 329–33). This contract form is used especially for foreign trade and working capital financing for circumstances in which banks will purchase raw materials, goods or equipment and sell them to a client at cost, plus a negotiated profit margin, to be paid normally within a fixed period of time or in instalments. When a *murabaha* sale is made on a deferred payment basis, it is called *murabaha-bi-muajjal* (Ahmed, 1997). With *murabaha*, Islamic banks do not share in profits and losses, but instead assume more of the role of a classic financial intermediary. In the traditional *murabaha* in *fiqh* (jurisprudence) books, the mark-up differs from interest in that it is not to be explicitly related to the duration of the loan but instead computed on a transaction basis for services rendered and not for deferring payment. Figure 3.2 illustrates a trade financing through *murabaha*. This might be arranged under a letter of credit (LC) requesting the bank to purchase/import the goods specified. The bank will issue the LC and pay the proceeds to the negotiating bank. The bank sells the goods to the customer on their arrival.

It may appear at first glance that the mark-up is just another term for interest as charged by conventional banks, interest thus being admitted through the back door. Yet the legality of the traditional type of *murabaha* is not questioned by any of the schools of Islamic law (although there are disputes about some forms of *murabaha* which have come into use where the factor of time commitment is added). What makes the traditional *murabaha* transaction in *fiqh* books Islamically legitimate is that the bank first acquires the asset for resale at profit, so that a commodity is sold for money and the operation is not a mere exchange of money for money (Wilson, 1983, p. 84–5). In the process the bank assumes certain risks between purchase and resale; for example, a sudden fall in price could see the client refusing to accept the goods. That is, the bank takes responsibility for the good before it is safely delivered to the client. The services rendered by the Islamic bank are therefore regarded as quite different from those of a conventional bank which simply lends money to the client to buy the good.

While the *murabaha* is employed predominantly in the context of trade financing, the technique has been adapted for a variety of other uses. It is utilised as a vehicle for syndication, on the classic lead manager and co-managers format, enabling a number of banks to participate in the financing. One such application involved the acquisition, and financing on a deferred basis, of equipment for a power generation project. Another has been to finance home purchase whereby a designated residence is purchased at a specified price by a financial institution, which, in turn, resells the property to the consumer, with the purchase price (including a profit component) to be paid in instalments over a period of five years (Buckmaster, 1996).

Murabahas are also used by Islamic banks for the investment of idle funds on a sale and repurchase basis, much as a conventional bank might do with a 'repo' but using commodities rather than *riba* instruments (Rahman, 1999). The bank's agent contacts a commodity broker and obtains a quote for the purchases of quantity of permissible commodities (often metals) at a set price for delivery against payment. At the same time, the agent enters into a transaction for the simultaneous resale of the same commodities to another broker, delivery to be made on a current basis but payment to be deferred for a specified time period (generally one, two or three months). The difference between the higher deferred purchase price and the original price represents, after the agent's fee, the rate of profit to the Islamic institution. This rate of

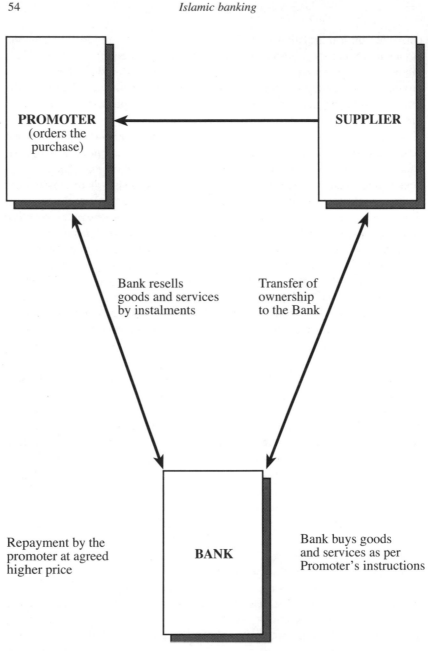

Source: Dresdner Bank (1966).

Figure 3.2   Trade finance through Murabaha

return is an Islamically-acceptable alternative to placing (that is, lending) money in an interest-bearing time deposit or using a bond repurchase.

Bai Bi-thamin Ajil (BBA)

This is similar to *murabaha* except that BBA is a deferred payment by instalments while *murabaha* is also a deferred payment but in a lump sum. With *murabaha* the purchaser should be aware of the cost price, which is in contrast to BBA. Some Islamic economic authors make no reference to BBA as it is incorporated into *murabaha*, for example in Pakistan (Yasin, 1997). However, in Malaysia BBA is used separately and distinct from *murabaha* for the specific purpose of the acquisition of assets such as buildings and machines for longer periods of time (for example, 10 to 30 years), while *murabaha* is for financing working capital (that is, within 30 to 120 days).

Bai'Muajjal (Deferred Payment)

Islamic banks have been resorting to purchase and resale of assets, products and properties on a deferred payment basis, which is termed *bai'muajjal*. Both BBA and *mudaraba* fall under this category of sale, because this transaction allows the sale of an item on the basis of deferred payment in instalments or in a lump-sum payment. The price of the product is agreed to between the buyer and the seller at the time of the sale and cannot include any charges for deferring payments. It is considered lawful in *fiqh* (jurisprudence) to charge a higher price for a good if payments are to be made at a later date. The general *shari'a* rules on sales apply, namely that the object must be in existence, be owned and possessed by the bank, the sale is instant and absolute, and the price is certain, with no conditions attached. According to *fiqh*, this does not amount to charging interest, since it is not a lending transaction but a trading one. This system is widely used in Pakistan and Bangladesh.

Bai'salam (Prepaid Purchase)

Reference must also be made to 'advance payment sale' or pre-paid purchase of goods, which is termed *bai'salam*, as a means used by Islamic banks to finance production. Here the price is paid at the time of the contract but the delivery takes place at a future date. This is a method which is really the opposite of the *murabaha*. There the bank gives the commodity first, and receives the money later. Here the bank pays the money first and receives the commodity later. It is a method which is normally used to finance agricultural products. The bank pays the value of the crops in advance, at a predetermined price, and receives the product later at the harvest time. The method is, of course, applicable to other trade activities that the bank may be interested to finance, and where there is a 'necessary. sale' denoting the need of the contracting parties to enter into this type of 'advance sale'. This mode enables an entrepreneur to sell his output to the bank at a price determined in advance. Islamic banks, in keeping with modern times, have extended this facility to manufactures as well (see next).

Istisnaa (Manufacturing)

This is a contract to acquire goods on behalf of a third party where the price is paid to the manufacturer in advance and the goods produced and delivered at a later date. It is a contract for production of specified items where a person or a company may ask the bank for production of such items, with inputs provided by the maker, at an agreed price. Such contracts are used for the financing of aircraft manufacture, equipment installation of factories, construction, and so on, where the subject matter needs manufacturing (while in *bai'salam* this is not necessarily the case).

Ju'alah (Commission)

Derived from the Arabic word *ju'l*, originally reward and now meaning fees, *ju'alah* means a transaction on a commission basis. The concept of *ju'alah* is similar to *istisnaa*. In *istisnaa* the seller provides a physical commodity; but in *ju'alah* the seller provides a service. In a *ju'alah* contract, a seller will offer a definite service to be provided as agreed upon whereas the buyer will pay a definite price for this service under the principle of *al-ujr*. This mode usually applies to transactions such as consultations and professional services, fund placements and trust services.

Ijara and *Ijara wa Iqtina* (Leasing)

Leasing or *ijara* is also frequently practised by Islamic banks. *Ijara* literally means 'to give something on rent', and technically it relates to transferring the usufruct of a particular property to another person on the basis of a rent claimed from him. The difference between sale (*bai*) and *ijara* is transfer of ownership *vis-à-vis* transfer of the usufruct (*manfa'a*). That is, the leased property remains in the ownership of the lessor and only its usufruct is transferred to the lessee.

Consequently, an *ijara*, or operating lease, is based on a contract between the lessor and lessee for use of a specific asset. The lessor retains the ownership of the asset and the lessee has possession and use of the asset on payment of specified rentals over a specified period. An *ijara wa iqtina*, on the other hand, is more like a financing lease. The rentals during the term of the lease are sufficient to amortise the leasing company's investment and provide an element of profit.

Under this mode of financing, the banks would buy the equipment or machinery and lease it out to their clients who may opt to buy the items eventually, in which case the monthly payments will consist of two components, that is, rental for the use of the equipment and instalments towards the purchase price. The original amount of the rent for the leased assets should be fixed in advance, but some incentive related to business success can be added. The client can also negotiate for the purchase of the asset at the end of the period. In such a case, the lease rentals paid in advance will be part of the price less the bank remuneration.

The profit element in an *ijara wa iqtina* is permissible, despite its similarity to an interest charge. According to Islamic jurists, the *shari'a* allows a fixed charge relating to tangible assets (as opposed to financial assets) because by converting financial capital into tangible assets the financier has assumed risks for which compensation is permissible. An *ijara wa iqtina* can either have a purchase option or a purchase obligation at the end of its term.

Since the distinguishing feature of *ijara* is that the assets remain the property of the Islamic bank, it has to put them up for rent every time the lease period expires so as not to have them remain unutilised for long periods of time. Under this mode of finance the bank bears the risk of recession or diminishing demand for these assets. Leasing also has been justified on the grounds that by retaining ownership the bank runs the risk of premature obsolescence. The rental equipment is often used in a transient manner, whether the situation is one of 'rental' or 'rent', the lessor is charged with the responsibility for maintenance. In the case of 'rental' especially the lessor is also charged with the responsibility for coping with the product's obsolescence, so that it may be regarded as a service-oriented business.

Islamic leasing is a major activity for Islamic banks. Although used primarily to finance high-valued equipment, such as aircraft, it is also being used increasingly to finance smaller items of equipment, such as medical equipment required by medicos in their private practice. A UK financial institution has established a programme to provide financing, structured in the manner of a financing lease, to individuals, aimed primarily at Gulf country nationals, who are interested in making property purchases in the UK.

Ijara Thumma Al-iqtina/Al-bai' (Hire Purchase Finance)

This, as we have noted, is one application of *ijara* in modern Islamic banking, when the bank rents the asset to the customer who promises to purchase the asset within a specified period. The rental payment could be a fixed amount or a percentage directly tied to the cash flow of the project (important for project finance) and consists of the bank's share in the net profit plus the rental charges. When the total rental charge equals the cost of the asset, ownership of the asset transfers to the customer.

Housing Property Finance

A combination of a diminishing *musharaka* and *ijara* forms the basis of home finance provided by Islamic banks in a number of countries. This concept requires the financier and the client to participate in the joint ownership of a property. The share of the financier is further divided into a number of units. The client is then able to purchase those units one by one periodically so that the equity held by the bank reduces progressively over time. Eventually, the bank will have zero equity and will cease to be a partner.

Justice Usmani (1999) considers the validity of such an arrangement based on the following transactions:

● The first step is to create a joint ownership in the property. There is no objection from Islamic scholars against structuring this transaction.
● The second part of the arrangement is that the financier leases his share in the house to the client and charges rent to him. Islamic scholars also permit this transaction insofar as the property is leased to the partner himself. All are unanimous on the validity of this *ijara* leasing transaction that eventually results in full ownership.
● The third step in the arrangement is that the client purchases different units of the undivided share of the financier. If the undivided share relates to both land and building, the sale of both is allowed according to all the Islamic schools.

There is then the question whether this transaction may be combined in a single arrangement, although each is permissible *per se*. It is a well-established rule of the Islamic legal system that one transaction cannot be made a pre-condition for another, and thus the agreement of joint purchase, leasing and selling different units of the share of the financier should not be tied up together in one single contract. However, the joint purchase and the contract of lease may be joined in one document, while at the time of the purchase of each unit, sale must be effected by the exchange of an offer and acceptance at that particular date. This example illustrates the complexity of Islamic law and the importance of *shari'a* advice when designing Islamic banking products.

Qard Hasan (Beneficence Loans)

This is the zero return type of loan that the Holy Qur'an urges Muslims to make available to those who need them. The borrower is obliged to repay only the principal amount of the loan, but is permitted to add a margin at his own discretion. The *qard hasan* borrowers also benefit from various services and financial and moral support rendered by the bank. This loan is often provided to charity institutions for the financing of their activities. Repayments are made over a period agreed by both parties. A levy of a modest service charge on such a loan is permissible provided it is based on the actual cost of administering the loan, and is not related to the amount or maturity of the loan.

Qard hasan funding may also be a way of cementing and facilitating existing business relationships. Al-Harran (1993, p. 99) gives examples of circumstances where it might be advisable for Islamic financial institutions to make use of *qard hasan* finance.

(a) In the case of *musharaka* between the institution and the client, it often happens that not all of the institution's shares in the project can be earmarked for the right to participate in profits. The institution's participation may be split into two parts: one constitutes a share in the partnership capital and the other a share in the working capital provided through *qard hasan*. However, under Islamic law, a question mark would exist about this *qard* because there is benefit derived out of it.

(b) A *qard hasan* can also be provided to a client with cash-flow problems.

(c) A third use of *qard hasan* may occur when a customer who has a blocked savings account which generates no interest encounters an urgent need for short-term finance.

Islamic Securities

Islamic financial institutions often maintain an international Islamic equity portfolio where the underlying assets comprise ordinary shares in well-run businesses, the productive activities of which exclude those on the prohibited list (alcohol, pork, armaments) and financial services based on interest income.

This general area has been one of considerable expansion over the last decade (as it has amongst conventional banks). In turn, there have been stimulated developments in investment-related instruments, such as Islamic mutual funds or unit trusts. Another development is the *muqarada*. This technique allows a bank to float what are effectively Islamic bonds to finance a specific project or direct investment. Investors who buy *muqarada* bonds take a share of the profits of the project being financed, but also share the risk of unexpectedly low profits, or even losses. They have no say in the management of the project, but act as non-voting shareholders, as indeed is the case with the other investment accounts offered under the *mudaraba* principle.

Other Activities

Besides their range of equity, trade financing and lending operations, Islamic banks worldwide also offer a full spectrum of fee-paid retail services that do not involve interest payments, including checking accounts, spot foreign exchange transactions, fund transfers, letters of credit, travellers' cheques, safe-deposit boxes, securities safekeeping, investment management and advice, and other normal services of modern banking.

CONCLUSION

It is clear from the above outline that Islamic banking goes beyond the pure financing activities of conventional banks. Islamic banks collect money from the depositors on the basis of *mudaraba* and invest the same in different projects/business/trading under different investment techniques using the funds under two-tiered or triple *mudaraba*. This system allows the institutions to collect funds from a large number of investors (depositors) on a profit-and-loss-sharing basis and then employ these funds as agent (*mudarib*) in equity arrangements and commodity (trade) investments which are in conformity with the Islamic principles explained in the previous chapter.

By its very nature, Islamic banking is a risky business compared with conventional banking, for risk-sharing forms the very basis of all Islamic financial transactions. To minimise risks, however, Islamic banks have taken pains to diversify risks and have established reserve funds out of past profits which they can fall back on in the event of any major loss. They have also shown a marked preference for particular types of contract. This becomes clear in later chapters.

NOTES

1. Modernist views are outlined in Rahman (1958, 1964), Rippin (1993), Brown (1996), Rayner (1991) and Saeed (1996).
2. The nature of Arab society is examined in Atiyah (1955) and Lindholm (1996).
3. Excellent accounts of profit-and-loss-sharing partnership techniques are contained in Al-Harran (1993) and Nyazee (1994, 1995, 1999). We follow Nyazee in dividing the traditional law of business organization into two categories, both being types of contract partnership. In the first category (for example *musharaka*), management and participation is stipulated for all partners, whether or not all partners actually participate in the management. In the second

category (for example, *mudaraba*), management is stipulated for one of the partners and the other partners are simply investors who share the profits in return for the capital they have provided.

4. Contractual partnership (*shirkah al-uqood*) has been divided in the *fiqh* books into four kinds: *al-mufawadah* (full authority and obligation); *al'-inan* (restricted authority and obligation); *al-abdan* (labour, skill and management); and *al-wujuh* (goodwill, creditworthiness and contracts). *Skirkah al-abdan* is where the partners contribute their skills and efforts to the management of the business without contributing to the capital. In *shirkah al-wujuh* the partners use their goodwill, their creditworthiness and their contracts for promoting their business without contributing to the capital. Both these forms of partnership, where the partners do not contribute any capital, would remain confined essentially to small-scale business only.

5. Two types of accounting policies are typically applied by Islamic banks. The first approaches separate the equity and invested amount 100 per cent. The second covers those deposits for 3, 6, 9 months, one year and two years. The revenue and expenses between that type of investment are allocated according to the proportional share of investment. For example, if the bank bought/built a building as an investment 'common portfolio' the income would be allocated between the investors and shareholders according to the proportional share. If a particular investor gets into a deal with the bank as 'specific investment', the total incomes of this deal are allocated for the investor and the bank charges its fees.

6. IAIB, *al-Mawsuat al-Ibniyya* quoted by Saeed (1996), p. 99.

7. There are different opinions among the scholars as to whether the ratio of profit must conform to the proportion of capital invested by each partner. The principle of proportionality between the capital contributed and share of profits is visible in all categories of partnership according to the Malikis, except the *mudaraba*. This is stated in the *Mudawwanah*: 'Partnership (sharing of profits) is not permitted, except in proportion to the *amwal* (capital contributed) (Sahnun, 1905, vol. 5, p. 41). However, this view has not won general acceptance. The Shafis do not allow the profit-sharing ratio to diverge from the capital contribution ratio (and thus no need for it to be specified in advance), but there is considerable flexibility in the basis for determining the ratio amongst the Hanafi and Hanbali schools. However, one of the most fundamental principles of *fiqh* is that losses from an investment must be divided in proportion to the initial capital contribution.

4. Islamic banking and financial intermediation

FINANCIAL MARKETS AND INTERMEDIARIES

In the previous chapter we examined the principles of Islamic banking and showed how the institutions collect deposit funds from investors, both by means of *mudaraba* investment accounts and other deposit accounts, on one side of the balance sheet, and then invest these funds in a variety of Islamically-acceptable forms, on the other side. That is, we considered how they operate as financial intermediaries in financial markets. Nevertheless, they conduct financial intermediation in ways quite different from conventional banks since profit-and-loss modes of finance and investment in trade and commodities feature extensively in their activities. There is a large literature in banking theory and finance that examines the optimality of the interest-based instruments used by conventional banks. In order to explore the differences that may result from substituting the Islamic financing instruments for the conventional techniques of banking, we need to review the theories of financial intermediation.

Financial markets are a means whereby the resources arising from acts of savings are made available to investors. The functions performed can be summarised as follows:

1. Indirect financing: transferring resources (funds) from those who have them (savers) to those who can make use of them (borrowers or investors). There is never a perfect coincidence between those who have funds and those who can make use of those funds.
2. Accumulating capital: many projects require more capital than that of any one saver or any small set of savers.
3. Providing liquidity: those providing funds may wish to lend them for shorter periods and on different terms than those borrowing funds. These different 'liquidity preferences' must be reconciled.
4. Selecting projects: there are always more individuals who claim that they have good uses for resources than there are funds available.
5. Monitoring: ensuring that funds are used in the way promised.
6. Enforcing contracts: making sure that those who have borrowed repay the funds.

7. Managing, transferring, sharing and pooling risks: capital markets not only raise funds, but determine the rules which govern repayment and who bears what risks.
8. Diversification: by pooling a large number of investment projects together, the total risk is reduced.
9. Recording transactions: running the medium of exchange and system of payments.

As we shall see, the distinction between monitoring and enforcement, on the one hand, and risk sharing, on the other hand, is important for considering the differences between Islamic and traditional banking.

An intermediary facilitates trade in goods and services by acting as a 'go between' for transactors. Financial intermediaries[1] can be defined in like manner as enterprises which come between (that is, intermediate) borrowers and lenders, often themselves engaging in the acquisition and sale of financial securities. Left to their own devices, lenders of funds would have to search out potential borrowers and verify their financing proposals, design appropriate financial contracts, monitor borrowers' behaviour, and possibly take actions to enforce the conditions of payment. None of these would matter in a world of perfect markets, but this is to assume away the existence of transactions costs, adverse selection due to information asymmetries (in effect hidden information), and incentive problems and moral hazard (in essence hidden actions).[2] These transactions cost and information problems must in practice be dealt with by financial markets. Markets must also cope with the need for liquidity when real investment is long-lived and those providing finance have unexpected consumption demands. Financial intermediaries supply these information and liquidity services, and as such they are central to the efficient operation of financial markets.

Sometimes financial intermediation is contrasted with direct financing via financial markets. In such a dichotomy the exchange of funds between savers and investors is accomplished either by a direct exchange of credit between borrowers and lenders or by an indirect exchange through a financial institution. This is a distinction which we shall make use of below; nevertheless we should note that it is misleading in a number of respects. Those issuing securities under direct financing invariably make use of the services of financial intermediaries – investment banks, merchant banks, broking houses. Those buying or tendering for these securities often do so with the intention of on-selling them to other securities firms as well as to various clients. When the securities are sold in the secondary markets, the services of financial intermediaries such as brokers, dealers and market-makers are employed. Few transactions take place directly between the saver and the investor, at least in relatively developed financial systems. Often many layers of intermediaries are involved.

A somewhat different distinction is between financial intermediation which involves no change to the instruments exchanged, and that in which portfolio transformation does occur. The first is illustrated by investment bankers and brokers. They provide advice, process information for resale and evaluate credit risks but do not alter the assets transferred. Other financial intermediaries, by contrast, undertake portfolio transformation by substituting their own liabilities for those of ultimate borrowers in lenders' portfolios. In some cases, such as with a mutual fund (unit trust), the substitution takes place with relatively little change in the terms and conditions, since their liabilities are simply claims on repackaged marketable securities. At the other extreme, in the case of banks and depository institutions there is a considerable contrast between claims issued and held. Liabilities of banks are liquid: they are redeemable at par and are very short term, many payable on demand. Assets of banks, by contrast, are risky: the market value of securities fluctuates with interest rates and some loans will inevitably go into default. In addition, many bank assets such as commercial loans have low marketability and because of this lack of liquidity cannot be sold at short notice without substantial loss. The same is not true of a mutual fund which is holding money market paper and other readily marketable securities, or indeed of many insurance companies, which have large portfolios of stocks and bonds. Much of the literature of financial intermediaries consequently addresses this 'specialness' of banks (and by implication depository intermediaries more generally).

Underlying this distinction between the two classes of financial intermediaries is a conception of financial markets as being of two categories: organised markets in which contracts and trading are relatively standardised (for example for bonds, shares, foreign currencies, call money, futures and traded options); and the other informal or bank-based markets dealing with differentiated contracts which are created by, or exist within, financial enterprises (for example for mortgages, consumer credit and commercial loans). Thus it has long been customary to distinguish between two broad types of financial system: the 'market-based' Anglo-Saxon (UK, US) type in which organised securities markets are highly developed and banks are not closely involved in the financing and managing of nonfinancial companies, and the 'bank-based' German/Japanese type of system in which securities markets are less developed and banks occupy key positions in the control and finance of industry. This distinction was made by historians as early as the beginning of the twentieth century and has been given renewed prominence (for example Mayer, 1988; Lewis, 1996). In many respects, as we shall argue below, Islamic banking can be regarded as constituting a third and distinctive type of system – an 'equity-based' system. This point will become clearer after we consider the theories of financial intermediation and banking.

THEORIES OF FINANCIAL INTERMEDIATION[3]

Traditional analyses of banks focused on their role in mediating between the different preferences with respect to maturity and liquidity of lenders and borrowers, and on their ability as specialised intermediaries to benefit from a variety of economies of scale. As an example, Gurley and Shaw (1956, 1960) in their studies of banks and financial intermediation took the existence of banks as given and cited economies of scale in the management of investments, risk reduction through diversification, and the ability of banks to rely upon the law of large numbers when managing liquidity as factors underpinning their operations. While dubbed by Greenbaum (1996) as the 'era of boring banking' (in comparison with the later 'explosion' of new perspectives), this strand of the literature continues with what is effectively an industrial organisation approach which considers that banks essentially offer services to their customers, and that financial transactions are only the visible counterpart to these services. It then models theories of bank behaviour explaining how banks provide these services. A survey by Swank (1996) identifies these as risk management theories, portfolio models, imperfect market models and real resources models.[4]

The 'Existence' Literature

By contrast, the newer literature primarily deals with the reasons why banks exist or, more abstractly, the conditions under which intermediation is viable and what form this takes. In this category of studies, usually referred to as 'financial intermediation theories', factors such as transaction costs and problems of imperfect information and market signalling are of critical importance. That is, the presence of banks and the form of their intermediation must be explained, and their existence is traced to various transactions costs or what can be termed 'information economies'.[5]

The origins of this 'existence' literature can be traced to Coase (1937) who posed the now well-known question: if the price mechanism is the most efficient mechanism for allocating resources in a market economy, why do firms exist? His answer was that economic agents incurred transaction costs when using the price mechanism, and that the firm can be seen as an alternative to market transactions as a way of organising activities because some procedures, such as the allocation of workers to tasks and the co-ordination of their efforts, could be more cheaply done by command rather than by price. Firms expand the range of activities (and define their boundaries) to the point where gains from saving transactions costs due to internalising certain (previously external) productive (or service generating) functions do not justify the cost involved in expanding. Building on this insight, Alchian and Demsetz (1972) added the idea of the firm as a monitor and enforcer of the incentive structure, while Williamson (1980) introduced uncertainty and bounded rationality, with the firm existing to economise on the costs of explicit outside contracting. In effect, uncertainty, idiosyncrasy, complexity, informational asymmetry and opportunism are inherent to transactions, which make it difficult to coordinate highly interdependent production and distribution processes through the market mechanism alone. Firms are a device to reduce the costliness of transactions by bringing more activities within the umbrella of one governance structure.

These ideas all have direct parallels in banking and finance, and indeed in general terms can be applied to the special case of Islamic banks. Owing to the nature of the instruments with which they deal (and the inherent adverse selection and moral hazard problems therein), a direct stake in the business (rather than acting strictly as a mediator) reduces transactions costs and may offer more profitable investment avenues. An extended vertical involvement, expanding the bank boundaries, may be perfectly understandable on Coasian grounds. But here we have jumped ahead of ourselves, for we need to examine the new literature which has informed the standard theories of banking and financial intermediation.

Perhaps the first question to be asked is why the 'existence question' took so long after the classic analysis of Coase to reach the theory of banking, one answer being the inheritance of the 'perfect markets paradigm' in financial analysis for, in one form or another, all of the major hypotheses which make up the modern theory of finance draw upon perfect market assumptions. There is no need for intermediation in hypothetical ideal environments such as those of Arrow (1964) and Debreu (1959). In their models there are no transactions costs and, by investing in perfectly divisible securities defined using states of nature with known probabilities, all transactors can achieve utility outcomes with certainty. In such an ideal world of complete and perfect capital markets, with full and symmetric information amongst all market participants, economic decisions would not depend in any way upon the financial structure (Modigliani and Miller, 1958). Following Modigliani and Miller's contribution, the view that 'finance is a veil' became very widely accepted. If the financial structure of firms is irrelevant, and if financial intermediaries are redundant, then monetary policy can have only a transitory impact on real variables through unanticipated changes in the money supply. In the real business cycle models that were developed subsequently, finance does not play any role.

With the Arrow/Debreu assumptions about information, there is no possibility of learning, and all transactions in securities must be completed through an auctioneer, before any outcomes are realised. Thus, their models are essentially static. All of the potential gains from adding banks are assumed away because every transactor is completely informed and honest about the environment, and frictions and indivisibilities do not exist. Households and firms have the information to arrange their own maturity transformation and undertake their own risk diversification (Fama, 1980).

Role of Information

In complete contrast to the perfect markets paradigm, the 'existence' literature (asking why banks exist) focuses upon imperfect markets. Imperfections arise from incomplete information and from an inadequate number of securities, relative to the possible states of nature. Information is incomplete in part because no person or group knows all of the possible states or nature of the probabilities of their occurrence. Further, information is distributed asymmetrically so that some people know more than others and can exploit their informational advantage. The number of securities is inadequate because of incomplete information and because of the potentially enormous real costs of issuing and maintaining markets for securities, each defined relative to a state of nature.

Some as a result argue (for example, Stiglitz and Weiss, 1981 and 1988) that financial markets are inherently imperfect to the extent that there is uncertainty about the completion of financial transactions. What is being dealt with in finance is a set of promises to deliver at some future date. Unlike many commodity market transactions which involve a contemporaneous two-way exchange of commodity and means of payments, with no obligation for a future transaction, and in which the identity of the transactors is often irrelevant, the value of a financial promise to a potential lender depends upon the perceived character of the individual issuing the promise (as regards honesty, unwarranted optimism and future prospects, and so on) together with expectations of how future events may influence the worth of that promise. In standard economic analysis (for example Arrow–Debreu), individuals may borrow with repayments contingent upon various states of the world and thus not under their control. Incentive problems are, however, excluded so that individuals cannot influence those circumstances. Also excluded from consideration is any adverse selection problem arising from the identity of those making the promises.

Consequently, in the existence analysis 'agents' or 'coalitions' of agents – loosely identified as banks or financial intermediaries – emerge as an endogenous response to the market imperfections by providing information services of one kind or another. The new literature began with a redefinition of financial intermediation, the centrepiece of which was Diamond's (1984) notion of 'delegated monitoring'. This brought asymmetric information to the fore and led in turn to a wider variety of issues, including attributes of the optimal loan and deposit contract. An important function of financial intermediaries becomes that of discovering the distribution of project value outcomes and asset values, while at the same time acquiring knowledge about the integrity and ability of clients. Refining and updating an information base that enables the best decisions to be taken is costly, if only because the stock and value of information are always changing. Nevertheless, it is a core activity of any financial firm. In this way, intermediaries thereby fill the gap which would otherwise exist due to imperfect information and non-zero transactions costs.

It may be helpful to summarise the information costs that inhibit the financing process.[6] First, there are search costs. Potential transactors must search out, obtain information about, select, meet and negotiate with potential other parties to a contract. Second, there are verification costs. These arise from evaluating borrowing proposals when lenders are unable to assess the future prospects of a borrower accurately, particularly when some borrowers may have an incentive to paint an overly-optimistic picture of the future. Adverse selection can occur when an asymmetry in information costs exists due to lenders' inability to observe the attributes of borrowers and the contingencies under which they operate. Third, monitoring costs are incurred when overseeing the actions of the borrower for consistency with the terms of the contract, and ensuring that any failure to meet the delivery promised is for genuine reasons. Moral hazard refers to the problems which may flow from the inability of lenders to ascertain and exercise control over the behaviour of borrowers, either with respect to the choice of investment project or the effort and diligence with which the business is managed. Fourth, enforcement costs arise should the borrower be unable to meet the commitments as promised, and a solution must be worked out between the borrower and lender or other aspects of the contract (for example, collateral) may need to be enforced. These four costs define the functions of banks as producers of information.

Left to their own devices under direct financing, potential holders of securities have access to information provided by rating agencies, newspapers and financial journals at low cost. Routine accounting information and knowledge about the issuing firm's past history in meeting timely payments of interest and other regular commitments can be gathered relatively cheaply. But detailed information about the firm's prospects is hard to acquire, and it is too costly for individual savers, as 'outsiders' not intimately connected with the running of a firm, to keep themselves informed about happenings inside the firm and influence its behaviour. Market analysts and investment bankers are unwilling to keep track of the activities of the many small firms which might turn out to be occasional minor borrowers. In particular, small companies and individuals face the problem that because of a lack of widespread information about their activities, investor interest in them is too limited for the substantial costs involved in the establishment and operation of secondary markets. These market 'gaps' define the role for banks.

Banks as Information Producers

Banks are seen as producers of information, supplementing or substituting for the information available through other sources. Their role as financiers is shaped by characteristics of the market for information. Because of the information asymmetries between 'insiders' and 'outsiders', a prospective lender needs to be given full details of the prospects of the investment project. Provision of this information by the borrowing enterprise involves it in the risk that the knowledge advantage it has may be given away in the process. 'The entrepreneur needs the lender, but once the lender has the information he no longer needs the entrepreneur' (Casson, 1982, p. 211). Banks have evolved in different ways to resolve this potential conflict of interest.

One solution is for the bank to take an equity interest in the firm or to have business links with the firm through interlocking directorships or shareholdings. This, broadly speaking, is the German and Japanese tradition mentioned earlier where banks acquire stock of companies and often sit on the board (German) or form part of linked groups (Japan). It also typifies the activities of the French *banque d'affaires* which originate participations in a company and retain sufficient holdings to control its policy.

An alternative way of resolving the conflict of interest, more in the Anglo-Saxon tradition, involves creating an arm's length relationship but nevertheless one in which there is a confidential transfer of information. In effect, banks establish a reputation for handling knowledge about a firm's plans responsibly. An implicit contract is made with the customer in which the bank is provided with a regular flow of price-sensitive information which it voluntarily undertakes not to exploit in competition with the customer: the information is instead 'internalised' in the bank's loans to the customer's business. This implicit contract may be reinforced by explicit legislation separating banking from 'commerce' (as in the US) or by unwritten rules discouraging acquisition of banks by 'commercial' enterprises (as in the UK). Accompanying the Anglo-Saxon tradition there has tended to be a greater reliance upon equity finance, with well developed and open securities markets. Financing under the alternative tradition is much more credit-based and capital markets are less developed, although this position is beginning to change, in both Germany and Japan.

Delegated Monitoring

If banks have access to privileged sources of information, it gives them special information advantages over other market participants and enables them to provide credit or market-enhancing guarantees for activities which, because of price-sensitive information or high evaluation, monitoring and enforcement costs, cannot easily be funded by the issue of securities in the open market. By engaging in indirect finance, the saver, as a depositor, does not have to monitor the financial condition and performance of the borrower; this task is delegated to the intermediary. For most savers, this choice is a rational one because, as outsiders, they do not have the time, inclination, money, or skill to evaluate the performance of insiders. Accordingly, they pass the agency problem and costs on to the intermediary, which acts as their agent. Outsiders are better off (in terms of costs saved) by delegating the task of monitoring insiders to those financial intermediaries such as banks with human and reputational capital invested in the monitoring process.

Here we have a central feature of the modern literature – the role of banks as delegated monitors. Since banks serve as agents for depositors by monitoring the performance of borrowing firms, these firms may benefit in the marketplace by having some debt on their balance sheets that is 'approved' by recognised monitors in the financial system. In addition, banks are not the only monitors in the financial system. Insured depositors receive the additional benefit of monitoring by deposit insurers and bank regulators. This prompts the question: who monitors the monitor?

Who Monitors the Bank?

Depositors face the same agency problems when delegating their financing to a bank as they would under direct financing. To some degree, they may be able to rely on the bank's shareholders to monitor the bank for them. As residual claimants, shareholders have a direct interest in ensuring that all prior claims on the bank are met fully; yet they too face agency problems in making sure that management looks after their interests.

Here the literature falls back on a story familiar to those schooled in the traditional theory: portfolio diversification and risk pooling. Diamond (1984) shows that the depositors' cost of monitoring the bank (the 'delegation cost') becomes arbitrarily small as the bank monitors a large portfolio of loans, diversified by firm and market. By means of the law of large numbers the fraction of loans of good and bad outcomes can be predicted increasingly accurately as the loan portfolio grows larger, and as it becomes more diversified. Loan losses will still occur: that is inherent in the nature of the loan contract. Pooling of loans reduces risk in the sense that the variability of losses approaches zero, and actual defaults approach those that can be anticipated, as the number of independently defaulting borrowers included in the group increases. It is more likely as a result that loan losses will be covered by the default premium built into interest charges.

In essence, the optimal contract between depositors and the bank in Diamond's model of 'delegated screening' is one for which the bank is committed to fixed payments to depositors with default unlikely. Default is unlikely because the bank lowers default losses on its loans by careful screening and monitoring of loans and investments, and then reduces its own probability of bankruptcy by exploiting advantages of size and diversification.

On the liabilities side of the balance sheet, it would seem to be the case that the theory of financial intermediation provides a theoretical justification for an interest-based deposit contract, although it may be argued (with some justification) that the literature here has followed what banks do rather than what banks could do; one is reminded of the old adage to the effect that 'economic theorists are people who observe something that works in practice and ask whether it can be made to work in theory'. In the associated part of the modern literature, addressing the role of banks as liquidity insurers, there is in fact a strand of the literature which favours an arrangement something like that in Islamic banking, known as mutual fund (or unit trust) banking. We now examine what the modern literature says about the contracting relationship between the bank, as financier, and the borrower, as entrepreneur or investor, as well as that between depositor and bank.

THE DESIGN OF BANK CONTRACTS

Twinning the modern theory of financial intermediation, an evolving literature has attempted to identify the optimal form of the financial contract between lender (bank) and entrepreneur, and between depositor and bank. The choice is usually posed in terms of 'debt versus equity', that is, in terms of whether contractual payments are fixed, state-independent ones in the form of debt contracts that promise providers of finance a specified return in 'normal', non-default states and first claim to the issuer's assets in default states; or whether the repayments are contingent on output or profit performance, as with equity-type claims that give holders a claim on an issuer's residual income (that is, its profit) and ultimate control over its assets provided the issuer does not default. Traditionally, theories of financial behaviour focused on the supply of and demand for these financial instruments, but had relatively little to say about why those particular contract forms are used in the first place. The question of 'security design' or 'contract design' was neglected.

From the perspective of this volume, one of the most important results that has emerged from the contract design literature is that debt contracts are often optimal transacting vehicles because they minimise the costs associated with asymmetric information or unobserved actions. Three circumstances have been the subjects of examination: costly verification, moral hazard and adverse selection.

Costly Verification

Costly verification and/or monitoring points to the optimality of the standard debt contract: the borrower pays the lender a fixed payment for good outcomes, when no verification or monitoring takes place, but must hand over the whole proceeds in the event of a bad outcome when the fixed repayment cannot be met and bankruptcy occurs. Gale and Hellwig (1985) provide the starting point for the modern literature on financial contracting. Their model analyses the case in which the outcome of an investment project undertaken in the current period in terms of revenue received in the future period depends both on the size of the investment and the state of nature. While it is assumed that the entrepreneur can observe this outcome at no cost in the second period, the lender can observe it only by declaring the borrower bankrupt, which involves certain costs for the lender (such as a fall in the value of the business from loss of reputation or the fact that its scrap value is less than its value as a going concern), and also for the entrepreneur (in the form of the loss of his equity in the firm). From these assumptions they then derive the optimal incentive-compatible contract. Incentive-compatibility requires the payment of a fixed sum by the entrepreneur to the lender in all non-observed states, since otherwise the entrepreneur would have an incentive to declare a state worse than the true state in order to pay a lower return to the lender, and this incentive for the entrepreneur to deceive would mean that the contract would not be agreed. Efficiency requires a contract where costs of observation are avoided as far as possible.

Hence Gale and Hellwig's optimal contract involves the following conditions: (i) the payment of a fixed sum when the firm is solvent (and the state is not observed); (ii) the firm to be declared bankrupt if it cannot pay this fixed sum; and (iii) that in case of bankruptcy, the lender receives the firm's actual revenue and remaining assets minus the costs of bankruptcy. The third condition maximises the return to the lender in case of bankruptcy, and therefore minimises the return which has to be paid in solvent situations in order to give to the lender an expected return equal to his reservation price, that is the opportunity cost of funds as determined in a competitive capital market. The second condition (in conjunction with the third) ensures that the entrepreneur has no incentive to go into default except in case of genuine bankruptcy. In this way, Gale and Hellwig establish that the optimal contract is the 'standard debt contract', for it has these three characteristics. Note, however, that their result depends on returns being costly to observe; the loan contract ceases to be optimal if the lender has information about the project (Williamson, 1986).

Moral Hazard

Hidden actions or moral hazard point to the optimality of the same type of contract: a requirement to make debt payments independently of the state of the world may be a check against moral hazard. This issue has been analysed within the principal–agent framework. The principal–agent literature[7] is concerned with how one individual, the principal (say an employer), can design a compensation system (a contract) which motivates another individual, his agent (say the employee), to act in the principal's interests. A principal–agent problem arises when there is imperfect information, concerning what action the agent has undertaken or should undertake. Obviously, in many situations, the actions are not easily observable. Should there be the possibility that output depends on the agent's hidden actions which the principal finds costly to monitor then there is a moral hazard problem (Arrow, 1965). The hidden action usually referred to is the agent's choice of endeavour, and the moral hazard problem in this context relates to the tendency of the agent to reduce effort on the grounds that some (perhaps most) of any extra effort would accrue to the principal. If output is observable at no cost and the agent's wealth provides no binding constraint, Harris and Raviv (1979) show that moral hazard over an agent's level of effort in the face of costly monitoring leads to an optimal contract in which the agent makes a fixed payment in all states of nature. The idea is that contract form gives the entrepreneur the appropriate incentive to work by rewarding him with all of the marginal returns beyond the fixed repayment amount specified in the contract.

Verification costs and moral hazard both tend to encourage the parties involved to make debt contracts. Debt contracts are preferable under these conditions because they reduce the impact of hidden information (since it will often not matter *ex post* that the investor does not directly see the output) and also of moral hazard (since debt gives the entrepreneur a strong incentive to work hard and capture the residual returns).

Adverse Selection

Debt contracts may also be optimal, in certain circumstances, when there is the problem of adverse project selection. There is a problem when some important feature of the investor's project (or choice of project) is not observed by the investor. One such situation is where the investor does not observe the (appropriately defined) 'quality' of the project. In this case, debt contracts are still optimal over a wide range of circumstances (Innes, 1993; Dowd, 1996). The reason is that the entrepreneurs with better quality projects would prefer debt contracts to maximise their residual profits, while the entrepreneurs with poor quality projects would need to imitate them so as to avoid revealing themselves.

However, there can also be adverse selection relating to the riskiness of the investment project, and in this case debt contracts may no longer be optimal. Equity contracts dominate debt contracts in the presence of this form of adverse selection because they eliminate (or at least substantially reduce) the possibility that the entrepreneur could pass expected losses back to the investor. With an equity contract, the investor gets a given proportion of the net income from the project, and so the entrepreneur cannot manipulate the investor's expected profit or loss by choosing a more risky project. Since profits are shared, if the entrepreneur chooses a project to maximise his own expected profit, he also maximises the investor's expected profit as well. The investor would then have no reason to object to the project choice even if he somehow got to find out what it was. The equity contract thus gets around the problem posed by adverse project selection and delivers the best result.

Note that this outcome depends on the output from the project being verifiable at negligible cost. If output is not verifiable at all, the entrepreneur could reduce the payoff to the investor by declaring that output was lower than it actually was, and the investor would never be able to prove that he was lying. In fact, the entrepreneur would always want to declare that output was at its minimum possible level. Knowing that he had this incentive, the investor would presumably prefer not to invest, or at least to invest elsewhere.

Contract choice may act as an important signalling device. When entrepreneurs know better than lenders of the riskiness of the projects they want to finance, one response of lenders envisaged in the literature is for them to offer contracts designed to encourage entrepreneurs to self-select appropriately. Naturally, in seeking to mitigate adverse selection and moral hazard, the banker will be concerned with evaluating the worth of the project and the capacity of the borrower to repay the debt within an acceptable period, using personal knowledge and past records to assess the character and financial acumen of the client. But an additional consideration will be the extent of 'insider equity', signalling the degree to which proprietors are prepared to back their own ventures. Other things equal, the larger is inside equity, the safer is the venture to finance.

Collateral

In a similar vein, the extent and quality of collateral also acts as a screening device aimed at selecting the honest entrepreneur (profitable project) from the dishonest one. The entrepreneur who is convinced that the project is profitable will be prepared to offer collateral as security. Otherwise he will not risk his personal wealth, unless he chooses to engage in a strategic default, that is, the value of the collateral is lower than the expected extent of the default. Collateral thus has the potential of reducing the adverse selection problem in the credit markets. By choosing the size of the amount of collateral, a bank will be able to screen the riskiness of the entrepreneur, who is obliged to identify his/her risk attributes from the extent of collateral offered.

Such collateral may take the form of a title over the shareholders' personal assets, the pledge of company assets such as property, accounts receivable or inventories, or (as used in the UK) a floating charge over all of the company's assets.[8] Usually a banker will also seek to reduce the risk of loss on his loan by writing 'covenants' into the loan agreement, so that he is able to demand immediate repayment of the loan if there is a serious risk that the firm will be unable to carry out its obligations. Covenants usually seek to prevent excessive dividend payments, prevent claim dilution from further borrowings, and prevent investment decisions which raise business risk. Borrowers usually go along with them to obtain cheaper finance.

An implication of the points in the previous paragraph is that banks may be able to reduce individual loan risks by designing and enforcing incentive-compatible loan contracts, so improving the prospect of loans being repaid. When there is repeated lending between the banker and firm, and knowledge of any interruption may be publicised, the implied threat of withholding future financing can be a very inexpensive substitute for other monitoring methods. Moral and social sanctions are not entirely absent from loan markets, and there is as well the exemplary effect of a few foreclosures on other borrowers. Finally, the banker is well placed, by virtue of his knowledge of a customer's business, to know when to waive temporarily some covenant and tailor-make a 'workout' which takes cognisance of the borrower's financial and trading position.

Other Factors

Of course, the real difficulty comes when all of the conditioning factors – costly verification, adverse selection, monitoring costs, moral hazard, enforcement costs, bankruptcy costs, and risk aversion – are examined simultaneously (which is not and probably cannot be done theoretically). Bank contracting choice is complicated further by the fact that the institution must design contracts suited to both borrowers and depositors, and additional work in this field has attempted to identify the optimal form of the financial contract between lender (bank) and entrepreneur, and between depositor and bank simultaneously (Williamson, 1987). For example, equity is a more flexible risk-sharing contract than debt, and the possibility of making the payment to the lender different in each state of the world reduces the borrowers' probability of bankruptcy. But under 'delegated screening', depositors cannot observe directly the lending bank's investments. Since the bank's payoffs cannot be credibly revealed, depositors seem unlikely to accept claims which promise returns contingent on what is, in effect, private information. It follows that mutual fund (unit trust) type contracts, in which returns and risks of the loan portfolio directly flow on to the lenders of funds, may be ruled out. A borrower's risk of bankruptcy may then be reduced by ensuring that repayments to the bank be as unvarying as possible, subject to the borrower's ability to repay. That is, the standard fixed (or pre-determined) interest rate debt contract again emerges as the optimal arrangement.

ISLAMIC BANKING AND THE INCENTIVE PROBLEM

The literature surveyed in the previous section has obvious implications for the theory and practical viability of Islamic banking. While the optimal bilateral financial contract depends on a variety of factors – the cost of output verification and/or monitoring against moral hazard, the presence of adverse selection, the degree to which wealth constraints bind the parties involved, and the parties' attitudes towards risk – there are a large number of circumstances in which debt contracts appear to be optimal. In addition, particular features of real-world debt contracts, among them the use of collateral and credit rationing, covenant restrictions of various kinds, the ongoing monitoring, workout and re-financing of loans gain theoretical support as being incentive-compatible.

Many economists (for example Dowd, 1996) take comfort from the fact that debt contracts are defensible in theory given that they figure so prominently in real-world financial arrangements and have done so for a very long time in conventional banking markets. It is rather less than reassuring from the viewpoint of the theory of Islamic banking. The standard debt (*riba*) contract, collateral requirements, loan covenants, and enforced workouts – measures designed to ameliorate adverse selection and moral hazard – are all prohibited in Islamic financing. At the same time, Islamic banks go beyond pure financial intermediation of the traditional sort, and have direct participation in business and investments with profit-and-loss-sharing along equity lines. How does the Islamic bank overcome the incentive problems which theory suggests would follow?

Characteristics of *Mudaraba*

Before addressing this question, we remind ourselves of the basis of a *mudaraba* contract. Unlike a conventional bank which is basically a borrower of funds on one hand and a lender of those funds on the other, an Islamic bank is essentially a partner with its depositors except in the case of current accounts and non-funded banking services, on one side, and also a partner with its clients on the other side as a manager of depositors' funds. It solicits funds from the community through a *mudaraba* contract which can be limited by time, or purpose or both, and thus becomes a managing partner for the duration of the contract.

Once the Islamic bank enters into the *mudaraba* contract with the 'depositor', it then turns around and employs those funds through the various *shari'a*-accepted contracts; *mudaraba, musharaka, murabaha, ijara* and so on. In the case of a *mudaraba* contract, the following conditions apply:[9]

1. The bank provides the entire capital needed for carrying out a project.
2. The entrepreneur offers only his labour and effort, that is, his wealth is effectively zero and he is thereby unable to offer any collateral.
3. The contract between the bank and the entrepreneur is an exclusive one, that is, the entrepreneur is not allowed to engage in other activities.
4. The compensation paid to the entrepreneur is a share of the net profit of the project. This share is fixed in advance. In the literature, the share of the entrepreneurs is recommended to be two thirds of net returns. This sharing ratio, which is said to be based on earlier Islamic tradition, is assumed to be fair for both parties.
5. In the event of negative returns, the bank loses some or all of its capital, and the entrepreneur does not receive any remuneration for his labour.
6. As soon as the contract is accepted by both parties, the bank cannot monitor or enforce the entrepreneur by legal devices to undertake any additional actions.
7. Finally, the contract will be automatically cancelled in case of death, insanity, or apostasy from Islam of either party.

The contrast between this type of contract and the standard debt contract is sharp, and can be formalised as follows (Karsten, 1982). Let P_0 denote the amount of principal lent to the borrower in period t_0 and P_1 the agreed amount of capital that has to be returned in t_1. If $P_1 > P_0$, then the difference between P_1 and P_0 is the additional amount (*riba*), or interest in the orthodox Islamic sense.

$$r = P_1 - P_0 \tag{4.1}$$

Profits and losses (*PL*) involve an element of uncertainty. Each partner in a *mudaraba* business is sharing an agreed proportion ϕ of the expected difference between total revenues R and total cost C. Expected profits for a participant in a joint venture are consequently:

$$\pi = \phi\, E\,(R - C) = \phi\, E\,(PL) \tag{4.2}$$

where E denotes expected value. Revenues can be shared on a pro rata basis among the various units of production after deducting incurred expenses. The distribution of profit shares is determined by a bargaining process between the investor (borrower) and the bank and, in turn, between the saver and the bank under a 'two-tiered' or 'triple' *mudaraba*. But, in comparison with interest, profit is not predetermined and fixed, but is uncertain and variable, and may even be negative.

Incentive Issues

These characteristics of the *mudaraba* contract *vis-à-vis* the standard interest-based loan create, at least potentially, three incentive problems on both sides of the balance sheet, and can be interpreted in terms of a principal–agent problem in that the bank cannot monitor perfectly the actions of those to whom it advances funds, nor can bank depositors monitor the actions of the bank, yet in both cases the action of one has an effect on the other. Further, from agency theory, there are reasons for believing that conflicts of interest could arise between the parties involved.

Consider, to begin with, the bank's investment of funds involving a *mudaraba*-type contract. Potential incentive problems exist in three aspects. First, the absence of a collateral requirement will aggravate the adverse selection problem in an Islamic banking system. According to the theory of Islamic banking, funds provided on a profit-sharing basis have to be offered without any collateral. The lack of collateral requirement will likely attract entrepreneurs with a limited size of wealth. In particular, the PLS contract will encourage new entrepreneurs who do not possess any assets except their efforts and skills, and without collateral would be considered to be high risk. In order to overcome the adverse selection problem, and discriminate between a high-risk project and a low-risk project, the lack of collateral may oblige an Islamic bank to ration the supply of funds to this sort of financing mode.

Second, a *mudaraba* contract will accentuate the moral hazard problem, because the bank cannot enforce the entrepreneur to take the appropriate action (or the required level of effort). According to this contract, the compensation to entrepreneurs takes the form of a predetermined share in the outcome of investment. This payment does not necessarily produce the 'right' incentive for the entrepreneur to provide the level of effort needed for the maximisation of outcome. In addition, the bank cannot *ex ante* constrain the activity of the entrepreneur by determining the intensity of his effort, for example by specifying in detail his expenditure budget. The entrepreneur is guaranteed full freedom in managing the project.

Third, as the expenditures on the venture are borne entirely by the bank, this contract provides an incentive to the entrepreneur to expand expenditures beyond the level needed for profit maximisation. In particular, a *mudaraba* contract gives the entrepreneur an incentive to increase consumption of non-pecuniary benefits at the expense of a pecuniary return. This is due to the fact that the increased consumption is partly borne by the bank, while the benefits are entirely consumed by the entrepreneur. An entrepreneur has access to a number of on-the-job consumption opportunities and perquisites, which have a positive value for him, such as shirking or expanding staff, large office space, executive services, and so on. The expansion of staffing may induce a higher organisational security, power, and status. Moreover, the PLS contract cannot include subject matters expected to occur in the future. Such a contract is considered as illicit according to Islamic law. In this sense, the bank cannot insist on a contract where the share of the entrepreneur in the outcome will be altered, if a high level of expenditure (or a lower level of effort) has been observed.

Many of the same issues surface on the liabilities side, but in this case the bank is the agent (*mudarib*) and the depositor is the principal. Under the trustee arrangement for investment accounts, depositors act as financiers by providing funds, and the bank acts as an entrepreneur by accepting them. Neither the nominal capital value nor a predetermined rate of return on deposits is guaranteed. Depositors effectively become shareholders.

If the bank makes profits then the shareholder–depositor would be entitled to receive a certain proportion of these profits. On the other hand, if the bank incurs losses the depositor is expected to share in these as well, and receive a negative rate of return. Accordingly, from the depositor's perspective, dealing with an Islamic bank is in many respects similar to investing in a mutual fund or investment trust.

Mutual Fund Banking

This comparison of an Islamic bank to a mutual fund-type organisation is an interesting one in a number of respects. Although it is in some ways a digression, it is worth noting that mutual fund banking[10] has been advocated in the context of a conventional banking system as one solution to the problem of bank failure due to withdrawal of deposits (that is, a 'bank run'). The classic work in this area is the article by Diamond and Dybvig (1983) which models banks' provision of 'liquidity insurance' and the difficulties posed for banks by early withdrawal of deposit balances.[11] However, there is nothing in their model which prevents banks from offering equity-type contracts, and a debt-type deposit contract is simply imposed arbitrarily. An equity contract could be like a mutual fund, and it has been argued that a mutual fund-type style of organisation would render banks run-proof. The idea is that banks would value and redeem deposits under a market value accounting system at the current market value of their assets (which could be more or less than face value). Were this feasible, it is argued, the source of bank runs would be removed.

Of course, the idea has proven not to be feasible to implement in conventional banking markets, but it does serve to bring out the point, first made by W.M. Khan (1985) and later by M.S. Khan and Mirakhor (1989) and Iqbal (1997), that an Islamic banking system is effectively structured along these lines since bank portfolio risk is borne by both deposit-holders and stock holders. Correspondingly, this system is likely to be more stable, that is, run-proof, than a conventional banking system.[12] Their argument runs as follows. If there is a decline in the value of the bank's assets then it will not be to the advantage of depositors to withdraw their money because their share would consequently decline. Also, the financial position of a depositor does not depend on the actions of other depositors because each gets a share in the bank's value which is independent of whether some decide to withdraw their balances while others do not. In fact, there may be a greater incentive to remain in the bank when it suffers a decline in the value of its assets because otherwise there is acceptance of a loss on the initial deposit, whereas retaining shares in the bank leaves hope for a revaluation of the bank's assets in the future.

This argument is the same as that of the advocates of mutual fund banking, but does depend on the nature of the bank investment portfolio. Where the portfolio is of short-term, low-risk assets like Treasury bills, there are clear limits to the downside risk from early conversions. When there are long-term assets, or assets of low marketability, an incentive to 'beat the market' in the face of an expected price decline could still exist. So long as maturity transformation (funding short, investing long), is undertaken, the risk of bank runs remains.

An Equity-based System?

Returning now to the question of incentives, the parallel of Islamic banking to a mutual fund or investment trust (company)[13] is instructive. Despite the apparent similarity, there are basic differences between the two forms of investment. In the case of an investment company, say, the shareholders own a proportionate part of the company's equity capital and are entitled to a number of rights, including receiving a regular flow of information on developments of the company's business and exerting voting rights corresponding to their shares on important matters, such as changes in investment policy. They are thus in a position to take informed investment decisions, monitor the company's performance, and influence strategic decisions. If they are dissatisfied with the performance, they can simply exit by selling their shares in the stockmarket.

Islamic banks, by contrast, accept deposits from the public rather than issuing and selling shares (although they do issue a 'prospectus' setting out the conditions governing the investment of funds). Depositors are entitled to share the bank's net profit (or loss) according to the PLS ratio stipulated in their contracts, but have no voting rights because they do not own any portion of the bank's equity capital, and under the *mudaraba* contract cannot influence the bank's investment policy. Investment deposits cannot be withdrawn at any time, but only on maturity and, in the best case, at par value. With Islamic deposits, it is not the market value which matters; there is none as they are not traded. Nor is the market value equal to the underlying value of the assets in which the bank has invested, unless these are deposits. What is important is the profitability of the investment.

An Islamic banking system, in short, is essentially an equity-based system in which depositors are treated as if they were shareholders of the bank, as earlier writers have argued (for example M.S. Khan, 1986; Al-Harran, 1993). However, the depositors are a very special type of shareholder. In effect, they are non-voting shareholders. Normally, someone with ownership rights in a company can express their disappointment with the company's performance by either getting rid of their shares or in some way expressing their concern. Hirschman (1970) called this the dichotomy between 'exit' and 'voice'. Expressed in these terms, the Islamic depositor *cum* non-voting shareholder has little 'exit' and no 'voice'.

We now go on to consider some of the implications of these arrangements. However, one thing is apparent. Errico and Farahbaksh (1998) note that, because of the lack of protection for investment depositors (in the form of deposit insurance, for example), Islamic bank depositors have more incentives to monitor bank performance than conventional depositors. Information disclosure should be more important in an Islamic banking environment.

IMPLICATIONS FOR ISLAMIC BANKING

These potentially serious incentive difficulties faced by Islamic banks and/or their depositors in terms of the conventional theory of financial intermediation cast a question mark over whether the system can be made to work. As such, they effectively frame the issues upon which we need to focus when the actual operations of Islamic banks are examined in the chapters which follow this conceptual analysis. At this juncture, however, a number of observations are warranted.

Intermediation Costs

First, in order to avoid the adverse selection problem, Islamic banks may need to undertake extensive evaluation and information-gathering activities. Consequently, Islamic banking will necessarily involve higher intermediation costs than conventional banking due to the larger monitoring costs. The viability and the profitability of every project must be judged separately before profit shares can be negotiated.

Such intensive evaluation and monitoring is not necessarily a bad thing, and it can be argued that if conventional banks had done rather more of it, most of the lending disasters of recent decades might have been avoided. In the period preceding the third world debt crisis of the 1980s, for example, many banks took their lead from Walter Wriston of Citicorp who insisted that sovereign lending must be safe, ignoring the history lesson of the Medici bank which was ruined by bad loans to Edward IV of England (Lewis and Davis, 1987). In the property lending boom of the late 1980s, banks were attracted into commercial property by the apparent security of collateral of 'bricks and mortar'. However, the collateral proved to be illusory when the vast expansion in available floor space saw a collapse in rentals and property values (Lewis, 1994).

In less developed economies, where rural financing is important, some external effects will likely flow from more intensive evaluation activities, providing something of an offset to the monitoring costs. Technical and economic skills are often scarce in such environments. This shortage, plus the high cost of information, may lead to weak performance in many projects. In order to be able to judge the viability of projects, the banks must employ certain experts. Their skills can be used not only for project appraisals, but also for guidance and advice about the management of projects, either directly via the participation or through spillover effects.

M.A. Khan (1994) outlines a number of models of rural financing by Islamic techniques, indicating how Islamic banks can provide assistance in terms of feasibility planning, project management and skills training. He also makes the interesting suggestion that auditing laws could be altered to make it mandatory for firms receiving finance from Islamic banks to have 'performance auditing' before final settlement of their accounts, both to improve management performance and reduce banks' monitoring costs. Hopefully, then, in these various ways, some of the higher administration cost may be balanced by improved performance (as indeed appears to have been the case in Sudan).

Depositors' Risks

Second, the implication that Islamic banks need to engage in more extensive monitoring would seem to carry corollaries for the behaviour of depositors if the focus of attention is shifted from the bank–borrower relation to the depositor–bank relation in a context of a number of banks. The fact that Islamic banks do not offer directly comparable fixed interest payments to their depositors, and undertake risk-sharing contracts with borrowers, implies that depositors need to take more trouble to choose and monitor the activities of their banks, not merely to avoid placing their funds with banks that default but also to obtain the highest return. Profit-and-loss-sharing returns on investment accounts are less readily observable than posted interest rates, while past performance may not always be a good guide to future prospects with respect to either expected returns or the institution's safety.

In terms of safety, however, there are some grounds, as we have noted, for arguing that Islamic banks may be more stable than conventional ones. In a conventional interest-based system the possibility of bank runs arises from the fact that banks' assets can vary in value but their liabilities are fixed in nominal terms. In an Islamic system, except for current accounts, deposits are profit-and-loss-sharing and any fall in the asset returns of a bank due, for example, to the impact of an economic downturn on the default rate, will be matched immediately (unless cushioned by reserves built up earlier) by a corresponding fall in the profit returns on the bank's liabilities, with the value of the investment deposits varying to reflect any losses sustained by the bank. In this particular respect Islamic banks can be regarded as closer to mutual funds rather than conventional banks, offering a form of 'equity-based' contracts (albeit of a rather special kind).

Contract Form

Third, we recall that from the viewpoint of financial sector efficiency, the standard debt contract is not invariably the optimal financial arrangement – all depends on the extent of monitoring costs and whether there are extensive scale economies in information collection. These issues have been addressed within the framework of Islamic economics by W.M. Khan (1985, 1987). He sets out to compare the 'fixed return scheme' (FRS) of debt contracts with the 'variable return scheme' (VRS) of Islamic *mudaraba* partnerships. Initially he assumes that monitoring costs are zero, that is, both lender and entrepreneur can observe without cost the realised return on a project and that the return is independent of the way the project is financed. Also assumed is the existence of a large number of mutually uncorrelated investment projects and the ability of lenders to put infinitely small amounts of money into each project. This allows lenders to diversify away all risk so that, if interest rates and profit-sharing ratios are set such that the expected returns in the FRS and VRS are equivalent, lenders will be indifferent between the two schemes. Borrowers' preferences then determine the choice between the two financing modes. For risk-neutral borrowers the choice does not matter (the standard Modigliani–Miller irrelevance theorem holds). However, if borrowers are risk-adverse (which given mutually uncorrelated investment projects is relevant because they are not allowed to diversify across projects), then the VRS is superior to FRS and full equity is also superior to any combination of debt and equity, since equity spreads risk more optimally than debt. VRS dominates FRS because under the former the lender in effect shares some of the risk which under the latter is borne entirely by the entrepreneur.

Obviously, monitoring costs must be introduced into the analysis and Khan then goes on to discuss extensions of some models, notably Stiglitz (1974), Jensen and Meckling (1976) and Grossman and Hart (1983) in which lenders can observe the outcome of investment projects only at a cost, and there is a tradeoff between the incentive effects of debt and the benefits of risk-spreading under equity. These models are used to show that expected monitoring costs are in general lower under FRS than VRS. The intuitive explanation is that in the fixed return scheme only reported returns below the fixed interest rate are regarded as suspicious by the lenders. The choice of FRS versus VRS depends on the costs of less than optimal risk-sharing versus the benefits of less monitoring costs in FRS. If the degree of risk-aversion is low, FRS dominates.

In summary, the overall comparison between the two contract types involves a trade-off between lower monitoring costs under FRS conditions and better risk-sharing under VRS arrangements. The frequency of use of debt contracts in practice is explained by supposing that the former often outweigh the latter (Ahmed, 1989). But, equally, there undoubtedly exist situations where this position is reversed, establishing a theoretical case for Islamic banking practices for certain types of projects where monitoring and evaluation can be undertaken with relative ease. For this theoretical case to be realised in practice, however, clear contracting arrangements and monitoring procedures would need to be put in place. One way in which this might occur is through the development of *musharaka*, where the bank can bring in technical assistance in the form of preparing feasibility studies, planning, coordinating and managing project development. Another is by putting in place more sophisticated regulatory-auditing procedures; for example, we noted earlier Khan's (1994) proposal for mandatory performance auditing.

Religious Precepts

Fourth, we must consider the 'religious variable' and the view that an analysis of Islamic financing cannot be carried out from a strictly economic viewpoint. On the deposit side of the balance sheet, there presumably will be many depositors choosing Islamic banks on purely ideological grounds and they will not be motivated solely by the returns available. Equally, on the asset side, the 'religious variable' may act as a counter to the incentive difficulties. Indeed, certain Muslim economists have argued that in a proper Islamic economic environment, incentive problems will not exist. In effect, Islamic religious ideology acts as its own enforcement mechanism to reduce the inefficiency that arises from the asymmetrical information and moral hazard. Their argument is twofold. On the one hand, the writers contend that an Islamic bank will overcome these problems by eliciting the right amount of information when a *mudaraba* contract is written so that it specifies the appropriate level of the actions of the entrepreneurs. The argument that an Islamic bank will induce full information in the contract is advanced, for example, by Haque and Mirakhor (1986). They argue that Islamic banking will overcome the problem of moral hazard by means of a profit-sharing contract

> such that all relevant information is used to deduce the state that is realised when, in fact, it is realised. To this end an incentive compatibility constraint, which is essentially like a truth-telling constraint, is utilised. Such a contract can be written to ensure that in each state the desired level of investment takes place. (p. 12)

At the same time, these authors maintain that, in an Islamic society, the actions of the entrepreneur are shaped by the Islamic normative system, which will restrict him from acting contrary to what is socially acceptable. Thus, the argument given by Muslim scholars for the absence of incentive problems in Islamic banking is that the Islamic moral code will prevent Muslim entrepreneurs from behaving in ways that are ethically unsound. In effect, Islamic ideology will act in a way that minimises the transaction costs arising from incentive issues, because a Muslim entrepreneur will always act honestly. As has been stated:

> to remain faithful to the terms specified in the contract, so much so that faithfulness to the terms of contracts is considered a distinguishing characteristic of a Muslim. The maxim that 'Muslims are bound by the stipulations' is recognised by all schools of Islamic thought. (ibid. pp. 3–4)

Our Agenda

These four issues – the costs of intermediation, the behaviour and attitudes of depositors, the importance of monitoring costs for contract form, and the role of religious precepts in reducing incentive problems – are obviously central to the success of the special Islamic modes of finance, and these are matters which we can assess empirically in the following chapters, when we examine Islamic banking in practice. As we shall see in Chapter 5, much depends on the legal framework surrounding the operation of Islamic banks; for example, whether there is a dispute-settlement tribunal operating to settle claims under *mudaraba* contracts like that which has been established in Pakistan.

In the absence of such mechanisms, an Islamic bank may be obliged to restrict the use of *mudaraba* and (to a lesser extent) *musharaka* contracts and instead provide funds by using available financial instruments, where incentive problems are less serious. Other financial instruments which can be used by the Islamic bank include mark-up (*murabaha*), and leasing and lease-purchase (*ijara, ijara wa iqtina*). The characteristics of these instruments, as have been outlined in Chapter 3, are much more similar to those provided by the traditional banking system. In particular, collateral is embodied in the asset or has to be provided in order to obtain finance, while the rates of profit associated with these instruments are largely determined in advance. Consequently, the risks associated with these instruments are mainly (if not in their entirety) borne by the entrepreneur, and to this degree not shared with the bank. How important these instruments are in practice is something which we will consider, especially in Chapter 6. This incentive-inefficiency problem is crucial in the competitive financial environment of the mixed systems, where Islamic and traditional banks operate side by side.

NOTES

1. The various types of financial intermediaries are examined in Lewis (1992a, 1995b).
2. Since these terms recur, some definitions might be useful. First, asymmetric information means that all economic transactors do not have the same information about all economic variables. Consider a market in which items of varying quality are exchanged and there exists asymmetric information in that only sellers can observe the quality of each unit sold. Without some device for buyers to identify good from bad, bad products will always be sold with the good products. Such a market illustrates the problem of adverse selection. This problem can be translated into what is known as the principal–agent model in which the principal delegates to the agent the responsibility for selecting and implementing an action. Adverse selection arises when the principal is not privy to some information which is relevant to the action, whereas the agent can make use of this information in selecting an action. By contrast, moral hazard occurs when the principal and agent share the same information up to the point at which the agent selects an action, but thereafter the principal cannot observe the action, only the outcome.
3. This section has benefited considerably from surveys of the extensive literature by Chant (1992), Cobham (1992), Dowd (1992, 1996), Hester (1994), Lewis (1991, 1992c) and Llewellyn (1999). The original references are given in these surveys and are not referred to here in great detail.
4. Briefly, risk management theories regard the individual bank as a risk-neutral agent that maximises expected profits while allowing for a particular type of risk. In portfolio models, banks are considered risk-averse investors, maximising a concave utility function in profits. According to imperfect-market models, the individual bank maximises (expected) profits or size by exploiting a set of market demand and supply functions through interest rate setting.

In real resource models, the bank is conceived of as a business firm producing financial services by combining labour and physical capital.

5. The most quoted references include Benston and Smith (1976) on transaction costs, Leland and Pyle (1977), Diamond (1984) and Fama (1985) on asymmetric information and signalling, and Diamond and Dybvig (1983) on liquidity insurance. These articles are reproduced in Lewis (1995b).

6. These also define our subsequent discussion, with the exception of search costs. There is surprisingly little analysis of search costs in the modern literature. Chan (1983) provides a model of intermediation based on spreading search costs amongst many investors, but it offers only a rationale for an information broker such as an introduction agency or marriage bureau, acting as a clearing house for would-be backers and seekers of venture capital (much like some agencies for enterprise or venture capital).

7. The term principal–agent problem is due to Ross (1973). Other early contributions to this literature include Mirrlees (1974, 1976) and Stiglitz (1974, 1975).

8. The law relating to the application of floating charges over collateral is explained by A. Lewis (1991).

9. Of course, the same conditions apply for all *mudaraba* contracts, including naturally that between a depositor and the bank in the case of investment accounts.

10. Giddy (1986), Kareken (1986), McCulloch (1986) and Goodhart (1988) developed the ideas.

11. The model has a number of key features: uncertainty about people's preferences for expenditure, which produces demands for liquid assets; private information about these preferences (that is about people's types); a demand deposit contract that allows depositors fully to withdraw their deposits on demand; a sequential service constraint that has banks honouring these withdrawals in the order they are received; and real investment projects that are costly to restart if they are interrupted. From these ingredients, Diamond and Dybvig develop a model of financial intermediation which has a 'bad' outcome, whereby a run on the 'bank', however triggered, proves to be self-fulfilling, in that the promised value of deposits plus interest cannot be met from the liquidation value of bank assets. A recent assessment, and critique of the model is provided by Green and Lin (2000). However, it is interesting to observe that in the United States, in the years shortly after Diamond and Dybvig's article was published, around 1000 banks and 1000 savings and loan associations failed, draining the deposit insurance fund and costing the taxpayers about $150 billion.

12. Following the Asian financial crisis of 1997/1998, there has been a renewed interest in Islamic banking on these grounds, in the light of the experience of the Islamic bank, Bank Muamalat Indonesia, which weathered the crisis better than most of the conventional banks (*Jakarta Post*, 5 March, 2000).

13. Mutual funds (unit trusts) and investment companies are different. The latter are closed-ended trusts, and the value of shares in an investment trust is determined in the stock market directly, invariably at a discount relative to the net asset value of the portfolio. In the case of a unit trust or mutual fund the value is based on a weighted basket of the underlying shares which are traded in the market, because they are open-ended and new units (shares) can be issued (or destroyed). Bid and offer prices of units are calculated frequently from market prices of the underlying assets. See Davidson (1992).

5. Islamic financial systems

OBJECTIVES OF AN ISLAMIC FINANCIAL SYSTEM

This chapter examines the appropriate structure of a complete financial system based on Islamic principles. Three countries which have sought to develop such a system are Pakistan, Iran and Sudan. Pakistan was the first to move in this direction, and a major part of this chapter is devoted to a study of the legal framework and the legislative and other changes instituted in Pakistan to bring this about. The transition in Iran and Sudan has been abrupt, in the wake of political transformations. But, to begin with, we outline the objectives and then the ideal structure of an Islamic financial system.

An Islamic banking and financial system exists to provide a variety of religiously acceptable financial services to the Muslim communities. In addition to this special function, the banking and financial institutions, like all other aspects of the Islamic society, are expected to 'contribute richly to the achievement of the major socio-economic goals of Islam' (Chapra, 1985, p. 34). The most important of these are: economic well-being with full employment and a high rate of economic growth, socio-economic justice and an equitable distribution of income and wealth, stability in the value of money, and the mobilisation and investment of savings for economic development in such a way that a just (profit-sharing) return is ensured to all parties involved. Perhaps the religious dimension should be presented as a further explicit goal, in the sense that the opportunity to conduct religiously legitimate financial operations has a value far beyond that of the mode of the financial operation itself.

The validity of these general objectives is seldom questioned. However, there is no consensus about the proper structure of the overall financial system needed to achieve them. This chapter will outline two alternative structural settings for Islamic banking. But first we consider the objectives of Islamic banking and finance in more detail.

From an Islamic perspective, the main objectives of Islamic banking and finance can be summarised in the following terms:

- the abolition of interest from all financial transactions and the reform of all bank activities to accord with Islamic principles;
- the achievement of an equitable distribution of income and wealth; and

- the promotion of economic development.

These are examined in turn.

Abolition of *Riba*

The first objective of abolishing interest and introducing Islamic principles is a religious one, and it is therefore difficult to measure the degree of its success or failure in purely secular terms. Nevertheless, Islamic scholars have sought to provide a theoretical basis for the prohibition in terms of morality and economics. The reason for this endeavour is straightforward: while the basic source of the ban is the divine authority of the Holy Qur'an, it gave no rationale for why interest is unjustified.

Early writers emphasised the social welfare aspects, in terms of those activities which increase utility (*musalih*) and those that do not (*mafasid* or disutilities). For example, Ghazali (who died in 1127CE) rejected lending because 'whoever uses money in *riba* practices becomes ungrateful and unjust', since money is 'not created to be sought for itself but for other objects'. And since 'hoarding money is injustice, it is meaningless to sell money for money except to take money as an end in itself which is injustice'.[1] As we shall see later, there are clear parallels here with the attitudes of medieval Christian scholars toward the Christian Church's prohibition of usury. (Both, in fact, would seem to have been influenced by the early views of Aristotle and other Greek philosophers on this subject.)

Twentieth century scholars[2] have moved away from equity considerations, and have taken to task the conventional theories of interest for equating interest with either 'impatience' or 'waiting', on the savings side, or with the 'productivity of capital', on the investment side of, respectively, the supply and demand for loanable funds. These writers question the view that interest is a reward for saving in the form of 'abstinence', arguing that such reward could be justified, from an economic standpoint only, if savings were used for investment to create additional capital and wealth. Their contention is that the mere act of abstention from consumption should not entitle anyone to a reward. As to the rationalisation on the grounds of 'productivity', the Islamic economists would reply that although the marginal productivity of capital may enter as one factor into the determination of the rate of interest, interest, *per se*, has no necessary relation with capital productivity. Interest, they argue, is paid on money, not on capital, and has to be paid irrespective of capital productivity.

Such arguments, we should note, have a very respectable heritage in conventional economic theory. The Austrian economist Eugen von Boehm-Bawerk (1922), for example, made much the same points. He rejected the 'sacrifice' or 'pain' theory of value implicit in the 'abstinence' theory by arguing that the utility of goods in productive use was the relevant consideration. At the same time, he objected to the 'productivity' theories of interest since if the capital investment produced nothing, it would presumably be of no value. Indeed, what Joseph Schumpeter (1951) called the 'dilemma of interest' has troubled a number of writers. Schumpeter himself was unable to resolve whether the equilibrium rate of interest is positive, that is, whether interest could exist in equilibrium (Schumpeter, 1951, especially pp. 159–69).

Another approach to the question of *riba* revolves around the Islamic law of property rights. The essence of the argument is that interest on money (*riba*) leads to the creation of unjustified property rights. As a result, the payment and receipt of interest is in violation of the *shari'a*. Two individual claims to property are recognised by the *shari'a*: property that is a result of the combination of individuals' creative labour and natural resources; and property the title of which has been transferred by its owner as a result of exchange, remittance or rights of others in the owner's property, outright beneficence grants by the owner to those in need and, finally, inheritance. Money is a claim of its owner to property rights created by assets that were obtained through one of the above means. Lending money is a transfer of this right and all that can be claimed in return is its equivalent and no more, that is principal only. By contrast, when the financial resources of the lender are used in partnership with the labour of the entrepreneur, the lender's right to his property is not transferred and remains intact, thus making him a co-owner of the enterprise. His money then has a legitimate claim and a right to share in the wealth it helps to create (Khan and Mirakhor, 1987).

On all three grounds, it can be said that the emergence of Islamic banking has accordingly given Muslims the opportunity to undertake interest-free and thereby *halal*, or licit, financial transactions. Two models have been advanced for how this should be done. The first, advocated by Siddiqi (1980, 1982), Chapra (1985) and Uzair ([1955]1978), is based around the two-tier or triple *mudaraba* outlined in earlier chapters. The bank's earnings from all its activities are pooled and are then shared with its depositors and shareholders according to the terms of their contract. Banks are allowed to accept demand deposits that earn no profit and on which may be levied a service charge. This model, although requiring that current deposits must be paid on the demand of the depositors, has no specific reserve requirement. Under the second model, proposed by Khan (1985), the liability side of the banks' balance sheet is divided into two windows, one for demand deposits (transaction balances) and the other for investment balances. The choice of the window would be left to the depositors. This model requires 100 per cent reserves for the demand deposits but stipulates no reserve requirement for the second window. This is based on the presumption that the money deposited as demand deposits is placed in trust or fiduciary relationship (*amana*) and must be backed by 100 per cent reserve holding. Money deposited in investment accounts, on the other hand, is placed with the depositor's full knowledge that his deposits will be invested in risk-bearing projects, and therefore no guarantee is justified. Both models consider the losses incurred as a result of investment activities by the banks as being reflected in the depreciation of the value of the depositor's wealth.

In either model, there exists the opportunity for interest-free investments at the individual level. Admittedly, there is some disagreement about the mode of operation of some (or perhaps most) Islamic banks. Some scholars argue that not all available and legitimate forms of Islamic financial contracts satisfy the requirements embodied in *shari'a* (Siddiqi, 1986, pp. 59–61). The most acceptable forms of financing, they argue, are equity participation schemes conducted along *mudaraba* and *musharaka* principles. A major part of banking business should be of this type. Yet, a large share of financing of Islamic banks is conducted by *murabaha* (mark-up) and *ijara* (leasing) contracts. These contracts yield a pre-fixed and known income and therefore have effects similar to those of interest-based transactions (Atiya, 1986, p. 9). This position is considered to be at variance with the value system of an Islamic economy.

In this respect, it might therefore be appropriate to distinguish between interest-free or *halal* banks, which obey the letter of the Holy Qur'an but not quite its spirit, and true Islamic banks, which have an explicit socio-economic responsibility (Khan, 1986, pp. 2–3). On this division, most of the present Islamic banks should be referred to as *halal* banks. Nevertheless, even in this case, the first objective is at least partly fulfilled. Individually, Muslims can choose to deal with banks which make interest-free financial transactions, even though Islamic principles concerning the use of funds may not be fully realised in terms of strict orthodoxy. It should also be noted that the distinction between an Islamic and a *halal* bank has not been recognised in jurisprudence.

Nevertheless, the emphasis placed on equity-oriented transactions in Islamic banking, especially the *mudaraba* mode, has been questioned in some sources. It has been argued that the replacement of predetermined interest by uncertain profits is not enough in itself to render a transaction Islamic, since profit can be just as exploitative as is interest, if it is 'excessive' (Naqvi, 1981). One response to this criticism is to note that one must distinguish between profit and profiteering, and Islam has prohibited the latter as well as interest. Naqvi has also pointed out that there is nothing sacrosanct about the institution of *mudaraba* in Islam. He maintains that *mudaraba* is not based on the Holy Qur'an or the *hadith* but was a custom of the pre-Islamic Arabs. Historically, *mudaraba*, he contends, enabled the aged, women and children with capital to engage in trade through merchants for a share in the profit, all losses being borne by the owners of capital, and on these grounds it cannot claim any special sanctity. Yet the fact remains that the Prophet (peace be unto him) raised no objection to *mudaraba*, so that it was at least not considered un-Islamic.

Distribution of Income

The objective of achieving an equitable distribution of income and wealth can be interpreted in several ways. It may be seen as an effort to spread the ownership of the productive resources of the society, or it may be interpreted as a striving to change the distribution of the production results between labour (including entrepreneurship) and capital. On the first interpretation, it seems obvious that Islamic banking will affect the ownership structure of the economy. Owing to the wider equity participation of Islamic banks, ownership is transferred from entrepreneurs to other sectors of the economy. It is, however, far from clear whether this transfer can be equated with a more equitable distribution of wealth. Ownership is usually transferred to the bank and thereby ultimately to the shareholders of the bank, rather than to the depositors. One group likely to benefit as a result is bank shareholders, since the ownership of Islamic banks at present is highly concentrated.

How production results *ought* to be distributed between labour and capital is less clear-cut. Because of the hostile Islamic attitude toward interest in conventional banking, large bank profits are seen as undesirable. But some additional issues are posed if Islamic banking principles operate instead. For instance, how are the production returns divided between the bank and the entrepreneur in Islamic financing as compared with interest financing? Also, who are the recipients of bank profit shares, shareholders or depositors? And, if the latter, who are the banks' investment account depositors? If they are among the advantaged or more wealthy in society, then a larger total share for the bank could mean a more unequal distribution of income. If they are not, then a larger share accruing to capital owners might actually improve the distribution of income.

No definite conclusions on these points can be reached on the basis of existing data. There are, nonetheless, some suggestions that the income distribution may not be made more equal by Islamic banking. Its introduction in a developing economy will change the distribution of productive returns in favour of the capital owners, who tend to be the banks' depositors. Also, minimum deposit limits for investment deposit accounts could restrict holders of PLS accounts to the middle class. Both factors could accentuate an unequal income distribution. But a necessary condition for this conclusion to apply is that Islamic banking and the institution of PLS arrangements does not expand the physical production possibilities of the economy in question, resulting in larger total investments and increased labour incomes. Such an eventuality is possible, particularly in less developed economies with severe shortages of management skills. In these circumstances, Islamic banks may provide various management services to projects and thus increase total efficiency and output. Furthermore, the differences in risk-taking between Islamic banks and conventional banks must be taken into account. If Islamic banks engage in projects with higher risk, higher capital yields are justified.

The redistributive effects of *zakat*, the wealth or religious levy must also be considered insofar as *zakat* is seen as a duty of Islamic banking. The fact that *zakat* is proportional and set at only 2.5 per cent of wealth suggests that it may not by itself be an effective redistributive instrument. In this context, a distinction between an equitable and an acceptable distribution of income needs to be made. *Zakat* may well generate sufficient funds to ensure *nisab*, a minimum acceptable standard of living, for all members of the Muslim community, but its impact on narrowing income differentials may turn out to be negligible.

In fact, the significance of *zakat* in Islam is different from a welfare programme, and *zakat* is different from a tax as it is understood today. A tax in a modern society is an obligation of individuals and other entities towards the state, whereas *zakat* is an obligation of a Muslim not only to society and the state, but also to *Allah*. In other words *zakat* is not merely a 'contribution', but it is also a 'due' or a 'claim'. A person paying *zakat* is not primarily doing a favour to the recipient or beneficiary of *zakat*, but is rather meeting a claim on himself by purifying wealth. Of course, the same is true of a Muslim who eschews interest. Neither obligation can be judged in earthly terms alone. Nevertheless, in all, it must be concluded that the introduction of Islamic banking and finance alone cannot be expected greatly to improve the distribution of income and wealth.

Economic Development

The third objective of Islamic banks, the promotion of economic development, consists of an optimum rate of growth, consistent with stability in the value of money as well as a religious aspect. From an Islamic point of view, as we have emphasised on a number of occasions, the economic objectives cannot be isolated from the religious and ideological aims. This complicates the analysis of success within the Islamic framework, since for example achievements in reaching full employment must be weighted with the value of possessing a financial system which is legitimate according to the rules of *shari'a*. This amounts, in other words, to a particular Islamic definition of economic development, which lies beyond the present study to attempt to define or analyse (see, however, Ahmad, 1980; Kazarian and Kokko, 1987; Kazarian, 1991; and M.F. Khan, 1995).

Increasingly, the achievement of macroeconomic stability is seen as a desirable prerequisite or accompaniment to economic growth, and this is a topic which has been extensively analysed by Islamic economists. The question at issue is whether an Islamic system, based on PLS-sharing rather than interest, can work and deliver an acceptable degree of economic stability. Their answer to both is yes, and a representative example is M.S. Khan's chapter in Khan and Mirakhor (1987). He examines these questions by considering a variant of a standard IS-LM model in which there are no bonds and banks act as pure intermediaries. There are no transactions deposits, banks hold no reserves and have zero net worth. Consequently, money consists only of currency. Despite its simplicity, his model is useful in showing that a well-defined equilibrium in an IS-LM type model with no bonds can be achieved, and is robust in the face of real (IS) disturbances. In the model, the Islamic-type banks issue equity-type claims (and in fact are no different from any other firm in the economy that issues only equity). Their response (and that of the system) to a real shock is quite different from that of standard banks. In standard banking, with a guaranteed nominal value of deposits, the short-run effect is a divergence between real assets and liabilities and the possibility of a banking crisis. With the Islamic banks, following an IS shock, the real value of the banks' liabilities adjusts instantaneously when the nominal value of investment deposits is not guaranteed. Thus, there is no divergence between real assets and liabilities, reducing the likelihood of a bank run. As we noted in Chapter 4, Islamic banks with investment accounts behave much like mutual fund banks.[3]

There are some interesting similarities between this analysis and that of a conventional (that is interest-based) banking system under de-regulation (for example, Davis and Lewis, 1982, 1992). These authors' argument is that in a de-regulated, competitive environment, deposit interest rates will be driven to equality with the average yield on banks' asset portfolios (less the resource cost of providing intermediation services). In their model, the bank asset portfolio comprised bonds and other financial assets only. For an Islamic banking system the portfolio would comprise only capital assets, but in other respects the conclusions are much the same. Davis and Lewis find that when deposit rates track asset returns, and are not subject to a ceiling, the system exhibits greater stability in the face of economic shocks. Asset yields are more variable, but these serve to stabilise the economy and reduce income variability.[4]

IDEAL STRUCTURE OF THE SYSTEM

Two conceptions of an ideal Islamic financial system have been provided in the literature on Islamic economics. One vision is the framework proposed by Chapra (1985) and Siddiqi (1983). The other is that of Ismail (1986). They differ in terms of what behaviour is expected from the constituent institutions.

Chapra's Model

Chapra suggests a system comprising the following institutions: central bank; commercial banks; non-bank financial institutions; specialised credit institutions; deposit insurance corporation(s); and investment audit corporations. Although on the surface this structure appears to be much the same as that for a conventional financial system, Chapra envisages that there are differences in the functions, scope and responsibilities of the institutions concerned. Each of the institutions is seen as an essential component of the integrity of the system and as such necessary for the achievement of the desired objectives outlined earlier in this chapter.

An Islamic central bank is supposed to perform all of the same functions as other central banks, namely the issuing of currency, acting as banker to the government and commercial banks, serving as the lender of last resort, and guiding, supervising and regulating the financial system.[5] Unlike conventional central banks, however, the Islamic version should also act to hinder the concentration of wealth and power in the hands of vested interests through the financial institutions. This socio-economic purpose, together with the very comprehensive supervisory responsibilities and its central function of promoting Islam, differentiates the Islamic central bank from its conventional counterparts.

Islamic commercial banks in this setting would differ from traditional commercial banks in two main ways. The first and most significant difference would be the abolition of *riba*. In turn, this prohibition would force banking to new methods of operations based primarily around PLS arrangements, corresponding in Chapra's framework with the first of the two models outlined earlier. A second principal difference would be that funds which come from the public should be used to serve the common interest and not individual gain. Thus banking transactions should not be solely profit-oriented, but instead be aimed at the needs of the Islamic society overall. In order to achieve these twin goals, Islamic banks would thereby tend to become universal or multi-purpose banks instead of purely commercial banks: a 'cross-breed of commercial and investment banks, investment trusts and investment-management institutions...' (Chapra, 1985, p. 154). They would therefore more closely approximate to the German or Continental European tradition than to the Anglo-Saxon tradition, and this mode of operation would have additional consequences for the term structure of funds, the distribution of risk, and the relations between banks and customers.

Non-bank financial intermediaries consist of investment trusts and funds, credit unions, credit co-operatives, other investment-management institutions and insurance companies. Their purpose is to supplement the commercial banks and to mobilise capital through equity participations and profit-sharing deposits for investment purposes. These institutions would be distinguished from each other according to the nature of financing activity undertaken and in consequence the maturity of the funds. Apart from mobilising capital, these intermediaries would help to spread the ownership of business interests and reduce the concentration of wealth.

Those projects and sectors of the economy which might not be attractive to commercial banks or other profit-motivated institutions, but nevertheless important from a wider communal perspective, would be financed by the specialised credit institutions. Their field of operation could include farmers, artisans, and other small businesses and entrepreneurs. Funds for these purposes could be directed through the specialised institutions from the central bank or the government, and provided in non-inflationary ways adopting practices used in standard development banking.

The deposit insurance fund and the investment audit corporation would be government-sponsored organisations set up respectively to insure demand deposits in commercial banks and to safeguard the interests of profit-sharing investors and equity holders. There is no equivalent to the investment audit corporation in Western banking because of the importance of the PLS principle in Islamic finance and the auditing function is vital not only in terms of safety but would fulfil an important function for the integrity of the financial system. For these reasons, the auditing process would reach beyond conventional auditing principles in the West to consider investment projects and the reliability of management practices, so as to ensure an equitable division of the returns between shareholders and profit-sharing depositors.

In summary, the main characteristic of Chapra's framework is the dispersal of social welfare responsibilities and religious requirements to all levels of the financial system, ranging from the central bank to private commercial banks to the deposit insurance and audit corporations. This communal role explicitly adds an extra parameter to the objective function of the Islamic financial agent.[6]

Ismail's Framework

An alternative setting for Islamic banking is proposed by Abdul Halim Ismail (1986), who argues for a more thorough division of responsibilities. He sketches an Islamic economic system which consists of three sectors, namely: *siasi*, the government sector, which encompasses public finance and central banking; *ijtimai*, the welfare sector, with responsibility for the administration of taxes, and *tijari*, the commercial sector, which covers all private sector commercial activities. In each of these sectors there would be several different types of institutions, all of them working on the basis of general *shari'a* principles but applied to the particular operations undertaken. The Islamic financial system constitutes institutions from all of the three sectors.

Within this framework, the Islamic commercial banks obviously belong to the *tijari* or the commercial sector. Their responsibilities thereby predominantly are limited to commercial activities. The task of ensuring an equitable income distribution does not burden the Islamic bank, but rather it concerns the *siasi* as a task of public finance. Likewise, the collection and distribution of taxes is not a commercial bank task but rather the responsibility of different *ijtimai* institutions.

This example highlights the differences between the two structures. According to Chapra, each of the institutions in an Islamic economic system must explicitly take responsibility for the fulfilment of the general economic and social objectives, sometimes at the cost of individual profitability. The operations should consequently be biased in favour of socially, but not necessarily financially profitable, projects. In Ismail's framework, by contrast, Islamic banks are overridingly commercial institutions, with responsibilities essentially to shareholders and depositors; society is served by them pursuing their self-interest (Adam Smith's invisible hand), augmenting profit and income, along with *zakat* distributions. A probable consequence of this difference in approach is that modes of operation will likely vary between banks in the alternative systems. Although the set of legitimate financing operations and practices is common to both settings and applies to all Islamic institutions, some activities may be preferred over others depending on the objectives. An examination of the actual workings of Islamic banking in practice should therefore be studied with these distinctions in mind.

Market Structure

Before doing so, however, we should observe that the world has moved on since these early contributions and so has the structure of financial systems. Securitisation has proceeded apace in Islamic financing as it has in financial systems generally. Banks and financial institutions still play an important role in the securities markets, but they do so in a different way. In the previous chapter we draw a distinction between intermediation activities that involve little change to the instruments exchanged, and those in which significant portfolio transformation takes place. This distinction matters a great deal in conventional banking and financial markets, where there is a significant difference between a broker who does not alter the assets traded and a bank which engages in substantial portfolio transformation converting long-term risky loans into short-term deposits with a guaranteed nominal capital value. Islamic banking represents a middle way between these two positions. Under the pure form of the two-tiered *mudaraba*, for example, liabilities of the banks, the suppliers of investment accounts, are claims on the profit returns on repackaged investments. Information gathering is centralised in the bank, and returns on the assets are pooled and diversified, but the residual, undiversified risk is shared and passed on in the agreed proportion to account holders.

In this respect, as we have noted before, Islamic banking bears some similarities with the mutual fund-type arrangement (the parallel is complete in the case of the hypothetical mutual fund banking). The difference, of course, is that with a mutual fund the risk falls fully upon holders of the units, and the sponsor acts as trustee/agent on a 'best efforts' fee basis. Nevertheless, it would seem to be a short step from the traditional *mudaraba* contract with investment account depositors to a pure investment fund arrangement, and this is the route along which many Islamic banks have gone when expanding their securities markets services to clients (see Chapter 9).

Two major difficulties arise when seeking a full Islamic financial system in which both banks and the direct investing public are looking for *shari'a* – acceptable investments. The first of these relates to private sector securities, for the Islamic financial system needs to develop appropriate instruments. Appropriate in this context is two-fold. They must, on the one hand, be religiously acceptable. Generally speaking, any instrument representing a position in real assets and having risk-bearing characteristics for which the rate of return is variable and tied to the performance of the asset is considered acceptable. At the same time, the securities need to be attractive to savers. This requires the development of risk-bearing instruments that can provide the investors with a sufficient degree of liquidity, security and profitability to encourage their holding. Proposals along such lines rely on the development of instruments corresponding and parallel to the permissible forms of transactions. These include such instruments as *mudaraba* and *musharaka* certificates, short-term profit-sharing certificates and leasing certificates (Al-Jarhi, 1983; Mirakhor, 1995).

Provision of liquidity is a major task of any system, for financial markets must simultaneously satisfy the portfolio preferences of those savers who have unexpected needs for spending with those investors wanting a guaranteed supply of long-term finance for investment projects. Banks do this by allowing depositors to withdraw their funds at short notice while making longer-term loans. Under direct financing, an individual who wishes to withdraw funds prior to the maturity of the security must be able to sell his share or participation in the investment in a secondary market. For secondary markets to be able to transform an asset into a reliable source of cash for an economic unit whenever needed, they will generally need to be dealer markets in which there will be position-takers who will trade significant amounts of assets (Lewis, 1990, 1992d).

On this basis, an Islamic financial system needs more than the institutions envisaged by Chapra and Ismail. It must create as well a full range of primary and secondary markets which, along with brokers, dealers and middlemen of various sorts, exist in conventional systems. Derivatives are also important in enabling financial engineering – the process whereby the risk–return characteristics of securities can be altered at low cost (Hodges, 1992; Lewis, 1997). Not all such contracts are acceptable in religious terms, however, because of the provisions in Islamic law about *gharar*.

Public Sector Finance

Public sector financing poses the second major difficulty when Islamic principles are applied to the whole financial system. Invariably, existing techniques for financing government expenditure involve the issue of bonds and other interest-bearing securities, either to the financial sector or directly to the public. How is the government to finance its expenditure in an economy with no fixed (or variable) interest debt?

Mannan ([1970]1986) has an interesting discussion of this issue and reaches a number of conclusions. First, government spending that is permanent or recurring, such as normal compensation of employees, would be financed by taxation. Second, temporary spending for specific projects would be financed by loans from the private sector on a profit-and-loss-sharing (PLS) basis. Third, the central bank would also be allowed to invest directly in the real sector on a PLS basis and choose how much of the government's equity to monetise through the usual kinds of open market operations, with the only difference being the nature of the securities being traded. Finally, nonproject-specific temporary spending by the government (emergency spending to finance a war, for example) would be financed through compulsory zero interest loans from the private sector.

It is the second of these recommendations which poses the greatest challenge. How can defence, health, education and infrastructure and such 'public goods' be provided on a PLS basis? One obvious reply is along the lines that many of these activities should not be funded from borrowings in the first place. There is a longstanding debate in the standard theory of public finance about the 'burden of the debt' (Buchanan, 1958), and the situations in which it is appropriate to borrow. Buchanan argues that debt issue imposes a burden upon future generations, who must repay the indebtedness with higher taxation. Borrowing is thus deferred taxation, as recognised by a recent report

by the International Institute of Islamic Economics (1999).[7] It would seem
fitting to borrow only if the future debt (that is, tax) burden shifted to the
future is accompanied by a commensurate benefit accruing to future
generations, such as may come from infrastructure projects or public utilities
or even defence procurement.

Fortunately, these sorts of expenditures lend themselves readily to PLS
techniques and other financing methods which are *shari'a* compatible. One
possibility is for the public sector to engage in public–private sector
partnership arrangements for the provision of infrastructure (see Grimsey and
Lewis, 1999). With projects so commercialised, they could conceivably be
financed through PLS techniques. Another possibility is for public entities to
be 'corporatised', with shares quoted on the stock market. Then there are other
choices. PLS certificates could be floated to finance for transport and
communications activities, or 'revenue bonds' issued with returns a proportion
of operating income. Leasing might also be used to purchase equipment.
Goods required for the provision of government services (for example
hospitals) could be acquired on a *murabaha* mark-up basis with deferred
payments if necessary.

Thus there are a number of options which would seem to be acceptable in
principle and practical enough to implement given the political will, although
all would require new institutions and alteration to existing bureaucratic ways.
Many Western governments have revolutionised the finance of infrastructure
over the last decade (Mustafa, 1999). None, of course, have ventured down the
PLS route (for obvious reasons), but this would not seem to be an
insurmountable hurdle given the innovative financial engineering applied to
existing deals.[8] Chapter 9 returns to the theme of infrastructure financing by
Islamic investment banks.

ISLAMIC FINANCIAL SYSTEMS IN PRACTICE

In Chapter 1 we noted that the development of Islamic banking or financial
institutions, which has gained momentum since the second half of the 1970s,
has basically taken two forms. One has been an attempt to establish Islamic
financial institutions side by side with traditional banking, and we examine the
cases of Egypt, Malaysia and some other countries in the next chapter. A
second form has involved an attempt to restructure the whole financial system
of the economy in accord with Islamic concepts. This has taken two directions,
one in which the entire economy and its institutions, including financial, are
transformed rapidly into an Islamic one, as in the Islamic Republic of Iran and
Sudan, and the other where Islamisation of the economy is undertaken through
a gradual process, as in Pakistan.

Iran

Iran switched to Islamic banking in August 1983 with a three-year transition period, although the process of Islamisation began earlier and has passed through three phases. In the first phase (1979–82), the banking sector was nationalised and restructured. In the second phase (1983–86), Islamic banking was introduced. The third phase, which began in 1986, defined a role for the banking system different from the earlier phases, in that the system was expected to be an integral part of the Islamic government. It was also to be an instrument for social and economic development, along with reconstruction in the wake of the economic crisis brought about by capital flight, the influx of 2 million Afghan refugees, the war with Iraq, and drastic reductions in oil revenues.

The Law for *Riba*-Free Banking was passed in August 1983, and came into force in March 1984, giving a very short deadline of one year for the banks to convert their deposits in line with Islamic law and their total operations within three years from the date of the passage of the law. It also prescribed a list of legitimate methods of transactions on both the liabilities and assets side of financial institutions. These permissible modes of financing are set out in Table 5.1.

Iqbal and Mirakhor (1987) and Khan and Mirakhor (1990) noted that the conversion to Islamic modes was much faster on the liability than on the asset side. The Iranian system allows banks to accept current and savings deposits without having to pay any return, but it permits the banks to offer incentives

Table 5.1   Islamic Republic of Iran: modes of permissible transactions corresponding to types of economic activity

Type of activity	Permissible mode
Production (industrial, mining, agricultural)	*Musharakah,* lease-purchase, *Salaf* transactions, instalment sales, direct investment, *Muzara'ah, Musaqat* and *Jo'alah*
Commercial	*Mudarabah, Musharakah, Jo'alah*
Service	Lease-purchase, instalment sales, *Jo'alah*
Housing	Lease-purchase, instalment, *Qard al-Hasanah, Jo'alah*
Personal consumption	Instalment sales, *Qard al-Hasanah*

Source: Khan and Mirakhor (1990), based on information supplied by Bank Maraqkazi (Central Bank of Iran).

such as variable prizes or bonuses in cash or kind on these deposits. Term
deposits (both short-term and long-term) earn a rate of return based on the
bank's profits and on the deposit maturity. Unlike non-Iranian Islamic banks
that mobilize funds using investment accounts based on the *mudaraba*
principle, term deposit accounts in Iran are based on the attorney-client
contract of *Al-wakalah*, for which the banks have the power of attorney
and are authorised to charge their clients appropriate legal fees (Yasseri,
2000).

On the asset side, profit-sharing modes such as civil partnerships (short-
term and project-specific partnerships) and legal partnerships (long-term and
firm-specific partnerships) took some time to take hold. Under the Iranian
Civil Code, there are two forms of partnership in Iranian banking contracts:
civil partnership and equity partnership. The latter is based on a bank's
participation in production through acquiring stocks and shares in a company,
whereas with a civil partnership there is a co-mingling of assets and ownership
rights in a profit-seeking venture. In such project-specific partnerships, banks
usually delegate management to the other partner(s), but they can require the
others to bear any capital loss and can utilise collateral security as protection
against mismanagement.

Table 5.2 shows that such partnership financing modes along with
mudarabas represented nearly one-quarter of the financing extended by Iranian
banks during the year ended March 1998 (Iranian year 1377). Nonetheless, by

*Table 5.2   Islamic financing modes employed by banks in the Islamic
Republic of Iran, 1995–98 (per cent of total credit facilities)*

	1995	1996	1997	1998
Instalment sales	45.0	43.4	56.0	56.1
Musharakah (civil partnerships)	19.4	19.6	11.6	9.4
Equity partnership	2.7	3.8	4.7	6.9
Mudharabah	6.8	6.7	6.4	6.3
Salaf transactions	5.5	5.0	5.2	5.9
Ghardhal-hassan	4.7	4.5	4.6	5.0
Jo'alah	7.0	6.6	1.6	1.5
Direct investments	1.7	2.8	2.5	1.7
Hire purchase	1.0	1.1	0.8	0.6
Other	6.2	6.5	6.6	6.6
Total	100	100	100	100

Source: Central Bank of the Islamic Republic of Iran, reported in Yasseri (2000).

far the most important financing method employed was that of instalment sales
– the Iranian version of *murabaha* – accounting for 56.1 per cent of financing.
Jo'alah is the Iranian variant of *istisnaa,* while *salaf* is the equivalent of
bai'salam. Iranian banks raise some deposit funds by means of *Ghardhal-
hassan* deposits, that is current and savings accounts, which are regarded as in
the nature of loan contracts, repayable on demand or when they become due,
and on the asset side advance funds on the same basis. Of the other financing
modes permitted, as per Table 5.1, *muzara'ah* and *mussaqat* are exclusively
designed for agriculture, and now little used in the Iranian banking system.

One of the peculiarities of the Iranian experience is the extent of banking
sector financing of government, for it has resolved a major obstacle to
Islamisation that we identified in the previous section, that is converting the
public sector to acceptable financing modes. *Riba,* according to the principles
of Islamic banking in Iran, required four conditions to be met. These are: the
existence of indebtedness; the existence of a debtor independent from the
creditor, or vice versa; the presence of a pre-agreement for the receipt of an
extra amount over the principal of the debt; and, finally, receipt of the extra
amount. Any lending with these four elements has the necessary and sufficient
condition to create *riba.* However, in the absence of one or more of these
factors, though the lending may exist, the extra amount received is not
considered to be *riba* (Mahdavi, 1995).

It was on the second condition that the solution turned; *riba* is created if,
and only if, the borrower has an identity independent from the lender.
Complete dependence of the borrower on the lender nullifies the existence of
lending from an Islamic point of view, and hence *riba* is not, in that case,
created. This interpretation provided the vehicle which has enabled Iranian
banks to circumvent the ban on *riba* in the case of the government and
government agencies. All banks in Iran have been nationalised and thus are
fully government-owned. If the government as a whole is considered to be one
body, or one legal entity, borrowing and lending between two sub-bodies of
this main body, though supported by documentation, and valid from this
perspective, does not have the characteristics of borrowing as there is no real
indebtedness. In effect, the borrower and the lender are the same entity, that
is, the government. As a result, the payment and receipt of the extra amount in
excess of the principal of the borrowing is not considered *riba.* This being the
case, it has been possible to finance, using traditional borrowing methods, the
central government and fully government-owned agencies and corporations
using the banks' own capital, current accounts, savings accounts and any
credit balances.[9]

On similar grounds, loans belonging to a specific person granted by one of
the branches of a business firm to another branch, would be deemed to lack the
independence feature of debtor and creditor. Another example would be loans

granted by one company to another when both companies have common shareholders. A third example would be inter-branch loans of a specific bank. None of these loan agreements create 'true' indebtedness under the Islamic banking procedures now operating in Iran, even though they have the 'appearance' of being interest-based. Nevertheless, while these transactions can continue in the traditional way, there is also nothing which excludes them (and government borrowings) from being replaced by the alternative Islamic financing techniques.

Sudan

For many years, Islamic banks in Sudan operated alongside conventional banks (which had earlier been nationalised in 1970).[10] The Faisal Islamic Bank of Sudan began operations in 1978 under a special decree, followed in 1983 by El-Tadamon Islamic Bank, the Sudanese Islamic Bank, and the Islamic Cooperative Development Bank (owned by cooperative unions) and in 1984 by Al-Baraka Bank (Sudan) and Islamic Bank of Western Sudan. However, the position changed in September 1984 when the whole banking system was 'Islamised'.

President Bumeiry of Sudan decided that the banking system should operate along Islamic lines, and he issued orders to the Governor of the Bank of Sudan, the central bank, to implement this transition immediately. The result was that in July 1984 the Governor instructed the conventional banks to change their business activities to be consistent with Islamic principles within two months. This was done, but often more by following the letter rather than the spirit of the law. Given the abrupt nature of the transition, many of the banks could do little more than to replace the word 'interest' with the word 'profit', undertaking virtually all business under *murabaha*. The central bank also continued with its pre-existing money supply control techniques which involved setting credit ceilings for each bank. These restricted the ability of the original Islamic banks to invest funds accepted on a trustee basis in investment accounts.

A more complete transition to Islamic banking took place from 1990, after years of political turmoil and military government. The new government took the following steps to implement the *shari'a* in the banking sector:

1. Revision of the Bank of Sudan Act to eliminate all articles related to interest.
2. Revision of the Banking Regulation Act with a view to eliminating all articles conflicting with Islamisation. All changes were to be made under the guidance of the Religious Board.
3. Appointing a Supreme Religious Board in the Bank of Sudan to supervise

the work of the Bank of Sudan as well as that of the other banks.

4. Instructing every individual bank to appoint religious researchers to ensure that its daily operations complied with the *shari'a*, referring difficult cases to the Superior Religious Board of the Bank of Sudan.
5. Strengthening the relevant departments in both the Bank of Sudan and the commercial banks.
6. Initiating special training seminars for the staff of the Bank of Sudan and the commercial banks with the help of the Islamic banks.
7. Restructuring the syllabus of the Institute of Banking Studies to cater for the needs of Islamic banking.[11]

Meanwhile, some of the Islamic banks have made significant headway in fashioning Islamic financing instruments to the agricultural conditions in Sudan, especially in the case of finance provided under the *musharaka* contract. Following low returns on its first *musharaka* transaction, the Faisal Islamic Bank introduced a system of monitoring and supervision of the financing partner, which they see as help and coordination rather than interference. Basically, the system ensures that the right quality of raw materials, in the right quantities, was purchased at the right time for the right price. Difficulties in production, storage and marketing are discussed and solved with the partner. The upshot of applying this system was that the Islamic banks then incurred relatively fewer bad debts and fewer non-performing assets compared with conventional banks (Mudawi, 1995).

The Sudanese Islamic Bank (SIB) has also experimented with and adapted the *musharaka* as a device for financing rural development (Al-Harran, 1993). A number of partnership arrangements have been fashioned according to the nature of the activity. Unlike the models suggested by Khan (1994), which generally included Islamic non-government or government bodies in the financing arrangements, these partnerships involve the bank and the farmer. In the agricultural financing model, for example, the bank provides fixed assets such as tractors, ploughs, harrows, water pumps, and inputs such as seeds, fertilisers, pesticides, fuel, jute sacks and co-management, marketing, storing and extension. The farmer, on the other hand, contributes his land, labour, part of the running expenses and management. From the net profit the farmer gets 30 per cent for management. The remaining profit (70 per cent) is divided between the bank and the farmer according to their equity share. The model is illustrated in Figure 5.1, and is modified according to the method of irrigation, for example canal irrigated schemes, pump and rainfall scheme. For a canal irrigation *musharaka*, for example, as well as land, labour and management, the farmer has to contribute part of the capital. The SIB prepares the land, provides inputs, transportation, storage and part of the capital. From the net profit the farmer gets 25–40 per cent for management. The remaining profit is

SIB contribution

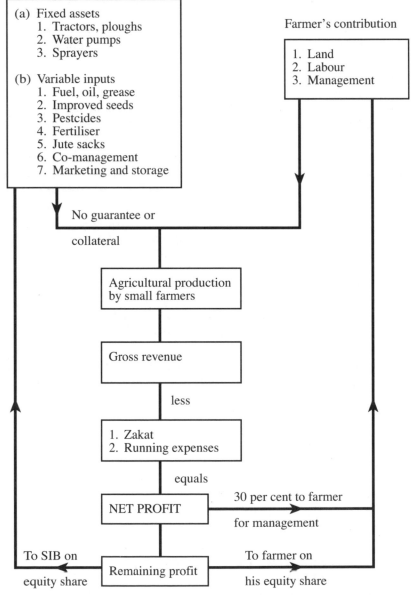

Farmer's contribution

Source: Based on Al-Harran (1993).

Figure 5.1   Sudanese Islamic Bank, Rural Development Department Agricultural Financing Model

divided between the farmer and SIB according to their capital contribution. Another model has been developed for poultry production.

As a consequence of such innovations, *musharaka* has become the largest type of financing undertaken by SIB, representing 52 per cent of financing at December 1995. In addition to rural financing, *musharaka* partnership financing is used for trade, fixed assets in industry and for working capital. Generally, the *musharaka* work as follows. First, the bank evaluates the project presented by clients in order to assess its viability. Upon approval of an application, a *musharaka* contract is signed between the bank and the client (who becomes a partner). The contract specifies all the details relating to the contribution of each partner in capital, management and profits as well as the procedures governing relations between the two partners. Any goods purchased from the partnership fund would normally be kept under due custody of both partners, thus serving as a form of collateral (even though no overall guarantee or collateral can be sought). To ensure compliance with the contract, the bank undertakes general supervision and monitoring of the progress of operations.

In the previous chapter, we noted that in traditional banking, the amount of insider equity committed by the borrower serves as an important signalling device to the financier. *Musharaka* involves active participation of both the Islamic bank and its client, and has a number of incentive-compatible features. The Islamic financial institution depends on revenues in the form of a percentage of net profit rather than interest, and this encourages close scrutiny and assessment of the viability and implementation of their investment transactions. On the other hand, the clients who become partners contributing capital are presumably eager to ensure the success of the transaction to increase the volume of total profits and, by extension, the volume of their share in these profits. The ultimate result is that both partners have a distinctive contribution and an interest in the success of the venture.[12]

Pakistan

The Pakistani experience differs from the others because Pakistan opted for a gradual Islamisation process which began in 1947 when Pakistan came into being as an independent and sovereign state. The process became more formalised in the latter part of the 1970s and was generalised in the middle of 1985. This gradualist approach has allowed the law to keep up with the requirements of the time, but it has also allowed the reform agenda to get bogged down in lengthy legal process and appeals.

Contract and property rights
A rigorous legal framework is central to Islamic banking, at the core of which

are the issues of contracts and property rights which underline the prohibition of predetermined interest. Islamic law provides freedom of contract, so long as the terms do not conflict with the *shari'a*. In particular, it permits any arrangement based on the consent of the parties involved, so long as the shares of each are contingent upon uncertain gain and are a function of productive transformation of resources. These provisos are crucial, since the *shari'a* condemns even a guarantee by the working partner to restore the value of invested capital, not only because it removes the element of uncertainty needed to legitimise the agreed distribution of the possible profits but also because the lender would not be remunerated to the extent of the productivity of his financial capital in the resulting profit (Iqbal and Mirakhor, 1992).

Islamic law recognises two types of individual claim to property: (1) property which is a result of the combination of an individual's creative labour and natural resources, and (2) property the title of which has been transferred by its owner as a result of exchange, remittance of the rights, other benefits, grants and inheritance. Money represents the monetised claims of its owner to property rights created. Lending money, in effect, is a transfer of this right, and all that can be claimed in return is the principal (Murvat, 1992). Funds are used either productively or unproductively. In the first case, when funds are combined with creative labour, the lender may ask for a portion of the created wealth but may not ask for a fixed return, irrespective of the outcome of the enterprise. In the second case, the money lent, even if legitimately acquired, cannot claim any additional property rights, since none are created.

Process of Islamisation

Implementation of the Islamic financing system in Pakistan is usually dated from February 1979 when the President of Pakistan announced that interest was to be removed from the economy within a period of three years. But the process of Islamisation began much earlier. Steps along the way included:

- Passing of the Objectives Resolution on March 7, 1949 by the first Constituent Assembly which laid down the ideological foundation of Pakistan in terms of the teachings of Islam as set out in the Holy Qur'an and the *sunna*.
- At the same time, the Government of Pakistan established the Talimat-i-Islami Board headed by Syed Sulaiman Naqvi – an eminent scholar of Islam – to make recommendations as to the incorporation of Islamic provisions and related matters in the Pakistan Constitution.
- The Pakistan Constitution of March 23, 1956 contained the earlier Objectives Resolution with slight verbal changes and established the Islamic Republic of Pakistan. Notably, Chapter 1 contained article 198:

198 – (1) No law shall be enacted which is repugnant to the Injunctions of Islam as laid down in the Holy Qur'an and Sunna, hereinafter referred to as Injunctions of Islam, and existing law shall be brought into conformity with such Injunctions.

Nevertheless, the legislature remained supreme and the courts of law could not be used to bring existing laws into conformity with the injunctions of Islam.

- The Chief Martial Law Administrator promulgated a constitution on June 8, 1962. The Principles of Policy included the elimination of '*Riba* (Usury)', but were purely advisory in nature, since they were non-justiciable.[13]. Hence the Principle that 'no law shall be repugnant to the teaching and requirements of Islam' continued to remain only a pious wish.

Financial reforms

Thus we come to 5 July, 1977, when the Constitution was suspended, 1 January, 1978, when the Courts were empowered to declare as void any law repugnant to the Holy Qur'an and *sunna*, and 1979 when a constitution of Shariat Benches was ordered to declare what laws were repugnant to Islam.

Measures to eliminate interest from the financial system of Pakistan were announced, along with other Islamisation measures by the President of Pakistan on 12th Rabiul Awal, 1399, which corresponds to 10 February, 1979. The Council of Islamic Ideology in 1980 (CII, 1983) and experts (Naqvi *et al.*, 1980) recommended a step-by-step approach, but the President ruled that interest was to be removed within a period of three years.

Almost immediately, three of the specialised credit institutions – the House Building Corporation, National Investment Trust and Mutual Funds of Investment Corporation of Pakistan – removed interest from their financing operations. The House Building Finance Corporation made housing finance available on a 'rent-sharing' basis, of up to 15 years. The National Investment Trust ceased investment in fixed rate-of-return securities. The Investment Corporation of Pakistan began a disinvestment of all the interest-bearing securities and in 1980 launched a PLS scheme (Dawn, 1981; Shah, 1981). By 1981 these specialised credit institutions had converted their operations to PLS-type financing modes.

However, the task of eliminating interest from commercial banking has proved difficult and complicated. The CII envisaged that banks' financing operations would be based on PLS, but it did not recommend any changes in the institutional structure of the banking and financial system, allowing the Islamisation process to be undertaken in phases. In this respect, the Pakistan example accords more closely with the second of the ideal systems examined in the previous section.

Banking – the first phase

In the first phase, which ended on 1 January 1985, domestic banks operated both interest-free and interest-based 'windows'. Separate counters were introduced on 1 July, 1981 for the domestic banks (which had all been previously nationalised) to accept deposits on a PLS basis. Opening of such counters by foreign banks was optional, and one of the foreign banks did start accepting PLS deposits. PLS deposits could not be mingled with their interest-based operations. In this way, interest-based transactions operated alongside interest-free banking.

In order to provide a legal cover for these changes and to facilitate the successful implementation of the transition phase, it was considered necessary to pass new laws, the most significant of which was the Mudaraba Companies and Mudaraba (Flotation and Control) Ordinance (1980, 1981). This ordinance provided for registration of *mudaraba* companies; the flotation, management, and regulation of *mudaraba;* and matters connected. It defines *mudaraba* as 'a business which a person participates with his money and another with his efforts or skill or both his efforts and skill' and includes 'Unit Trusts and Mutual Funds by whatever name called', and a *mudaraba* company as a company engaged in the business of floating and managing *mudaraba.*

A *mudaraba* may be either multi-purpose or for a fixed period or indefinite, and divided into *mudaraba* certificates (that is, a certificate of denomination issued to the subscriber of the *mudaraba* acknowledging receipt of the money subscribed) listed for trading on the Stock Exchange. They are analogous to close-ended mutual funds, and invest primarily in leasing, equities and commercial financing.

The *mudaraba* certificate is one of the many new financial instruments devised since 1980. On the most recent count there were 54 *mudarabas* operating, although new flotations have fallen away since tax-exempt status was withdrawn in 1992 (whereas leasing and mutual funds have continued to expand). Using *mudaraba* certificates for investment in such *mudaraba* businesses is one corporate method of employing savings along Islamic lines. Significantly, in terms of the adverse selection and moral hazard issues raised in the previous chapter, a *mudaraba* can be wound up by a Tribunal, constituted for the purpose by the federal government, on the application of the Registrar of Mudarabas under certain circumstances. The Tribunal also has powers to expeditiously decide all claims by a holder of *mudaraba* certificates against the *mudaraba* company or by a *mudaraba* company against any other party with whom it has entered into a business transaction relating to the *mudaraba* fund.

All *mudarabas* are first registered with the Registrar, who allows their operations after a body of religious scholars, headed by a High Court judge, called the Religious Board, evaluates the permissibility of the activities in terms of the *shari'a*. Then, until recently, *mudaraba* business was subject to the scrutiny of the Directorate of Non-Banking Financial Institutions of the State Bank of Pakistan. In April 2000, new prudential regulations covering *mudarabas* were issued by The Securities Exchange Commission of Pakistan. These regulations include the creation of a reserve fund, limits on exposure, provisioning for non-performing assets, restrictions on the types of investments, the power to appoint special auditors and a code of conduct. The new regulations came into force on 30 June, 2000.

Banking – the second phase
In the second phase of the transformation process, the banking system was required to operate all transactions on the basis of no interest, the only exceptions being foreign currency deposits, foreign loans and government debts. Hence, in June 1984 it was announced that the dual windows would be discontinued within one year. From 1 July, 1985, all financial operations of the banking and financial system, except the foreign currency deposits earning fixed interest, were brought under the non-interest-based modes of financing.

With outstanding loans, there was a concern that the existing legal framework in the country could not adequately protect the banks against undue delays and defaults, and so the government enacted the Banking Tribunal Ordinance in 1984. Twelve tribunals were set up with specific territorial jurisdictions, each headed by a high-ranking judge and required to dispose of all cases within 90 days of the filing of the complaint, with provisions for an appeal procedure. In this way, the Pakistani model took care to ensure that the new modes of financing did not upset the basic functioning and structure of the banking system. This, and the gradual pace of transition, made it easier for the banks to adapt.

In terms of new financing, the State Bank of Pakistan in 1984 laid down three permissible forms of financing. These are: (i) finance by lending (zero interest, *Qard Hasan*); (ii) trade-related financing (mark-up on goods, trade bills, goods subject to buy-back, leasing, hire purchase, property with a development charge); and investment (PLS) modes (*musharaka*, shares and equity participation, *mudaraba* certificates and participation term certificates, rent-sharing). For the third category, it was made clear that 'should any losses occur, they will have to be proportionately shared among all the financiers'. There are the allowable options. The appropriate mode of financing to be adopted in any particular case is settled by agreement between the banking company and the client. Some suggested modes of financing for various transactions are shown in Table 5.3.

Table 5.3   Possible modes of financing for various transactions in Pakistan

Nature of Business	Basis of Financing
I. *Trade and Commerce* (a) Commodity operations of the Federal and Provincial Governments and their agencies.	Mark-up in price.
(b) Export bills purchased/negotiated under letters of credit (other than those under reserve).	(i) Exchange rate differential in the case of foreign currency bills. (ii) Commission or mark-down in the case of rupee bills.
(c) Documentary inland bills drawn against letters of credit purchased/discounted.	Mark-down in price.
(d) Import bills drawn under letters of credit.	Mark-up in price.
(e) Financing of exports under the State Bank's Export Finance Scheme and the Scheme for Financing Locally Manufactured Machinery.	Service charge/concessional charge.
(f) Other items of trade and commerce.	*Fixed Investment* Equity participation, PTCs, leasing or hire-purchase. *Working Capital* Profit and loss sharing or mark-up.
II. *Industry*	*Fixed Investment* Equity participations, PTCs, *Mudaraba* certificates, leasing, hire-purchase or mark-up. *Working Capital* Profit- and loss-sharing or mark-up.
III.*Agriculture and Fisheries* (a) Short-term finance.	Mark-up. In the case of small farmers and small fishermen who are at present eligible for interest free loans finance for the specified inputs etc. up to the prescribed amount may also be on mark-up basis. The mark-up amount may however be waived in the case of those who repay the finance within the stipulated period and payment of the mark-up made by the ☐State Bank to banks by debit to Federal Government Account.

Table 5.3   Continued

Nature of Business	Basis of Financing
(b) Medium and long-term finance. (i) Tube-wells and other wells	Leasing or hire-purchase. In addition to ownership of machinery, banks may create charge on the land in their favour as in the case of other loans to the farmers under the Passbook System.
(ii) Tractors, trailers and other farm machinery and transport (including fishing boats, solar energy plants, etc.)	Hire-purchase or leasing.
(iii) Plough-cattle, milch cattle and and other livestock	Mark-up
(iv) Dairy and poultry	PLS/mark-up/hire-purchase leasing.
(v) Storage and other farm construction (viz. sheds for animals, fencing, etc.)	Leasing or rent sharing basis with flexible weightage to the bank's funds.
(vi) Land development	Development charge.
(vii) Orchards, including nurseries	Mark-up, development charge or PLS basis.
(viii) Forestry	Mark-up, development charge or PLS basis.
(ix) Water course improvement	Development charge.
IV. *Housing*	Rent sharing with flexible weightage to bank's funds or buy-back cum mark-up.
V. Personal advances (other than those for business purposes and housing). (a) Consumer durables (cars, motor cycles, scooters and household goods).	Hire-purchase.
(b) For consumption purposes.	Against tangible security with buy-back arrangement.

Source: State of Pakistan, Banking Central Department, Circular No. 13 (20 June, 1984).

Just as was the case in Iran, the liability side of the Pakistani banking system quickly converted to Islamic modes, with the banks becoming portfolio managers for depositors. Indeed, the revealed preference of the depositors was more meaningful in Pakistan because, unlike Iran, depositors had a choice between interest- and non-interest-based deposits until July 1985. Khan and Mirakhor (1990) show that the ratio of Islamic deposits to total deposits more than tripled from 1981 until July 1985, when the interest-based deposit windows of the commercial banks were closed.

By contrast, the asset side of the banking system showed a far slower tendency to progress toward PLS financing. When the nature of the transaction is such that it does not lend itself to profit-sharing modes, Islamic law provides for alternative modes. One such procedure is what is referred to as 'mark-up', according to which the seller is allowed to charge a mark-up over and above his costs. This was a method that the CII had listed among permissible non-interest-based modes of trade financing, and the banks showed a strong tendency to substitute mark-up for interest. In 1984 short-term assets constituted over 80 per cent of bank portfolios, while PLS financing was only 13.2 per cent of the total.

This bias in bank lending and investments was strongly criticised by Pakistan's Federal Shariat Court (FSC) in a judgement delivered in November 1991. The FSC argued that the concept of mark-up is appropriate for trade but not for banking, since banks are not trading organisations. It had been permitted in banking as a temporary measure only, on the understanding that it would be used sparingly during the transition period, but had become the mainstay of the 'interest-free' banking system and served as a 'back-door for interest to creep in'.[14] The FSC therefore directed the government to delete references to mark-up from legislation. Somewhat similar views were expressed by the FSC about leasing, another non-interest-based mode of financing, although in this case the Court stopped short of directing the deletion of legislative references.

Banking – the third phase

The 1991 Judgement of the Federal Shariat Court regarding the laws involving interest sparked the next phase. The Court decreed that the laws held to be repugnant to the injunctions of Islam would cease to have effect as from 1 July 1992. However, appeals for relief were made by banks and by the government (worried by the implications for its own Eurobond issues and financing for the Hub River Project and Pakistan Telecom). In terms of the constitutional provisions, the Judgement could not come into effect until all appeals were heard.

After a lengthy process, the Supreme Court on December 23, 1999 eventually dismissed all government and bank appeals against the Federal

Shariat Court Judgement. It outlawed 'interest' in every form and called by whatever name and laid down specific guidelines for a completely interest-free economy by June 2001. The transactions declared un-Islamic and, therefore, unconstitutional include mark-up, *murabaha*, *bai'muajjal* (deferred sale) and any so-called interest-free modes insofar as elements of *riba* (usury and interest) have crept in to them. Any amount, big or small, over and above the principal in a loan or barter transaction, whether obtained for consumption or for commercial or productive activity, is prohibited.

The timetable laid down in the ruling means that domestic inter-government borrowings as well as the borrowings of the federal government from the State Bank shall be interest free. The Federal Finance Ministry has to find out ways to convert the domestic borrowings into project-related financing and to establish a mutual fund that may finance the government on that basis. Thus the types of alternatives to public debt that we suggested earlier in this chapter have been proposed. The main obstacle which remains is that the ruling requires repeal and enactment of various laws by legislative assemblies, not all members of which are sympathetic to the changes.

ISLAMISATION: AN ASSESSMENT

Most of the problems that have been encountered in Pakistan, especially in banking operations, relate essentially to the difficulties in moving away from traditional short-term financial operations and toward medium-term and long-term equity operations involving profit-and-loss-sharing. Owing to legal and institutional constraints, banks have continued to concentrate, as in the past, on short-term financing and the provision of working capital on a mark-up or instalment basis.

It has been suggested (for example, by Mirakhor, 1987) that this short-term financing is the result of the risk-averse attitude of the policymakers and bankers in the Islamisation process. The highly regulated environment in Pakistan does not allow market realities to be reflected in the rates of return, in that both the rates of return to the banking system and to the depositors are strongly influenced by regulation rather than by market data. Given this situation, it is a rational reaction on the part of bankers to ration funds and select minimum-risk portfolios that may not be effective in promoting Islamic banking and the national interest.

However, the financing pattern may also reflect a basic incompatibility in the system. On one side, there are the depositors, motivated by religious preference, who place their funds within the banking system, but run the risk that their funds will not be utilised, as anticipated, in strictly PLS projects. On the other side, the banking system has the perception that it runs a risk of bankruptcy should it place a large portion of its asset portfolio in *musharaka* and *mudaraba* financing. So long as the business community does not adopt Islamic ethical norms in its operations, the evaluation and monitoring costs of profit-sharing projects will be excessively high due to adverse selection and moral hazard difficulties.

Addressing this inconsistency may necessitate reforms in other areas of the economy and economic policy. Dar (1999) points out that corruption in financial and commercial dealings, tax evasion, maintaining two books for profit/loss statements, default on loans, and a bureaucratic structure all are hostile to partnership or PLS, necessitating heavy contracting costs for banks and *mudaraba* companies. In particular, the existing income-tax system in Pakistan is viewed as burdensome. Therefore, business owners have attempted to conceal genuine profits. The existence of multiple books of account in the business community, motivated by tax avoidance, does not allow efficient monitoring of an entrepreneur's operation, thus discouraging partnership financing by the commercial banks. Also, the absence of precise legal definitions of various modes of financing constrains their future evolution, as the new system in Pakistan was introduced without fundamental changes in the laws governing existing contracts and mortgages. One suggested remedy is the adoption of the Islamic Law of Contracts, which will then permit contracts between banks and their clients to be representable in the courts as legal documents, which is the case in Iran.

In addition, business attitudes have to change, since without such alteration, entrepreneurs are unlikely to enter into profit-and-loss-sharing operations. Under PLS arrangements, the formula for determining profit-sharing ratios is arbitrary and this might bias profit shares in favour of shareholders and against depositors. In principle, shareholders and depositors should be treated evenhandedly. So far in Pakistan, the differential treatment has been prompted by the banks' perceived need to accord higher returns to those who have supposedly taken greater risks by tying up their resources for longer periods. This concept of relating returns to time creates a problem under the Islamic system.

In this respect, then, the existing financial infrastructure may be inadequate. There may be too few people with sufficient knowledge of the *shari'a* and a dearth of the expertise needed to determine costs and benefits, as well as profits and losses, under Islamic banking. At the same time, there is a need for well-developed and open secondary and primary capital markets that can provide liquidity to depositors and to ensure the marketability of assets. Without such markets, the banking system will not be able to move easily from short-term, trade-oriented operations to profit-and-loss-sharing ones. These markets might develop at an international level, as we argue later.

Finally, government borrowing poses special problems, both in Pakistan and Iran, underscoring the need to devise suitable interest-free instruments.[15] Iran as we saw, has decreed that government borrowing on the basis of a fixed rate of return from the nationalised banking system does not amount to interest and is permissible. The officiai rationale is that, since all banks are nationalised, interest rates and payments among banks will cancel out in the consolidated accounts. (This argument of course, abstracts from the banks' business with non-bank customers.) In Pakistan, financing of government deficits also has continued to be on an interest basis, with serious implications for the transformation of the system, because payments by the Pakistani Government on these borrowings are fixed and are not related to the returns from its investments or expenditures. In fact, the position has been accentuated by the offering of national savings accounts, auctioning Treasury bills and federal (interest-bearing) investment bonds, all of which has meant that government financial operations have become progressively more interest-based (El-Gamal, 1999a).

Overall, though, while some problems have emerged, Pakistan's experience has been favourable. Some deepening of the financial market has taken place through the creation of *mudaraba* and leasing-related instruments, and the mobilisation of savings has continued unabated. There has been a trend away from fixed returns and toward lending and borrowing based on variable returns. In the process, there has been a movement toward equalising financial rates of return and real rates of return. But much remains to be done to move closer to the 'ideal' structures outlined earlier and to convert the system fully to Islamic principles if the deadline of June 2001 is to be sustained. There is a case for arguing that these institutional innovations are more likely to occur if the pace of change is speeded up; the old saying is that a coming execution concentrates the mind wonderfully.[16]

NOTES

1. The views of Ghazali and others on these issues are outlined in Ahmad (1980, chapter 1). The particular quotations come from Ghazali, pp. 21–92 as cited in Mirakhor (1995, p. 31).
2. Some of the leading works are Ahmad (1952), Chapra (1985), Siddiqi (1980, 1982), Khan (1985) and Abu Su'ud (1980).
3. Khan's model assumes an Islamic banking system structured in accordance with the second principal model of Islamic banking discussed earlier. If demand deposits are backed by a 100 per cent reserve requirement, the run-associated features of fractional reserve banking will be eliminated. In the other 'window' the banks accept deposits as if they are equity shares the minimal value of which is not guaranteed and the rate of return of which is variable. The overall finding that there is stability in response to certain shocks implies that a two-window Islamic banking system, in which demand deposits will have a 100 per cent reserve requirement and investment deposits will carry no guarantees, has desirable safety attributes.
4. In effect, when translated into an IS–LM framework, they imply an LM curve which is less

elastic with respect to absolute rates of return.

5. In line with practice in continental Europe, and many other countries (including UK and Australia), the supervisory functions could be handled by a regulatory agency separate from the central bank. Goodhart (1995, chapter 16) discusses the pros and cons of the two alternatives, while Lewis and Mizen (2000, chapter 16) give an update on the present situation.

6. It is perhaps worth noting that much of Islamic economic analysis exhibits a strong emphasis on social justice. Some (for example Wilson, 1998) see this as a way of modifying a market system in line with the *shari'a*. Others (for example Ali, 1996) speak of building a 'third economic system', the Islamic economic system, as a counterbalance to capitalism and Marxism.

7. The report was especially concerned about the issue of foreign borrowing in a fully Islamised financial system. It listed four major international transactions (debt servicing, defence procurement, development projects financing and balance of payments needs) in which a government gets involved. While arguing that past debt and debt-servicing commitments must be honoured, it recognised that borrowing is deferred taxation, and fresh borrowing should be avoided whether in the name of aid or otherwise. As for almost all other cases, such as defence procurement and project financing, Islamically admissible options are available. Most borrowings for the balance of payments could be obviated by adopting a flexible exchange rate.

8. One illustration of the type of innovation which could occur comes from the State of Victoria in Australia. In 1988, the Victorian Equity Trust (VET) was launched with the stated objective of raising 'equity'-type funds for Victorian government business enterprises. The VET was a unit trust-type vehicle, the unit prices of which were quoted on the Australian Stock Exchange. Minimum subscription to the trust was 1000 units of $1 each, and the funds raised were to provide public equity capital for Victorian government statutory authorities. Returns to unit holders took the form of a declared dividend based on profits from those authorities and the potential profits from a put option granted to holders enabling them to resell their units to the Victorian government at the end of 1992 at a price inversely related to the level of distributed profits over the previous four years and positively related to the value of the Australian Stock Exchange's All Ordinaries Index. Thus, the cost to the Victorian government, and the return to investors, was related (in a complex manner) to the overall stock market return on equity capital. It in fact attracted little funds from individuals, one explanation being the complexity of the put option, which reduced the range of investors who could easily understand the potential risk and rewards relative to the interest returns on offer in debt markets (Davis, 1997).

9. Such liabilities are considered as the banks' own resources, which can be utilised by them for any form of credit facilities. Profit earned on such credit facilities belongs to the bank itself. By contrast, investment accounts are not considered to be the bank's resources since the bank is acting purely as a trustee for the depositors. Hence, these funds cannot be utilised to finance government financial needs in the way specified.

10. The objective of nationalisation was mainly to improve the provision of banking services to the rural areas, and to control the flow of funds to capital investment.

11. These are reproduced from Mudawi (1995).

12. Al-Harran (1993, chapter 11) provides a detailed analysis of the experience of SIB in *musharaka* financing.

13. See All Pakistan Legal Decisions (PLD) 1963, S.C. 51.

14. To others, the technique might be seen as a legal subterfuge (*hiyal, hila*). We examine this point in the next chapter.

15. Some Muslim countries have introduced what are called 'Muqarada Bonds', the proceeds of which are to be used for income yielding public utility projects such as the construction of bridges and roads. The bond holders have a share in the collection of tolls and other receipts.

16. 'Depend upon it, Sir' said Dr Johnson, 'when a man knows he is to be hanged in a fortnight it concentrates his mind wonderfully'. Boswell's *Life of Johnson*, vol. 1, p. 167, 19 September, 1777.

6. Islamic banking in mixed systems

GROWTH OF ISLAMIC FINANCIAL INSTITUTIONS

Modern banking was introduced into Muslim countries in the late nineteenth century.[1] Leading banks based in the home countries of the imperial powers established branches in the capitals of the colonies and they catered mainly to the import–export requirements of the foreign enterprises. Banking was generally confined to the capital cities, and the general population remained largely untouched by the banking system. Local traders avoided the 'foreign' banks for nationalistic as well as religious reasons. However, over time it became difficult to engage in trade and other activities without making some use of the commercial banks. Even then, many confined their involvement to transaction services such as current accounts and money transfers. Borrowing from the banks and depositing savings with the banks were generally avoided in order to avoid dealing in interest.

With the passage of time, and along with other socio-economic forces demanding more involvement in national and international economic and financial activities, interactions with the banks became more commonplace. Indigenous banks were established on the same lines as the interest-based foreign banks for want of an alternative system and they began to expand within the country bringing the banking habit to more local people. As countries gained independence the need to engage in banking activities became more urgent. Governments, businesses and individuals began to transact with the banks, with or without necessarily liking it. This state of affairs attracted the attention and concern of Muslim intellectuals. The story of interest-free or Islamic banking effectively begins at this point.

Development of the Islamic Banking Concept

The earliest references to the reorganisation of banking on the basis of profit-sharing rather than interest are found in the writings of Qureshi ([1946]1991), Siddiqi (1948), Ahmad (1952), Mawdudi ([1950]1961).[2] Over the next two decades interest-free banking attracted more attention. This was in part because of the political interest it attracted in Pakistan, in part because of the emergence of young Muslim economists, but also because the involvement of institutions and governments resulted in the establishment of the first interest-free banks.

These intellectual and institutional developments came to a head at the Third Islamic Conference of Foreign Ministers, held in Jeddah in 1972, when a programme to abolish interest from Islamic financial institutions was presented by the finance ministers of 18 participating countries. A comprehensive plan to reform the monetary and financial systems of the Islamic communities according to *shari'a* principles was laid out concurrently (Kazarian and Kokko, 1987). Several countries afterwards undertook various efforts, including the establishment of Islamic banks, to support and realise these ambitions. Measures to 'Islamise' the financial system were introduced in such countries as Egypt, Saudi Arabia, Kuwait, Sudan, the United Arab Emirates (UAE), Bahrain, Jordan, Malaysia and, of course, Pakistan and Iran.

Islamisation

In general, Islamisation has consisted mainly in founding Islamic banks which operate without charging or paying fixed interest rates on loans or deposits. Such banks are usually exempt from taxation, but they have to pay *zakat*, or wealth contribution, in the form of a levy on capital. Assets of Islamic banks are also usually immune from seizure because the majority of Islamic banks have been established by special laws which protect them and their companies from future confiscation and nationalisation. Such protection presumably encourages many investors to undertake ventures in cooperation with an Islamic bank. Also, given such a guarantee, savers may also be encouraged to deposit their funds at an Islamic bank. In these ways, the growth of Islamic banking has been politicised, to some degree, and the resulting increase in market segmentation likely assists Islamic banks by improving their access to particular sections of the market seeking religiously legitimate banking facilities.

In some countries, the Islamisation process has extended beyond the sphere of commercial banking, and includes development banks, investment companies, holding companies and other quasi-banking institutions. The more radical reforms in Iran, Sudan and Pakistan outlined in the previous chapter have added central banks to the list of Islamic financial institutions. Here we focus on the countries where individual Islamic banks co-exist with conventional banks.

FORMATION OF INDIVIDUAL BANKS

Islamic banks were established in the late 1970s and 1980s in a wide range of countries. Table 6.1 traces the growth from 1963 to 1999. Many of the banks are parts of international groups, notably the Dar al-Maal al-Islami (DMI) group (which includes the various Faisal Islamic banks) and the Al-Baraka group. Both of these groups have their origin in private capital in Saudi Arabia which was not allowed formally to set up banking operations there, and have created international networks based elsewhere. Other Islamic banks are autonomous locally-owned banks.

A large number of Islamic financial institutions are working in the informal financial markets of several countries, particularly in the Muslim minority countries such as India, Australia, Canada, US, UK and other countries of Europe. These include saving and loan associations, credit associations, cooperative societies, cooperative funds, Islamic funds and cooperative credit societies. All of these institutions make an effort to conduct their activities without dealing in interest, in conformity with Islamic principles. However, often very little is known about them.

If we include the Islamic financial institutions operating in the informal sector in some Muslim as well as non-Muslim countries, the total number of institutions which adhere to Islamic principles, and could be described as Islamic, may well be close to 1000. Due to a lack of reliable information about many of these, our analysis is confined to Islamic financial institutions operating in the organised sector.

In terms of ownership structure, Islamic banks can be classified into international Islamic banks, publicly-owned Islamic banks, joint venture Islamic banks and privately-owned Islamic banks. The Islamic Development Bank is an example of an international bank in the sense that the governments of different member countries have all subscribed to its share capital. All Islamic banks in Iran and some major banks in Pakistan are in the public sector. Most of the dedicated Islamic banks in Sudan are joint-venture banks with ownership split between Sudanese and foreign capital. Islamic banks elsewhere are predominantly privately owned.

Most Islamic banks are joint stock companies, and their organisational structure is not much different from the usual structure of such companies. The company is floated either by a few individuals or governmental agencies. Sometimes certain restrictions are imposed on the subscription to these shares according to the law of the land or as the situation may demand. For instance, only Kuwaiti nationals are allowed to hold the shares of the Kuwait Finance House. Such restrictions do not have a lot to do with the nature of Islamic banking but reflect the general philosophy and business ethos of the country concerned. The operation of the Islamic banks is also quite similar to the operation of other joint stock companies in that the shareholders elect a shareholders' committee and a board of directors headed by a managing director or chairman, who may also be responsible for the day-to-day functioning of the company. Differences come from the distinctive corporate culture of an Islamic institution and the separate supervisory/auditing function

Table 6.1 Establishment of Islamic banks and financial institutions, 1963–99

Year	No. set up during the year	Name of Islamic institution
1963	1	Tabung Haji (Pilgrims Management and Fund Board), Kuala Lumpur.
1971	1	Nasir Social Bank, Cairo.
1975	2	Islamic Development Bank, Jeddah; Dubai Islamic Bank, Dubai.
1977	5	Islamic Investment Company of the Gulf, Sharjah, UAE; Abu Dhabi Islamic Bank, UAE; Faisal Islamic Bank of Egypt, Cairo; Faisal Islamic Bank, Sudan; Kuwait Finance House, Safat.
1978	3	Islamic Finance House Universal Holding; Islamic Investment Company of the Gulf, Bahamas; Jordan Islamic Bank for Finance and Investment.
1979	4	Bahrain Islamic Bank; Iran Islamic Bank; Islamic Finance House Universal Holding SA, Luxembourg; National Investment Trust, Pakistan.
1980	7	Alwatany Bank of Egypt, Cairo (One Islamic Branch); Banker's Equity Ltd, Pakistan; Egyptian Saudi Finance Bank; Islamic Finance House Co., Jordan; Islamic Investment Co., Bahrain; International Islamic Bank for Investment and Development, Cairo; Islamic Cooperative Housing Corporation, Toronto.
1981	2	Bahrain Islamic Investment Co.; Dal Mal al Islami Trust, Nassau.
1982	5	Al-Baraka Investment and Development Company, Jeddah; Faisal Islamic Bank of Kibris, Lefkosa, Kibris; Faysal Islamic Bank of Bahrain; Islamic Investment Company, London; Masraf Faisal Islamic Bank & Trust, Bahamas Ltd.
1983	20	Al-Baraka Islamic Bank, Sudan; Al-Baraka Investment Co., London; Bangladesh Islamic Bank; Bank al Tamwil al Saudi al Tunisi; Bank Islam Malaysia Berhad, Kuala Lumpur; Banque Islamique de Guinee; Banque Islamique du Niger; Banque Islamique du Senegal; Beit El-Mal Saving and

Table 6.1 Continued

Year	No. set up during the year	Name of Islamic institution
		Investment Co., Jordan; Faisal Islamic Bank, Bahrain; Islamic Bank for Western Sudan; Islamic Bank International of Denmark, Copenhagen; Islamic Coop Dev. Bank, Sudan; Islamic Investment and Development Company, Cairo; Islamic Investment Co., Qatar; Islamic Investment Co. of the Gulf, Bahrain; Masraf Faisal al Islami de Guinea, Conakry; Qatar Islamic Bank (SAQ); Sudan-Tunisian Finance House; Sudanese Islamic Bank, Sudan.
1984	13	Albaraka International Bank, UK; Albaraka Investment and Dev. Co., Saudi Arabia; Albaraka Islamic Bank, Bahrain; Albaraka Islamic Investment Bank, Bahrain; Dar al Mal al Islami Trust, Geneva; Faisal Islamic Bank, Guinea; Faisal Islamic Bank, Niger; Faisal Islamic Bank, Senegal; Faysal Investment Bank of Bahrain; Islamic Investment Co., Geneva; Islamic Investment Co., Niger; Islamic Investment Company of Guinea, Conakry; Tadamon Islamic Bank, Sudan.
1985	6	ABC Islamic Bank, Bahrain; Al-Ameen Financial and Investment Corporation, India; Al-Baraka Islamic Bank, Mauritania; Al-Baraka Turkish Finance House, Istanbul; Faisal Finance Institution, Istanbul; Islamic Investment Fund, Switzerland.
1987	5	Al-Amin Co. for Securities and Inv. Funds, Bahrain; Albaraka Bancorp (California) Inc.; Albaraka Bancorp (Texas) Inc.; Albaraka Bank, Bangladesh; Al Tawfeek Company for Investment Funds, Bahrain.
1988	4	Al Rajhi Banking and Investment Corporation, Saudi Arabia; Islamic Bank, South Africa; National Islamic Bank, Jordan; Saudi-Egyptian Finance Bank, Egypt.
1989	9	Albaraka Bank, Durban; Albaraka Bancorp (Chicago) Inc.; Albaraka Finance House, India; Al-Jazeera Investment Company, Doha, Qatar; ANZ Global Islamic Finance, London; Banque Albaraka Djbouti;

Table 6.1 Continued

Year	No. set up during the year	Name of Islamic institution
1990	5	Muslim Community Cooperative (MCCA), Melbourne; Turkish–Kuwaiti Finance House, Istanbul; Turkish–Kuwaiti Finance House, Qatar.
1991	4	Amanah Islamic Investment Bank, Manila; Arab Islamic Bank, Bahrain; Faisal Finance (Switzerland) SA.; Faisal Holding, Luxembourg; Qatar International Islamic Bank.
		Banque Al Baraka D'Algerie; Dallah Al Baraka (Malaysia) Holding; Pan Islamic Consultancy Services Istishara, Switzerland; Perbadanan Tabung Amanah Islam, Brunei.
1992	6	Al Baraka Bank, Lebanon; Arab Albanian Bank; Bank Muamalat Indonesia; Ibn Majid Emerging Marketing Fund, Cayman Islands; The International Investor Advisory Group, London; The International Investor, Kuwait.
1993	3	Dallah Albaraka Europe, London; International Investment Group, Kuwait; Iraqi Islamic Bank for Investment and Development.
1994	2	Amana Income Fund, US; Arab Gambian Islamic Bank.
1995	4	Al-Arafah Islami Bank, Bangladesh; Lariba Bank, Alma Ata, Kazakhstan; Prime Bank, Bangladesh; Social Investment Bank, Bangladesh.
1996	8	Adil Islamic Growth Fund, Labuan, Malaysia; Al Meezan Commodity Fund, IES, Dublin; Citi Islamic Investment Bank, Bahrain; Faisal Finance Jersey; First Islamic Investment Bank, Bahrain; Ibn Khaldoun International Equity Fund, Virgin Islands; Tadhamon Islamic Bank, Yemen; Yemen Islamic Bank for Finance and Investment.

124

Table 6.1 Continued

Year	No. set up during the year	Name of Islamic institution
1997	1	Saba Islamic Bank, Yemen.
1998	4	Al Manzil Islamic Financial Services, New York; Badr Bank, Moscow; Islamic Bank of Brunei Berhad, Brunei; Islamic International Arab Bank, Jordan.
1999	6	Bank IFI (*syariah* unit); Bank Syariah Mandiri, Indonesia; Habib Nigeria Bank (6 Islamic Windows), Nigeria; Bank Bumi-Muamalat Malaysia Bhd, Malaysia; Gulf Finance House, Bahrain; Bank for Agriculture and Agricultural Cooperatives (30 Islamic Branches), Thailand.

Source: Institute of Islamic Banking and Insurance.

carried out by the *Shari'a* Supervisory Board or Adviser. These differences are considered in Chapter 7.

As to the question of who forms Islamic banks, holding companies, governments, religious organisations, government bodies, and so on have subscribed to the capital of different Islamic banks. Some Islamic banks have subscribed to the capital of some other Islamic banks. The Islamic Development Bank also has equity shares in a number of Islamic banks working in different countries. In addition, many of the Islamic banks themselves have subsidiaries providing investment banking, leasing, *takaful* insurance, unit trusts, and other specialist services. This is obviously the case of the two large Islamic holding companies, the DMI and Al-Baraka groups.[3]

Earlier we spoke of the 'politicisation' of Islamic banking. Many Islamic banks are indeed closely linked to government entities. Various ministries of the Kuwaiti government have 49 per cent equity in the Kuwait Finance House. Several governments have subscribed to the capital of the Bahrain Islamic Bank, which is as follows: Kuwait government 17.4 per cent, Bahrain government 10.4 per cent, Islamic Development Bank 13.0 per cent, Kuwait Finance House 8.7 per cent, Dubai Islamic Bank 4.4 per cent and private shareholders 3.7 per cent. In some instances, religious bodies and governments have jointly subscribed to most of the capital. In the case of Bank Islam Malaysia, the government contributed 37.5 per cent, Pilgrims Management and Fund Board 10 per cent, Muslim welfare organisations of Malaysia 5 per cent, state religious councils 17 per cent, state religious agencies 6 per cent and federal agencies subscribed 12 per cent. The government of Bangladesh has 51 per cent shares of the subscribed capital of the Islamic Bank of Bangladesh.

Among the Islamic banks there are a number which could be better described as specialised Islamic development banks. The Islamic Bank of Western Sudan was established specifically to promote the development of Western Sudan, and is fast emerging as an Islamic financing institution which is specialised in the area of rural development, agricultural financing and small-scale industries. Similarly, the Islamic Cooperative Development Bank is devoted to the development of cooperative societies in Sudan. However, the emergence of such special purpose Islamic banks is still a rarity.

OPERATIONS IN THE FORMATIVE YEARS

Based on studies of Islamic banking in the 1980s, various 'inconsistencies' have been observed between the liability and the asset side of banks' balance sheets when putting the concept of Islamic banking into practice. Before considering why this might be the case, we look at some of the evidence prompting the observation made. We have chosen two banks which can be studied both in their early years of operation and in more recent years.

The Faisal Islamic Bank of Egypt

The Faisal Islamic Bank of Egypt (FIBE) was incorporated in 1977, and commenced operations in 1979. The statutes authorise all banking, financial, commercial and investment operations in Egypt as well as abroad within the framework of Islamic *shari'a*. Special provisions in the law of incorporation exempt the FIBE from various rules and regulations in the context of these operations: for example other commercial banks are prohibited from engaging in trade and are not allowed to own direct investments. FIBE is the only private economic institution in Egypt which is secured against confiscation or nationalisation by law. This is important in Egypt, which has had a history of the confiscation and nationalisation of private property.

FIBE's founders were financiers, with strong political and financial clout. Overall, 51 per cent of the initial capital of the bank, which is highly concentrated in the hands of a few owners, was provided by Egyptians and 49 per cent by Saudi citizens. In both groups are parties who can be readily identified in political and economic terms.[4] As is apparent from the name, FIBE is affiliated with the DMI group.

The financial power of its founders, combined with the freedom from nationalisation, presumably induces a feeling of security for depositors that the bank will be supported in the event of any financial difficulties. To some degree, the peculiar situation of FIBE may explain the strong growth and composition of deposits. From its foundation, over three-quarters of deposits have been placed in investment accounts, and in 1995 these constituted over 95 per cent of the deposit base of FIBE. The small remainder is deposited in current and savings accounts. FIBE has maintained its minimum deposit amount fixed at a considerably lower level than the minimum deposit of competing banks, so that investment accounts have thereby become viable alternatives for a large number of depositors who have not been able to meet the deposit requirements of other banks. Deposits can be held in foreign currency accounts, with the yields for these accounts quoted in the respective foreign currencies.

The Bank Islam Malaysia Berhad

The Bank Islam Malaysia Berhad (BIMB) was incorporated by the Islamic Banking Act (No. 276) in March 1983 and started up its operations in July of the same year. With authorised capital of M\$ 500 million, the initial paid up capital of M\$ 80 million was distributed among the Malaysian government and five other institutions, namely State Religious Councils (20 million), Federal Agencies (12 million), State Religious Agencies (3 million), The Pilgrims Management and Fund Board (10 million), and The Muslim Welfare Organisation of Malaysia (5 million).

The bank accepts deposits from customers in current accounts, saving accounts and general investment accounts for maturity periods ranging from one month to five years. The bank also accepts deposits from institutional clients in special investment accounts. Savings accounts have the largest number of depositors, but general investment accounts have attracted the largest share of funds, as the average investment account balance is over thirty times that of saving accounts. One reason for the popularity of savings accounts is that the BIMB has chosen to distribute a return to savings accounts, although the contract form does not guarantee any return, which has been quite competitive with that offered by conventional banks.[5]

Comparing the Two Banks

Differences between the two are exhibited in terms of the sources and uses of funds, in the financial results, in various administrative practices, and even in the basic objectives of the banks.

Considering the latter first, we recall the two 'ideal' conceptions of Islamic financial systems given in Chapter 5. In one, owing to Siddiqi and Chapra, financial institutions are meant individually to take account of wider Islamic social objectives. In the other, due to Ismail, the public-sector institutions pursue the socio-economic goals, leaving the other intermediaries free to pursue narrower commercial interests.

In these terms, we note that the provision of banking facilities and services according to Islamic principles is stated as an objective of both FIBE and BIMB. However, the remit for FIBE also emphasises the 'endeavour to achieve social development and solidarity', as stated in its annual reports. Thus FIBE's charter recognises a socio-economic purpose, whereas BIMB's emphasises its commercial charter. This is indicative of a basic difference in the view of the role of Islamic banks. FIBE accords with Siddiqi's and Chapra's concepts of Islamic banking. BIMB, on the other hand, follows Ismail's model of *tijari* (commercial) banking. For many years, Professor Dr Ismail was the managing director of the BIMB.

Different conditions apply to the distribution of profit. FIBE was exempted from all governmental taxes for the first 15 years of its operations, while BIMB is taxed. In addition, the calculation of profit shares differs between the banks. FIBE deducts all intermediation costs from the gross income from financing operations before dividends and deposit yields are calculated. BIMB divides the incomes from financing operations into one pool for depositors and another for the bank's operational expenses and the shareholders' remuneration. These points make it difficult for a direct comparison to be made of returns.

However, the balance sheets of the two institutions can be compared (Kazarian and Kokko, 1987; Kazarian, 1991). Table 6.2 sets out the comparison of the deposit structure of the two banks as of 1985/86. The funding sources of FIBE and BIMB appear to be relatively similar when aggregate data are considered as the bulk of deposits in both banks were placed in investment accounts. For FIBE, over 85 per cent of total funds were investment deposits, while the corresponding figure for BIMB was 75 per cent. Unlike BIMB, FIBE has not rewarded savings deposits.

Table 6.3 compares the financing activities of the two banks, also for 1985/86. Both FIBE and BIMB conducted the bulk of their financing operations on a short-term basis. *Murabaha* (mark-up) and *ijara* (leasing) contracts were the most common forms of financing. The share of short-term operations for FIBE was around 80 per cent, while the corresponding figure for BIMB was up to 90 per cent. The medium- and long-term operations – *mudaraba, musharaka* and direct investments – were relatively more important for FIBE. These operations are also often more risky than the short-term contracts. The main part of FIBE's operations was concentrated in financing to industry, housing and transportation. BIMB, on the other hand, focused more on trade financing and the financing of consumers' house purchases. Overall, however, the similarities rather than the differences seem to be the striking factor, especially in terms of the usage of short-term financing instruments.

Table 6.2   A comparison of the deposit structure of FIBE and BIMB, 1985–86

	FIBE	BIMB
(a) Distribution by type of account (percentage of funds)		
Current accounts	5	10
Savings accounts	10	14
Investment accounts	85	76
(b) Deposit size (US dollars)		
Total	2 000	1 800
Savings accounts	n.a.	260
Investment accounts	n.a.	10 000

Source: Bank Islam Malaysia Berhad and the Faisal Islamic Bank of Egypt.

Table 6.3   A comparison of the lending operations of FIBE and BIMB, 1985–86

	FIBE	BIMB
(a) Term structure (percentage of total financing)		
Short-term	80	90
Medium-term	15	8
Long-term	5	2
(b) Distribution by sectors (percentage of domestic financing)		
Agriculture	7	3
Industry	38	14
Housing and transportation	42	21
Trade and other sectors	13	62

Source: Bank Islam Malaysia Berhad and the Faisal Islamic Bank of Egypt.

Additional evidence relating to the formative years is set out in Table 6.4. This table illustrates much the same pattern, although the data for this table are of the term structure of investments by a sample of 20 Islamic Banks operating in a number of countries in 1988. Less than 10 per cent of the total assets went into medium- and long-term investment. Real estate financing and particularly short-term investments (*murabaha*) accounted for the great bulk of investments.

THE FORMATIVE YEARS: SOME ISSUES

Tables 6.2–6.4 illustrate the 'inconsistencies' noted earlier between the conversion to Islamic partnership arrangements on the deposit and asset sides of the balance sheets. These inconsistencies may reflect in part conceptual problems inherent in the principles of Islamic banking, and in part may be the consequence of practical difficulties in actually implementing the principles.

Consider, first, the theoretical issues. In Chapter 4 we argued that, in the light of modern theories of financial intermediation based around information asymmetries, Islamic banks operating in a conventional banking environment may face special difficulties. In particular, there is likely to be an adverse selection problem. An entrepreneur with low profit expectations is likely to prefer equity finance from an Islamic bank, while an entrepreneur with high profit expectations may opt for a fixed interest loan from a conventional bank (Cobham, 1992). Also, Islamic banks may find that a high proportion of firms

Table 6.4   Term structure of investments by 20 Islamic banks, 1988

Type of investment	Amount*	% of Total
Short-term	4909.8	68.4
Social lending	64.2	0.9
Real-estate investment	1498.2	20.9
Medium- and long-term investment	707.7	9.8

Note: *in thousands of US dollars.

Source: Aggregate balance sheets prepared by the International Association of Islamic Banks, Bahrain, 1988.

seeking loans from them are ones who have been refused by conventional banks (Ariff, 1988). Furthermore, the entrepreneur may have an incentive to present an overly optimistic view of the investment project in an attempt to persuade the Islamic bank to accept a lower profit-share (Nienhaus, 1983, 1988).

According to some proponents of Islamic banking, these incentive issues may be counter-balanced by the 'religious variable', encouraging truthfulness and straight-dealing by the Islamic businessman. Yet this factor might apply with less force in a mixed financial system than in one which has been entirely Islamised according to Muslim laws and customs. If so, these problems all suggest a need for extra monitoring by banks which lend on a PLS basis in competition with other banks, resulting in potentially higher costs of intermediation.

Here, second, practical difficulties exemplified in the cases of Pakistan, Sudan and Iran, considered in Chapter 5, seem instructive. In both Iran and Pakistan it turned out to be relatively straightforward to make the banks' deposits non-interest-bearing, but much more difficult to make their loans profit-and-loss-sharing. In both countries bank asset portfolios were dominated by various forms of short-term financing, notably instalment sales in Iran and mark-up (*murabaha*) in Pakistan.

Among the factors cited by Khan and Mirakhor (1990) – the source for most of this information about Iran and Pakistan – to explain both the relatively low level of PLS financing and the expectation that it would increase only slowly, include in the case of Iran the general uncertainty about the intended role of the private sector under the new regime, and the segmentation of the banking system between specialist banks unable to raise deposits themselves and commercial banks with weak project evaluation and monitoring skills, due to the lack of personnel with adequate relevant banking expertise. For Pakistan, the factors include: the extreme caution of both policymakers and bankers because of heavy-handed regulations in a nationalised banking environment; the obstacles to effective monitoring posed by the tax system and the existence of multiple account books amongst business firms; and the fact that rates of return to both the banking system and depositors are strictly controlled and do not accurately reflect project outcomes. In addition, it is worth noting that in neither of these countries have the problems associated with the financing of government deficits been solved. In Iran, the government borrows extensively from the banking system at zero interest, arguing that it owns the banking system itself so that interest payments merely reshuffle money within the public sector. In Pakistan, the government borrows from the private sector at fixed rates which in many instances actually exceed those paid on investment deposits in the banking system.

Instead of facing up to these problems, banks in both countries – and Pakistan in particular – largely contented themselves with avoiding the issue and concentrating on short-term *riba* alternatives consistent with *shari'a* principles as laid down in the letter of the law. These are mark-up and lease financing arrangements.

This then is the position revealed by a study of Islamic banking during the formative years. Before drawing any definite conclusions on this evidence, we need to examine the present situation.

GLOBAL OPERATIONS TODAY

A number of case studies below examine the present day operations of a variety of Islamic banks. As a preliminary to these individual cases, we look at the overall situation.

Worldwide – the Present Position

The International Association of Islamic Banks collects data from 176 banks, and Table 1.2 above gave details of the capital, deposits and assets, classified by region for 1997. Some other information is relevant.

- Financing of trade is the single largest activity accounting for 32 per cent of financing. Other areas were industry (17 per cent), real estate (16 per cent), services (12 per cent), agriculture (6 per cent) and other finance (16 per cent). Over the past 5 years, real estate and construction financing has expanded relative to agriculture and industry (although the sample has not remained unchanged).
- The 176 banks operated a total of 22 639 local and overseas branches.

- In terms of employment, the 176 banks had in all 293 635 employees.
- As to the corporate structure, 65 banks are classified as public or joint-stock companies, while 76 banks are under private ownership, one is a cooperative, and the remaining 34 are fully or partly government-owned.
- Considering *shari'a* supervision, the data indicate that 133 institutions have a *shari'a* Adviser and/or Board (59 have both). The rest, mostly banks Islamicised by government legislature in Iran, Pakistan, and Sudan operate within total Islamic economies and therefore do not require specific *shari'a* services on an individual basis.

Investment Pattern Worldwide

Table 6.4, we recall, considered the investment pattern in 1988 of 20 Islamic banks reporting to the IAIB. Table 6.5 provides an update for 1997, but in this case for the 119 banks (out of 176) reporting Islamic financing modes to the IAIB, classified by region of operation (with the three complete systems, Iran, Sudan and Pakistan, shown separately).[6] It is immediately apparent that *mudaraba* and *musharaka* feature more prominently, at least in certain areas. Because of the different coverage of the tables, however, it is difficult to tell whether this reflects different behaviour or the larger sample of institutions included.

Dar Al-Maal Al-Islami

One group of Islamic financial institutions with a worldwide focus is the DMI group. The Dar Al-Maal Al-Islami (DMI) group was established by His Royal Highness Prince Muhammad Al-Faisal Al-Saud, of Saudi Arabia in 1981. Earlier the Prince was instrumental in establishing the Faisal Banks in Egypt (FIBE) and Sudan (FIBS), and the Islamic Investment Company of the Gulf in 1978. Foundation of the DMI Trust in the Bahamas three years later with paid up capital of US$320 million initiated a move to establish Islamic Faisal banks, Islamic investment companies, Islamic insurance (*Takaful*) companies, and business enterprises throughout the world. Figure 6.1 sets out the structure of the DMI Trust group. FIBE and FIBS are affiliated institutions. DMI Trust affairs are administered by Dar Al-Maal Al-Islami (DMI) SA located in Geneva, Switzerland, which focuses upon group strategy, accounts and treasury, coordination of investments and technical assistance. It carries out its activities in accordance with the directives given by the Board of Supervisors of the Trust. The operating subsidiaries of DMI run their day-to-day affairs through their network of branches.

In the Islamic banking field, DMI Massaref (Islamic banks) provide a

Table 6.5 *Financing instruments of Islamic banks, by region, 1997*

Region	No. of reporting banks	Assets of reporting banks $ million (per cent)[1]	Murabaha (per cent)	Musharaka (per cent)	Mudaraba (per cent)	Ijara (per cent)	Others (incl. equities) (per cent)
Pakistan	23	9 534 (25)	24.98	0.17	1.92	2.05	70.87
Sudan	21	957 (85)	50.57	23.21	4.15	0.40	21.70
Iran	8	45 286 (67)	1.29	24.55	17.38	9.47	47.29
Gulf countries[2]	15	8 450 (41)	59.02	9.59	2.01	5.93	23.46
Middle East[3]	15	14 696 (94)	34.16	50.88	13.40	0.23	1.28
South Asia[4] (excl. Pakistan)	6	755 (100)	32.81	1.62	11.65	18.73	35.19
Africa[5] (excl. Sudan)	7	451 (92)	39.96	24.92	1.23	14.84	19.04
South East Asia[6]	19	924 (40)	2.92	0.21	0.53	12.59	83.75
Western Countries[7]	5	842 (92)	12.02	50.90	0.51	6.67	29.90
Total	119	81 895	17.10	24.66	12.63	6.59	38.97

Notes:
1 Assets of banks recording financing modes as percentage of assets of all reporting banks in region.
2 Bahrain, Kuwait, Qatar, Saudi Arabia, UAE.
3 Egypt, Iraq, Jordan, Lebanon, Turkey and Yemen.
4 India and Bangladesh.
5 Algeria, Djibouti, Gambia, Guinea, Mauritania, Niger, South Africa, Senegal, Tunisia.
6 Brunei, Indonesia, Malaysia, Philippines.
7 Europe, Americas, Australia.

Source: International Association of Islamic Banks.

comprehensive range of Islamic banking and financial services and are involved in local, regional and international business activities. DMI Massaref accept deposits and provide for a variety of call, fixed, special purpose and private investment accounts. Like other Islamic banks, for the participating account, the Massaref invests the funds on behalf of its clients and the resulting profits are shared in agreed percentages between the clients and the Massaref. They also provide short- and long-term financing to their clients. Short-term financing includes trade finance and working capital while long-term finance includes equity financing, project financing, lease financing and lease purchase financings. A wide range of international trade and currency-related transactions is undertaken.[7]

In the case of the investment companies, the principal sources for mobilising funds are through various *mudarabas* which are launched to attract deposits from a broad base of investing customers. These are tailored to the needs of the clients, both private and institutional. There is a real sense in which it can be said that these reflect the investing preferences of the client rather than the institution (so long as they are *shari'a* acceptable).

Table 6.6 sets out the capital, assets, deposits and Islamic financing instruments employed for investment purposes by 14 of the DMI group institutions. While the short-term *murabaha* is the most commonly employed financing instrument, there is a considerable diversity from bank to bank. FIBE, the first established bank, is by far the largest in terms of balance sheet aggregates. In comparison with the earlier figures given in Table 6.3 above, it is now the case that *musharaka* and *mudaraba* together account for over one-third of FIBE's investments. Moreover, a study of FIBE's operations by Saeed (1995) showed that FIBE appears to invest more in long-term projects than do the other commercial banks in Egypt. In particular, FIBE participates in the equity of several companies in the areas of industry, agriculture, commerce, health and housing, consistent with the economic and social development plan of the government.

Malaysia

In the earlier part of this chapter we examined the formation of Bank Islam Malaysia Berhad (BIMB) in 1983 and its operations in the early years of the mid-1980s. Over the decade or so since then, its activities have expanded considerably, so much so that other Malaysian banks have introduced 'Islamic counters', or 'Islamicised' their own banking business under the interest-free banking system instituted by Bank Negara Malaysia in 1992. In addition, another bank, Bank Raykat, began converting to Islamic banking in 1993. Bank Raykat was originally set up to help farmers gain access to cheap credit but the bank found that many rural people were reluctant to use the banking

Dar Al-Maal Al-Islami Trust
Nassau, Bahamas

Dar Al-Maal Al-Islami (DMI) SA
Trust Administrator, Geneva, Switzerland

Massrafs (Banks)	**Investment Companies**	**Business Companies**	**Takafol and Tetakafol (Insurance and Reinsurance) Companies**
• Massraf Faysal Al-Islami (Bank & Trust) Bahamas Ltd	• Islamic Investment Company of the Gulf – Sharjah	• Islamic Leasing Company, Bahrain EC	• Islamic Takafol and Retakafol (Bahamas) Company Limited
• Massraf Faysal Al-Islami of Bahrain EC Branches in Pakistan	• Islamic Investment Company of the. Gulf (Bahrain) EC	• DMI Administrative Services Limited, Jersey	• Islamic Takafol Company, Luxembourg
• Faisal Finance Institution AS, Turkey	• Faisal Holding (Luxembourg) SA	• International Islamic Trading (IIT) Limited, Bahamas	• Takafol Islamic Insurance, Company, Bahrain EC
• Banque Islamique du Senegal	• Islamic Investment Company Limited, Jersey	• International Islamic Trading (IIT) Limited, (Geneva branch)	
• Banque Islamique du Niger	• Islamic Investment Company Limited, UK	• Pan Islamic Consulting Trust, Bahamas	
• Banque Islamique du Guinee	• Islamic Investment and Development Company, Egypt	• Pan Islamic Consulting Services SA, Istishara, Geneva	
• Massraf Faysal Al-Islami (Jersey) Limited	• Islamic Investment Company of the Gulf (Bahamas) Ltd	• Pan Islamic Consulting Services Limited, England	
• Faisal Finance (Switzerland) SA (Finance company subjected to art. 7–8 of the Federal Banking Law)			
• A/S Islamic Bank International of Denmark			
• Al-Faysal Investment Bank, Pakistan			

Source: Institute of Islamic Banking and Insurance.

Figure 6.1 Corporate structure of the Dar Al-Maal Al-Islami Trust Group

Table 6.6 Financing instruments of DMI group institutions, 1997

Name of institution	Country	Paid-up capital US$000	Total assets US$000	Total deposits US$000	Modes of financing (per cent)				
					Murabaha	Musharaka	Mudaraba	Ijara	Others
Al Faysal Investment Bank Ltd	Pakistan	16 927	272 811	228 213	100.00	0.0	0.0	0.0	0.0
Faysal Bank Ltd	Pakistan	27 469	485 434	357 664	79.6	0.0	0.0	16.1	4.3
Banque Islamique de Guinee	Guinea	4 500	15 691	5 723	42.00	0.0	0.0	0.0	58.0
Banque Islamique du Niger	Niger	3 017	9 487	6 533	91.00	0.0	0.0	0.0	9.0
Banque Islamique du Senegal	Senegal	4 919	10 114	3 421	40.0	5.0	10.0	5.0	40.0
Faisal Islamic Bank of Sudan	Sudan	1 053	58 928	37 135	47.5	17.5	0.0	0.0	35.0
Faisal Islamic Bank of Egypt	Egypt	132 000	1 843 600	1 787 800	62.4	13.3	19.8	0.0	4.5
Faisal Finance Institution Inc	Turkey	9 807	186 305	166 407	98.5	1.5	0.0	0.0	0.0
Faisal Islamic Bank of Kibris	N. Cyprus	1 100	21 322	16 341	48.0	8.6	25.8	9.6	8.1
Faysal Invest. Bank of Bahrain	Bahrain	44 015	52 544	N/A	30.3	0.0	0.0	69.7	0.0
Faysal Islamic Bank of Bahrain	Bahrain	100 000	311 585	1 251 367	61.5	0.6	12.5	20.7	4.7
Islamic Investment Co. of the Gulf	Bahrain	40 000	65 191	821 495	73.0	0.0	0.0	0.0	27.0
Islamic Invest. Co. of the Gulf - Bahamas	Bahamas	20 000	26 000	N/A	42.9	2.4	0.2	6.5	48.0
Faisal Finance (Switzerland) SA	Switzerland	13 800	53 000	645 000	78.0	5.0	8.0	4.0	5.0

Source: International Association of Islamic Banks.

system because of the interest taken and paid. As a consequence of these developments, there is much greater competition for Islamic deposits. Nevertheless, we focus for continuity upon BIMB.

BIMB's initial paid-up capital, we recall, was RM80 million subscribed by various government and Islamic bodies. In 1990/91 the bank took steps to expand its equity and shares were listed on the Kuala Lumpur stock exchange. The paid-up capital of the bank is now RM133.4 million, supporting operations in 43 branches and 30 'mini-branches' (in 1996) along with the following subsidiaries:

- *Al-Wakalah* Nominees Sdn Bhd – this is a wholly-owned nominee company
- *Syarikat Takaful Malaysia* Sdn Bhd – the purpose of this subsidiary is to conduct Islamic insurance operations.
- *Syarikat Al-Ijarah* – this company was formed for the acquisition of immovable and movable fixed assets and is a wholly-owned leasing subsidiary.
- BIMB Securities and BIMB Unit Trust Management.

Tables 6.7 and 6.8 set out some details of the bank's deposit-raising and investments. The first table shows that in the wake of the competition for deposits, there is now an even greater concentration than before on current accounts and savings accounts, with these representing 22 and 19 per cent respectively of the total deposit funds (which in turn constitute 95 per cent of non-capital liabilities). The lower panels of Table 6.7 provide further details of the deposit base, showing that funds are drawn from individuals, business enterprises and institutions. Religious bodies such as Lembraga Urusan dan Tabung Haji, state religious councils, Perkim and the Federal Baitulmal are depositors with BIMB. While the majority of the bank's customers are Muslims, surveys have shown that the bank is also popular with non-Muslims, as the profit paid to investors is generally comparable to that of commercial banks. Nevertheless, with investments accounts having a short-term profile (80 per cent maturing within 6 months), depositors are sensitive to the dividend rate. Overall, a statistical study by Samad and Hassan (1999) of BIMB's performance relative to other commercial banks from 1984 to 1997 found a roughly comparable result; there is little difference in overall profitability, BIMB is somewhat more liquid and somewhat less risky than the other banks.

Table 6.8 gives information on the Islamic investments (which, incidentally, were not included in the IAIB data considered earlier in the section). Most of the instruments will now be familiar to readers, except perhaps for *Bai Bithaman Ajil*. This is similar to a *murabaha*. With a

Table 6.7   Deposit structure of Bank Islam Malaysia Berhad, 1994-96

	1994	1995	1996
Total deposits	2 547 799 (RM '000)	2 865 963 (RM '000)	3 196 281 (RM '000)
(a) By type of account (per cent)			
Current account	17.27	20.78	22.96
Savings account	15.02	16.32	19.15
Investment account	67.66	62.84	57.79
Others	0.05	0.06	0.10
(b) By type of customer (per cent)			
Business enterprises	14.80	15.86	17.93
Individuals	41.23	40.18	49.27
Others	43.97	43.96	32.80
(c) Investment Account, by maturity (per cent)			
Due within six months	66.29	62.24	81.00
Six months to one year	14.94	23.01	15.85
One year to three years	17.57	11.80	2.39
Three years to five years	1.19	1.94	0.08
Over five years	0.00	1.01	0.68

Source: Bank Islam Malaysia Berhad Annual Reports (various).

murabaha, the customer requests the bank to acquire the goods using its own financing. The bank sells the goods to the customer at cost plus profit margin for settlement by cash or on a deferred payment (*bai bi-thamin ajil*) basis. Where the deferred payment is by instalments, it is called *Bai Bithaman Ajil* (BBA), while in this framework *murabaha* is the description reserved for a deferred payment by a lump sum. However, not all schools of jurisprudence accept this distinction between the two (Yasin, 1997).

BBA is essentially a sales contract, differing from a cash sale by virtue of the fact that payments are deferred in instalments to some future dates. The profit derived from a BBA sale is legitimate because it comes from a trade rather than a debt transaction (*al-bai* being trade and commerce). If a bank is to comply with the spirit of *al-bai* as the *shari'a* has rightfully intended, it must hold risks of possession of the property before resale. Doing so will make the profit generated from the BBA sale licit as it involves the element of risk-taking, namely risks of holding and possession of property. The determination

Table 6.8   Financing operations of Bank Islam Malaysia Berhad, 1994–96

	1994	1995	1996
Total financing	1 027 096 (RM '000)	1 495 267 (RM '000)	2 046 435 (RM '000)
(a) By instrument (per cent)			
Al-Bai Bithaman Ajil	68.36	59.01	65.96
Al-Ijarah	8.74	6.65	7.12
Al-Musyarakah	1.72	1.19	0.98
Al-Mudharabah	0.33	0.76	0.97
Al Murabahah	17.85	30.23	23.21
Al-Qardhul-Hassan	0.09	0.11	0.08
Staff financing	2.58	1.93	1.67
Bai Al-Dayn	0.34	0.12	0.01
(b) By period of maturity (per cent)			
Maturing within one year	26.83	39.60	18.30
One year to three years	16.02	6.78	5.18
Three years to five years	16.11	12.51	15.26
Over five years	41.03	41.11	61.25
(c) By sector (per cent)			
Agriculture, mining and quarrying	4.26	2.73	2.38
Manufacturing	24.76	32.37	29.35
Real estate and construction	17.42	13.96	24.95
Housing	22.21	16.60	14.44
General commerce	6.71	9.91	6.03
Finance, insurance and business services	2.58	2.73	3.03
Consumption credit	2.32	2.89	4.85
Others	19.75	18.81	14.98

Source: Bank Islam Malaysia Berhad Annual Reports (various).

of the mark-up or selling price will depend on the stipulated annual rate of profit the bank desires from the transaction. Rosly (1999) gives an example. Suppose that the financing is $100 000 with a desired annual profit rate of 10 per cent and 60 months period of financing. An annuity factor of 0.0210714 using annuity tables is used to obtain the monthly instalment payments which are equal to $2107.14 per month. Multiplying $2107.14 by 60 will give the selling price, which is $126 428.70. The difference between the market price (cost price) and the mark-up price (selling price) is the profit over the instalment periods.

BIMB's usage of the BBA is for longer-term financing of assets such as buildings and machinery while *murabaha* is for short-term finance of working capital. Together, however, these two *murabaha* forms of financing accounted for 90.6 per cent of BIMB's Islamic investments in 1997. Over 60 per cent of these investments are relatively long-term (over 5 years), and the largest exposure is to the real estate market (commercial and residential) which represented 40 per cent of total financing.

This commercial financing structure has created risk problems for BIMB, not so much in terms of the entrepreneur's ability to maintain the instalments (although delinquency obviously can and does occur, especially for commercial real estate), but due to interest rate exposure. BBA is legitimate because it is a contract of sale. This requires the selling price to remain unchanged for the contract duration, since only one set of selling prices is allowed. This, in turn, necessitates that the rate of profit on each contract be fixed. From the viewpoint of bank risk management, BBAs are the equivalent of fixed rate assets. When the market interest rates rises, the Islamic bank's earnings and profit rates will remain unchanged. If conventional banks' assets are rate sensitive, these banks will tend to gain market share during periods of rising interest rates.[8]

Bangladesh

A recent study of Islamic banking in Bangladesh was made by Sarker (1999b). Islamic banks have been operating in Bangladesh for one and a half decades alongside the traditional banks. Out of over 39 banks only 5 banks (including one foreign Islamic bank) and two Islamic banking branches of a traditional bank, Prime Bank Limited (PBL), have been working on Islamic principles. The banks are:

Islami Bank Bangladesh Ltd (IBBL) was incorporated on 14 March 1983 as the first interest-free bank in Bangladesh. IBBL is a public limited company with limited liability and it is a joint venture multinational bank with 64 per cent of equity being contributed by foreign sources. It has over 100 branches. *Al-Baraka Bank Bangladesh Ltd* (Al-Baraka) is the second scheduled Islamic bank of the country and commenced business on 20 May 1987. It is a joint venture of Al-Baraka Investment and Development Company of Jeddah, Saudi Arabia, the Islamic Development Bank, a group of eminent Bangladeshi entrepreneurs and the government of Bangladesh. There are 32 branches in the country.

Al-Arafah Islami Bank Limited (Al-Arafah) was established on 18 June 1995 and started operation as the third Islamic bank in Bangladesh. By 1998, Al-Arafah had opened 21 branches.

Social Investment Bank Limited (SIBL), the fourth Islamic bank in Bangladesh, was incorporated on 5 July 1995, and launched its banking operations of 22 November 1995. It is a joint venture bank of some renowned Islamic organisations of the world and the Government of Bangladesh. By June 1998, SIBL had opened seven branches within the country.

Faysal Islamic Bank of Bahrain EC, Dhaka, Bangladesh (FIBB) obtained permission to open its branch in Bangladesh on 6 March 1997. The principal activities of the branch are to provide a wide range of commercial banking services to customers.

Prime Bank Ltd (PBL) is the only bank in Bangladesh which is operating branches on both a conventional interest-based and *shari'a*-based basis. At an operational level the two Islamic banking branches of PBL are maintained separately from the conventional banking ones. Other traditional banks in the country are moving to open fully-fledged Islamic banking branches.

IBBL is by far the largest of the six banks, with a market share of 63 per cent of total Islamic bank deposits (the next largest being Al-Baraka with 25 per cent of Islamic deposits). Around 80–85 per cent of IBBL's deposits are received under the *mudaraba*-PLS sharing principle. IBBL offers a variety of investment accounts, including general investment accounts (which are pooled), limited period investment accounts, unlimited period investment accounts, and specified investment accounts, where the funds are invested in a specific project or trading activity, with the bank acting as agent for an agreed fee.

Table 6.9 shows the Islamic financing instruments employed by the six banks. Overall, *murabaha, bai-muajjal,* and hire purchase are the most commonly employed instruments. *Murabaha* and *bai-muajjal* are used for trade financing, and hire purchase for term financing. *Musharaka* have a negligible proportion and no *mudarabas* are reported. Sarker (1999b) reports that:

> under-reporting of profit by the entrepreneurs to evade taxes widely matters to the application of PLS modes since both *Mudaraba* and *Musharaka* are profit sharing contracts between the bank and the entrepreneurs, maintenance of proper accounting and declaration of actual profit by the entrepreneurs are extremely essential for the bank. Under-reporting of profit is one of the severe moral hazards in Bangladesh. This has been established as a rule rather than an exception. (p. 20)

Jordan

The next case that we consider is the first Islamic bank in Jordan, Jordan

Table 6.9   Financing modes of Islamic banks in Bangladesh, 1997 (per cent of total)

Mode	IBBL	Al-Baraka	Al-Arafah	SIBL	FIBB	PBL
Murabaha	42.45	–	27.09	53.18	82.05	0.85
Musharaka	2.61	–	0.14	0.87	–	–
Bai' muajjal	19.87	62.49	10.70	10.02	–	1.09
Hire purchase	20.47	19.31	3.05	19.98	–	95.46
Qard Hasan	4.80	5.10	9.02	7.29	–	1.53
Purchase and negotiation	9.64	–	–	0.32	–	1.07
Investment in shares and securities	0.15	–	1.58	0.02	-	–
Others	–	13.10	48.42	8.33	17.95	–
Total	100	100	100	100	100	100
Memo Taka million	13 095	5203.38	1791.20	368.31	42.00	102.54

Source: Based on data reported in Sarker (1999b).

Islamic Bank for Finance and Investment (JIB), examined by Alrawi (1997). JIB was established in 1978 according to a special temporary law (No. 13) then made permanent law in 1985 (No. 62). The bank was registered as a public limited company with a capital amounting to 15 million JD, of which most was paid, and began operations in 1979. The bank's aim is to enhance the economic and social developments through banking services by opening as many regional offices as possible. There were 44 branches in 1997.

Deposits received through the branch network provide 82 per cent of the bank's investible resources, and are made up as follows:

Current and demand deposits	18.0 per cent
Savings accounts	8.5 per cent
Term investment accounts	73.5 per cent

Like other Islamic banks, JIB obtains a share of the profit of the latter without bearing any loss, provided it is not a result of the bank's negligence as *mudarib*.

Table 6.10 sets out JIB's financing activities. In common with many other Islamic banks that we have examined, JIB makes use of *murabaha* for financing trading activities and such financing is 57 per cent of the portfolio. *Musharaka* and *mudaraba* represent only 2 per cent of investments. Early in its operations, JIB attempted to utilise the *mudaraba* to invest its funds, but after losses had to limit its use. Diminishing *musharaka* have been used for some real estate activities.

These experiences are in line with those of many other Islamic banks. Where JIB has differentiated itself from others is in terms of direct investments and joint ventures of various types. Together, these make up 40 per cent of the bank's investments. Activities in which the bank has engaged include housing scheme projects and commodity investments. This extent of direct involvement in productive investment is unusual, even amongst Islamic banks.

Australia

So far we have focused on Islamic institutions operating in predominantly Muslim countries. In this example, we consider an institution operating in a country where Muslims are only 1.1 per cent of the 18 million population. The Muslim Community Cooperative (Aust) (MCCA) was established in February 1989 with 10 members and initial capital of $22 300, operating in Burwood, a suburb of Melbourne, Victoria. Ten years later there are 3822 members and capital of $18 million. There is one branch in Lakemba, a suburb of Sydney (800km away).

Table 6.10   Financing operations of Jordan Islamic Bank, 1994-95

	1994 (per cent)	1995 (per cent)
Murabaha	52.73	57.37
Mudaraba and *Musharaka*	2.10	1.97
Direct investment	12.23	12.30
Joint venture	8.83	6.19
Investment in external goods	2.78	3.59
Investment in stocks	14.67	12.79
Investment in buildings	6.29	5.41
Other investments	0.40	0.37
	100	100
Total financing JD 1000	356 105	418 154

Source: Based on information in Alrawi (1997).

As a cooperative society, all members are shareholders. Under new registration procedures ruling in Australia, MCCA obtained approval in 1999 to form a credit union, Muslim Community Credit Union (MCCU), the first Islamic financial institution in Australia, and chartered to operate with a banking licence. This licence enables MCCU to operate across Australia and overseas, and to provide current account (cheque) services to businesses as well as to individuals. Via the services corporation which operates throughout Australia for all credit unions, MCCA and MCCU will have access to these support facilities, while members will eventually have access to linked ATMs and other electronic systems.

MCCA's basic objectives, however, will not change, and these are to act as a housing cooperative that assists with the purchase of mainly residential properties for and on behalf of its shareholders. The purchase of other asset classes is undertaken in a similar fashion, mostly the purchase of motor vehicles, computers, and some limited business finance, all in accord with *shari'a* principles. The main forms of investment, both roughly equal in amount, and making up nearly 90 per cent of the total investments are *musharaka* property finance and *murabaha* with deferred payment by instalments, as shown in Table 6.11.

Table 6.11 Balance sheet of Muslim Community Cooperative (Australia) Ltd, 1998–99

	Share capital			
	1998 A$000 $11 834		1999 A$000 $18 035	
Invested as follows:	A$000	per cent	A$000	per cent
Cash in hand	230	2	1 463	8
Investment in commodity finance (*Murabaha*)	5 225	44	7 567	42
Investment in property finance	5 347	45	8 133	45
Commercial finance (*Mudaraba*)	730	6	506	3
Qard Hassan and other funds	302	2	366	2
Total	11 834	100	18 035	100

The shared equity & rental scheme is an equity form of financing used in financing the purchase of owner-occupied residential or commercial property. Under this diminishing *musharaka* partnership arrangement, MCCA and the occupant (the buying member) agree jointly to purchase the property. Based on the share of each party's beneficial ownership, both parties agree to a fixed rental, which is divided proportionally between the parties on the basis of such an ownership. The occupant (the buying member) also agrees to purchase MCCA's beneficial ownership in the property over a deferred period. As MCCA's share declines, its share of the rental income also declines. This process continues until the property is solely owned by the occupant (the buying member). As a means of rationing supply, members have to serve a six-month qualifying period and must have at least 20 per cent of the property purchase price invested with MCCA prior to being eligible to apply (MCCA will not invest more than 80 per cent of the purchase price).

The murabaha scheme (cost plus profit deferred instalment sale contracts) involves an instalment sale agreement (effectively *bai bi-thamin ajil*) between the ordering member and MCCA where the member requests MCCA to purchase outright a tangible commodity in their favour. After the Cooperative has acquired the commodity fully and has it in its possession, the ordering member is invited to purchase the commodity from the Cooperative at a fixed price that includes a pre-agreed profit. Once a formal sale agreement has been executed, the commodity is surrendered to the ordering member who then has exclusive title to the commodity and is required to meet the agreed deferred instalments. This arrangement is used for capital goods, motor vehicles and other durables, and a three-month qualifying period applies.

The mudaraba/musharaka scheme (commercial investment) is the method of providing business finance. Those meeting the screening criteria are offered a *musharaka* facility, which is an investment agreement between MCCA and the business manager (the applying member) in which all terms and conditions are pre-arranged including the sharing (by way of proportion) of the profit (or loss) of the commercial operation. MCCA, as a rule, does not exercise any significant control or influence over such operations except in a recovery situation.

The qard hassan scheme (interest/cost-free loans) is the only form of permissible lending. The *qard hassan* fund is maintained solely as a benevolent function for the social advancement of members and non-members alike. As a fund consisting solely of donations and temporary placements, it is made available to those experiencing genuine and emergency financial crisis under an interest/cost-free loan agreement.

Bad debts have been a problem for commercial investments, especially by means of *mudaraba*. MCCA has responded by reducing its exposure to this instrument, as well as introducing increased screening and monitoring procedures. Because of abnormally high write-offs in 1999, the dividend declared on (all) shares was 4.01 per cent, much lower than the average of 7.1 per cent over the three previous years, but not far below money market rates at that time.

Finally, like other Islamic institutions, a *zakat* fund is maintained and distributed. A *shari'a* adviser assists with this and other related matters, in an unpaid capacity. There is a Board of Directors, mainly non-executive.

ISSUES IN ISLAMIC BANKING

The expansion of Islamic banks worldwide, both in numbers and funds under control, along with the operations examined in this chapter for Egypt, Malaysia, Bangladesh, Jordan and Australia, along with Sudan, Iran and Pakistan earlier, all point to a central conclusion: Islamic banking is clearly feasible and Islamic banks can and do operate in a variety of countries, fulfilling a range of functions and employing different instruments. While many of the banks have attracted generous capital support and patronage from governments and prominent Muslim families, they have relied on much more than this in the competitive market environment of the mixed Islamic–conventional banking systems.

Our case studies, based in two instances on experiences ten years apart, show that Islamic banking is an evolving market and that there are differences in the applications of the basic principles to different locations. For example, on the deposit side, current accounts are operated mainly on the principle of *al-wadiah*. Saving deposits, too, are accepted on this basis, but 'gifts' to depositors are given entirely at the discretion of the Islamic banks on the minimum balance, so that the depositors also share in profits. In Malaysia, Islamic savings accounts compete in their returns directly with those of conventional banks. Investment deposits are based on the *mudaraba* principle, but there are considerable variations. Thus, for example, the Islamic Bank of Bangladesh has been offering PLS Deposit Accounts, PLS Special Notice Deposit Accounts, and PLS Term Deposit Accounts, while Bank Islam Malaysia has been operating two kinds of investment deposits, one for the general public and the other for institutional clients. There are also interesting variations in the pattern of resource utilisation by the Islamic banks. For example, *musharaka* has been important as an investment mode in Egypt and Sudan, while in Malaysia these hardly feature. Diminishing *musharaka* have been adopted for partnership financing of housing in Australia. The Jordan Islamic Bank has invested directly in housing and other investment schemes.

Nevertheless, there are some issues to be addressed if further progress of the concept is to occur. These matters relate to the legal arrangements, the continued attraction of deposits and the pattern of financing operations undertaken. They are considered in this order.

Legal System

In all except the last case study examined, the banks concerned were chartered under special legislation enacted for the purpose. This is the normal state of affairs, and for good reason, as existing banking laws in most countries do not permit banks to engage directly in business enterprises using depositors' funds, or at least strictly limit such investments to funds supplied by shareholders. Since this is the basic way that Islamic banks are meant to acquire assets, new legislation and/or government authorisation is needed to establish these banks. In Iran, comprehensive legislation was passed to establish Islamic banks, while in Pakistan the central bank was authorised to take the necessary steps. In other Muslim countries the authorities actively participated in the establishment of Islamic banks on account of their commitment to religious principles, so creating a mixed system offering customers the choice of Islamic or conventional banking modes.[9] This is not the case in non-Muslim countries. In them, establishing Islamic banks involves conforming to the existing laws of the countries concerned which generally are not conducive to PLS types of financing in the banking sector.

Witness, for example, the position taken by the Bank of England. Sir Robin Leigh Pemberton, then Governor of the Bank of England, told the Arab Bankers' Association in London in 1984:

- A central feature of the banking system of the United Kingdom as enshrined in the legal framework is capital certainty for depositors. It is the most important feature which distinguishes the banking sector from the other segments of the financial system.
- Islamic banking is a perfectly acceptable mode of financing but it does not fall within the definition of what constitutes banking in the UK.
- The Bank of England is not legally able to authorise under the Banking Act, an institution which does not take deposits as defined under that Act.
- The Islamic facilities might be provided within other areas of the financial system without using a banking name.

Consequently in countries working under conventional laws, the authorities are generally unable to grant permission to institutions which wish to operate under the PLS scheme to function as commercial banks. The upshot is that Islamic banks must operate in most non-Muslim countries as non-bank financial intermediaries or as investment houses. It is thus encouraging for its future market growth that MCCA has been able to structure itself as a credit union, rather than a cooperative, in Australia and provide banking services, consistent with a banking licence.

Attraction of Deposits

When established, Islamic banks operating in mixed Islamic–conventional banking environments have obviously relied heavily on their religious appeal to gain deposits. This emphasis has continued. To give one example, Saeed (1995) reports that the Faisal Islamic Bank of Egypt (FIBE) is actively involved in attracting Muslims, particularly those who believe in the unlawfulness of interest, to its deposit mobilisation schemes. To attract such customers in an increasingly competitive financial environment, FIBE utilises several means:

- Attracting leading *'ulama* (religious scholars) to propagate the prohibition of interest, and advocate that interest income is unlawful, and that lawful income on capital can be gained by depositing the funds with the Islamic bank.
- Emphasising its Islamic credentials by means of the collection and distribution of *zakat*.
- Convening seminars and conferences to propagate the merits of Islamic banking.
- Attacking any potential threat to its *raison d'être*, fully utilising supportive *'ulama* and the mass media, as was indicated in the case of the Mufti Tantawi's opinion that interest on investment certificates was lawful.
- Offering modern banking facilities such as automatic teller machines and fast banking services by means of installing latest computer technology in banking operations.
- Giving depositors a return comparable to that given to the depositors of traditional banks.

While all of these factors are relevant, the last two are critical. The market is no longer in its infancy, and an Islamic bank cannot take its clients for granted. There are many institutions, including Western banks, competing with the original Islamic banks by means of Islamic 'windows', and the general lessons in financial, as in other, markets is that profit spreads and profit margins fall as new financial institutions enter the market. For example, securitisation and the entry of independent mortgage providers to the conventional housing finance market saw margins reduced by competition by over one percentage point (100 basis points) in the United States, UK and Australia.

There have been a number of studies of the factors prompting bank patronage of Islamic and conventional banks using survey data: Erol and El-Bdour (1989) and Erol, Kaynak and El-Bdour (1990) for Jordan; Haron, Ahmad and Planisek (1994) for Malaysia; while Gerrard and Cunningham (1997) undertook an analysis of the awareness of Islamic banking in Singapore. (Since no Islamic banks, only *Takaful* institutions operate in Singapore it is perhaps not surprising that most of the users of Singapore's underground transport system who were polled were generally unaware of the culture of Islamic banking.) The main results of these studies are, first, that religion did not appear to be the main, or even a major, motive prompting people to use an Islamic bank. Second, all of the studies found efficiency to be an important factor, in that people wanted their transactions to be completed as quickly and as efficiently as possible. Efficient use of technology was valued. Third, customers of Islamic banks were profit-oriented and expected the banks to be as profitable or more profitable than conventional banks.

Financing Difficulties

This last consideration is important in view of the constraints which are imposed upon the investments of Islamic banks. One factor is a lack of very short-term financial instruments. At present there is no equivalent of an inter-bank market operating on a non-interest basis where banks could place, say, overnight funds, or where they could borrow to satisfy temporary liquidity needs. Obviously, the creation of suitable financing instruments is a pressing need as Islamic banks are placed at a distinct disadvantage relative to conventional banks in the range and maturity structure of instruments on both the liability and asset sides of their balance sheets. A new international initiative along these lines is discussed in Chapter 9. At present, Malaysia has made the most steps in this direction with the introduction of Government Investment Certificates which are held by Malaysian Islamic banks when complying with their liquid asset requirements. These are a sort of Islamic variant of Treasury bills and, while they are issued on a *qard hasan* basis with only the principal guaranteed, there is a 'satisfactory' rate of return paid voluntarily to holders.

Another issue is government finance. In most countries government borrowing constitutes a major component of the demand for funds – both short-term and long-term. Unlike business loans these borrowings are not always for investment purposes, nor for placement in productive enterprises. Even when invested in productive enterprises they are generally of a longer-term type and provide low yields in purely economic terms. This latter consideration only accentuates the difficulties in estimating a rate of return on these funds if they are granted under PLS schemes. Obviously, Islamic banks cannot invest in government bonds if they are of the standard fixed interest rate form, but equity participation modes are ruled out except for asset-creating expenditure (for example infrastructure and development) undertaken on an economic basis where returns can be assigned to individual equity claims or to various leasing-type arrangements for equipment.

But it is the private-sector financing operations of Islamic banks which create the most serious problems, in both theory and practice. In theory, there is a central analytical dilemma facing Islamic banking operations. Islamic law forbids the payment of interest, but standard debt contracts have incentive compatibility features which make them clearly preferable in many cases. The inability to offer fixed interest loans imposes on Islamic banks the need to monitor their borrowers much more intensively than conventional banks would do if true PLS arrangements are to operate on the lending side. So far it has not been possible fully to develop a system of contracts which allows for equity partnership between the lender (the bank) and the borrower while keeping monitoring costs at a reasonable level and eliminating the moral hazard issues which arise when the lender and the investor have asymmetric information on the profits from an investment venture.

Three types of finance have proved difficult to implement. One is the working capital of businesses, where the flexibility of overdraft facilities along UK lines has not been easy to replicate in Islamic terms. PLS type schemes are not well suited to cater to this need, although they can be adapted to a degree. *Musharaka* have been employed where a special account of a customer is debited with a pre-determined rate of profit (rather than interest), but then adjusted up or down in line with the trading results and profit returns. Even if there is complete trust, reliable accounting and a full exchange of information between the bank and the business, it is difficult or costly to estimate the contribution of a particular short-term financing line on the return of a given business. Neither is the much used cost plus mark-up system suitable in this case.

Second, financing of small business has also been difficult to provide under the PLS scheme without the devices employed by Western banks such as personal or family guarantees, mortgages over personal assets, floating charges upon business assets, and loan covenants. Leasing or hire purchase might be used, but otherwise the observations of Iqbal and Mirakhor (1987, p. 24) in the case of Iran are instructive:

Given the comprehensive criteria to be followed in granting loans and monitoring their use by banks, small-scale enterprises have, in general, encountered greater difficulties in obtaining financing than their large-scale counterparts in the Islamic Republic of Iran. This has been particularly relevant for the construction and service sectors, which have large shares in the gross domestic product (GDP). The service sector is made up of many small producers for whom the banking sector has not been able to provide sufficient financing. Many of these small producers, who traditionally were able to obtain interest-based credit facilities on the basis of collateral, are now finding it difficult to raise funds for their operations.

Third, many Islamic banks have been unable or unwilling to participate in long-term projects, although this is not as true as it once was with the use of diminishing *musharaka* and Islamic project finance. The need to participate in an enterprise on a PLS basis involves time-consuming, complicated assessment procedures and negotiations, requiring expertise and experience. As yet, there are no commonly agreed upon procedures and 'credit-scoring' criteria for project evaluation based on PLS partnerships, although some banks have introduced them. Each single case has to be treated separately with due diligence, and each venture has to be assessed and the contract negotiated on its own merits. Many Islamic banks are small by conventional banking standards, and cannot afford to set up specialist evaluation teams.

Other reasons for the lack of long-term PLS financing are that such investments tie up capital for very long periods, unlike in conventional banking where the funding is recovered in regular instalments almost right from the start or the asset can be securitised and on-sold to other holders. Further, the longer is the maturity of the project, the longer it takes to realise the returns and banks consequently cannot pay a return to their depositors as quickly as conventional banks are able to do.

In practice, almost all Islamic banks – whether operating in financial systems which have been 'Islamicised' or in conventional environments with mixed arrangements – have reacted to these problems by utilising, to varying degrees, financing where there is no PLS element. Use of *murabaha* overcomes the monitoring problem, but these contracts create difficulties of their own, especially when repayments are on a deferred basis, as with *murabaha-bi-muajjal* or *bai-bi-thamin ajil*. First, the delinquency problem is a real one, accentuated because late payments cannot be penalised, whereas in the interest system late payments would attract increased interest charges. Second, repossessions are costly, as any finance company knows – hence the high charges they apply. Third, because the selling price is fixed under the sale contract, the financing is essentially fixed rate. In effect, *murabaha* techniques create the Islamic equivalent of 'interest rate risk'. The banks are exposed to declining profits when market interest rates rise, since their returns are fixed, while when market rates fall, they face 'pre-payment risk'.[10]

HOW ISLAMIC IS THE FINANCING?

There seems to be general agreement amongst Islamic writers (although bankers see it differently), that Islamic banks' failure to participate more extensively in long-term projects is a very unsatisfactory situation, both from the viewpoint of development and growth policies in the countries concerned, and in terms of *shari'a* principles. In many instances, the equity participation, *musharaka*, instrument has been used for carrying out the banks' own direct investments in Islamic financial institutions, insurance companies, and investment companies for financing trade, housing, and services activities, while the share of investments in the agricultural and industrial sectors has been declining.[11] This is one part of a broader criticism of Islamic banking practices by Muslim scholars (and some Western observers).

A major part of the funds provided to customers by Islamic banks, over 90 per cent of the total in the case of BIMB, are on the basis of mark-up contracts and variants (leasing, deferred sale). A feature of these contracts is that the funds are secured, because the goods bought and sold or leased act as collateral, or other security can be sought. In addition, the cost of funds (rate of profit) is determined in advance by the banks.

From the viewpoint of Islamic banking principles, these contracts embody a number of characteristics which are seen to be less than satisfactory. The finance charges are determined in advance, governed by type of activity, the security offered by the investors, and the duration of the transaction. Different margins of profit apply for various economic sectors. These are explicitly added to the amount of funds provided. In addition to the direct cost associated with the transactions, other costs associated with the transaction have to be added, such as the costs of information, travel and time. The purchased goods also serve as collateral, and the ownership of them transfers successively from the bank to the investor in proportion to the sum paid for the goods. Thus, the financial risk taken by the banks has been minimised (if not altogether removed). Most risks are shifted to the investor/borrower.

Observers point out that use of *mudaraba* financing has declined to almost negligible proportions. There has been a greater employment of *musharaka* techniques, but finance provided via this form of investment remains low relative to *murabaha* variants and *ijara* and other less Islamically-approved modes of financing. Such financing practices have invoked considerable hostility from Muslim scholars. A number of the critiques are reproduced below.

First, Dr Ghulam Qadir (1994, p. 105) on practices in Pakistan:

Two of the modes of financing prescribed by the State Bank, namely financing through the purchase of client's property with a buy-back agreement and sale of goods to clients on a mark-up, involved the least risk and were closest to the old interest-based operations. Hence the banks confined their operations mostly to these modes, particularly the former, after changing the simple buy-back agreement (prescribed by the State Bank) to buy-back agreement with a mark-up, as otherwise there was no incentive for them to extend any finances. The banks also reduced their mark-up-based financing, whether through the purchase of client's property or through the sale of goods to clients, to mere paper work, instead of actual buying of goods (property), taking their possession and then selling (back) to the client. As a result, there was no difference between the mark-up as practised by the banks and the conventional interest rate, and hence it was judged repugnant to Islam in the recent decision of the Federal Sharia Court.

As banks are essentially financial institutions and not trading houses, requiring them to undertake trading in the form of buy-back arrangements and sale on mark-up amounts to imposing on them a function for which they are not well equipped. Therefore, *banks in Pakistan made such modifications in the prescribed modes which defeated the very purpose of interest-free financing*. Furthermore, as these two minimum-risk modes of financing were kept open to banks, they never tried to devise innovative and imaginative modes of financing within the framework of *musharaka* and *mudaraba*.

Next, Professor Khurshid Ahmad (1994, pp. 46–7) writes:

Murabaha (cost-plus financing) and *bai'mu'ajjal* (sale with deferred payment) are permitted in the *Sharia* under certain conditions. Technically, it is not a form of financial mediation but a kind of business participation. The *Sharia* assumes that the financier actually buys the goods and then sells them to the client. Unfortunately, the current practice of 'buy-back on mark-up' is not in keeping with the conditions on which *murabaha* or *bai'mu'ajjal* are permitted. What is being done is a *fictitious deal which ensures a predetermined profit to the bank without actually dealing in goods or sharing any real risk. This is against the letter and spirit of Sharia injunctions.*

While I would not venture a *fatwa*, as I do not qualify for that function, yet as a student of economics and *Sharia* I regard this practice of 'buy-back on mark-up' very similar to *riba* and would suggest its discontinuation. I understand that the Council of Islamic Ideology has also expressed a similar opinion.

Dr Hasanuz Zaman (1994) is more critical still:

It emerges that practically it is impossible for large banks or the banking system to practise the modes like mark-up, *bai' salam*, buy-back, *murabaha*, etc. in a way that fulfils the *Shari'ah* conditions. But in order to make themselves eligible to a return on their operations, the banks are compelled to *play tricks with the letters of the law*. They actually do not buy, do not possess, do not actually sell and deliver the goods; but the transition is assumed to have taken place. By signing a number of documents of purchase, sale and transfer they might fulfil a legal requirement but *it is by violating the spirit of prohibition*. (p. 208)

Again,

> It seems that in large numbers of cases *the ghost of interest is haunting them* to calculate a fixed rate per cent per annum even in *musharaka, mudaraba,* leasing, hire-purchase, rent sharing, *murabaha, (bai' mu'ajjal,* mark-up), PTC, TFC, etc.[12] The spirit behind all these contracts seems to make a sure earning comparable with the prevalent rate of interest and, as far as possible, avoid losses which otherwise could occur. (ibid., p. 203)

He sums up in the following words:

> many techniques that the interest-free banks are practising are not either in full conformity with the spirit of *Shari'ah* or practicable in the case of large banks or the entire banking system. Moreover, *they have failed to do away with undesirable aspects of interest*. Thus, *they have retained what an Islamic bank should eliminate*. (ibid., p. 212)

In considering these criticisms, the first thing that should be resisted is the notion that the financing techniques violate the *shari'a*. While the Holy Qur'an prohibits usury, it actively encourages trade. The criticised financing methods are the principal ways by which Islamic banks finance trade. A letter of credit under the *murabaha* principle enables buyers to take delivery of goods for trading purposes, with the bank acting as intermediary (see Figure 3.2).[13] We saw earlier that financing of trade is the single largest activity of Islamic banks, constituting 32 per cent of financing. It follows that the more international the bank, and the greater is its involvement with the financing of trading and commercial activities, the larger is likely to be its usage of mark-up instruments. Similarly, the more international the region, for example the Gulf countries, the greater is likely to be the trade financing activities of the Islamic banks in the area.

Second, the mark-up technique used for trade accords with the classical principles of good banking. In the days before conventional banks began investing funds (and losing billions of depositors', shareholders', and taxpayers' money) in loans to developing countries (see Lewis and Davis, 1987) and on commercial real estate developments (Lewis, 1994, 2000), they followed a number of rules of 'sound banking'. One of these, the basis of the 'real bills doctrine' (see Mints, 1945), was the idea that banks should confine their lending to 'self-liquidating' paper. An example is the discounting of trade bills. Taking in deposits and lending against trade bills would be considered to be 'self-liquidating' on the grounds that deposits can be repaid from the receipts of the maturing loans. This is not a lot different from a *murabaha* transaction, except that the bank is in this instance buying and selling a commodity rather than a debt security, and must carry the different risks inherent in commodity markets.[14]

Third, these risks may not be very large in some cases, but our theoretical analysis in Chapter 4 concluded that PLS financing is not practicable for all economic activities, and it would appear that Islamic banks have found this out the hard way and learnt from it (Zaman, 1994). In any case, it is not really the banks' preferences which ought necessarily to count; they are acting as trustees for depositors and investing their clients' money, not that of their own shareholders. *Murabaha* is a good instrument for low-risk, low-return investors. If they are not satisfied with this pattern of returns they will make their preferences known over time by not renewing investment account balances. In the competitive environment of a mixed financial system, the return paid to depositors is a major competitive tool and an important barometer of a bank's solvency and performance. Unfortunately, PLS financing techniques do not always guarantee the banks a reliable return available for distribution to depositors.

NOTES

1. To our knowledge there is no overall study of this phenomenon. Baster (1934) examined the expansion of British banks in Turkey, Tunisia and other locations in the 'Near East'. Landes (1958) provides a colourful account of the expansion of British and French banks in Egypt. The operations of the Standard Chartered group in the Gulf in the first half of last century are examined by Wilson (1987), while the general expansion of European banks overseas in the nineteenth and twentieth centuries is studied by Born (1983).
2. These developments are outlined by Siddiqi (1980) and surveyed more recently by Gafoor (1995).
3. DMI is examined later in this chapter. The Al-Baraka Holding Company consists of the following: Al-Baraka Investment and Development Company, Saudi Arabia; Beit-et Tamwill Saudi-Tunisi, Tunis; Al-Baraka International Ltd., England; Al-Baraka International Bank Ltd., England; Al-Baraka Turkish Finance House, Turkey; Al-Baraka Islamic Investment Bank, Bahrain; Al-Baraka Islamic Bank of Mauritania; Al-Baraka Islamic Bank, Bangladesh; Al-Baraka Bancorp, Texas, USA; and Al-Baraka Bancorp, California, USA. It also has financial institutions in Djibouti, India and Pakistan.
4. Several influential and wealthy Egyptians like Osman Ahmad Osman, Ibrahim Al-'Ayuti, 'Isa Isma'il al-'Ayuti, 'Abdul 'Aziz Azzam and Yusuf Mustafa Nada, and even public bodies like the Egyptian *Awqaf* (Islamic endowments) authority had subscribed to the capital of the bank. The 49 per cent of the shares allocated to the Saudi side was subscribed to by Prince Muhammad al-Faisal, Prince Sa'ud b. Fahd, Saudi businessmen Salh Kamil, Muhammad 'Ali 'Adil Azzam, Ahmad Azmi Azzam and Tawfig al-Shawi (Saeed, 1995).
5. Profit-sharing ratios and procedures vary from country to country, and in Malaysia profits are provisionally declared on a monthly basis. BIMB aims to distribute about 70 per cent of profits to depositors and retain around 30 per cent for reserves, various fees and bonuses, and shareholders. The share devoted to depositors is divided among the different accounts according to a specific formula. The lowest weight is given to savings accounts and the highest to investment accounts. The yields on general investment accounts are dependent on the period of maturity. The distribution of profits to special investment accounts is individually negotiated with the institutions concerned.
6. Figures of financing for each region are weighted averages for the banks supplying data, the weights determined by the assets of the banks in the total for the area indicated.
7. The international banking services include foreign exchange operations, parallel purchase

and sale of currencies and commodities, transfer of funds, Islamic securities, letters of credit, pre- and post-shipment financings, letters of guarantee, Islamic syndication, leasing and collections.

8. This may have happened already. Rosly reports the following deposit returns for 1997.

Commercial banks	Al-Wadiah	Al-Mudarabah Investment Account (3 months)	Al-Mudarabah Investment Account (6 months)
Bank Islam Malaysia Berhad	4.14	5.98	6.33
Arab-Malaysian	5.50	7.23	7.27
Bank Bumiputra	5.09	7.44	7.54
Southern Bank	5.00	9.03	9.60
Hong Leong	4.25	5.43	5.74
Pacific Bank	4.08	5.74	5.84
Bank Utama	7.62	8.90	9.99

1997 was a year of higher interest rates and BIMB, which makes greater use of *murabaha* with deferred payments than the other banks, recorded lower returns – the only bank to have done so (Rosly, 1999). As a result, BIMB's investment accounts declined by 30 per cent, while those of the other interest-free banks increased by 37 per cent.

9. One interesting exception is Saudi Arabia. Despite being the home of DMI, Al-Baraka and Al-Rajhi, the Saudi Arabian Monetary Agency refuses to grant banking licences giving Islamic banks equal status with other banks. Islamic banks have nonetheless operated there for a number of years, even though they have no legal status and are unlicensed and unsupervised (El-Gamal, 1999a).

10. There are a large number of primers on interest rate risk management. Lewis (1992c) provides an overview, while Lewis and Morton (1996) give a case study of a UK retail bank. Other references are given therein.

11. For all Islamic banks reporting to IAIB on the sectoral distribution of financing, agriculture financing declined from 13.3 per cent in 1993 to 6 per cent in 1997, while the industry sector financing fell from 30 per cent in 1993 to 17 per cent in 1997.

12. PTC (participation term certificate) and TFC (term finance certificate) are two Pakistani instruments to provide long-, medium- and short-term finance. See Chapter 5 above.

13. El-Gamal (1999b) argues that the mistake made by scholars stems from the early writers in Islamic economics, who suggested that any fixed rate of return over a known time period is forbidden under the banner of *riba*.

14. There are other differences as well between *murabaha* and *riba* transactions. Homogenous things cannot be bought on *murabaha*, so that one cannot ask the bank to buy gold on deferred payments in cash as both are of the same genus, that is medium of exchange. The items need to be sufficiently heterogenous, that is a car for cash, to qualify. In addition, if the instalment payment is delayed, the bank cannot impose a mark-up on the late payment or ask the customer to pay more with the next instalment. Some scholars allow a fixed monetary penalty for late payments, for example, $x per late instalment, but the penalty should go to charity and cannot be treated as a revenue to the bank. It goes without saying that the boundary line between *murabaha* and *riba* has caused considerable trouble to the jurists.

7. Corporate governance in Islamic banking

INTRODUCTION

Previous chapters have examined the overall deposit-gathering and financing activities of Islamic banks, supplemented by case studies of operations in Iran, Sudan, Pakistan, Egypt, Malaysia, Bangladesh, Jordan and Australia (in the order discussed). This chapter provides a study of three banks in Bahrain, but within the context of the literature on corporate governance.

From the viewpoint of corporate governance, Islamic banking embodies a number of interesting features since equity participation, risk and profit-and-loss-sharing arrangements form the basis of Islamic financing. All have one essential aspect to them, in the sense that they must be real transactions and not purely financial ones, and all parties to the contracts must share in the risk of the transaction by means of profit-and-loss-sharing arrangements.

These financial arrangements imply a quite different degree of involvement, and by corollary governance structures, from the conventional model since depositors have a direct financial stake in the bank's investments and equity participations. In addition, the Islamic bank is subject to an additional layer of controls to be observed since the suitability of its investments and financing must be in strict conformity with the *shari'a* and meet the expectations of the Muslim community. For this purpose, Islamic banks employ an individual Religious Adviser and/or Board.

Our examination of these issues begins with an outline of corporate governance and governance in conventional banking. The chapter then compares the Islamic banking and financial model and its implications for governance structures with the position under conventional banking. Next, using interview and survey evidence, the chapter considers the governance structures and the role of the religious supervisory system in the actual operations of Islamic banks. The study focuses on Bahrain, which is the country with the largest number of Islamic banks and other financial institutions operating alongside conventional banking institutions.[1]

CORPORATE GOVERNANCE

Ever since Berle and Means (1933) characterised modern corporations as having a separation of ownership from control, the question of how to align the interests of owners, managers and other stakeholders in the corporate entity has been an active issue, although the expression 'corporate governance' did not come into use until relatively recently. The Cadbury Committee (1992) defined corporate governance as the system by which companies are 'directed and controlled'. Formally, 'Corporate Governance can be defined as the whole system of rights, processes and controls established internally and externally over the management of a business entity with the objective of protecting the interests of all stakeholders' (Lannoo, 1995).

This definition then begs the further question of who are those with an interest in the corporation. In the literature on corporate governance, the groups involved range from shareholders along with the Board of Directors at one end of the spectrum to all entities which have an interest in the enterprise, at the other end (Blair, 1995; Gelauff and den Broeder, 1997). These entities might include owners, managers, employees, consumers, suppliers and competitors. Sometimes, the expression 'work governance' is used to describe the relationship between management and workers, while 'contractual governance' covers the links between supplying and procuring firms, leaving the expression 'corporate governance' to refer more narrowly to the relationships between those supplying capital and finance to the firm and its management – that is, to what others (ourselves included) would prefer to call 'financial governance'. On the broader view, however, corporate governance embraces financial governance, contractual governance and work governance structures.

But, in all instances, we are dealing with the institutional arrangements and relationships through which companies and institutions are directed and controlled. According to the dominant paradigm of agency theory, governance structures are needed because the interests of principals and agents diverge. Hart (1995), for example, argues that governance structures arise whenever there is a potential agency problem, or conflict of interest, between the stakeholders which cannot be resolved through a contractual arrangement – some future actions have not been (and perhaps cannot be) specified in the initial contract. The potentiality for an agency problem is due to the process of delegation inherent in the indirect ownership of productive real assets (Lewis, 1990). While owners might prefer to manage their own companies, this is not possible because of the capital requirements of the large corporation, necessitating that equity and other funds be raised from a large number of investors.

Thus the modern corporation has many owners, and there is a separation between the ownership and managerial control of assets. This separation enables risks to be spread over a large group of shareholders when attracting equity capital, and facilitates the hiring of professional managers with more information and expertise on management issues than the ultimate owners of corporate wealth. But management might invest too much in projects that require little managerial effort or in projects that increase salaries, power and status. A major part of corporate governance is thus concerned with the design of checks and balances on management behaviour.

However, corporate governance is not only about designing control mechanisms and resolving principal–agent conflicts by keeping an agent's self-serving opportunistic behaviour in check. Corporate governance arrangements may also serve to build trust, elicit cooperation and create a shared vision amongst those involved in the firm which may prevent agency problems from arising. This outcome seems especially likely where the governance structures can build upon a set of pre-existing shared values, beliefs, concepts, traditions and moral attitudes which give those involved with the organisation a common bond, such as that which may derive from religious precepts. Here the contrast is between agency theory, which sees managers and employees as agents whose interests may diverge from those of their principals, and stewardship theory, which views them as stewards who can be motivated to act in the best interests of the principals in a spirit of partnership for the good of the firm (Davis, Schoorman and Donaldson, 1997).

Issues of stewardship and control apply not only to those who supply capital, since the entire group of interested parties or 'stakeholders' is affected to some degree by the economic performance of the company. How broad this mandate might be is illustrated by Figure 7.1. It distinguishes first between those governance structures with an internal focus (the inner circle) and those of an external character (the outer circles). Within the latter, a further distinction can be made between formal and informal relations. Informal links concern the relationship between the company and industry and society generally, while the formal relations derive from legal and contractual arrangements. Included in these in the case of financial organisations are the prudential requirements imposed by financial supervisory bodies. A further distinction can be made between the direct stakeholders (namely, shareholders, employees and those with contractual relationships) as opposed to indirect stakeholders (in other words, all other parties involved). Finally, it should be noted that in addition to laws and contracts, codes, customs, social and ethical norms of behaviour also exert a considerable influence. Indeed, corporate governance in this broad sense is embedded in the entire framework comprising the cultural identity of the society or group. This fact becomes apparent when we consider Islamic banking structures. But first we look at the conventional bank.

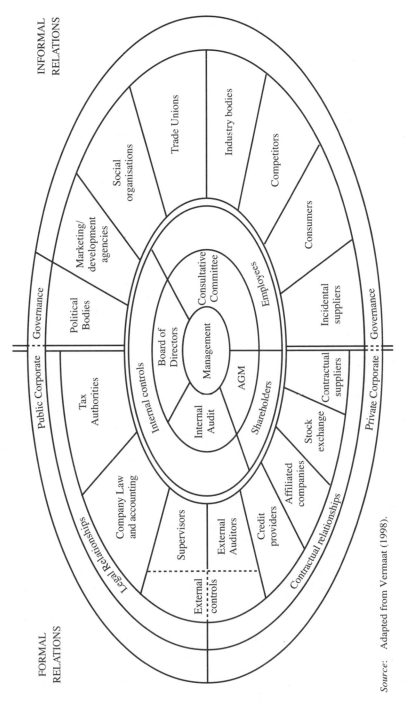

Source: Adapted from Vermaat (1998).

Figure 7.1 A taxonomy of corporate governance

161

GOVERNANCE IN A CONVENTIONAL BANK

At least four direct stakeholder groups can be identified for a bank:

- shareholders/subordinated debt holders
- depositors/creditors
- management
- government insurance agencies/supervisory bodies.

Since the *raison d'être* of a bank is the presence of heterogeneous and costly information in financial transactions, it would hardly surprise if agency problems were important in banking. Agency problems can occur when control over resources is delegated by one party (the 'principal') to another (the 'agent'), but their interests do not coincide and the principal cannot assess accurately the agent's actions and exert control over them. The information which is routinely generated by banks as part of their business activities is not readily available to those parties with an interest in the banking firm, while client confidentiality rules out the dissemination of much of the information about lending decisions and other matters. As we noted in Chapter 4, banks may be 'delegated monitors', in the description of Diamond (1984), but who monitors the monitor?

Potential agency conflicts involving depositors and shareholders and government and shareholders have been the most studied. Those between depositors and shareholders reflects the typical conflict between debt-holders and stockholders, which has been studied extensively. As Smith and Warner (1979) point out, stockholders can take decisions such as excessive dividend payouts, increased leverage (claim dilution), higher risk activities (asset substitution) which transfer wealth from bondholders to themselves. If depositors suspect that this is happening, they can discipline shareholders by withdrawing resources, but at the cost of 'bank runs' to emerge as a rational economic response (Diamond and Dybvig, 1983). In this case, governments may step in to provide depositor protection in some form or other. Explicit deposit insurance is one approach, while explicit or implicit guarantees of deposits is another. Either way, public funds are committed and there may then be an incentive for the bank's owners to take greater risks with borrowed funds, secure in the knowledge that depositors' balances are not at risk. So as to reduce this incentive, authorities may put limits on the range of activities (thereby possibly limiting the risk of the organisation), link deposit insurance premiums to risk, and tie capital adequacy requirements to business risk – thereby enforcing some element of risk-sharing between government and owners.

While such agency issues are normally considered in the context of depositors and/or government deposit insurance agencies *vis-à-vis* bank shareholders, they also seem likely to arise in the case of management and shareholders. Further, there may be a range of overlapping interests between the various groups: information required under prudential supervision may enable shareholders to monitor the behaviour of management better; enhanced shareholder monitoring may substitute for government monitoring. In fact, the position in banking is even more complex than is normally envisaged since in addition to shareholders, managers, creditors (depositors) and government there is another group of stakeholders – other banks. When one bank lends to another interbank, it is effectively adding its own capital to the capital base of the other bank in support of that bank's activities and, to that degree, sharing in the risks (Lewis, 1991).

GOVERNANCE IN THE ISLAMIC BANK

Under Islamic banking, governance issues are quite different from those above because the institution has an overriding obligation to obey a different set of rules – that of Islamic law, the *shari'a* – and generally comply with the expectations of the Muslim community by providing partnership financing on the basis of profit-and-loss-sharing (PLS) arrangements or other acceptable modes of financing. These profit-and-loss-sharing methods, in turn, imply different stakeholder relationships than under interest-based borrowing and lending.

Figure 7.2 sets out the key stakeholders in an Islamic bank. There are two major differences from the conventional framework. First, and foremost, an Islamic organisation must serve *Allah* and develop a distinctive corporate culture. Second, following on from this obligation, the bank must provide and design acceptable financial instruments and products. It is in both aspects that the concept of 'stewardship', noted earlier, is valuable for understanding the behaviour of those involved with the organisation. The Islamic concept of *amana*, or trust, signifies 'that wealth belongs to God and man is, individually and collectively, custodian of wealth' (Ali, 1999, p. 13). Wealth can only be employed for defined ends.

Corporate Culture

Hofstede (1994, p. 180) defines 'corporate culture' or 'organisational culture' as the collective programming of the mind which distinguishes the members of one organisation from another. It has been conceptualised in two fundamentally different ways (Smircich, 1983; Schreyogg, Oechsler and Wachter, 1995). The first approach regards organisational culture as part of a

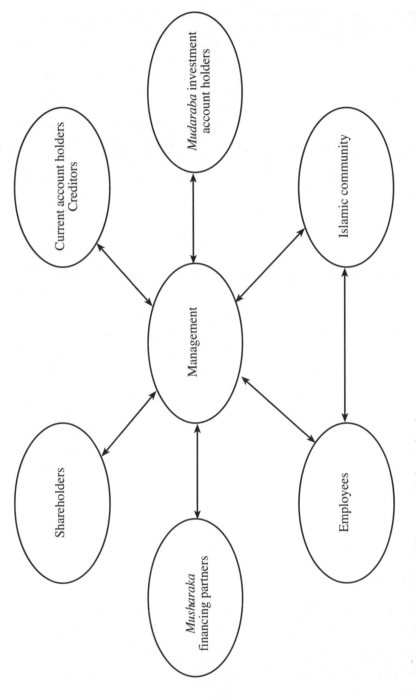

Figure 7.2   Key stakeholders in an Islamic bank

superior whole; culture is something which an organisation has or can acquire. Here, culture is seen as one of a series of variables (technology, planning and so on) which shape an organisation and the behaviour of its members. The other approach regards the organisation itself as a culture. Organisations are referred to as social constructs, as systems of shared meanings and patterns of symbolic discourse. Organisational culture is understood as a sort of language in which all organisational actions are embedded. Culture is no longer seen as an external or imposed variable, it is the basis of organisational life. Two implications of this second view are that, first, organisational culture is basically an implicit phenomenon; organisational cultures are systems of shared meanings which characterise the organisation's identity and definition of itself. Second, organisational culture is shared, that is it refers to the orientation, values, and so on that organisational members have in common. Therefore, it is a collective experience which shapes the thinking and actions of individual members.

On this second approach, any organisation, irrespective of the nature of its activities, has its culture which is shaped by and reflects that of the society of which the organisation is a structured and organised group. Organisational culture can be viewed as a pattern of assumptions including shared values, beliefs, perceptions, norms, symbols, language, rituals and myths, used by individuals and groups to act within organisations and to deal with the external environment. The culture sets out appropriate behaviour and bounds, motivates individuals and governs internal relations and values. It results in shared norms and attitudes such as dress code, business practice, and so on.

Viewed in these terms, the corporate culture of an Islamic bank should be one in which Islamic values are reflected in all facets of behaviour ranging from internal relations, dealings with customers and other banks, policies and procedures, business practices through to dress, décor, image, and so on consistent with Islam as a complete way of life. The purpose is to create a collective morality and spirituality which, when combined with the production of goods and services, sustains the growth and advancement of the Islamic way of life. To quote Janahi (1995):

> Islamic banks have a major responsibility to shoulder ... all the staff of such banks and customers dealing with them must be reformed Islamically and act within the framework of an Islamic formula, so that any person approaching an Islamic bank should be given the impression that he is entering a sacred place to perform a religious ritual, that is the use and employment of capital for what is acceptable and satisfactory to God, the Almighty. (p. 42)

There are equivalent obligations upon employees:

> The staff in an Islamic bank should, throughout their lives, be conducting in the Islamic way, whether at work or at leisure (p. 28)

Islamic banking

Further, obligations also extend to the Islamic community (the *umma*):

> Muslims who truly believe in their religion have a duty to prove, through their efforts in backing and supporting Islamic banks and financial institutions, that the Islamic economic system is an integral part of Islam and is indeed suited for all times ... through making legitimate and Halal profits. (p. 29)[2]

Financial Governance

The Islamic concept of *umma* or solidarity amongst Muslims is closely linked to that of *amana* or trust: wealth is to be acquired, used and distributed within the framework of the *shari'a*. No person has an absolute right to use his wealth as he wishes but can only use it for those purposes which are consistent with Islamic values. The same concept of *amana* also means that Islamic banks act as trustees for those investors whose funds they manage, and they have to fulfil their obligations responsibly and with due diligence.

Interest-free banking in its purest form is based on the concepts of *shirkah* (partnership) or *musharaka,* and *mudaraba* (profit-sharing). An Islamic bank is conceived as a financial intermediary mobilising savings from the public on a *mudaraba* (trustee) basis and advancing capital to entrepreneurs on a PLS partnership basis. A two-tiered profit-and-loss-sharing arrangement operates.

With *mudaraba* financing by a bank, the project is managed by the client and not by the bank, even though the bank shares the risk. Certain major decisions such as changes in the existing lines of business and the disposition of profits may be subject to the bank's consent. The bank, as a partner, has the right to full access to the books and records, and can exercise monitoring and follow-up supervision. Nevertheless, the directors and management of the company retain independence in conducting the affairs of the company.

Many of the same restrictions apply to *musharaka* financing, except that in this instance the losses are borne proportionately to the capital amounts contributed. The Islamic bank provides funds which are mingled with the funds of the business enterprise (and perhaps others). All providers of capital are entitled to participate in the management of the project, but are not necessarily required to do so and generally the bank would leave the management to the partner. Profits are distributed among the partners in pre-determined ratios (which may differ from that of losses which are borne by each partner in proportion to the contribution of capital).

These conditions give the finance many of the characteristics of non-voting equity capital. From the viewpoint of the entrepreneur, there are no fixed annual payments needed to service the debt as under interest financing, while the financing does not increase the firm's risk in the way that other borrowings do through increased leverage. Conversely, from the bank's viewpoint, the returns come from profits – much like dividends – and the bank cannot take action to foreclose on the debt should profits not eventuate.

Agency Problems

Viewed in terms of conventional banking analysis, such financing characteristics raise, at least potentially, three incentive issues. First, the absence of collateral may aggravate the adverse selection problem. 'Those borrowers who expect their projects to supply high non-monetary benefits but low realised profits will choose PLS financing because they will enjoy high total returns at an artificially low cost of capital' (Sarker, 1999a, p. 9). Second, a *mudaraba* contract will accentuate the moral hazard problem, because the bank cannot enforce upon the entrepreneur the action and effort needed for maximisation of outcome. Third, 'in PLS contracts, borrowers have every incentive to under-report or artificially reduce declared profit. They can deflate profit by taking excessive perquisites or extra leisure or resorting to accounting subterfuges' (Sarker, op. cit., p. 9). As the two quotations above show, the existence of such potential agency issues is recognised in Islamic banking circles.

Similarly, there are agency issues on the other side of the financing equation where, unlike in a conventional bank, a sharp distinction has to be drawn between current and investment accounts. Current account balances are the bank's non-contingent liability to pay on demand. Investment accounts operate under the PLS scheme – capital is not guaranteed, nor is there a predetermined return. Current account holders are akin to ordinary creditors. Holders of *mudaraba* investment accounts are closer to shareholders, at least with respect to downside risk. In the event of a loss, the *mudaraba* depositor and the bank shareholder share the loss. However, the bank (shareholders) may be held liable for losses resulting from actions that are beyond those originally provided for in the *mudaraba* investment contract.

Clearly, from the perspective of the standard theory of financial intermediation, agency issues are certainly not absent from Islamic banking. Yet to some degree, the Islamic bank providing PLS finance can borrow from the standard agency theory literature and employ various incentive systems. Among the techniques suggested in this literature, with the aim of aligning the behaviour of the agent with the interests of the principal, is the idea of offering the agent profit-related remuneration or stock options. In much the same way, an Islamic bank could adopt 'specific incentive mechanisms such as providing a stake in the ownership, linking transfer of ownership through granting bonus shares on the performances, build reserve scheme[s] to induce [people] to hold company shares and provision for profit-related pay linking with the declaration of profits, etc.' (Sarker, 1999a, p. 10).

However, it is possible to envisage interests being aligned in quite different ways. As Arrow (1974) has noted, 'trust is an important lubricant of a social system. It is extremely efficient; it saves a lot of trouble to have a fair degree of reliance on other people's word' (p. 23). What he calls the 'invisible institutions' of ethics and morality are important in reducing agency costs and transactions costs more generally. Governance itself can be viewed as a mechanism to increase trust, and the significance and rewards attached to cooperative outcomes might induce the agent to act in a principled, honest manner. One of the strands of the 'stewardship theory' concerns the role of corporate culture in eliciting appropriate responses through structures that promote cooperation rather than coercion and control. Those who identify with the organisation's mission, vision and objectives are more likely to act as stewards and custodians. These are the very circumstances in which the special nature of the governance structures of the Islamic bank come into play.

Governance Structures

When examining governance structures, it is useful to begin with the distinction made in Figure 7.1 between the processes of internal regulation and those of external regulation. The latter include the external audit function along with the associated reporting requirements under company law and accounting codes of best practice, as well as the actions of shareholders and the role of the Stock Exchange. Internal regulation encompasses the activities and functions of boards of directors, non-executive directors, the audit committee and the internal audit. These must be supplemented by internal control systems which have the objective of ensuring the reliability of financial reporting, compliance with relevant laws and regulations, along with the efficiency of operations.

These structures are depicted in Figure 7.3, along with some very important additions for an Islamic bank relating to the process of *shari'a* supervision. Islamic banks employ eminent scholars of Islamic law, usually on an advisory or consultancy basis, in order to ensure that the day-to-day policies and activities of the bank are in accordance with the *shari'a*. In some banks, such as the Jordan Islamic Bank, there is only one religious consultant. In many others, like the Faisal Islamic Bank of Egypt, the advisers constitute a separate Supervisory Board (something along the lines of the two-tiered Board structure in Germany, although the composition and purpose obviously differ).[3]

Thus, central to the framework of corporate governance for an Islamic Bank is the *Shari'a* Supervisory Board (SSB) and the internal controls which support it. The SSB is vital for two reasons. First, those who deal with an Islamic bank require assurance that it is transacting in accordance with Islamic law. Should the SSB report that the management of the bank has violated the

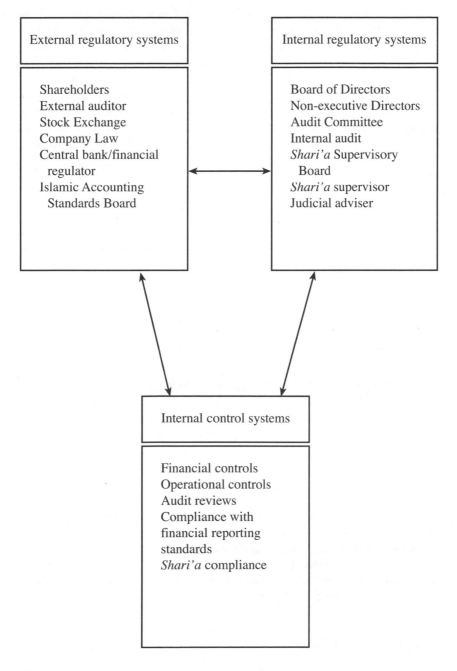

Figure 7.3   Corporate governance in an Islamic bank

shari'a, the bank would quickly lose the confidence of the majority of its investors and clients. Second, some Islamic scholars argue that strict Islamic religious principles will act as a counter to the incentive problems outlined earlier (Haque and Mirakhor, 1986). Muslims believe in a hereafter in which honesty is rewarded and dishonesty is punished. Membership of the *umma* creates rights and duties. Solidarity is the basis of the Islamic social order and the argument is that the Islamic moral code will prevent Muslims from behaving in ways which are ethically unsound, so minimising the transaction costs arising from incentive issues. In effect, Islamic religious ideology acts as its own incentive mechanism to reduce the inefficiency that arises from asymmetric information and moral hazard.

> Islamic banking has an intrinsic advantage in this [ethics] since Islam, through the *Shari'a,* encourages and compels the industry to engage in and facilitate trade that is socially, morally and ethically responsible. It is all the more imperative in light of all these developments, that Islamic banking practitioners now take a more proactive position in the area of promoting the practice of ethical behaviour. (Ayoub-Bey, 1999, p. 14)

Such matters are obviously basic to the successful operation of Islamic modes of finance, and they are assessed in the next section when we examine Islamic banking in practice.

FINANCIAL GOVERNANCE IN BAHRAIN

In this section we analyse the operations of three Islamic banks in Bahrain. Our other cases dealt with banks operating in national financial systems, Egypt, Malaysia, Bangladesh and Jordan. Bahrain is a very different type of economy and financial market, at a quite different stage of development. Altogether, Bahrain – with a population of only 538 085 inhabitants – has 19 full commercial banks, 7 incorporated in Bahrain and the rest branches of foreign banks. There are 47 offshore banks operating offshore banking units (OBUs), along with 23 investment banks licensed to carry out investment business. Add to these 40 representative offices, 5 money market brokers, 27 licensed money changers, 15 insurance companies and two specialised banks, and it is obvious that Bahrain has a large and very international financial system. The operations of Islamic banks in this very different environment offers something of a contrast to the earlier analysis.

Islamic Banks in Bahrain

This country has established itself not only as a leading regional and international centre for conventional commercial banking and financial activities, but also for Islamic banking operations. It now hosts over 30 Islamic financial institutions dealing in diversified activities including commercial banking, investment banking, offshore banking, funds management, and Islamic insurance. An interesting addition is Citi Islamic Investment Bank, incorporated in 1996 in Bahrain as a wholly owned subsidiary of Citicorp. This is the first Islamic bank established by a major international bank as a dedicated and separately capitalised subsidiary.

Bahrain is also of interest because it aims to be the main global centre for Islamic banking and finance (Algaoud and Lewis, 1997). It has been able to attract a relatively large number of banks to its shores due to its strategic geographical position in the heart of the Gulf region. Besides, Bahrain has an advanced infrastructure such as its excellent telecommunications facilities, while possessing the supporting services and professional capabilities that provide the country with a conducive banking environment. These characteristics make Bahrain well qualified to become a convenient base for Islamic banks since it can put at their disposal a wide range of available resources and facilities. Already, Bahrain hosts the Accounting and Auditing Organisation for Islamic Financial Institutions, which was established as a private board in Bahrain in 1991. In addition, the Bahrain Institute of Banking and Financial Studies provides training courses in Islamic Banking.

The banks chosen for case studies are the two Islamic institutions in Bahrain with a commercial banking licence, the Bahrain Islamic Bank (BIB) and the Faisal Islamic Bank of Bahrain (FIBB), along with an Islamic investment bank, Al-Baraka Islamic Investment Bank (AIIB). These three banks offer something of a contrast. BIB was established in 1979 as the first Islamic bank incorporated in Bahrain and the third such bank in the Gulf area. The two other banks are subsidiaries of the two large Islamic holding companies – the DMI group and the Al-Baraka group respectively. Incorporated in 1982, FIBB was one of the first subsidiaries of the DMI group, which was itself formed in 1981 and operates an extensive network of subsidiaries and related companies spread all over the world. FIBB now holds a full commercial banking licence, and is the only Islamic bank with overseas operations, having a subsidiary in Karachi and 11 branches in Pakistan. A merger of FIBB with the Islamic Investment Company of the Gulf (Bahrain), a sister company of the DMI group, created in 2000 the Shamil Bank of Bahrain (Islamic Bankers). The other Islamic holding company – the Al-Baraka group – was established in 1983 and its subsidiary AIIB is licensed as an offshore Islamic investment bank in Bahrain.

Two sets of written surveys and in-depth follow-up structured interviews were held with senior management at the institutions: one in September 1996 and the other in March 1997. The first focused on the banks' financial operations generally and their financial stewardship, and was supplemented with financial data and balance sheet information. The second set of questionnaires and interviews focused specifically on the nature of the *shari'a* supervision, and associated related policies, in each of the banks.

Financial Operations

The banks' financial operations shape the nature of stakeholder relationships. We have noted, for example, that contractual arrangements and custodianship requirements differ as between current accounts and the *mudaraba* investment account, where the banks act as trustees for those investors whose funds they manage. At one extreme, the Islamic bank could conceivably raise funds entirely by means of individual unrestricted *mudarabas* with depositors and channel these resources into *musharakas* and *mudarabas* with entrepreneurs – the two-tiered PLS system. At the other extreme, the Islamic institution could to all appearances look like a conventional bank, investing savings deposits into, say, leasing-type financing. Risk factors would differ markedly between the two situations. In fact, as we shall see, a direct hybrid of these two polar positions more or less seems to be the norm.

Tables 7.1–7.3 compare aspects of the operations of the banks. The first of these tables provides a comparison of the three in terms of assets, Islamic financing operations, liquidity, deposits, shareholders' funds, income and earnings. Investment accounts are treated differently in the banks' accounting and the table is structured to allow for these different approaches. BIB includes *mudaraba* investment accounts along with current accounts (demand deposits, cheque accounts, savings accounts), whereas FIBB argues that the fiduciary nature of these accounts makes them equivalent to private investment portfolios and they are accordingly maintained separate from the bank's own capital, current accounts and other non-fiduciary elements.

AIIB takes a middle course between these two positions and divides *mudaraba* investment accounts into two categories. Joint investment accounts are included in the balance sheet along with current accounts, while specific *mudaraba* investment accounts are treated as 'funds under management' and put with commitments and contingent liabilities. The interviews revealed that funds in the former and returns on the investments are pooled, and the profit-sharing ratio applied for calculating returns is governed by the term of the investment in the pooled fund. Specific investment accounts, by contrast, are invested entirely in specific businesses or investment transactions, and the minimum amount for opening such accounts is presently US$500 000. Profits are distributed when the specific investment matures.

In distributing profits between the bank and its depositors, two methods are

Table 7.1   Comparison of financial position of Faisal Islamic Bank, Bahrain Islamic Bank and Al-Baraka Investment Bank, 1997 (millions of US dollars)[1,2]

	FIBB		BIB		AIIB	
Assets		2109.8		404.0		355.8
Related to equity/others	356.0		392.3		155.6	
Funds under management[3]	1260.5		–		81.4	
Contra accounts[4]	493.3		11.7		118.8	
Islamic financing		982.2		359.9		203.0
Murabaha	708.7		338.0		169.2	
Ijara	107.5		–		4.2	
Musharaka	1.9		16.1		17.1	
Mudaraba	–		–		3.2	
Qard Hasan	–		0.3		–	
Islamic securities	164.1		5.5		9.3	
Liquidity		317.5		14.2		22.7
Cash and balances	27.3		13.6		14.2	
Short-term liquid funds	290.2		0.6		8.5	
Deposits		1331.2		345.5		170.8
Current accounts	70.7		25.3		11.7	
Mudaraba investment accounts	859.9		320.2		73.1	
Private investment portfolio	400.6		n.a.		81.4	
Shareholders' funds		116.3		38.2		56.8
Authorised share capital	200.0		61.0		200.0	
Issued and fully paid	100.0		30.5		50.0	
Reserves	16.3		7.7		6.8	
Net income		13.9		4.3		4.1
Gross income	53.1		23.0		14.2	
Expenses, taxes, provisions etc.	39.2		18.7		10.1	
Return on equity		11.9%		11.2%		7.2%

Notes:

1   Balance sheet date of 7 May, 1997 for Bahrain Islamic Bank, 31 December, 1996 for Faisal Islamic Bank and Al-Baraka Investment Bank.
2   Converted from Bahraini Dinars at the rate US$0.377.
3   Funds deposited with Faisal Islamic Bank for investment purposes and managed by the bank on a fiduciary basis are maintained separate from the bank's own capital and deposits treated as the bank's liability.
4   Commitments related to letters of credit and guarantees.

Source: Faisal Islamic Bank, Bahrain Islamic Bank and Al-Baraka Investment Bank.

available: (a) the invested amount is charged with all expenses and then the net amount is divided between the depositor and the bank in accordance with agreed proportions; (b) the profit is divided according to agreed proportions and then the expenses are charged to the bank's share. AIIB, in common with the rest of the Al-Baraka Group uses the second procedure, on the grounds that, in this way, the bank is given an incentive to look closely at expenditure, which it might not do if the expenses were charged to the common profit.

Islamic financing constitutes almost 90 per cent of the assets of BIB, 57 per cent of the assets of AIIB and 47 per cent of the assets of FIBB. The latter has an extensive Islamic leasing portfolio (*ijara*). This particular mode of financing is one of the specialities of the DMI group, which undertakes leasing activities in both Muslim and non-Muslim countries. The Al-Baraka group specialises in inventory financing on a global basis, and nearly 40 per cent of the Islamic financing of AIIB consists of commodity *murabaha* financing.

Table 7.2 shows the geographic distribution and industry allocation of the assets and liabilities of the two banks for which comparable data are available. BIB draws all of its liabilities from the Middle East, and attracts funding

Table 7.2   Geographic distribution and industry distribution of assets and liabilities of Faisal Islamic Bank and Bahrain Islamic Bank, 1997 (per cent of total)

	Faisal Islamic Bank		Bahrain Islamic Bank	
	Assets	Liabilities	Assets	Liabilities
Geographic region				
Europe	} 8.3	} 1.5	4.1	
North America			3.7	
Middle East	49.6	57.5	89.2	100.0
Asia	42.1	41.0	3.0	
Industry sector				
Trade and manufacturing	19.0	8.7	6.9	36.6
Banks and financial institutions	65.3	61.4	71.4	14.9
Other	15.7	29.9	21.7	48.5
	100.0	100.0	100.0	100.0

Source: Faisal Islamic Bank and Bahrain Islamic Bank.

extensively from the personal sector. FIBB raises funds from a number of regions and has extensive links with other banks. This bank pioneered Islamic syndications, and has been active as a lead agent with major Islamic financial institutions, regional banks and conventional banks participating. Syndication has been applied to *murabaha* and *ijara* lease financing transactions.

Finally, Table 7.3 focuses on profitability and gives the ROE of the two quoted Islamic banks relative to four Bahraini-based commercial banks and eight offshore or investment banks. Both Islamic banks have generally had ROE's in double figures and earnings are relatively stable *vis-à-vis* the others included in the sample.

Interviews with Banks

As noted, interviews were conducted with executive vice-presidents of the three banks on two separate occasions, supplementing written responses and other materials. The first set of interviews included questions about the banks' overall strategies and their investment policies. All three banks volunteered a strong customer orientation and emphasised the range of specialised services, and the extension of them, consistent with customer needs and *shari'a* principles. There are probably two good reasons for this approach. Many of those depositing funds with Islamic banks are strongly committed to *shari'a* principles, and the competitive advantage of an Islamic bank over a conventional bank lies in meeting these expectations with a wide range of products which are acceptable to those engaged in the profit-and-loss-sharing arrangements. In addition, an Islamic bank is subject to a layer of corporate governance from which a conventional bank is exempt, since the investments and financing undertaken must be in strict conformity with Islamic law. This latter relationship formed the basis of the second set of interviews.

It is apparent from the data in Table 7.1 that the great bulk of funds are raised via individual *mudarabas*. Liabilities under PLS-type arrangements constitute 95 per cent of total deposits for FIBB, 93 per cent for BIB and 90 per cent for AIIB. The market niche targeted by both group banks is that of individual Islamic investors of high net worth status, principally from Saudi Arabia but also from Bahrain and the Gulf region generally, along with Pakistan, Indonesia and Bangladesh. Institutions are also of importance as a source of deposits (Table 7.2). Here other Islamic institutions invest funds with third parties, using FIBB or AIIB as their agent (*mudarib*). Returns paid on investment accounts or funds under management primarily are measured against those paid by other Islamic banks. Because of the importance of foreign currency accounts, attention was also paid to LIBOR, with one bank seeking an average rate of return of 2 per cent over LIBOR. BIB, by contrast, focuses most directly on the Bahrain market, where its market share of

Table 7.3 Return on equity (ROE) of selected banks (per cent)

Company Name	1991	1992	1993	1994	1995	1996	1997
Islamic banks							
Bahrain Islamic Bank	10.69	11.17	9.81	10.00	10.74	11.46	11.18
Faisal Islamic Bank of Bahrain	14.74	13.93	13.00	17.33	12.53	11.94	14.45
Banks sector							
National Bank of Bahrain	13.67	14.81	18.77	13.75	11.51	14.65	15.73
Bank of Bahrain & Kuwait	26.41	13.48	14.00	10.20	11.17	12.51	31.76
Al-Ahli Commercial Bank	19.26	11.82	18.03	14.20	14.64	15.14	15.08
The Bahraini Saudi Bank	6.87	7.72	11.24	11.32	10.96	11.50	11.89
Banks and investment sector							
Arab Banking Corporation	3.19	5.57	9.42	7.38	7.53	7.79	8.43
United Gulf Bank	9.77	6.66	8.84	4.89	7.04	7.11	9.89
Bahrain International Bank	6.54	7.20	7.94	8.74	9.59	10.85	14.10
Investcorp Bank	18.79	19.42	18.05	12.55	15.32	17.52	18.37
Bank of Bahrain & Middle East	1.45	−22.43	6.80	3.05	5.68	8.89	15.64
Bahrain Commercial Facilities Co.	11.89	15.27	9.91	9.27	3.79	6.84	11.40
United Gulf Industries Corp.	4.77	3.22	1.43	−4.74	0.70	1.28	n.a
Taib Bank	3.65	4.35	6.49	9.58	9.31	9.64	6.69

Source: Bahrain Stock Exchange

deposits has increased steadily, and is presently about 5.5 per cent. Returns on deposits are broadly comparable with those offered by the conventional banks, and this relationship is used as a marketing tool.

Turning now to investment policies, the three banks identified trade finance and commodity finance as the principal categories. In fact, two of them aimed at having around 70–80 per cent of Islamic financing in terms of short-term (up to 2 years) trade-related financial transactions covering import–export and commodity *murabahas*, where a customer wishing to purchase equipment or goods requests the bank to purchase them on his behalf and sell them to the client on a cost-plus basis. Profit margins (mark-ups) reflect the interplay of market prices and, notably, the need for returns on investment accounts to be competitive with those of conventional banks and other Islamic banks. In addition, the banks initiate and participate in syndicated transactions and international commodity trading and leasing operations. Real estate developments are undertaken jointly with the client, with the bank's own resources under supervision and management (for example *musharakas*). Only AIIB has *mudaraba* investments (1.6 per cent of Islamic financing), while *musharakas* represent 8.4 per cent of Islamic financing for AIIB, 4.5 per cent for BIB, and less than 1 per cent for FIBB.

Much the same pattern of intermediation can be observed for other Islamic banks in other countries that we (in the previous chapter) and others[4] have studied. On the liabilities side, Islamic banks have been successful in attracting funds on a PLS basis. But the same degree of transformation to PLS financing has not occurred on the asset side of the balance sheet. For this lack they have been strongly criticised. A number of scholars (for example, Qadir, 1994; Ahmad, 1994 and Zaman, 1994) have denounced the *murabaha* mark-up and buy-back schemes as effectively interest-based lending under another name (see Chapter 6). Kuran (1995) contends that the banks are aping interest-rate remuneration on their investment accounts as well.

Of course, perhaps the pressure to match conventional banks' deposit rates has encouraged the development of mark-up financing modes. Or, perhaps the spread of mark-up financing results in interest equivalent returns on deposits. Doubtless there is some truth in both. From the viewpoint of depositors, we have described their unique status under trustee investment accounts as the equivalent of non-voting shareholders, sharing in the profits and losses of the bank, but unable to influence the banks' investment policies except by 'voting with their feet' when invested funds are due to be rolled over. Two implications ought to follow from this position: other things equal, investors might be expected to demand higher returns from an Islamic bank to compensate for the greater risk, while full shareholders would accept lower returns because their investment risk is being shared with the investors. However, other things may not be equal and in particular Islamic banks, aware of their fiduciary responsibilities and stewardship under *amana*, may have chosen a low-risk portfolio. Certainly, for example, Al-Baraka boasts that its depositors have not lost on any investment since formation in 1982.[5]

For their part, the Islamic banks reject the charge that mark-up is merely *riba* in another guise. They argue that even if the predetermined mark-up was the same as the prevailing interest rate, there is one difference between the *murabaha* contract and interest lending: ownership of the item concerned is transferred to the bank which must bear the risks (breakage, theft, fire) entailed. The banks interviewed also raised some practical concerns about *mudaraba* and *musharaka* contracting. While they recognise that these modes of financing are the most *shari'a* acceptable, they pose special problems because of the high risk and the long waiting period for returns in comparison with *murabahas,* which (using our terminology) are mostly 'self-liquidating', in terms of classical banking principles, within one year. Assignment of profit or loss to individual credit lines, as required under *mudaraba* and *musharaka* financing is extremely difficult for large corporate entities, where joint costs have to be allocated across a number of activities. This fact, the bankers argue, makes the financing techniques more suited for venture capital-type investments than for the great bulk of bank financing.

It is also important to understand the nature of the banks' operations in Bahrain. None of the banks has a large staff. Total employment in BIB is about 110, of which 90 per cent is Bahraini and 10 per cent is foreign. AIIB has 35 employees in all, while FIBB has a staffing of around 90 which includes the offshore unit (head office), the commercial branches in Bahrain, and marketing offices in Saudi Arabia. These staff levels reflect the international/ private banking/wholesale/investment banking character of the operations of these two group institutions. The international character of their activities not only biases financing towards trade and services provided to other institutions, but internationality creates an extra dimension of riskiness, with funds being raised in one jurisdiction and used for financing in others creating additional problems of moral hazard due to the difficulty of monitoring cross-border actions.

Equity-type participations are being sought by other means, and the two group banks in particular engage in capital market activities in a variety of countries (including Bahrain).[6] But, for the time being, it would seem that it has not been possible to develop a system of PLS contracts between the lender (the bank) and the entrepreneur that can keep monitoring costs at a reasonable level and eliminate the moral hazard issues which arise when the parties have asymmetric information on the prospects and outcomes of an investment venture. In their absence, Islamic banks have felt obliged to restrict the use of *mudaraba* and *musharaka* contracts and instead provide funds by using other available financial instruments, such as *murabaha* and *ijira* where incentive problems are less serious.

These other financial instruments must still satisfy the Islamic code of conduct, and here we turn to the role of *shari'a* supervision and other regulatory constraints peculiar to the operations of Islamic banks. These issues were covered in the second round of interviews.

SHARI'A SUPERVISION

In order to ensure strict adherence to the *shari'a*, each of the banks maintains a comprehensive system of controls, based around the *Shari'a* Supervisory Board (SSB). Banaga, Ray and Tomkins (1994, pp. 10–11) list the functions of the SSB as:

- Answering the enquiries that come from the community at large.
- Issuing formal legal opinions according to the Islamic law (*Fatawa*) and enquiries submitted by bank management or any other interested party.
- Reviewing and revising all the dealings and transactions which the bank enters into with clients so as to ensure that these agree with *shari'a*. If any deals or transactions contradict *shari'a* principles, such transactions would not be approved.
- Reviewing researches on any particular subject and issuing their opinion.
- Holding regular meetings to discuss all enquiries received. The minutes of these meetings are usually recorded.
- Receiving enquiries from the management or others and presenting them to the Board of Directors.
- Preparing draft opinions and delivering them to all those who are concerned.
- Issuing opinions in final form if the Board does not have any second opinion on the subject.
- Preparing contracts in collaboration with the legal adviser of the bank.
- Participating in the preparation of drafts of decrees, decisions and orders presented by the bank, and preparing explanatory notes thereto.
- Preparing the studies and researches required to direct the *zakat* resources towards the deserving parties and determining the rate or the percentage that in the light of the *shari'a* rules could be invested from the resources of the *zakat*.
- Carrying out the technical review and follow up to make sure that the

shari'a controls are implemented by the bank, its branches and its affiliated companies.

Figure 7.4 compares the structure of *shari'a* supervision across the three banks. In BIB, the SSB comprises four scholars representing the main schools of thought. In addition, BIB employs a qualified religious supervisor (RS) as an in-house supervisor, reporting both to the SSB and to the general manager. So there are two levels of religious supervision in the bank. The highest level is the SSB involved in product design and inspection of the bank's operational activities and all other issues relevant to *shari'a* supervision. The second level is the in-house RS who practises his responsibilities through regular perusal of

	FIBB	BIB	AIIB
Group level	Group SSB		
Bank level	SSB	SSB	SSB
In-house supervisor	SSB member		
		RS	AGM (operations)
Compliance function	Control Division member		

Figure 7.4   Shari'a *supervision in three banks*

all new contracts on a daily basis to ensure compliance with the *shari'a*. A random sampling method is adopted for checking old contracts. The RS makes most necessary corrections for deducted errors and prior violations at the time of the inspection.

AIIB also has a two-tiered structure of compliance. Its SSB meets at least four times a year to review the contracts, documentation and deals of the bank. The Board is involved in product design and new operations and activities where it often suggests alternative ways of doing things. In fact the SSB sometimes interferes in the allocation of assets, investments and products, that is to avoid concentration of risk. In addition, the bank's AGM (Operations and Administration) acts as a secretary to the SSB. He works as liaison between the SSB and the bank to ensure compliance and to put in place an awareness amongst staff of *shari'a* obligations.

In FIBB, there are three levels of supervision. Like the other banks, the SSB monitors and checks the bank's operations, and all new activities require its prior approval. Board members are drawn from five different countries. In a second layer, one of the SSB members is deputised to undertake field inspections of the bank's operations. The third layer comes from within the bank. One of the members of the Control Division conducts a separate audit of operations for all types of investments. In fact, there is really a fourth level, since the SSB for the DMI Group as a whole provides advice from time to time.

All of the SSBs conduct an annual review and issue an annual report to shareholders and investors in which they must indicate whether they are satisfied with the investment activities, projects handled and contract documentation of the bank. Usually at this time, the SSB oversees the collection of the *zakat* and its distribution to deserving parties.

A common approach operates across the banks for breaches of *shari'a*. When the SSB feels that a transaction may not accord fully with, or be in breach of, the *shari'a* the following steps are taken:

1. Finding alternative ways to make the transaction accord with *shari'a*.
2. If no alternative suggestions can be made, the transaction is not processed.
3. If, however, the transaction has been executed and later on it is discovered that it has violated *shari'a*, the SSB puts its qualified opinion to shareholders and the management makes steps to take out the income generated from that transaction from the income account and have it distributed to a charity account. There is thus a potential financial penalty for non-compliance as well as adverse publicity.

While in these ways broadly similar supervisory procedures operate in the banks, this does not mean that they will reach identical solutions. The SSBs 'are guided by their moral beliefs and obligations to religious peers and community' (Karim, 1990, p. 39), and inevitably scholars and Boards may interpret the matters differently. For example, there are still questions about the Islamic acceptability of *murabaha*, as noted earlier. This mode also raises a number of conceptual issues, such as at what point the property title passes to the customer. Also, *murabaha* principles allow the customer to refuse to purchase the goods financed if, because of subsequent market conditions, it may result in a loss. In this circumstance, the unsold goods are the bank's risk. But not all banks follow this edict (Banaga, Ray and Tomkins, 1994).[7]

It was in order to resolve some of these questions that the Accounting and Auditing Organisation for Islamic Financial Institutions (AAOIF) was established in Bahrain. Initially, it concentrated on defining Islamic financial instruments and fashioning standards for their accounting. In 1999, this organisation set up a 15 member Central *Shari'ah* Board with the aim of harmonising and converging concepts and their application amongst the SSBs of Islamic financial institutions. The objective is to avoid inconsistencies between the individual boards and assist with developing new products.[8]

Finally, we note that most of the governance structures in place for a conventional bank apply also to the Islamic counterpart. Here we refer to company law, the stock exchange and financial regulation. One issue concerns the role of the external auditor *vis-à-vis* the SSB.[9] Some contend that the external auditor is not qualified to contribute to religious supervision. Others argue that they are required to do so, since adherence to the *shari'a* is included in the bank's Memorandum of Agreement and Articles of Association, which the auditor must uphold. Amongst the banks studied here, there is no formal interaction between the SSBs and the external auditors. However, as one of them observed:

> The auditors of Islamic Banks usually tend to know obvious *shari'a* breaches, hence they do require a *shari'a* clearance on those transactions before finalisation of the financials.[10]

CONCLUSION

Corporate governance structures assume considerable significance for an Islamic bank. This system of banking revolves around the substitution of profit-and-loss-sharing principles for interest-based borrowing and lending activities. Instead of charging or paying *riba* (interest), Islamic banks invest predominantly by engaging in trade and industry, directly or in partnership with others, and sharing the profits. The partnership arrangements have the potential to give rise to severe agency problems. Moreover, the profit-sharing contract cannot allow for events expected to take place in the future.

Covenants, collateral and other incentive-compatible devices employed in conventional financing are prohibited. These conditions, we argue, have the effect of converting what would otherwise be debt into the equivalent of non-voting equity capital.

Despite these apparent handicaps, strong growth in a large number of countries shows that Islamic banking is clearly feasible, and can operate successfully. How does the Islamic bank succeed in overcoming the difficulties? Based on the study of banks in Bahrain we conclude that two factors have been significant. One is the adoption of contracting modes and engaging in activities which promise adequate returns while mitigating the risks to financing partners and other stakeholders. The other is strict adherence to Islam, achieved by means of a special supervisory Board, in-house judicial advisers and compliance officers. This extra layer of corporate governance applying to Islamic banks is essential for retaining the confidence of depositors and investors seeking the 'fairness' inherent in the Islamic financial relationships.

The Islamic community has always relied on voluntary compliance by Muslims with the injunctions in the Holy Qur'an against usury (*riba*). Islamic banks, as we have seen, have cooperated with religious bodies and relied on educational campaigns to encourage adherents to use the interest-free banking facilities that they provide. But then it has been left to the individual's conscience. This is in marked contrast with Christianity in enforcing its ban on usury. We now examine these different experiences.

NOTES

1. This chapter draws on Algaoud and Lewis (1997, 1999).
2. This treatise, first published in 1990, is distributed by the Bahrain Islamic Bank.
3. In Germany and other European countries such as Austria and the Netherlands, there is an executive Board of Directors and a separate supervisory Board, the latter comprising outside experts and employee representatives. See Lewis (1999b) for a comparison of the arrangements for corporate governance in a number of countries.
4. For example, based on an examination of Islamic banks in Pakistan, Iran and Dubai, Saeed (1996) notes a general pattern that approximately 75 per cent of assets constitute short-term *murabaha* financing. The Dubai Islamic Bank in 1989 had 3 per cent of 'investments' in *mudaraba* and *musharaka* financing.
5. As in conventional banking markets, there is also the question of whether there would be implicit state support should a prominent Islamic bank get into serious trouble. Many were established with the encouragement of government and religious bodies, and prominent members of ruling families feature as shareholders and Board members.
6. In Bahrain, BIB founded the Bahrain Islamic Investment Company, the DMI group has the Faisal Investment Bank of Bahrain, Islamic Investment Company of the Gulf (Bahrain), Islamic Leasing Company Bahrain, while Al-Baraka has the Al-Tawfeek Company for the Investment of Funds and the Al-Amin Securities Company.
7. This is in fact the opposite of the scenario suggested by Saeed (1996, p. 116), who criticises the Boards for unduly moulding solutions suggested by management.

8. Reported in *New Horizon*, February 1999, p. 2.
9. Hood and Bucheery (1999) investigate this 'audit gap' and consider five different possibilities in terms of the interrelationship of the religious and financial auditors, namely no interaction, minimum interaction, financial auditor in control, religious auditor in control and cooperation (with independence). They, and the majority of the respondents to their survey, favoured the last scenario.
10. As recorded in conversation during an interview.

8.   Islamic and Christian attitudes to usury

THE LESSONS OF HISTORY

Islam is the only major religion which maintains a prohibition on usury. Yet, it was not always so. In Ancient India, laws based on the Veda, the oldest scriptures of Hinduism, condemned usury as a major sin and restricted the operation of interest rates (Gopal, 1935; Rangaswami, 1927).[1] In Judaism, the Torah (the Hebrew name of the Law of Moses or the Pentateuch, the first five books of the Old Testament) prohibited usury amongst the Jews, while at least one authority sees in the Talmud (the Oral Law which supplements the Written Scriptures for orthodox Jews) a consistent bias against 'the appearance of usury or profit' (Neusner, 1990). Under Christianity, prohibitions or severe restrictions upon usury operated for over 1400 years. Generally, these controls meant that any taking of interest was forbidden. But gradually only exorbitant interest came to be considered usurious, and in this particular form usury laws of some sort preventing excessive interest remain in force today in many Western countries (and some Muslim ones).

This chapter examines the attitudes of the Christian Church to usury, and compares Christian doctrine and practice with the Islamic position.[2] Our major focus naturally will be upon the medieval Christian Church. The Middle Ages usually refers to the period in Europe, between the disintegration of the Western Roman Empire in 476 CE and the onset of the Italian Renaissance, and covering an area stretching from Sweden to the Mediterranean. This was the period when the Church had vast secular and religious authority and was a universal and unifying force across Christian countries much like Islam is today amongst Muslims. For our purposes, we need to extend the analysis to at least the sixteenth century, for the great medieval unity of Christendom – and its views on usury – went largely unchallenged until the Protestant Reformation and the rise of Calvinism.

The Islamic ban on usury rests on the unparalleled authority of the Holy Qur'an in which the prohibition is frequently and clearly enunciated. What was the authority for the Christian opposition to usury? What rationale was provided by the clerical authorities? How do these compare with those of Islamic jurists? How was the Christian ban enforced? Was it honoured more in the breach than in the practice? What devices were used to avoid the ban? Why did the Christian

Church remove the prohibitions upon usury? Are there lessons for Islamic countries from the Christian experience? These are some of the questions we shall endeavour to answer. One interesting finding that we unearth is that some of the devices used by Christians in response to the prohibition were remarkably similar to financing instruments used by Islamic banks today.

FOUNDATIONS OF THE CHRISTIAN POSITION

To medieval Christians, the taking of what we would now call interest was usury, and usury was a sin, condemned in the strongest terms. For Muslims, the prohibition on *riba* in the Holy Qur'an is equally clear-cut. English versions of the Holy Qur'an translate the Arabic word *riba* as interest or usury.[3] On the face of it, the Islamic position on usury would seem to be little different from the official Christian position in the Middle Ages.

While this parallel is essentially correct, the process of getting there is greatly complicated by the origins of the words themselves. Interest derives from the medieval Latin word *interesse*. Usury comes from the Latin word *usura*. The problem is that theologians and ecclesiastical law treated the two as different in kind. In particular, *interesse* was permitted and *usura* was forbidden (Nelson, 1949, p. 17). *Usura*, meaning enjoyment, denoted money paid for the use of money, and under canonical law meant the intention of the lender to obtain more in return from a loan than the principal amount due. It equates to what we would today call interest, measured by the difference between the amount that a borrower repays and the principal amount that is originally received from the lender (Patinkin, 1968). Both usury and interest also correspond to *riba* which as we have seen literally means 'increase' or in excess of the original sum.

Medieval canon law thus prohibited payment for the use of a loan, which (following Roman law) it called *usura*. But while a person was prevented from charging money for a loan, he could demand compensation – *damna et interesse* – if he was not repaid on time. *Interesse* referred to the compensation made by a debtor to a creditor for damages caused to the creditor as a result of default or delays in the repayment of the principal, corresponding to any loss incurred or gain foregone on the creditor's part.[4] Because such *interesse* was lawful and conceptually distinct from unlawful *usura*, it is easy to understand why the term 'interest' has come to be universally adopted in post-medieval societies, and also why in the Middle Ages creditors had a strong incentive to seek to disguise usury as *interesse* and accordingly not fall foul of the Church.

What was the authority for the Church's rulings on these matters? It needs to be recalled that the Church was the single most powerful institution of the

Middle Ages, and held sway over people's lives by a combination of secular and spiritual power. Its land holdings made it the greatest of the feudal lords, and its estates were the source of much economic production and consumption. In addition, the Church had a doctrinal unity and claimed command over the totality of human relations. Like Islam today, Christianity then was not just a religion, but a way of life governing both conduct on earth and spiritual salvation in the other world.

Christian doctrine derived from three basic sources. First, there were the scriptures, especially the Gospels and the teachings of Jesus. Second, as the Middle Ages progressed and the Church became increasingly institutionalised, the words of Jesus were not sufficient to cover all eventualities and were supplemented, and to a large degree supplanted, by canon law based on the rulings of ecumenical councils and Church courts. Third, schoolmen and theologians laid the foundations of Christian theology, drawing on ethical principles developed by Greek philosophers such as Plato and Aristotle.

Biblical Sources

The Holy Qur'an – a work roughly the same length as the New Testament – contains four clear strictures on the subject of usury (s.2 A. 275–8; s.3 A. 130; s.4 A.161; s.30, A.39). The New Testament has three references to usury, and the Old Testament has four.

Of the three passages on usury in the New Testament, two of them are identical and relate to the parable of the talents (Matthew 25: 14–30 and Luke 19: 12–27). Both, it must be said, are decidedly ambiguous on the question of usury (Gordon, 1982). The servant who returns the talents as he received them is castigated by the nobleman for not having 'put my money to the exchanges, and then at my coming I should have received my own with usury' (Mt. 25: 27). If interpreted literally, this verse would appear to condone the taking of usury, yet at the same time the recipient is criticised for 'reaping that thou didst not sow' (Luke, 19: 21).

However, the other reference in the New Testament is clear:

> But love ye your enemies, and do good, and lend, hoping for nothing again; and your reward shall be great, and ye shall be the children of the Highest. (Luke 6: 35)[5]

Jesus himself exhibited a distinctly anti-usury attitude when he cast the money-lenders from the temple, while the Sermon on the Mount revealed strongly anti-wealth sentiments as well.

In the case of the Old Testament, three references to usury come from the Pentateuch, the Law of Moses, the other from Psalms and attributed to David.

In historical order, they are:

> If thou lend money to *any* of my people *that* is poor by thee, thou shalt not be to him as a usurer, neither shall thou lay upon him usury. (Exodus 22: 25)
>
> And if thy brother be waxen poor, and fallen in decay with thee; then thou shalt relieve him: *yea, though he be* a stranger, or a sojourner; that he may live with thee. Take thou no usury of him, or increase: but fear thy God; that thy brother may live with thee.
> Thou shalt not give him thy money upon usury, nor lend him thy victuals for increase. (Leviticus 25: 35-7)
>
> Thou shalt not lend upon usury to thy brother; usury of money, usury of victuals, usury of any thing that is lent upon usury:
> Unto a stranger thou mayest lend upon usury; but unto thy brother thou shalt not lend upon usury. (Deuteronomy 23: 19-20)
>
> Lord, who shall abide in thy tabernacle, who shall dwell in thy holy hill?
> He *that* putteth not out his money to usury, nor taketh reward against the innocent.
> He that doeth these *things* shall never be moved. (Psalm 15: 1,5)

In Exodus and Deuteronomy, the biblical (Hebrew) term for interest is *neshekh*, although in Leviticus the term *neshekh* occurs alongside *tarbit* or *marbit*. In the *Encyclopedia Judaica* it is argued that *neshekh*, meaning 'bite', was the term used for the exaction of interest from the point of view of the debtor, and *tarbit* or *marbit*, meaning 'increase', was the term used for the recovery of interest by the creditor (Cohn, 1971, p. 28). But in both meanings, it seems to be the case that the prohibition on interest is not a prohibition on usury in the modern sense of the term, that is, excessive interest, but of all, even minimal, interest. Cohn concludes that there is no difference in law between various rates of interest, as all interest is prohibited.

Three other features of the Mosaic injunctions are notable. First, in at least two cases, the ban on usury is connected to poverty and consumption loans (likely the main form of loan at that time). Second, two of the passages extend the ban to any form of loan, not just of money, by including food given for profit. Any time contingent contract might therefore be regarded as usurious. Third, all three make clear that the prohibition refers to loans to 'brothers', that is fellow members of the tribe or adherents to the common faith. Charging interest to 'foreigners' was acceptable. In this way, the Jews justified taking interest from Gentiles, and Christians charged interest to 'Saracens' (as Arabs and, by extension, Muslims in general were called in the Middle Ages).[6]

These three qualifications were to prove instrumental to the later removal of the ban. Even at the time, the 'Deuteronomic double standard', as Nelson (1949) termed it, was difficult to explain away by Christians, since Jesus had preached the oneness of friend and foe alike. In addition, the idea that usury to any group could be considered religiously sound, was contradicted by the passage from the Psalms quoted above. One possible way around this conundrum would have been to follow the lead of Jewish Church leaders who defended the practice of those of their brethren who lent at usury to Gentiles by arguing that the verse from the Psalms can be attributed to David who was Moses' disciple and could not, therefore, place himself in contradiction to his master by altering Mosaic law (Cohn, 1971).

Canonical Law

Islamic Law – the *shari'a* – grew out of the attempts made by early Muslims, as they confronted immediate social and political problems, to devise a legal system in keeping with the code of behaviour called for by the Holy Qur'an and the *hadith* ('traditions' or 'sayings' related to the life of Prophet Muhammad, peace be upon him). Scholars developed these systems by treating the Holy Qur'an as containing the general principles by which all matters should be regulated, and where the meaning of the Holy Qur'an was imprecise they sought clarification from the *hadith*. Thus the foundations of the *shari'a* were the clear and unambiguous commands and prohibitions to be found in these sources. With the passage of time, scholars came to agree increasingly on the basic laws and the principle of *ijma*, or consensus of the community of believers, was established (see Chapter 2 above).

Much of the same process of evolution took place in the early Christian Church, and canon law was fashioned by the ecumenical councils, the popes and the bishops. The early Church first condemned usury by the 44th of the Apostolic Canons at the Council of Arles, 314, followed by Nicea in 325, and Laodicia in 372. The first Canon law ruling against usury was the Papal Encyclia *Nec hoc quoque* of Saint Leo the Great, pope from 440–61 and a Doctor of the Church. The last Papal Encyclical against usury *Vix pervenit* was issued in 1745 by Pope Benedict XIV (although it was not an infallible decree). In between, the Catholic Church maintained its opposition to the practice, although the emphasis did change over time.

At first, the Church's prohibition on usury did not go beyond the clergy, although more general disapproval was expressed to laity by the first Council of Carthage (345). Roll (1953) argues that a wider prohibition was unnecessary. In the absence of a developed money economy and capital market, with most feudal dues rendered in kind, the Church was not only the largest production unit but also virtually the only recipient of large sums of money. Irrespective of the scriptures, for the Church to charge interest on consumption loans to the needy would rightly be seen as exploitation. Glaeser and Scheinkman (1998) suggest other reasons. Interest-free loans were 'good business' in that they generated enthusiasm amongst the people for religion. Also, to allow usury might encourage private profiteering by clerics and perhaps open the door for simony (the buying and selling of any spiritual benefit for a temporal consideration).

As trade and commerce expanded in the later Middle Ages, and the demand for loans increased, to combat 'the insatiable rapacity of usurers' the Church's prohibition was extended to laymen in ever more strident and stringent forms (Divine, 1967). These condemnations came from the great Lateran Councils,[7] Lyon II and Vienne. The Second Lateran Council (1139) condemned usury as 'ignominious'. Lateran III (1179) introduced excommunication (exclusion from the Christian community) for open usurers. Lateran IV (1215) censured Christians who associated with Jewish usurers. Lyon II (1274) extended the condemnations to foreign usurers. Finally, the Council of Vienne (1311) allowed excommunication of princes, legislators and public authorities who either utilised or protected usurers, or who sought to distinguish between allowable interest and usury.[8]

It was thus with good reason that Tawney (1926) described this period as the 'high-water mark' of the ecclesiastical attack on usury. It was also at this time that an extra dimension was added to the Church's arguments against usury in the revival of Aristotelian logic and its combination with Roman law by St Thomas Aquinas (1225–74).

Aquinas and Aristotle

The third influence upon the Church's view on usury came from the medieval Schoolmen and in particular the most important of them, Saint Thomas Aquinas, who is generally acknowledged as the greatest of the scholastic philosophers, ranking in status as a philosopher alongside Plato, Aristotle, Kant and Hegel (Russell, 1946). St Thomas succeeded in persuading the Church fathers that Aristotle's views should form the basis of Christian philosophy, and that the Arab philosophers especially Ibn Rushd (1126–98) the Spanish-Arabian and his Christian followers, the Averroists, had misinterpreted Aristotle when developing their views on immortality. Consequently, St Thomas's *Summa Theologica* sought to undo this close adherence to Arabian doctrines.

In the process, St Thomas resurrected Aristotle's views on usury. The Greeks themselves (like the Romans later) exhibited no compunction about the taking of interest, but Plato disliked usury and *The Republic*, his ideal state, was opposed to all credit transactions except those undertaken on the basis of friendship and brotherhood, and explicitly prohibited lending at interest.[9] Plato's pupil Aristotle also opposed interest, based on a distinction between natural and unnatural modes of production, the latter including income from money-lending. Interest thus violates natural law – a position with which St Thomas and the Church concurred.

WHY DID CHRISTIANS ABHOR USURY?

Having examined the sources of the Christian doctrine on usury in terms of the Bible, the canon law and the writings of the Fathers and Schoolmen overlaid on Greek philosophy, it is now time to pull the threads together. At least ten justifications could be offered by the medieval Churchmen for the ban on usury.

First, usury contravened the teachings of Jesus. Although the passages in the Gospels can be variously interpreted, the absence of a specific condemnation cannot disguise the fact that on the basis of Jesus's casting out of the moneylenders and the principle 'actions speak louder than words', the lending out of money at interest was regarded as the very worst form of gain.

Second, Hebrew law prohibited usury unambiguously. The only point at issue was to whom and how widely the ban applied. However, from the very earliest years, Christians at least should have had few illusions on that score. St Jerome (340–420) and St Ambrose (340–97) claimed that 'brothers' in Deuteronomy had been universalised by the prophets and the New Testament ('love thine enemies'). Consequently, there was no scriptural warrant for taking usury from anyone.

Third, the Scriptures also severely restricted loan-related activities. Much lending of money occurred against objects held in trust (a pawn or pledge) by the lender. The prohibition of usury also extended to the types of collateral which could be used. The usury restriction in Exodus is immediately followed by the injunction: 'If thou at all take thy neighbour's raiment to pledge, thou shalt deliver it unto him by that the sun goeth down' (Exodus 22: 26).

This and other limitations on pledges are given in Deuteronomy 24, and there are restrictions on collateral in the *Halakah* (Rabinovich, 1993). These presumably had the intention of reducing the power of the creditor, and preventing the debtor from having to observe usurious contracts (and thus himself commit a sin). Under Talmudic law, it is not only the creditor who takes interest who is violating the biblical prohibition, but also the debtor who agrees to pay interest, the guarantor who guarantees the debt which bears interest, the witnesses who attest the creation of an interest-bearing debt, and even the scribe who writes out the deed (Cohn, 1971).

Fourth, usury was contrary to Aristotle. Once canonists accepted Aristotle's distinction between the natural economy and the unnatural art of money-making, then it followed that the science of economics had to be seen as a body of laws designed to ensure the moral soundness of economic activity. Money, according to Aristotle, arose as a means of facilitating the legitimate exchange of natural goods in order to provide utility to consumers. As such, money was barren. Interest was the unnatural fruit of a barren parent, money.

The most hated sort [of wealth], and with the greatest reason, is usury, which makes gain out of money itself, and not from the natural object of it. For money was intended to be used in exchange, and not to increase at interest ... Of all modes of getting wealth, this is the most unnatural. (*Politics*, 1258)

In fact, usury (which of course meant all lending at interest) was doubly condemned. Through usury, the accumulation of money becomes an end in itself, and the satisfaction of wants is lost from sight. Those doing so are rendered 'deficient in higher qualities' (*Politics*, 1323).

Fifth, St Thomas Aquinas augmented the Aristotelian view with the doctrine of Roman law which divided commodities into those which are consumed in use (consumptibles) and those which are not (fungibles). Wine is an example of the former (although not a good one to use in this company). 'If a man wanted to sell wine separately from the use of wine, he would be selling the same thing twice, or he would be selling what does not exist: wherefore he would evidently commit a sin of injustice'. Since 'the proper and principal use of money is its consumption', 'it is by very nature unlawful to take payment for the use of money lent, which payment is known as interest' (*Summa Theologica,* II 78).

Sixth, closely related was the view that usury violated natural justice. When a loan of money is made, the ownership of the thing that is lent passes to the borrower. Why should the creditor demand payment from a person who is, in effect, merely using what is now his own property? To do so would be to rob from those who make profitable use of the money. Profits should rightly belong to those who make the money profitable.

Seventh, St Thomas also condemned usury because it 'leads to inequality which is contrary to justice'. The Biblical admonitions on usury are surrounded by references to the 'poor', 'widows and orphans' and those in poverty to whom one is encouraged to 'lend freely, hoping for nothing thereby'. Prohibitions on usury were allied to the notion of a 'just price', which featured in Aristotle's *Ethics* (Thomson, 1953). The moral justification for trade, and wealth derived from trade, depended on whether the exchange which was effected is just. A 'proportionate equality' between the parties prior to exchange is essential if justice is to underlie commercial transactions (*Ethics* Book V, Ch. 5, p. 152). This was unlikely to be the case when money was lent to needy persons for the purposes of consumption. Usury, and the search for gain for its own sake, was the basest aspect of trade, leading men to the desire for limitless accumulation. In this respect, usury laws were 'commands to be lenient, merciful and kind to the needy' (Maimonides, 1956).

Eighth, since interest was regarded as the means by which the wealthy received an 'unearned income' from the unfortunate, it cut across medieval views on work. Work was a positive virtue and supplied the only justification for any kind of economic increment and profit. Consider the scriptures: 'In the sweat of thy face shalt thou eat bread, till thou return unto the ground' (Genesis 3: 19). A university professor, for example, who might otherwise be accused of selling knowledge, which belongs only to God and cannot be sold, could at least argue on this basis that he is working and therefore merits a salary (Le Goff, 1979). But this defence did not help the usurer: 'The creditor becomes rich by the sweat of the debtor, and the debtor does not reap the reward of his labour' (Tawney, 1926, p. 115). Not only does the usurer not work, but he makes his money work for him. Even in his sleep, the usurer's money is at work and is making a profit. Nor does money observe the Sabbath. Even the peasant lets his cattle rest on Sundays. But the usurer does not let his money respect the day of rest (Baldwin, 1970, Vol. 2, p. 191).

Ninth, to the canonists, time was an important consideration in the sin of usury. Interest was a payment for the passage of time. Moreover, usury was defined broadly. Under Charlemagne, who first extended the usury laws to the laity, usury was defined in 806 CE as 'where more is asked than is given' (Glaeser and Scheinkman, 1998, p. 33), while in the thirteenth century usury or profit on a loan (*mutuum*) was distinct from other contracting arrangements. A usurer, in fact, was anyone who allowed for an element of time in a transaction, such as by asking for a higher price when selling on credit or, because of the lapse of time, goods bought cheaper and sold dearer (Tawney, op. cit., p. 59-61).[10] The sin was in exploiting time itself. Time belongs to God, a divine possession. Usurers were selling something that did not belong to them. They were robbers of time, medieval gangsters (Le Goff, 1979, pp. 34-5).

Finally, most damning of all was that interest was fixed and certain. It was a fixed payment stipulated in advance for a loan of money or wares without risk to the lender. It was certain in that whether or not the borrower gained or lost, the usurer took his pound of flesh (Tawney, op. cit., p. 55). What delineated usury from other commercial transactions was in it being a contract for the repayment of more than the principal amount of the loan 'without risk to the lender' (Jones, 1989, p. 4).

It was this last point which created an unbridgeable divide between commercial motives and divine precepts. According to Tawney, medieval opinion, by and large, had no objection as such to rent and profits, provided that they were not unreasonable and exploitive. In addition, the ecumenical authorities had endeavoured to formulate the prohibition upon usury in such a way as to not unnecessarily conflict with legitimate trade and commerce. But no mercy was to be shown to the usurer. In many areas of economic activity, temporally-based returns were permitted because they involved the taking of a certain amount of risk. But where no risk was considered to be involved, interest-taking was strictly forbidden. The usurer's crime was in the taking of a payment for money which was fixed and certain:

The primary test for usury was whether or not the lender had contracted to lend at interest without assuming a share of the risk inherent to the transaction. If the lender could collect interest regardless of the debtor's fortunes he was a usurer. (Jones, 1989, 118–19)

COMPARING ISLAMIC AND CHRISTIAN VIEWS

The Parallels

To those who had forgotten – or perhaps been unaware of – the extent to which Islam builds on, and sustains and fulfils, the message of its two monotheist antecedents, the similarities between the views in the previous section and those of Islam outlined in earlier chapters may well be surprising. In particular, the attitudes seeing usury as the worst form of gain, as lacking any scriptural warrant whatsoever, as involving unjustified collateral, forcing the debtor to sin, as unnatural and barren, as an unwarranted expropriation of property, as devoid of true work, and fixed, certain, and lacking in risk-sharing, all of these are echoed in (or echo) Islamic views. This parallel is especially so in the case of the last, in that a loan provides the lender with a fixed return irrespective of the outcome of the borrower's venture, whereas the reward to capital should instead be commensurate with the risk and effort involved and thus be governed by the return on the individual project for which funds are supplied.

There are other parallels as well. Islam comprises a set of principles and doctrines that guide and regulate a Muslim's relationship with God and with society. In this respect, Islam is not only a divine service, but also incorporates a code of conduct which regulates and organises mankind in both spiritual and material life. The Aristotelian idea that ethics should govern the science of economics would sit comfortably with an adherent, as would the view that the Church (Muslims would of course substitute God)[11] has command over the totality of human relations.

Yusuf al-Qaradawi (see Hussain, 1999) gives four reasons for the Islamic prohibition of interest (*riba*), similar to those quoted earlier of Razi ([1872]1938):

- Taking interest implies taking another person's property without giving him anything in exchange. The lender receives something for nothing.
- Dependence on interest discourages people from working to earn money. Money lent at interest will not be used in industry, trade or commerce all of which need capital, thus depriving society of benefits.
- Permitting the taking of interest discourages people from doing good. If

interest is prohibited people will lend to each other with goodwill expecting nothing more back than they have loaned.

- The lender is likely to be wealthy and the borrower poor. The poor will be exploited by the wealthy through the charging of interest on loans.

These are virtually identical to some of the early Christian views. There is also a shared concern about the time element in contracting. Compensation from licit forms of Islamic financing must differ from interest not only by being calculated on a pre-transaction basis but also cannot be explicitly related to the duration of the finance.

The Differences

However, there are differences too. The first, and most obvious, concerns the central scriptural authority. In the case of the Bible, there are enough ambiguities – New versus Old Testament, Mosaic versus later Hebrew law, and a very parabolic parable[12] – to keep an army of scholars employed (as indeed they did), whereas the injunctions in the Holy Qur'an are forthright. Second, while canon law and scholastic philosophy sought to augment scripture, the essential feature of that source was that it could – and did – change in response to the temper of the times and new religious thinking, whereas the Holy Qur'an provided a fixed and certain point of reference. Third, to the extent that Christian doctrine rested on an Aristotelian foundation it was vulnerable to the charge of being, at heart, anti-trade and commerce. Aristotle adopted the view, later followed by the Physiocrats, that the natural way to get wealth is by skilful management of house and land. Usury was diabolical and clearly the worst way of making money. But there was also something degraded about trading and exchanging things rather than actually making them, as summed up in the medieval saying, '*Homo mercator vix aut numquam Deo placere potest*' – the merchant can scarcely or never be pleasing to God. By contrast, the Holy Qur'an endorsed trade, so long as it was not usurious.

On all three counts, where Christianity was somewhat equivocal in comparison with Islam, its stand on usury was subject to erosion. Perhaps ironically, the one aspect on which it was more forthright than Islam probably served to reinforce that trend. This was in the area of punishment.

Christian Sanctions on Usurers

A Christian usurer faced five sanctions. First, he had eventually to face his Maker, and the Church left him in no doubt that he faced the fiercest of the fires of hell. In the scale of values, the usurer was linked with the worst evildoers, the worst occupations, the worst sins and the worst vices. Indeed, the prohibition of usury is even more rigorous than the commandment against murder; murder could be condoned in some circumstances, but nothing could excuse usury. Also, echoing Talmudic law, the sin is shared by all of those who conspire in the acts – public officials who sanction usury and even the debtors themselves. Debtors who contract to pay usury without explicitly demurring in some way are declared to share the creditor's sin: without the addict, the dealer could not survive.

Second, disclosure meant becoming a social outcast. It has been said that the usurer was 'tolerated on earth but earmarked for hell' (Lopez, 1979, p. 7), but this was not so. Public opinion was that usurers should be exterminated like wolves, and their bodies thrown on the dung hill. They should be condemned to death and hanged, or at the very least banished from the country and their property confiscated.[13] They were fit only to associate with Jews, robbers, rapists and prostitutes, but were worse than all of them. Thirteenth century society was classified according to two groupings: a classification by sins and vices, and a classification according to social rank and occupation. On both lists, usurers were at the bottom of the heap. They were publicly preached at, shamed, taunted and reviled.

Third, the usurer would be punished by the Church, and by the orders of the Church. The Lateran Councils laid down clear rules for offenders: they were to be refused communion or a Christian burial, their offerings were not to be accepted, and open usurers were to be excommunicated. There could be no absolution for them and their wills were to be invalid. Those who let houses to usurers were themselves to be excommunicated. No usurer could hold public office. Church courts and civil courts fought over the lucrative business of who would levy the fines.

Fourth, the only salvation for the usurer lay in restitution. Restitution had to be made to each and every person from whom interest or increase had been taken, or to their heirs. Were that not possible, the money had to be given to the poor. All property that had been pawned had to be restored, without deduction of interest or charges. And the ecclesiastical authorities could move against the usurers and their accomplices even if the debtors would not.

Fifth, the usurer risked condemning his wife and heirs to penury, for the same penalties were applied to them as to the original offender. They also faced a lifetime of humility and devotion. Certain actions of the living (alms, prayers, masses) could aid in the posthumous redemption of the usurer: the sinful husband might be saved by the faithful wife. By becoming recluses, and engaging in alms, fasts, and prayers, the wife and children might move God to favour the usurer's soul.

Islamic Sanctions

In comparison with these punitive measures, the sanctions imposed on the Islamic usurer seem less extreme. That the usurer will not fare well on the Day of Judgement is clear enough. Consider Zamakhsharî on Süra 2: 275/276:

> Those who consume interest (ar-ribä) shall not rise again (on the day of resurrection), except as one arises whom Satan has prostrated by the touch (that is, one who is demon-possessed): that is because they have said: 'Bargaining is just the same as interest', even though God has permitted bargaining but has forbidden interest. Now whoever receives an admonition from his Lord and then desists (from the practice), he shall retain his past gains, and his affair is committed to God. But whoever repeats (the offence) – those are the inhabitants of the fire, therein dwelling forever.[14]

However, no specific penalty was laid down in the Holy Qur'an, and it was left to the jurists to determine the scale of punishment, qualification and legal validity (Schacht, 1964, p. 12).

According to Islamic law, the following actions are punishable: (1) Injuries against life and limb, which justify blood revenge or the claim for expiatory money. (2) Offences for which a specific, unalterable punishment is prescribed either in the Holy Qur'an or in the *hadith*, that is, unchastity, slander with regard to this, the partaking of wine, theft, highway robbery, and according to some, also apostasy, for which the death penalty is given. (3) All other violations against the command of God, for which discretionary punishment (*al-ta'zir*) is determined by judges of the *shari'a* courts. There is in these cases (which includes usury) neither fixed punishment nor penance, and the ruler or the judge is completely free in the determination of the offences or sanctions (El-Awa, 1983).

As for the legal status of *riba* transactions, Islamic law recognises, first, a scale of religious qualifications and, second, a scale of legal validity. Interest is forbidden (*haram*), but on Schacht's (1964, p. 145) interpretation a contract concluded in contravention of the rules concerning *riba* is defective (*fasid*) or voidable rather than null and void (*batil*). Nevertheless, this distinction between the two is not recognised by all schools of Islamic law, and since *riba* is a special case of 'unjustified enrichment' by which the property of others is consumed (or appropriated for one's own use) for no good reason, the *riba* element cannot be enforced. It is a general principle of Islamic law, based on a number of passages in the Holy Qur'an, that unjustified enrichment, or 'receiving a monetary advantage without giving a countervalue', is forbidden, and he who receives it must give it to the poor as a charitable gift. The latter condition is the practice of Islamic banks when extant transactions are found to have violated the ban on interest, and the earnings are distributed by *shari'a* Boards to various *zakat* funds (see Chapter 7).

THE CHRISTIAN USURY BAN IN PRACTICE

Usury was clearly a sin but it was one that many Christians found difficult to resist, despite the severe temporal penalties exacted by the ecclesiastical authorities. It was much better for the interest element to be concealed and many a technique was developed in order to come to gain, while not violating the letter of the law. Of course, it hardly needs to be said that such stratagems are not unknown in Muslim economic life.

Our examination of these arrangements in medieval Christianity is grouped under five headings. First, there are the variations upon *interesse*. Second, there are those transactions which took advantage of the international dimension. Third, interest income could be converted into other permissible forms of income. Fourth, some of the legal fictions that were employed borrowed directly from those being used contemporaneously by the early Muslim community to circumvent the ban on *riba* (as others did from Jewish evasions). However, it is the fifth category which is particularly interesting. Intriguingly, some other practices followed seem virtually identical to those which have gained approval today in Islamic financing.

Interesse

A number of techniques rested on the distinction between *usura*, which was unlawful, and *interesse,* compensation for loss, which was lawful. Under the doctrine of *damnum emergens*, the suffering of loss, the lender was entitled to exact a conventional penalty from the borrower if he failed to return the principal at the agreed time, that is if he defaulted. This provision opened the door to the taking of interest, since the courts assumed that there had been a genuine delay and that a *bona-fide* loss had occurred. By making very short-term loans and simulating delay (*mora*) in repayment, interest could be concealed.

Payment could also be demanded under the doctrine relating to *lucrum cessans*. As well as compensation for damage suffered, the lender could be compensated for the gain that had been sacrificed when money was lent. A creditor with capital invested in a business could claim compensation on this account, and the growing opportunities for trade made it easier to prove that gain had escaped him. A wide range of financial transactions could be legitimised in this way, especially since a special reward could be claimed by the lender because of the risk which had been incurred.

International Transactions

The international dimension could also be utilized, using the 'Deuteronomic double standard', to charge interest to enemies such as the Saracens during the Crusades. But by far the most common activity involved foreign exchange. Lending gave rise to interest, which was contrary to nature and the law, but the sale of one asset for another (including coinage) was legitimate. If the asset was a foreign one, the price at which the sale was concluded could be used to conceal that the transaction was really the combination of a loan with a foreign exchange transaction.

The most typical case was that of the bill of exchange, and special 'foreign exchange fairs' which operated between 1553 and 1763 were held at regular intervals – usually four times a year – largely for the purpose of issuing bills payable there and organising foreign exchange clearing (Kindleberger, 1984; de Cecco, 1992). A rule endorsed by most scholastic writers exempted from the anti-usury laws the buying and selling of bills issued in terms of a foreign currency and payable in a foreign country – a sort of medieval equivalent of a Eurocurrency transaction today. A bill was an ideal vehicle because it involved an extension of credit in one place, used for the export of goods, and payment of the loan in another place, but in a different currency. This feature made it possible to disguise a domestic credit transaction in the form of currency exchange (Einzig, 1962).

Usually a medieval bill of exchange transaction consisted of the sale for local currency of an obligation to pay a specified sum in another currency at a future. It thus involved both an extension of credit and an exchange of currency. A modern-day bank would handle this transaction by converting the foreign into the local currency at the ruling spot rate of exchange, and then charging a rate of discount for the credit extended when paying out cash now for cash later. To do so then would have been usurious, for discounting was not an allowable activity. Consequently, by not separating the two elements involved, the medieval banker bought the bill at a price which incorporated both an element of interest and a charge for his services as an exchange dealer.

Of course, the banker then had an open book which had to be closed by reversing the transaction and buying a bill in the foreign location, and receiving payment in his own currency. The fluctuation of exchange rates provided a convincing case of risk, since the terms at which the reverse deal could be undertaken would not be guaranteed at the time of the original transaction. It was this risk that reconciled bill dealing with the laws.[15]

Once the bill of exchange became admissible, it was a short step to lend money domestically by means of fictitious exchange transactions involving drafts and redrafts between two places. For example, a merchant needing cash would get it from an Italian banker by drawing a bill on the banker's own correspondent at the fairs of Lyons or Frankfurt. When this bill matured, it would be cancelled by a redraft issued by the correspondent and payable by the borrowing merchant to his creditor, the banker. Thus, the latter would recover the money which he had lent. To confuse the theologian, the real nature of the *cambio con la ricorsa*, as it was called, was clouded in technical jargon and was further obscured by clever manipulations in the books of the banker and of his correspondent. But once these trimmings were stripped away, it was simply discounting taking place under the cover of fictitious currency exchanges (de Roover, 1954, 1963).

Many bankers had a guilty conscience about getting around the usury laws in this way, as reflected by those of their number who included in their wills and testaments a distribution to the Church or to the needy in restitution for their illicit returns (Galassi, 1992). Other bankers institutionalised their attempt to buy 'a passport to heaven'; in fourteenth-century Florence, the Bardi and Peruzzi banks regularly set aside part of their annual profits for distribution to the poor, holding the funds in an account under the name of *Messer Domineddio*, Mr God-Our-Lord (Galassi, 1992, p. 314).

Income Conversions

Converting interest income into permitted sources of earnings lay at the heart of all of the techniques, including those above. Some others can be briefly mentioned. The element of risk that avoided the charge of usury for bills of exchange also applied to, and was allowed in, the purchase of annuities, because the payment was contingent and speculative, not certain. Commissions could be charged for negotiating loan contracts or 'sweeteners' paid for the commitment to lend – much like American banks got around the interest rate ceilings by giving depositors gifts of toasters and such-like. Income from property was allowable, as well, for the fruits of the land are produced by nature, not wrung from man.

Land provided the vehicle for the one form of investment that was widely understood and universally practised, even by the Church itself. This was the rent-charge. Those with funds to lend could purchase a contract to pay so much from the rents of certain lands or houses or premises in return for the sum outlaid. For example, around 1500 CE, £10 a year for £100 down was about a normal rate in England. Such an investment was not regarded as usurious, despite being as fixed, certain and safe in medieval conditions as any loan. As in most legal systems, observance of the letter rather than the spirit of the law often took precedence.

Islamic-type Investments

Not surprisingly, the same pressures to follow 'form' over 'substance' in commercial dealings existed in the Islamic countries, and at much the same time. Commercial practice was brought into conformity with the requirements of the *shari'a* by the *hiyal* or 'legal devices' which were often legal fictions. Schacht (1964) defines the *hiyal* as 'the use of legal means for extra-legal ends, ends that could not, whether they themselves were legal or illegal, be achieved directly with the means provided by the *shari'a*' (p. 78). Frequently, he argues, these were the maximum that custom could concede, and the minimum that the theory demanded.

As in the West, Muslim merchants utilised the potential of the bill of exchange to (and perhaps beyond) the limits of the law. Another device consisted of giving real property as a security for the debt and allowing the creditor to use it, so that its use represented the interest; this transaction was not dissimilar to the rent-charge. Closely related to this transaction was the sale of property with the right of redemption (*bay' al-wafa', bay' al-'uhda*).

A popular technique consisted of the double sale (*bay 'atan fi bay'a*). For example, the (prospective) debtor sells to the (prospective) creditor an item for cash, and immediately buys it back from him for a greater amount payable at a future date; this amounts to a loan with the particular item concerned as security, and the difference between the two prices represents the interest. Schacht claims that there were 'hundreds' of such devices used by traders *cum* money-lenders, all with a scrupulous regard for the letter of the law.[16] It goes without saying, of course, that from an Islamic perspective these legal fictions or *hiyal* are strictly prohibited. The mention in the Holy Qur'an of the example of a Jewish community nullifying the Sabbath command leaves no scope for such a subterfuge (S2: 65).

It seems quite likely that many of these *hiyal* were conveyed to medieval Europe by Muslim traders presumably through the principles and practice of the triangular international trade and commerce which connected the Islamic countries, Byzantium and (at that stage) the relatively undeveloped West. Such transmission is suggested by the etymological sources of the vocabulary of medieval finance. For instance, we can cite the medieval Latin *mohatra*, from Arabic *mukhatara*, a term for the evasion of the prohibition of interest by means of a double sale, by the French term *aval*, from Arabic *hawala*, for the endorsement on a bill of exchange, by the term *cheque*, from Arabic *sakk*, 'written document', and by the term *sensalis (sensale, Sensal)*, from Arabic *simsar*, 'broker'.

Some of the more approved modes of Islamic financing also featured in medieval Europe. Since the legal form of the financing was what ultimately mattered, the owner and the prospective user of funds could, as an alternative to arranging a loan, form a partnership (*nomine societatis palliatum*), with profit *and* loss divided among them in various ways. What was of crucial importance, theologically, was that the provider of funds had to share in the partner's risk. That proviso rendered the arrangement broadly equivalent to that of the Islamic *musharaka* under which an entrepreneur and investor jointly contribute funds to a venture, and divide up the profits and losses according to a pre-determined ratio. Finance-based partnerships involving merchants find mention in Islamic sources around 700 CE, but the origins in the West (the *commenda* and the *compagnia*) go back no further than the tenth century (Lopez, 1979).

Of course, it was also possible to use the partnership form as a legal fiction to cloak what was really interest rate lending in all but name. For example, a person might have lent money to a merchant on the condition that he be a partner in the gains, but not in the losses. Another favourite method, used particularly in the City of London, was for the 'partner' providing funds to be a 'sleeping one' to conceal the borrowing and lending of money. Even more complicated devices such as the *contractus trinus* (triple contact), were devised which, while approved by custom and law, caused much theological strife.[17]

Although it takes us ahead further in time, it is perhaps worth mentioning at this juncture that the formation of partnerships (*hetter iskah*) established the basis for the Jewish 'legalisation' of interest. Cohn (1971) explains that a deed, known as a *shetar iskah*, was drawn up and attested by two witnesses, stipulating that the lender would supply a certain sum of money to the borrower for a joint venture: the borrower alone would manage the business and he would guarantee the lender's investment against all loss; he would also guarantee to the lender a fixed amount of minimum profit. The amount of the capital loan plus the guaranteed minimum profit would be recoverable on the deed at the stipulated time it matured. Cohn goes on to observe that over time this form of legalising interest became so well established that nowadays all interest transactions are freely carried out, even in compliance with Jewish law, by simply adding to the note or contract concerned the words *al-pi hetter iskah* (Cohn, 1971, p. 32).

Mudaraba Investments

More interesting still was the existence in Middle Ages Europe of *mudaraba*-type arrangements when the medieval banks took in funds from depositors. Under these types of account no fixed return was specified but the depositor was offered a share or participation in the profits of the bank. For example, on 17 November, 1190, a servant of the famous Fieschi family entrusted 'capital' of £7 Genoese to the banker Rubeus upon condition that he could withdraw his deposit on fifteen days' notice and that he would receive a 'suitable' return on his money (de Roover, 1954, p. 39). Much closer to present day *mudaraba* were the investment modes offered by the Medici Bank. For example, the famous diplomat and chronicler Philippe de Commines (1447–1511) placed with the Lyons branch of Medici a time deposit which instead of yielding a fixed percentage, entitled him to participate in the profits 'at the discretion' of the bank (*depositi a discrezione*). As another illustration, the contract between this same bank and Ymbert de Batarnay, Seigneur du Bouchage, concerning a deposit in 1490 of 10 000 *écus* does not mention any fixed percentage but states, on the contrary, that this sum was to be employed in lawful trade and the profits accruing therefrom were to be shared equally between the contracting parties (de Roover, 1948, p. 56).

The historian Raymond de Roover called this 'strange behaviour' and dismissed the practice as merely a legal deception to skirt the usury laws. Viewed from the perspective of current Islamic banking, however, the arrangement seems an entirely appropriate response, valid in its own right. It would thus be fascinating to know how widespread this type of contract was (it was obviously in operation for over 300 years), and why it later fell into disuse.

THE CHRISTIAN RETREAT

With the advent of the mercantile era (circa 1500–1700) the practice of the taking of interest, which had been forbidden by the Church, gradually came to be accepted (although cases involving usury were still being heard in England in the reign of Elizabeth I) and eventually sanctioned. Why did the prohibition on usury break down throughout Europe? As in any other area of enquiry, a number of strongly intertwined factors were involved, making it difficult to disentangle cause from effect.

'Deregulation'

Tawney was the first to connect this shift in religious thought with the rise in commerce. He argued that economic growth swelled the channels for profitable investment to such an extent that the divorce between theory and reality had become almost unbridgeable. Greater investment opportunities made the usury laws more costly and tiresome to enforce, while the devices to get around the prohibition had become so numerous that everyone was concerned with the form rather than the substance of transactions. In effect, the ban had become unworkable and the rulings themselves were brought into disrepute.

All of this can be interpreted in terms of the economic theory of regulation.[18] When the bans were introduced in the early Middle Ages, the Church itself was the centre of economic life, and canon law was concerned with ensuring that its own representatives were kept in line. As the outside market grew and commerce expanded, more and more activity moved outside the controlled (that is non-usury) sector. At first, the Church extended the regulations (that is the ban on usury) to the non-controlled activities. When the market continued to expand, and the legal devices to circumvent the regulations expanded also, the Church's condemnations became at first more strident and its penalties more severe as it tried to keep a lid on interest transactions. But at some point the tide turned. As the thinly disguised interest economy continued to grow, more and more were willing to seek immediate gains in the present world and take their chances in the hereafter, hoping that a deathbed confession and token restitution would ensure an easier route to salvation. The Church itself was forced to devote more of its energies to examining the accounts of money-lenders and merchants in order to root out the various subterfuges used to conceal usury. In short, the cost of maintaining the regulations increased. Regulatory theory predicts that a stage might be reached when the least-cost solution is to 'deregulate' and remove the irksome controls.

Then the problem, of course, is how to save face and break from the past, particularly when so much intellectual capital and moral fervour has been devoted to the issue. It was necessary to avoid the charge of hypocrisy or moral backsliding. Again, we can explain what happened in terms of the theory of regulation, by borrowing from what is known as the theory of regulatory 'capture'.[19] One strand of that literature concerns what happens if there are a number of competing regulatory agencies (as in US banking, for example), fighting over common turf and seeking to widen their constituency. Then 'competition in laxity' may be the result. Something like this may have happened with the Christian Church on usury: competition to the orthodoxy of Catholicism came from the rise of Protestantism associated with the names of Luther and Calvin, and laxity from the relaxation of the usury laws.

Calvin

Luther was rather ambivalent on the topic of usury, but Calvin was not. His denial (in a series of letters beginning in 1547) that the taking of payment for the use of money was in itself sinful has been hailed as a 'turning point in the history of European thought' (Ashley, [1888, 1893]1913), as the foundation stone of the 'spirit of capitalism' (Weber, 1930) and the 'Gospel of the modern era' (Nelson, 1949). Earlier, St Paul had declared that the 'New Convenant' between Jesus and the people had superseded the old covenant of Mosaic law, so that Judaic law was no longer binding on Christian society (Letter to the

Romans, Chapter 3). Calvin went further. He argued that neither the old Halakic code nor the rulings of the Gospels were universally applicable and binding for all time, because they were shaped by and designed for conditions that no longer exist. Rather they should be interpreted in the light of individual conscience, the equity of the 'golden rule' (do unto others as you would have them do unto you), and the needs of society.

Thus under Calvin's reformation the lender is no longer a pariah but a useful part of society. Usury does not conflict with the law of God in all cases and, provided that the interest rate is reasonable, lending at interest is no more unjust than any other economic transaction; for example, it is as reasonable as the payment of rent for land. Although Calvin repudiated the Aristotelian doctrine that money was infertile, he nonetheless identified instances in which the taking of interest would be an act of sinful usury, as in the case of needy borrowers oppressed by circumstances and faced with exorbitant interest rates. But these are problems inherent in the social relations of a Christian community, to be solved in the light of existing circumstances and the dictates of natural law and the will of God, not by blanket prohibition.

Redefining Usury

Calvin's doctrine has become the language of modern Protestant Christianity, but the practical reality of the time was that everyone who sought a more liberal approach to usury turned to Calvin for support. Throughout Protestant Europe, governments embraced his views to abolish the legal prohibition of interest. Earlier, after Henry VIII's break with Rome, a statute was enacted in England in 1545 legalising interest but limiting it to a legal maximum of 10 per cent, and legislation laying down a maximum rate in place of a prohibition of interest was made permanent by law in 1571. Such 'usury laws' became the norm thereafter in Protestant Europe.

The retreat of Catholic canon law was in general slower and involved the concession of exceptions while clinging to the principle. Nevertheless, in the nineteenth century, the Roman Catholic authorities also relented by the issuance of some 14 decisions of the Congregations of the Holy Office, the Penitentiary, and the Propaganda stating that the faithful who lend money at moderate rates of interest are 'not to be disturbed', provided that they are willing to abide by any future decisions of the Holy See. Nonetheless, the Church still provides in the Code of Canon Law (c.2354) severe penalties for those convicted of usury in the modern sense, that is excessive interest (Nelson, 1949: Divine, 1967).

Consequently the great achievement of Calvin and his followers was, in effect, to have turned Deuteronomy on its head. Finding a solution to the troublesome 'Deuteronomic double standard' had long worried Christian theologians imbued with ideas of universal fraternity. Amongst the early Church, the distasteful implication that usury was lawful when levied upon some ('foreigners') but unlawful and sinful when applied to others ('brothers') was initially resolved by not charging interest to anyone. Following Calvin, the resolution came about instead by charging usury to all, but at a rate deemed to be not injurious.

Some other factors may have featured in the erosion of the usury prohibition that we shall mention briefly. One was a shifting allegiance involving borrowers and lenders. In the Middle Ages, Church property was almost entirely in land, and landowners have always been borrowers rather than lenders. But when Protestantism arose, its support came chiefly from the middle class, who were lenders rather than borrowers. With this changing 'constituency' first Calvin, then other Protestants, and finally the Catholic Church sanctioned usury. Related to this argument is the distinction between consumption loans and production loans, which also features in some revisionist Islamic literature on *riba* (Shah, 1967; Rahman, 1964). In the early Middle Ages most loans would have been consumption loans, for which the potential for exploitation is presumably greater than for production loans. By the time of Calvin the position had reversed, and protection from exploitation could be achieved by proscribed maxima in excess of the 'natural' commercial rate.

Solving one problem often creates another and this proved to be the case with the switch from the outright prohibition of usury to permissibility within specified maxima. Consider the case of England, where a legal maximum of 10 per cent p.a. was installed by statute in 1545 and law in 1571. In 1624 the legal maximum was lowered from 10 to 8 per cent; in 1650 it was reduced to 6 per cent and in 1713 to 5 per cent. In each case these reductions followed upon a fall in the level of interest rates generally – perhaps reflecting declines in the 'natural' rate. Nevertheless, the maximum rates created difficulties for commercial borrowers because the usury laws did not apply to the State and the government was an habitual debtor. No matter how great was the need of industry for funds and however high was the return on investments, borrowers were not allowed to offer more than the legal maximum. Evasion was always possible, and not unknown, but the penalties were high and the law was generally respected. The government, by contrast, could offer whatever rate was needed, for there was no limit to the yield on government stock. Consequently, laws designed to ensure that the borrower was shielded from extortion unwittingly had the effect, at times, of diverting loanable funds from merchants, farmers and producers to the State.[20] In 1833 the Usury Act was repealed, although the aversion to extortionate interest rates did not disappear entirely and re-emerged in the Moneylenders Acts of 1900 and 1927 and the Consumer Credit Act of 1974.

CAN ISLAM SUCCEED?

At the beginning of this chapter we raised a number of questions about the Christian ban on usury and the lessons for Islamic countries from the Christian experience. While we have gone some way towards answering them, in other respects, more questions have been raised than answered. For example, some of the methods used to conform with the Church's opposition to usury were quite consistent with the spirit of the law and similar to the preferred modes of Islamic financing. Were these contracts an antecedent of *mudaraba* or were they copied from contemporary Muslims? This question would seem to be an interesting avenue to explore.

Another question concerns interest rate lending. Why was this so attractive and seductive to Christians? Why did lenders and borrowers strive to engage in this form of financing? The Church regarded usury as diabolical and, at base, exploitative. But it would be facile to see extortion as the only, or even major, reason for its popularity with lenders. The modern theory of financial intermediation (see Chapter 4) considers interest rate loans as 'optimal' incentive-compatible forms of contracting in the face of certain types of information asymmetries and moral hazard. If so, a question-mark has to be raised over the universal applicability of some Islamic financing techniques, such as *mudaraba* and *musharaka*, and the Islamic banks have in fact been circumspect in their use. This was examined in earlier chapters.

A more difficult question is posed by the historical interpretations of Tawney and Weber. Both of these authors trace the birth of capitalism to the rise of Protestantism and the relaxation of the ban on usury. To them, the abolition of the restrictions on usury was a necessary, if not sufficient, precondition for the development of an enterprise economy. They argued that the prohibition against usury had its roots in a peasant society, close to subsistence levels, in which the ethical problem is relatively simple. When a crop fails and a family goes hungry, a non-interest loan will often be a duty: fraternal brotherhood offers a charitable hand, not a self-seeking one. But it is an entirely different matter to extend this type of ethical kinship to the realms of a national, indeed international, capital market, in which the contracting is between relatively anonymous commercial lenders and borrowers. Such an attempt, it was said, risked either deception or failure, or both.

Exactly how important the relaxation of the usury laws was to the achievement of economic growth remains a controversial issue, since the alterations to the usury laws likely responded to the rise of commerce as well as perhaps influencing it (Iannaccone, 1998). It has been argued, on the one hand, that the prohibition of usury impeded the development of capitalism by restricting the supply of loanable funds and keeping interest rates high, since the laws undermined the enforcement of contracts (the authority of any civil law permitting interest was consistently denied by the Church which ruled such contracts to be null and void). On the other hand, some contend that the operation of the prohibition during the formative years of capitalism in the late Middle Ages may well have had the important effect of diverting funds, which might otherwise have been loaned out at interest, into equity-type investments which nurtured a spirit of enterprise and contributed to development in these formative years (Spiegel, 1992).

Nevertheless, on the central questions posed at the beginning of this chapter the answers seem clearer. The Christian Church maintained a prohibition on usury (interest) for over 1400 years and, once the terminological difficulties are sorted out and the doctrinal sources examined, it is apparent that the official Christian objection to usury was almost identical to the Islamic position.

There were differences, too. In fact, the divergences between the two religions on their stance about usury go a long way to explaining why Christianity relaxed and eventually retreated from the ban on usury, while Islam has not. One factor was the lack in the Christian creed of an overriding injunction on the subject like that in the Holy Qur'an. That deficiency, along with ambiguities on related issues such as the acceptability of trade, opened up Catholicism to the inroads of Protestant revisionist interpretations on usury and what we have called 'competition in laxity'.

Another difference came from the severity of the temporal penalties applied to usurers by the Christian ecclesiastical courts. These inhibited much legitimate trade and at the same time raised the incentive to evade the prohibition in the form of taking advantage of various legal loopholes, which brought the institution itself into disrepute because of the transparency of some of the devices. There is, of course, an obvious lesson here, which has not gone unheard in Islamic circles (for example Gafoor, 1995).

At the same time, however, it can also be claimed with considerable justification that in medieval Christendom too much time was devoted to evasion, and by the Church to condemning and rooting out the evaders, than to finding acceptable non-interest alternatives to usury. In Islam, compliance has been left as a matter for the individual (and his Maker), but the Islamic community and the Islamic bankers have spent much effort examining the legitimacy of particular transactions and formalising procedures which have enabled everyday banking, finance and commerce to be conducted on an *halal* basis.

On this interpretation, a key factor governing the success of Islamic banking and finance will be product innovation – fashioning instruments which remain genuinely legitimate, in the sense of meeting the spirit as well as the letter of the law, while responding to the ever-changing financial needs of business and commerce. The next chapter examines some of the recent developments.

NOTES

1. Veda is the literature of the Aryans who invaded North India about 1500 BCE. Vedic law operated until about 500 BCE.
2. Based on Lewis (1999c).
3. Chapter (*surah*) and verse references used here relating to *riba* are from the English translation revised and edited by The Presidency of Islamic Researches, 1413 AH.
4. The compensation originated from *id quod interest* of Roman law, which was the payment for damages due to the nonfulfilment of a contractual obligation (*Encyclopedia Britannica*, 1947 edn).
5. This and other passages below come from the Authorised Version or King James Version of 1611 prepared by scholars in England.
6. This practice was often rationalised as an instrument of warfare. Pope Alexander III in 1159 argued that 'Saracens and heretics' whom it had not been possible to conquer by force of arms would be compelled under the weight of usury to yield to the Church (Nelson, 1949 p. 15).
7. Named after the old Lateran palace in Rome, the scene of five ecumenical councils.
8. The Church's position is outlined in Jones (1989), Le Goff (1979, 1984), Nelson (1949), Noonan (1957).
9. Platonic and Greek economic thought is explained by Trever (1916) and Langholm (1984).
10. There is similarity here with the Rabbinic rulings in the Mishna, the collection of legal interpretations of Exodus, Leviticus, Numbers and Deuteronomy. Loans of goods and speculative trading in wheat are ruled as morally equivalent to usury (Baba Mesia 5:1) (Levine, 1987).
11. In Islam, there is no church in the sense of a religious hierarchy separate from the ruler (or *imam*), the religious leader of the people (rather like the Queen as head of the Church of England), nor does Islam have priests.
12. The description owes to Keen (1997).
13. All of these actions were recommended in Thomas Wilson's *Discourse upon Usury* (1572) quoted in Nelson (1949).
14. From the commentary of the Persian-Arab scholar Abu l-Qasim Mahmud ibn Umar az-Zamakhshari completed in 1134 CE, as reported in Gätje (1997).
15. Due to the slowness of communications at that time, even a sight draft was a credit instrument, since time elapsed while it was travelling from the place where it was issued to the place where it was payable. The theologians insisted upon the observance of the *distantia loci* (difference in place), but they tended to downplay the fact that the difference in place necessarily incorporated a difference in time (*dilatio temporis*). As the jurist Raphael de Turri, or Raffaele della Torre (c.1578–1666), put it succinctly: *distantia localis in cambio involvit temporis dilationem* (distance in space also involves distance in time). Although he could not deny that a *cambium* (exchange) contract was a loan mixed with other elements, he wrote a treatise full of references to Aristotle, Aquinas, and a host of scholastic doctors in order to establish that exchange dealings were not tainted with any usury. In other words, the exchange transaction was used to justify profit on a credit transaction (de Roover, 1967).
16. The first and simplest *hiyal* were probably thought out by the interested parties who felt the need for them, the merchants in particular, but it was quite beyond them to invent and apply the more complicated ones. They would have had to have recourse to specialists with knowledge of the *shari'a*. The early development of Islamic law is examined by Lindholm (1996).
17. The kind of loan which the Church condemned – a loan in which the creditor claimed interest from the beginning of the loan and stipulated the return of his principal, whether the

enterprise was successful or not – could be considered a combination of three separate contracts. The components were a *commenda* in the form of a sleeping partnership, an insurance contract against the loss of the principal, and an insurance contract against fluctuations in the rate of profit. What clearly was legal was that A could enter into partnership with B; he could further insure the principal against loss with C and contract with D against loss caused by fluctuations in profits. The essence of the triple contract was that it combined three separate contracts which were legal when struck in isolation between different parties, but when combined and made between just two parties had the effect of contracting for an advance of money at a fixed rate of interest. If it was lawful for A to make these three contracts separately with B, C and D, why was it not possible for A to make all three of them with B? This was the dilemma posed by the triple contract. Pope Sixtus V denounced the triple contract in 1585 in response to Luther's offensive against the Church's position in his *Tract on Trade and Usury*. Nevertheless, it led to a religious quandary and perhaps even hastened along the removal of the ban on usury (Nelson, 1949; Anwar, 1987; Taylor and Evans, 1987).

18. See, for example, Davis and Lewis (1992) for a summary.
19. The 'capture' theory of regulation is associated especially with Downs (1961), Stigler (1964, 1971) and Stigler and Friedland (1962). Stigler argued that regulation increases the well-being of the soliciting groups in the regulated industry, while Downs argued that the political process is geared up to supply those vested interests.
20. Usury laws also inhibited the Bank of England in its operation of discount policy (see Court, 1962, p. 97).

9. Directions in Islamic finance

TAKAFUL (ISLAMIC INSURANCE)

In 1999, there were 34 *Takaful* companies providing Islamic insurance. Table 9.1 shows the countries in which *Takaful* companies operate, and the organisations engaged in *Takaful* business. Many of these organisations were established wholly or partly, by Islamic banks, and the table indicates the associated bank, along with the date of formation (where known). Some of the factors underlying the *bancassurance* trend in Western markets are relevant for this diversification, but in addition there are complementarities because Islamic insurance operates under a set of rules and *shari'a* supervision not dissimilar to that for Islamic banking. By establishing their own *Takaful* companies to serve the Muslim community, the Islamic banks, in effect, lend credibility to their banking operations.

Problems with Conventional Insurance

Unlike its banking counterpart, Islamic insurance has been largely neglected in the literature,[1] for reasons which seem difficult to explain other than the specialised nature of insurance as a subject. From the viewpoint of Islamic law, there are three main problems with conventional, especially life, insurance.[2] First, it violates the prohibition of *gharar* (uncertainty) since the benefits to be paid depend on the outcome of future events that are not known at the time of signing the contract. This prohibition in particular nullifies a conventional whole-of-life policy contract because this type of policy is based on a time frame, the lifetime of the insured, which is not known and cannot be known until the event (death) itself occurs. Second, insurance is regarded as *maysir* (gambling) because policyholders are held to be betting premiums on the condition that the insurer will make payment (indemnity) consequent upon the circumstance of a specified event. For example, when policyholders take out a pure endowment policy they are taking a gamble that they will still be alive by the end of the term of the policy to receive the benefits stated in the contract. Third, all insurance policies (including general insurance) have a significant savings element built into them, as the insurer invests prepaid premiums on behalf of those insured (Covick and Lewis, 1997). Since the underlying investment activities of many insurance company contracts are

Table 9.1 Takaful *(Islamic insurance) institutions in operation, 1999*

Country	Organisation[1]
Australia	Australia *Takaful* Association Inc
Bahamas	Islamic *Takafol ReTakafoul*, Bahamas (DMI Group) – 1983
Bahrain	Al-Salam Islamic *Takaful* Company – 1992
	Islamic Insurance & Re-insurance Co. (Al-Baraka Group)
	Takaful International Company (formerly Bahrain Islamic Insurance Company (Bahrain Islamic Bank) – 1989
	Takafol Islamic Insurance Co. EC (DMI group)
Brunei	Insurans Islam Taib Sendiran Berhad IITSB (Perbadanan Tabung Amanah Islami Brunei) – 1993
	Takaful Ab Birhad – 1993
Ghana	Metropolitan Insurance Company Ltd
Indonesia	PT Asuransi *Takaful* Keluarga (Bank Muamalet Indonesia) – 1994
	PT Asuransi *Takaful* Umum (Bank Muamalet Indonesia)
	Takaful Asuransi
	PT Syarikat *Takaful* Indonesia (Bank Muamalat)
Jordan	Islamic Insurance Company Plc (Jordan Islamic Bank for Finance and Investment)
Luxembourg	*Takafol* SA (DMI group) – 1982
Malaysia	Asean *Retakaful* International (L) Ltd (Bank Islam Malaysia Berhad) – 1997
	The Malaysian Insurance Institute
	MNI *Takaful* SBN Berhad – 1993
	Syakirat *Takaful* Malaysia, SDN BH (Bank Islam Malaysia Berhad) – 1984
	Takaful Nasional Anda – 1993
Saudi Arabia	International Islamic Insurance Co.
	Islamic Arab Company for Insurance
	Islamic Arab Insurance Co. (Al-Baraka Group) – 1979
	Islamic Corporation for the Insurance of Investment and Export Credit (Islamic Development Bank) – 1994
	Islamic Insurance Co. Ltd, Riyadh
	Islamic Insurance and Reinsurance Co. Bahrain (Al-Baraka Group) – 1985
	Islamic International Company for Insurance, Salamat – 1985
	Islamic Rhajhi Co. for Cooperative Insurance, Al-Aman – 1985

Country	Organisation[1]
	Islamic *Takafol* & *ReTakafol* Company (DMI Group) – 1986
	National Company for Cooperative Insurance – 1986
	Takafol Islamic Company, Riyadh (DMI Group)
Singapore	AMPRO Singapore
	Syarikat *Takaful* Singapura – 1995
Senegal	Sosar Al Amane (Al-Baraka Group)
Sudan[2]	The National Reinsurance Company (Sudan) Ltd
	The United Insurance Company (Sudan) Ltd – 1968 (1992)[2]
	Watania Cooperative Insurance Co. (Islamic Cooperative Development Bank) – 1989
Trinidad	*Takaful* T & T
Tunisia	B.E.S.T.–RE (Al-Baraka group)
Turkey	Ihlas Sigorta As
Qatar	Qatar Islamic Insurance Co. – 1994
UAE	Islamic Arab Insurance Co. (Al-Baraka group)
	Oman Insurance Company, Dubai
USA	*Takaful* USA Management Services – 1996

Notes:
1. In brackets the name of any Islamic Bank with a full or part shareownership is shown, along with the date of establishment, where known.
2. All insurance companies in Sudan have been deemed to operate on an Islamic basis, since 1992.

Source: Directory of Islamic Insurance (*Takaful*) 2000.

riba-based, conventional insurance policies, therefore, contravene the *shari'a*. For example, interest-rate bonds and securities accounted for about 80 per cent of the assets of US life insurance companies in 1988 (Lewis, 1992b), and in 1998 still accounted for 65 per cent of assets (ACLI, 1999).

Insurance, it must be said, remains a controversial matter within the Muslim community. Some argue that the calculation of probability involved might be seen as an act of defiance against *takdir*, God's predestination of events. House insurance, for example, is virtually unknown in some Arab countries. Muslehuddin (1982) surveys the *fatawa* (religious rulings) for and against the contract of insurance. As recently as 1995, Sheik Al-Azhar Al-Sheikh Jad-al Haq Ali Jad al-Haq, an Egyptian scholar, declared all life insurance to be prohibited under *shari'a* (Billah, 1999; Wahib, 1999). Others, however, argue that a system of life insurance can be worked out, based on mutuality, which avoids the presence of *gharar*, *riba* and *maysir* in conventional life insurance. This is the basis of *Takaful* insurance.

Takaful Policies

Takaful is a noun stemming from the Arabic verb 'kafal' meaning to take care of one's needs. It is descriptive of a practice whereby participants in a group agree jointly to guarantee themselves against loss or damage. If any member or participant suffers a catastrophe or disaster, he/she would receive financial benefit from a fund as defined in the insurance contract to help meet that loss or damage. Essentially the concept of *Takaful* is based on solidarity, responsibility and brotherhood among members where participants agree to share defined losses to be paid out of defined assets. It thus corresponds to what would be called in a different context mutual insurance, in that members are the insurers as well as the insured.[3]

Three types of *Takaful* products are on offer:

- *General Takafuls (Islamic general insurance)*
  These offer protection or coverage against risks of a general nature for companies or individuals (participants). Some of the products are motor insurance, fire and allied perils, worker compensation, marine cargo, engineering insurance, property, transport, and so on.
- *Family Takafuls (Islamic life insurance)*
  These provide coverage for participation by individuals or corporate bodies on a long-term basis and the maturity period generally ranges from 10 to 40 years. Some of the products are medical and health plans, education, accident, marriage, *hajj* and *umra* plans, lump-sum investments, savings plans, retirement plans, mortgage and so on.
- *Retakaful Coverage (Islamic reinsurance)*
  There are very few companies in this field and they are mainly located in the Bahamas, Malaysia, Saudi Arabia and Sudan. The *Retakaful* companies offer coverage for *Takaful* companies against risks, loss or dilution of its capital and reserves resulting from high claim exposures.

General *Takafuls* are short-term contracts for the protection of potential material losses from specified catastrophes. Members' premiums are called *tabaru* (contribution, donation). These are invested on a *mudaraba* basis by the *Takaful* company, with profits allocated between the *tabaru* fund and the management. Any surplus, after indemnity, reserves and operational costs are deducted, is then shared between either all participants or those who did not make a claim, depending on the company concerned. In short, the similarity with conventional insurance comes from the entire contribution of members being invested, like premiums, in a *tabaru* fund; the differences come from the *mudaraba* investment basis and the entitlement of participants to any surplus in the *tabaru* fund.

In the case of life (family) insurance, the basic objective of *Takaful* is to pay for a defined loss from a defined fund, which is set up mutually by policyholders, but is managed by a *Takaful* company. The policy is not so much to insure one's own life but is a financial transaction that relies on the principles of mutual cooperation for the welfare of the insured and/or his/her dependants. Second, the elements of *gharar* can be avoided if the policy operates on the principles of *mudaraba,* as a profit-sharing contract between the provider(s) of the fund, that is the policyholders, and the entrepreneur, that is the *Takaful* company, under defined profit-sharing ratios. Third, each policy also has a fixed period or term such as, say, 10 or 15 years so as to eliminate the uncertainty in the contract period, and prevent it from being a whole-of-life policy.[4]

Types of Conventional Life Insurance

So as to better understand how a *Takaful* life policy works, it may be valuable to review how standard life insurance operates.

Term insurance

Life offices could offer financial security against death by means of one-year contracts, with annual premiums rising sharply in line with the age of the life covered. Although it is possible to buy term insurance (or temporary life insurance) on this basis, this is not the usual way. Under the standard form of term life insurance policy, a contract period of a number of years' duration is specified and a constant annual premium is determined. If the person whose life is the subject of cover then dies during the contract period, and if the various other terms of the contract have been complied with, the insurer pays out the sum specified in the contract, and no further premiums are payable. If at the end of the contract period the relevant person is still alive, the obligations of the insurer simply end.

The fact that a constant annual premium is being levied when the likelihood of a claim arising on the policy is in fact increasing from one year to the next means that, during the early years of the contract, premium monies are being paid in excess of what would have been necessary to secure the same cover under one-year term policies for those years. In effect, then, the insurer is providing the insured with two distinct sets of services: death cover over the contract period via a sequence of one-year term policies (each with its own appropriate premium rate); and a 'premium-equalisation' service, consisting of the management of a balance of prepaid premiums on behalf of the insured.

Whole-of-life

Under a whole-of-life policy, the contract period is not a specified number of years: it is the remaining lifetime of the person whose life is the subject of the cover, with a constant annual premium rate again the norm. But both the insurer and the insured know with certainty that sooner or later a claim must arise. A pool of such whole-of-life policies serves an insurance function and a saving function. By the time the last of these contracts expires, the insurer will have paid out the sum insured on each and every policy. In the early years, when few claims are being made, the insurer must be accumulating the funds necessary for coping with the more rapid flow of claims in later years. The funds held are, in effect, an aggregate of a set of 'prepaid premium deposits' – one deposit per policy still in force. The insurer manages these deposits and simultaneously provides each insured with death cover.

To summarise, then, for term policies the insurer holds prepaid premiums on behalf of those insured. With whole-of-life policies the same principle applies, but on a larger scale. The other standard types of life insurance contract in existence can be regarded as outgrowths of these, and all in one way or another bundle together life cover with a substantial 'savings bank' type facility. For example, endowment insurance policies require the insurer to manage an accumulating balance of the insured's savings. Annuities require the insurer to manage a decumulating balance of the annuitants' savings (Covick and Lewis, 1997). However, a major difference comes from the new unit-linked policies.

Unit-linked

Unit-linked or investment-linked policies, as they are called in Britain, were introduced in the 1960s and have become very popular, largely displacing the traditional US-style policies outlined above (in the US the new policies are called variable life). Instead of bundling together death cover and a savings-type account, the unit-linked or investment-linked policies package the insurance cover with a unit trust (mutual fund) or a special management fund. Premiums are collected over the length of the contract and a determined minimum death benefit may be guaranteed (based upon an assumed but very modest rate of return on assets). A part of the premiums goes to pay for the insurer's expenses and another part can be regarded as going to provide the minimum life cover. The balance, rather than being invested in the normal life insurance fund, is used to buy units (shares) in a mutual fund or in one of the office's special funds consisting, say, of common stocks. Both funds contain assets which can be expected to increase in nominal value year by year and thus provide a hedge against inflation. When the policy matures or the person dies, all units credited to the policy are sold, with the value of the proceeds depending upon the growth of performance in the interim of the underlying fund or investment pool.

Takaful Life Insurance

This distinction between the US-style and the UK-style of life insurance is important for understanding *Takaful* life insurance, which is closer to the unit-linked policy than to the traditional. Figure 9.1 sets out the structure. Premiums paid by the participants are divided into a *Takaful*, also called *tabaru*, account (TA) and participants' *mudaraba* investment portfolio account (PA). Usually, depending on the formula used, which sometimes varies according to the age and participation period of the participants, between 2.5 per cent to 10 per cent of instalments go to the *Takaful* fund and the balance goes to the *mudaraba* portfolio account of the participants. Insurance benefits are paid from the *tabaru* fund. Profits from the *mudaraba* investments are shared between the participants and the companies in pre-agreed ratios, for example 6:4, 7:3, 8:2, and so on. Participants are entitled to reimbursements (of PA premiums and investment earnings and share of net surplus) upon maturity, withdrawal (PA funds only) and, in some cases, upon disablement. Upon death of a participant, his heirs are entitled to *Takaful* benefits, along with PA funds, which are reimbursed according to the Islamic inheritance laws, discussed earlier.

There are obvious similarities between the *Takaful* life and the unit-linked policy. In particular, both types of policies deduct a proportion of the premiums paid and credit it into a separate account, that is, a TA for the *Takaful* policy and a special management fund for the unit-linked policy, to cover the cost of any guarantees. Also, the sum assured for both policies depends on the investment performance of the remaining portion of the premiums, subject to a minimum guaranteed sum assured on death.

There are also important differences, which it may be useful to summarise:

1. Under unit-linked policies, only the remaining portion, which is put into a unit fund, is invested in a portfolio of assets, whereas under *Takaful*, both accounts, PA and TA, are invested.
2. There are no bid and offer values under *Takaful* like the ones being used under a unit-linked policy.
3. Under *Takaful* there is a fixed minimum premium which is the same for all policyholders of all ages, normally from 18 to 55. *Takaful* companies are not allowed to make profit from favourable mortality experience, and the policies taken out are regarded more as a means of the family saving for the future rather than as a means to get compensation in the event of death (or on survival) of the policyholder.
4. Conventional life companies usually charge an extra premium in addition to the normal amount for policyholders (for example smokers, those with dangerous jobs) who are deemed to pose extra risk and hence have higher

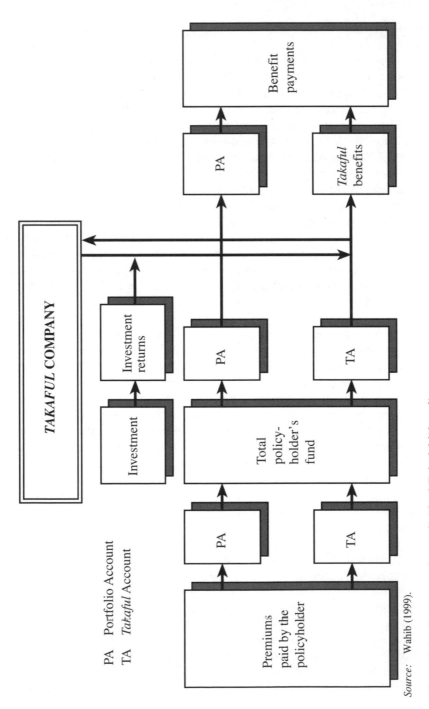

PA   Portfolio Account
TA   *Takaful* Account

Source: Wahib (1999).

Figure 9.1   *Structure of an individual Takaful life policy*

mortality rates than average. *Takaful* companies generally still charge the same fixed minimum premium.

5. Conventional insurance companies may not pay claims from death due to suicide or other unnatural causes. *Takaful* companies, by contrast, have to pay out the benefits regardless of the way any policyholder dies and this includes death by suicide or being killed while committing a crime. Muslims believe that the death of all creatures is ultimately determined by God, no matter how the creature dies.[5]

6. Finally, under the terms of the *mudaraba* investment arrangement, participants cannot interfere with portfolio selection as the management assumes full authority and the investment is made under utmost good faith, which may exclude firm contracts. However, if a loss occurs due to disrespect of *mudaraba* conditions, the *Takaful* companies will bear those losses.

Two Problems

This last feature, of 'non-interference', differs from the conventional unit-linked policies, under which provision for switching between funds is a feature. An office issuing unit-linked policies may provide a policyholder with a choice of, say, five different funds. There may be a specialised equities fund, a property fund for real estate investments, a fund of international shares, a fund of money market deposits (essentially a money market mutual fund), and a fund of longer-term fixed interest securities. Frequently, one switch per year is allowed free of charge. The companies are able to offer this switching flexibility to savers by conducting their own capital market, selling the units purchased from one saver to another saver switching into that fund. As the *Takaful* market develops, this is a feature which may well be adopted without departing from the *mudaraba* principle, since each separate fund's investments would remain at the *mudarib*'s discretion. Yet, at the same time, it would add to product variety, which is regarded as a problem for *Takaful* companies (Wahib, 1999).

As well as product variety, one of the other difficulties facing *Takaful* insurance has been in finding *riba*-free investments. With the move to unit-linked policies, many conventional insurers' investments have become more equity-oriented, whereas in the past they have been predominantly interest-based (and still are in the US). This trend ought to suit *Takaful* insurers, but a suitable portfolio requires knowledge of the degree of *riba* involved in a company's operations on a company-by-company basis; this knowledge can be tedious and costly to obtain for the many companies the shares of which are traded on exchanges. This is where developments in Islamic investments may help.

ISLAMIC UNIT TRUSTS

Islamic banks have long offered special investment accounts under an individual restricted *mudaraba* basis for high net worth individuals investing, say, $500 000 or more, as well as the unrestricted *mudaraba* for ordinary depositors. It was a short step to combine elements of these two investment modes in the form of closed-ended or open-ended unit trusts, utilising the pooling principle of the latter with the higher entry value of the former to offer a range of alternative investments, at different entry prices.

Closed and Open-ended

The most common form of closed-ended fund is a company which uses the funds provided by shareholders to 'invest' in the shares (stocks) of other companies. Shares in the investment company are simply bought or sold in the stock market. An example is the Faisal Fund for Egyptian Equities Ltd, organised under the laws of Jersey with participating shares listed on the Irish Stock Exchange. The Fund then invests mainly in listed Egyptian equities. It was established in 1997 and launched in 1998.

Because of the forces of supply and demand, the market price of closed-ended investment companies can differ from the market value of the underlying share portfolio. This cannot happen with open-ended funds, because the number of units or shares is not fixed or restricted like that of a closed-end fund (where, for example, participating shares may not exceed management shares by some specified ratio, for example 9:1), and thus the supply of shares or units, that is capital, can be increased or decreased according to demand. Accordingly, the market price or value of units will vary directly with the market value of the securities represented by those units. An example of such a fund is the Al-Safa Investment Fund, formed in the UK in 1999 as an open-ended investment company, with minimum investments of £1000 or £50 per month by regular savings, pooled and invested in selected UK equities. With tax-exempt Personal Equity Plan (PEP) status, it is suitable for the attraction of the savings of British Muslims.

All trusts offer a number of features (Lewis and Davis, 1987, ch. 2). First, they offer information services, in that participants acquire the services of professional investment management and administration of investments for a price, in the form of a management fee or expenses or profit share. Second, diversification is made possible by the size of the fund, the factor which prompted the formation of the first pooled fund in Britain in 1868. For example, the Al-Safa fund will normally have in excess of 40 stock-market holdings. Third, the funds offer liquidity, in that shares can be bought or sold before maturity or redeemed through the investment company at close to the current market value.

Types of Trusts

As well as the distinction between closed and open-ended, investment companies can be classified according to the types of investments made by the pooled funds. These can be divided into three groups:

1. *Islamic transactions.* A number of long-established funds have concentrated in a variety of Islamic portfolios. Thus, for example, the Al-Tawfeek Company for the Investment of Funds and the Al-Amin Company for Securities and Investment Funds, both part of the Al-Baraka group, were established in Bahrain in 1987. Both issue shares which participate in profits and can be bought and sold. Investments are made in a number of countries such as Morocco, Mauritania, Algeria, Turkey and Saudi Arabia. In 1998, Al-Amin's investments comprised lease contracts 46 per cent, *murabahas* 29 per cent and Islamic deposits 26 per cent.
2. *Specialised funds.* A number of funds specialise in particular activities such as leasing whereby the Trust finances equipment, a building or an entire project for a third party against an agreed rental. For example, in June 1998 the Kuwait Finance House launched a leasing fund in the United States, to invest in industrial equipment and machinery. The fund was established with $40 million in assets, and the minimum investment in the fund is $250 000. As another example of a specialised fund, The International Investor Kuwait Real-State Development Fund bought assets from the Kuwait government and then issued shares which were sold to the public and listed on the stock market. There are also specialised real estate and commodity funds.
3. *Equity funds.* These are simply trusts, both closed and open-ended, which invest funds in stocks and shares. Those funds investing in international equities cover the world's major stock markets. As at July 2000, there were 88 Islamic funds in operation, most established since 1995 (Al-Rifai, 1999; *New Horizon*, July 2000). We now examine the characteristics of these trusts.

Types of Equity Funds

Types of equity funds include:

- Global funds (Al-Rajhi Global Equity, NCB Global Trading Equity,

Wellington Hegira, Al Sawfa, Al Baraka, Al Fanar Investment
Holdings, Al-Dar World Equities, Riyad Equity Fund, Oasis
International Equity)
- Regional funds (Mendaki Growth, Al Rajhi Middle East, TII Ibn Majid, Al-Nukhba)
- Sector funds (TII Small-Capital, Amana Income, Hi Tech Fund)
- European funds (Al-Dar European Equities, European Trading Equity Fund)
- Country funds (Saudi Trading Equity, Al Rajhi Egypt, most Malaysian funds, US equity funds)
- Hedge funds (TII Alkhawarizmi Fund)
- Index Funds (Dow Jones Islamic Market Index Fund)

Interestingly, the first Islamic equity fund was established not in a Muslim country but in the United States. The Amana Income Fund was formed in June 1986 by members of the North American Islamic Trust (NAIT), an organisation in Indiana which oversees the funding of mosques in USA amongst other things. The fund still exists. Saturna Capital Corp., a small asset management company in Washington, manages the Amana Income Fund as well as the Amana Growth Fund. With about 7 million Muslims in America and an equal number living in Europe, some Islamic funds have been launched to tap this investment market. This is true of Al-Safa, noted earlier. It is also true of the Halal Mutual Investment Company based in Ireland which collects individual investment funds as small as £250 for placement into short-term trading facilities, much like a money market mutual fund. As another example, Commerzbank launched the Al-Sukoor European Equity Fund in January 2000 targeted at the Middle East and also at Muslims living in Germany.

Shari'a Acceptability

The principal question from the Islamic point of view is whether investments in international equity markets are acceptable under the *shari'a* (Hasan, 1995). There is no doubt that dealing in the supply, manufacture or service of things prohibited by Islam (*haram*), such as *riba*, pork meat, alcohol, gambling, and so on cannot be acceptable. But companies which are not involved in the above *haram* activities could be considered acceptable. The main objection against them is that in their own internal accounting and financial dealings they lend and borrow from *riba* banks and other institutions, but the fact remains that their main business operations do not involve prohibited activities. Essentially, non-Muslim entities cannot be expected to work under the Islamic code of conduct, and in any case only a negligible amount of interest may be involved. In this case, if some income from interest-bearing accounts is incorporated, the proportion of such income in the dividend paid to the Islamic shareholders must be given by them to charity. For example, if 5 per cent of the whole income of a company has come out of interest-bearing returns, 5 per cent of the dividend must be given in charity.

Islamic Market Indices

Quite clearly, ascertaining such information could be costly for an individual fund, but has been made less so by the creation in February 1999 of the Dow Jones Islamic Market Index (DJIM), launched in Bahrain, and in November, 1999 of the Financial Times–Stock Exchange Global Islamic Index Series (GIIS). Both indices are aimed at investors who follow Islamic investment guidelines, and classify quoted companies according to a number of screens. After removing companies with unacceptable core business activities, the remaining list is tested by a financial-ratio 'filter', the purpose of which is to remove companies with an unacceptable debt ratio. Both indices use a debt/asset ratio of less than one-third, while the DJIM uses two additional filters: accounts receivable/total assets must be less than 49 per cent and interest income/operating income must be less than 10 per cent. Both series report a dividend cleansing/impure income figure. Here 'tainted dividend' receipts relate to the portion, if any, of a dividend paid by a constituent company that has been determined to be attributable to activities that are not in accordance with *shari'a* principles and therefore should be donated to a proper charity or charities. However, such cleansing cannot be counted as part of *zakat* obligations. In this and other matters, both index compilers were advised by *shari'a* scholars.

In the case of DJIM, it forms part of the Dow Jones Global Index (DJGI) of nearly 3000 companies from 33 countries, covering 10 economic sectors and 122 industry groupings. After the *shari'a* screening, there were left about 600 companies from 30 countries. Indonesia and Malaysia are the only Muslim countries included in the DJGI (and Malaysia was put on hold when it imposed capital control restrictions in 1998). Dow Jones have also licensed Brown Brothers Harriman and Wafra Investment Advisory Group of Kuwait to create a tradeable fund based on the DJIM.

There are obvious parallels in this selection process with the ethical investment movement. A number of investment advisers, such as Buckmaster and Moore in the UK, have been providing investment advice for over three decades to clients who want to invest in ethical Unit Trusts, that is, those which do not invest in the shares of companies trading in tobacco, alcohol, gambling, arms or, until recently, in South Africa. The main difference is that the determination of whether an investment is ethical or unethical is made by the fund managers, based on information received from various professional bodies, including the Independent Investors Responsibility Research Centre of Washington DC and other specially constituted committees of reference. In the case of Islamic Unit Trusts, the ultimate approval comes from the Boards of Religious Advisers, and their rulings are binding on the fund managers.

ISLAMIC INVESTMENT BANKING

As the Islamic equity market develops, so too will the demand for investment banking services. This is already apparent. The International Investor (TII), the largest wholesale Islamic investment bank, pioneered the GIIS, discussed in the previous section. Al-Baraka Investment Bank, Saudi Arabia and London, and Faisal Finance, Switzerland have also been prominent as managers of Islamic equity funds. At the same time, many conventional investment banks and fund managers are employed as advisers or managers of Islamic equity funds. The major firms are: Wellington Management Co. USA; UBS Switzerland; Robert Fleming, Luxembourg; and Citibank, USA and Bahrain (Citi Islamic Investment Bank).

Investment Banking

Investment banking is not easy to define. Table 9.2 lists the activities associated with investment banking, but not each bank will undertake all – rather they will concentrate on their own mix of activities from within this range as well as innovating with new ones, for investment banking is more an approach to financial intermediation than a defined set of financial product and service lines. Traditionally, it relies on the quality of the bankers, rather than on the size of capital resources, and in this sense is more an attitude of mind – a flexible, creative and opportunistic approach to facilitating financial transactions.

When capital risk is incurred by an investment bank, it is usually only intended to be of a short-term, market pricing risk nature, for example underwriting of new issue securities, or secondary market trading. Confusion arises because, in the 1980s, US investment banks became involved in what they called 'merchant banking', seemingly involving equity-type and sometimes pure equity investment in corporations. For the most part, however, this reflected the investment banks' role in structuring and arranging equity investment on behalf of clients. The banks were primarily managing the funds of other investors (in leveraged buy-out funds, and so on) although they sometimes provided sizeable short-term 'bridge' financing, in the expectation of receiving equity-related returns.

Table 9.2   Range of investment banking activities

While the mix of activities varies by bank and over time, the following summarises the range of activities which have historically characterised investment banking in domestic and/or international markets.

Acceptances, bills of exchange, letters of credit, etc.
Commercial paper issuance and trading
Loans, short- and medium-term (including direct, but mainly syndicated)
Project finance (advice on structuring, concessions and tendering)
Export credit (advice, provision or negotiation)
Multi-option facilities, structuring and negotiation (mainly syndicated)
Debt trading (discounted loans)
Islamic finance
Government policy (general advice on economic and financial sector strategy)
Treasury bills issue and government securities underwriting, distribution and
    trading
Government policy (general advice on economic and financial sector strategy)
Treasury bills issue and government securities underwriting, distribution and
    trading
Government international market borrowings (advice and negotiation)
Privatisation (advice on structuring and execution involving underwriting,
    distribution and after market trading)
Investment advice and/or management (for governments, central banks, pension
    funds, unit trusts, mutual funds, investment trusts, corporations and high net
    worth individuals)
Custody services
Private banking
Corporate bonds, convertibles, equities, warrants – public issue underwriting,
    distribution and aftermarket trading, new listings, new issues/rights issues
Stockbrokerage, equity and fixed income market-making, with associated
    investment research
Futures, options and swaps broking and managed futures, with associated
    investment research
Private placements (debt, equity and investment funds)
Merger and acquisitions (strategy, company searches, advice on feasibility,
    valuations, negotiation or defence advice, and execution of debt and equity
    financing)
Corporate restructuring (advice and negotiation)
Venture capital (advice, structuring, financing and negotiation – MBOs/MBIs,
    specialist funds, etc.)
Foreign exchange trading and (through subsidiaries) moneybroking
Bullion and other commodity dealing
Property investment (advice and financing)
Estate agency (through subsidiaries)
Insurance broking (through subsidiaries)

Traditional investment banking is a peculiarly Anglo-Saxon phenomenon. In the US and the UK, it is commonplace for corporate, governmental and individual clients to pay them fees for financial advice relating to the broad spectrum of financial transactions, including equity, debt, corporate finance (including privatisation) and currency transactions. This is despite the fact that both countries have competitive, developed financial systems and also have an abundance of other fee-earning professional advisers (for example lawyers, accountants and management consultants), who are also used by these clients for specific, fee-based advisory services. US investment banks and UK merchant banks also export their skills into other capital markets outside the US and the UK, and they dominate the international capital markets. Even the European universal banks have had to acquire firms in New York and London in order to obtain the investment banking skills to match their global ambitions.

Islamic Activities

Not surprisingly, few Islamic investment banks have been able to succeed in this select company. Of course, many of the traditional activities are excluded to them, because they are bond- and bill-based, and they have naturally concentrated on those areas linked to Islamic financing. As an example of the types of activities we reproduce some extracts from the 1998 Annual Report of The International Investor[6] which emphasised four areas.

- Structured finance, which embraces corporate finance, project finance, venture capital, IPOs, mergers and acquisitions. 'There was increased demand throughout the region for investment banking and project finance, and the Company drew on its core strengths in structuring, placement and market knowledge to develop and expand this area of the business. Key assignments in Kuwait included the raising of equity and leasing facilities to finance the expansion of Al Mowasat Hospital and a mandate to arrange equity and debt for a new Spent Catalyst venture. Outside Kuwait, the Company provided a range of Islamic merchant banking services for clients in the UAE, Lebanon, UK and USA.'
- Advisory services that are long-term relationships where Islamic advisory services are provided to asset managers around the world. 'Significant progress was made during the year in the development of advisory services provided by the Company for asset managers wishing to enter the Islamic market. Attention was focused on responding to the increasing difficulty faced by conventional local and international industry players of entering the Islamic market, largely due to the rapid growth, dynamic and fast-moving nature of this niche market. The Company was designated by Japan Energy as regional investment

adviser for selected projects in Egypt and Jordan.'

- Franchising, where local institutions are helped to build an Islamic retail banking capability using the TII brand name. 'Initial franchising activities in Islamic retail banking with the Gulf Bank in Kuwait, and in Islamic Private Banking with Pictet and Cie in Switzerland both had an encouraging start. The Company is in progress of opening TII operations in Qatar and the UAE with local partners. A joint venture agreement was signed with the Bank of Bahrain and Kuwait to provide Islamic services in Bahrain.'
- Wholesaling, providing a range of Islamic investment products funds and unit trusts for distribution through others. 'Discussions in relation to wholesaling were initiated with leading financial institutions for the global distribution of TII's products.'

ISLAMIC PROJECT FINANCING

As well as a growth in advisory services around asset management, another area of expansion in the investment banking area seems likely to be around project finance, if Muslim countries follow the trends evident elsewhere. For most of the post-war period, government has been the principal provider of infrastructure (at least outside of the United States). Over the last decade, that position has begun to change. Faced with pressure to reduce public sector debt and, at the same time, expand and improve public facilities, governments have looked to private sector finance, and have invited private sector entities to enter into long-term contractual agreements which may take the form of construction or management of public sector infrastructure facilities by the private sector entity, or the provision of services (using infrastructure facilities) by the private sector entity to the community on behalf of a public sector body (Grimsey and Lewis, 1999).

The budgetary pressures which have forced the pace in the West seem particularly strong for countries such as Pakistan, seeking greater Islamisation of the financial system and looking for replacements to cover the removal of *riba*-based government borrowing. At the same time, there has been a marked revision in attitudes about whether governments have to be involved in the construction and finance of infrastructure. The old conviction was that infrastructure investment produced public goods, externalities and natural monopolies. The trend away from public to private provision of infrastructure has been underpinned by a marked change in thinking and practice on these matters. There has been the perception, for example, that a move from 'taxpayer pays' to 'user pays' (that is, from ability-to-pay to the benefit principle) in the provision of infrastructure services (water, power) is likely to be associated with a better economic use of the services and an improved allocation of resources. Many industries considered to be natural monopolies, for example electricity generation and telecommunications, have been broken up geographically into different regional firms or, with deregulation, separated into competitive (or potentially competitive) sectors *vis-à-vis* those sectors that remain natural monopolies (the distinction between power supply and high-voltage transmission, and between railway operation and rail track services). In those activities which have natural monopoly characteristics, third party access to certain facilities that are not economic to duplicate have widened competition in the upstream and downstream markets served by the facilities. All of this has laid the groundwork for joint public–private sector financing (PPS) arrangements.

Typical examples are BOOT and BOO agreements, although there are many variants. The acronym BOOT stands for Build-Own-Operate-Transfer. Under such an arrangement, a private sector developer finances, builds, owns and operates a facility which is transferred to the public sector at the end of the arrangement with or without payment in return. A classic example is the third Dartford Crossing of the River Thames in England. With a BOO (Build-Own-Operate) project, the private sector entity finances, builds, owns and operates an infrastructure facility in perpetuity. An example comes from water treatment plants in Scotland and elsewhere.

From the perspective of the project sponsors, PPS is essentially project financing, characterised by the low capitalisation of the project vehicle company and consequently a reliance on direct revenues to pay for operating costs and cover financing while giving the desired return on risk capital. The senior financier of private finance looks to the cashflow and earnings of the project as the source of funds for repayments. Funding security against the project company is not sought because the company usually has minimal assets and because the financing is without recourse to the sponsor companies behind the project company. The key principle for large PPS projects is to achieve a financial structure with as little recourse as possible to the sponsors, whilst at the same time providing sufficient support so that the financiers are satisfied with the risks.

Successful project design requires expert analysis of all of the attendant risks and then the design of contractual arrangements prior to competitive tendering that allocate risk burdens appropriately. This is where the investment bank comes in, and from the viewpoint of Islamic financing a number of financing instruments are available.

Ijara

The Islamic Development Bank (IDB) pioneered the use of leasing for project finance as early as 1977. Other Islamic finance houses have followed its lead. For example, recent project financing with an Islamic component occurred in the Equate project in Kuwait involving a US$1.2 billion joint venture between Kuwait's Petrochemicals Industries Corp. and Union Carbide of the United States. This project featured a US$200 million tranche raised by the Kuwait Finance House for two *ijaras* with maturity of 8 and 10 years, respectively. The *ijara* tranche of the project is reserved for supply of capital equipment to be structured either as a conventional lease or according to a prepayment system (Hamwi and Aylward, 1999).

While lease financing continues to be one of the most important modes of project financing used by the IDB, certain problems have been encountered in its application. For example, the asset in question is sometimes not eligible for leasing, either because it is not separately identifiable or because of its short useful life span. Moreover, the legal or tax regulations in the country of the prospective lessee may not make leasing an attractive or even a feasible proposition.

Murabaha/bai bi-thamin ajil

As a result of these limitations in the leasing mode, the IDB introduced an instalment sale in 1985. This is a contract of sale whereby ownership of the asset is immediately transferred to the buyer, while the purchase price is payable in instalments. This mode of financing fully conforms to the *shari'a* and falls within the deferred sale (*bai'muajjal*) scheme. Using the same technique, several Islamic and conventional banks, including Citibank, formed a syndicate in 1992 to provide a six-month US$110 million facility to the Hub River Power Company. The facility was used by the company to finance on a deferred basis the purchase of equipment needed for the project. The lead manager was Islamic Investment Company of the Gulf. Later, in another project, Citibank arranged a syndicated facility in July 1994 to provide a six-month US$115 million *murabaha* financing to the Pakistan Water and Power Development Authority that was used to buy engineering equipment (Buckmaster, 1996).

Istisnaa

An *istisnaa* facility is a contract for acquisition of goods where the price is paid in advance at an agreed markup, and the manufactured goods delivered at a later date. Such an arrangement can be used for the construction phase of a project. This was the idea with the M$1 billion Islamic financing structure for the Kuala Lumpur Light Rail Transit 2 project, known by the Malaysian acronym 'Putra'. The Islamic financing tranche which was negotiated by the co-arrangers was in two parts. The first was a four-year *istisnaa* facility. After a four-year construction phase, the facility was then designed to switch to an *ijara* whereby the owners of the equipment (switches, tracks, trains and so on) would lease the goods back to the railway operator, Putra, over the next 11 years. Under the project financing deal, the switch to a leasing structure after four years would allow the financing banks to issue asset-backed bonds because Islamic guidelines enable bonds to be issued if they are backed by physical assets equating to 51 per cent or more of their value.

Musharaka

If investment funds come from the sponsor(s) as well as the financier, the traditional method of *musharaka* could be used for project finance. Since the *musharaka* would have been effected from the very inception of the project, there should be no problem with regard to the valuation of capital. Similarly, the distribution of profits according to the normal accounting standards should not be difficult. Should the financier want to withdraw from the *musharaka* while the other party wants to continue the business, the latter can purchase the share of the former at an agreed price. If the sale of the share on one time basis is not feasible for the lack of liquidity in the project, the share of the financier can be divided into smaller units and each unit can be sold after a suitable interval. Whenever a unit is sold, the share of the financier in the project is reduced to that extent, and when all the units are sold, the financier exits the project totally. This would then be equivalent to a diminishing *musharaka*.

Equity

It may also be possible to finance the project by means of participating equity. Suppose that a build-operate-transfer (BOT) company has been awarded the concession for the construction of a toll road, on the condition that the project be financed by *shari'a* compatible means. If the BOT company is in need of funds in local currency, these sums could be raised by means of equity participation certificates issued as shares in the ownership of the bridge, entitling their owner to a proportional share in the collected toll. It would be as if the stocks actually consist of full ownership of a physical segment of the bridge. Since the owners obviously get income only if the entire bridge is intact, they should not care which shares they own, thus rendering those physical segments 'fungible', and capable of being traded in the same way that simple equity can be bought and sold.[7] A variant along similar lines suggested by Ebrahim (1999) is a 'revenue bond' which would promise a certain fraction of the net operating income from operations rather than any fixed rate of return. A revenue participating scheme along similar lines was undertaken by the Turkish government in the mid-1980s.

Thus there are a number of different ways by which the revenue stream from an Islamically acceptable project can support project financing contracts which accord with the *shari'a*. Such instruments would enable the large sums that are currently held mainly in short-term Islamic investments to be harnessed for investment in long-term infrastructure projects. Not only would this mobilisation be valuable in resolving the problems of public sector financing in Islamic countries, it is entirely consistent with Islamic precepts. By providing basic social goods such as power, water, transport, and communications services, infrastructure projects fit comfortably with the social responsibility ethos that is an essential feature of Islamic finance. In addition, limited recourse or non-recourse project financing structures are a form of asset-based financing that seem entirely consistent with Islamic law. When the complex financial structures that constitute these arrangements are stripped away, what is apparent is that project investors are sharing in the asset and cashflow risks of projects in ways that financiers are required to do under Islamic law.

INTERNATIONALISATION OF ISLAMIC BANKING

This section investigates whether there is potential for an international centre for Islamic finance. Our starting point is the contention that there is a strong actual and latent demand for Islamic banking and finance.

Latent Demand

The natural catchment area for Islamic banking comes from the Muslim community at a world level. In these terms, Islamic financing is potentially a global phenomenon, given both the large and growing percentage of the world's population (currently approximately 20 per cent) adhering to Islam, and the large number of Muslim states. In many of these Muslim countries, the market penetration of Islamic banking has been low, but may not remain so.

In Indonesia, for example, the largest Muslim country in the world, where Muslims account for 85 per cent of a population of 210 million, Islamic banking has a small presence: 0.15 per cent of total banking assets in December, 1999. One reason for this neglect in Indonesia is that a substantial proportion of the population, especially in Java, subscribe to the Pancasila ideology which is essentially secular in character. Nevertheless, from a low base, Islamic banking is expanding rapidly. In July 1999, Bank IFI opened an Islamic banking (*syariah*) unit, and in November 1999, Bank Susila Bhakti was transformed into Bank Syariah Mandiri. They joined Bank Muamalat Indonesia, established in 1992. In addition, as of February 2000, most commercial banks' branches in Aceh have been transformed or are in the process of being converted into *syariah* banks or units. Also, the central bank had given its approval to state-owned Bank Negara Indonesia to change five of its branches into *syariah* units. They are in Yogyakarta, Malang, Jepara, Pekalongan and Banjarmasin. State-owned Bank Rakyat Indonesia and Bank Tabungan Negara have also asked for the central bank's approval to convert a number of their branches into *syariah* units.[8]

There are other countries in a roughly similar position (for example Turkey), and a number where the Islamic market has not really been tapped (for example the 6.8 million Muslims in Thailand, 7.6 million Muslims in the Philippines and 50 million Muslims in China). Such considerations, along with the lack of familiarity in general with Islamic institutions and methods of financing, mean that the latent demand for Islamic finance is, for all practical purposes, virtually infinite. By latent demand is meant a demand from those Islamic investors who presently invest in conventional financing transactions but who would favour conversion into investments in 'Islamic-qualifying' transactions, provided that these were to have risk–return and portfolio diversification characteristics roughly comparable to those similarly available in conventional markets.

A pure Islamic-qualifying transaction could be seen as one which involves only adherents of Islam (that is, as investors, as users of funds and as intermediaries). So long as a transaction is structured to adhere rigidly to the most stringent interpretation of Islamic finance principles and with funds deployed in Islamic-qualifying projects it would be considered Islamic-qualifying by all *shari'a* (religious supervisory) boards globally. But a wider range of activities might be classed as qualifying if the criteria were to relate to its form, substance and purpose, and the other activities of the end-users, rather than to the general religious adherence of the participants. That is, the qualifying elements relate to the form and substance of a transaction and not the 'qualifications' of those who design, participate or manage the activity. Such an interpretation would conceivably allow many conventional (non-Islamic) financial institutions, governments, corporations and individuals to participate in the market, as indeed they do already and to a growing extent.

Financing Opportunities

Amongst Islamic banks there is something of an imbalance between the deposit side and the financing operations of the banks in the sense that, while it has been relatively easy to create a system in which deposits do not pay interest, and attract many deposits from those religiously-inclined to *shari'a* principles, it has been more difficult to implement profit-and-loss-sharing financial arrangements on the asset side. An accentuating factor is that many Islamic equity funds launched by European-based institutions have failed to gain the confidence of Gulf investors, partly because the institutions concerned and their *shari'a* advisers were not well connected with the Muslim community (Wilson, 1999).

The result is that at present, the demand for Islamic-qualifying transactions may be outstripping the supply of suitable investment outlets. KPMG Fakhro estimated the unsatisfied visible demand for Islamic investment vehicles in Saudi Arabia alone to be US$10 billion! This estimate represented the amount (known to KPMG Fakhro) of uninvested capital commitments specifically dedicated to Islamic finance (MOFNE, 1994). The most recent estimate of the potential market globally for Islamic investments is $100 billion to $150 billion.[9]

Past experience in the annals of finance would suggest that such financing imbalances can best be resolved by market means through the establishment of regional or international financial centres, along with the creation of new financial instruments. For example, the petrodollar recycling crisis in the 1970s was solved when London arose as the principal international centre for Eurodollars, and a new financial instrument – the syndicated credit – enabled long-term financing to be made (especially to developing countries) on the back of short-term deposits of dollars from OPEC countries (Lewis and Davis, 1987).

A similar conclusion comes from experience in the 1980s. Then, the financing problem was to recycle Japanese current account surpluses to finance the USA deficit, and again the international financial markets came to the rescue. In this case, however, the financial innovation took place off-the-balance sheets of the banks in the securities markets via securities derivatives (for example bond warrants and convertibles) and Euro-note facilities of various sorts which enabled short-term financial instruments to be transformed into longer-term funding (Lewis, 1988 and 1992c).

AN ISLAMIC INTERNATIONAL FINANCIAL CENTRE

By analogy, the contention here is that the Islamic finance imbalance might be solved if the 'surplus' deposits were on-lent to an international finance centre which could act as a funnel for the funds. For each individual bank participating in such a market, the funds provided might be on a short-term basis. But a series of such short-term funds by different banks when combined would exhibit greater stability and provide resources which could be channelled into longer-term investments. At the same time, the existence of this pool of resources would attract long-term investment vehicles, and so act as a magnet for investment avenues in need of funding. Thus at the aggregate level the existence of the market would enable a succession of short-term surpluses to be transformed into longer-term investments. This is exactly what happened with the London Eurodollar market and the international syndicated credit, and much the same sort of process could occur with Islamic finance.

Of course, in this particular instance, the new instruments and financial innovations required need to be equity- and real asset-based and not debt instruments. This is because debt instruments as such are not transferable under Islamic financing principles. But it is possible under *shari'a* to trade physical or real assets. Such assets can be paid for on a deferred payment basis. Hire purchase seems to be an acceptable method and leasing is widely acceptable. Therefore, it should be possible to develop tradeable Islamic-qualifying quasi-financial instruments which are based upon transferring the ownership of the physical asset, along with the attached hire purchase or deferred payment contract. Equity investments are certainly transferable and, therefore, tradeable, for example Islamic stocks quoted on markets such as the Bahrain Stock Exchange and participating shares in Islamic investment companies.

In addition, it ought to be possible to devise different categories of Islamic corporate liabilities on the basis of differing risk–return profiles for the sharing and timing of receipts of cash flows – much along the lines of the allocation of cash flows between different classes of investors (quick pay, slow pay) in conventional mortgage-backed securities. However, these securities would have to be structured along the lines of revenue bonds so that, in line with profit-and-loss-sharing principles, they would have different predetermined shares of cash flow, set in relation to relative rights of priority of receipt of cash flows, for their income, and also in relation to relative rights of priority of redemption. In essence, the idea would be to provide a range of liability/equity categories similar to those developed for the conventional corporate balance sheet, but with the important difference that no investors could enjoy predetermined rates of return nor receive any returns independent of the business performance of the underlying asset. In this way, by allowing some investors to share more of the risk in return for more of the cash flow, securitisation could attract medium- to long-term finance from Islamic finance sources.

Hence the argument is that the demand–supply position in Islamic financing at the present time and in the conceivable future affords plenty of scope for profitable innovation, as regional and international investment outlets are sought for the strong, visible (and even stronger latent) demand from actual (and potential) Islamic investors in the Gulf, Middle East region and elsewhere.

LOCATION OF THE INTERNATIONAL CENTRE

What factors govern the location of financial activities and enable some places to develop as international and regional financial centres? Decisions about where banks locate are made by financial enterprises engaged in producing financial services. Dunning (1981) suggested some 'location-specific variables' in his 'eclectic' theory of international production, namely:

- spatial distribution of inputs and markets;
- input prices, quality and productivity, for example labour, energy, materials, components, semi-finished goods;
- transport and communication costs;
- investment incentives and disincentives (including performance requirements, and so on);
- artificial barriers to trade in goods and services;
- infrastructure provisions (commercial, legal, educational, transportation);
- psychic distance (language, religious, cultural, business, customs and so on differences);
- economies of centralisation of R&D production and marketing.

Location in Finance

While all of these factors seem relevant in principle to the multinational banking firm (Lewis, 1999a) some apply with different force to financial services. For example, regulatory barriers are usually more important than trade and commercial restrictions (Lewis, 1996). Other factors such as the range of ancillary markets (foreign exchange, derivatives, wholesale funds) assume importance because of their liquidity and risk-sharing potential.

In a survey of European bankers, Abraham, Bervaes and Guinotte (1994) in fact identified no less than 47 potential factors! These included: regulatory environment, range of markets, track record of innovation, availability of complementary services, presence of foreign institutions, time zone, language, political and economic stability, communications infrastructure, business tax regime, staffing and office costs, quality of life, and so on. Moreover, their focus was upon international financial activities. In order to operate as a regional base, other factors such as access to local information and sources of finance would presumably also come into play.

Much obviously depends on what type of centre one has in mind, and what sort of activities might be undertaken. In this context Kindleberger (1974) distinguished traditional centres from Euro-centres. Dufey and Giddy (1978) drew a contrast between capital exporting centres, entrepôt centres, and offshore centres. Lewis (1995a) added a further distinction between market centres, where there is a concentration of trading in particular instruments and markets, and ancillary centres, which supply various ancillary and supporting services to other locations.

In addition to these factors, an international Islamic financing centre raises further issues such as compliance with *shari'a* requirements and the ability of the location concerned to attract a sizeable share both of Islamic investment money and of international financing activities which would qualify as being Islamically acceptable. This last consideration is obviously important. At present, there would seem to be two front-runners, Bahrain and London.

Attractions of London

London has undoubtedly emerged as the major Islamic finance centre in the West (Wilson, 1999). The attraction of London, including to all of the major Islamic banks, is the breadth of specialist financial services offered, the depth to the markets and the reputation of the major banks, which include all the leading global institutions in finance (Lewis, 1999b). Most Gulf businessmen and bankers have English as their second language, and many have long connections with the United Kingdom, where they and their families can interact with the Arab community in central London. A number of conventional banks provide an extensive range of Islamic financing services including investment banking, project finance, Islamic trade finance, leasing, private banking and mortgages. Islamic banks and businesses can utilise the expertise which these banks have, and their experience and contacts. City law firms provide legal advice on leasing and other Islamic financing techniques (Freeland, 2000). In effect, London has become a global ancillary centre for Islamic financing.

Nevertheless, London has drawbacks too. Relatively few institutions are themselves involved directly in Islamic finance. Only three Western-owned banks (ANZ International, Citibank, and Dresdener Kleinwort Benson) out of the hundreds operating in London have Islamic banking departments. There is no wholly Islamic institution functioning in London as a bank. The managed Islamic funds are based offshore in Luxembourg, the Channel Islands and Ireland to take advantage of the tax regimes in those locations (although much of the management takes place in London). Also, until relatively recently, the track record of funds introduced in London was 'disappointing' (Wilson, 1999, p. 437).

BAHRAIN AS CENTRE

In these areas Bahrain has certain competitive advantages. Already operating in Bahrain are two Islamic commercial banks, twelve Islamic investment banks, two offshore Islamic banking units, and four *Takaful* insurance companies along with several banks with Islamic 'windows' – a larger concentration than in any other country. In addition, we suggest seven other factors pertinent to Islamic financing needs.[10]

1. *Position*. There are the obvious locational merits of Bahrain. Islamic investors comprise specialist Islamic financial institutions and Islamic high net worth individuals, both of whom are heavily concentrated on Bahrain's doorstep in the Middle East and the Gulf, particularly in Saudi Arabia. Bahrain-based banks are already targeting this market segment in the Gulf, and have the necessary expertise. At the same time, Bahrain has local and expatriate connections to the peoples and governments of countries such as Pakistan, Egypt and Bangladesh. These countries are ripe for fiscal re-engineering, privatisation and infrastructure financing which seem likely to require financial know-how and international connections.

2. *Trading*. An Islamic finance centre would need to create a secondary, as well as a primary, market in equity and real asset-based instruments qualifying as *shari'a* investments. Conventional banks' expertise would be invaluable in the securitisation process, and Bahrain should benefit from its critical mass of Islamic and conventional financial institutions. The head offices, branches and associated companies of these financial institutions are well-versed in secondary market trading methods. Local and other Arab financial institutions also have experience of proprietary trading in international capital markets.

3. *Attraction*. Conventional banks (in Muslim countries as well as Western ones) like Dresdener Kleinwort Benson, Citibank, UBS, SBC and so on increasingly are participating in Islamic banking, albeit in a limited way. They offer Islamic banking products which provide Islamic banks with *murabaha*, *ijara* and *mudaraba* investment opportunities, a range of managed investments funds, and Islamically-permissible liquidity facilities. Bahrain offers a regulatory and cultural environment conducive to their continued participation in this market, as evidenced by the establishment of Citi Islamic Investment Bank.

4. *Innovation*. Bahraini-based institutions already have an established track record of financial innovations in Islamic finance. Islamic syndicated finance was introduced by the Faisal Islamic Bank of Bahrain in 1987, for example; Bahrain Islamic investment banks and investment companies

manage Islamic securities or unit trusts. Such securities are normally shares in issues or funds that represent contributions to an investment or a collection of investments for specific periods of time, with unit values determined weekly and negotiable at the market price.

5. *Infrastructure.* An international centre requires a wide range of supporting facilities in the areas of specialised staffing, computer technology, information services, legal advice, accounting and auditing needs, office space and facilities, and so on. Bahrain can offer a full range of facilities and has a well educated and trained labour force, along with facilities for advanced training in Islamic banking.

6. *Regulation.* A number of regulatory issues are posed by the growth of Islamic banking. Bahrain offers a supportive environment. The Bahrain Monetary Agency has a strong interest in Islamic financing and a good reputation internationally. Bahrain is also host of the Accounting and Auditing Organisation for Islamic Financial Institutions.

7. *Prime mover.* In order to attract others to its shores, a locale has to be recognised as an international centre of note and, with currently the highest concentration of Islamic financial institutions among actual and potential international financial centres, Bahrain possesses a beneficial starting position.

Nevertheless, Bahrain remains essentially a commercial banking centre, in the sense that commercial banking managerial and profession skills have underpinned its development. Future needs will likely revolve around investment banking and infrastructure and privatisation financing. The establishment in July 1996 of Citi Islamic Investment Bank in Bahrain was an important step. So too was the formation in late 1996 of the US$1 billion OIC Infrastructure Fund by the Bahrain-based Islamic Investment Company of the Gulf (IICG) in conjunction with the Islamic Development Bank (IDB). This fund is an equity and mezzanine financing vehicle dedicated to providing Islamic *istisnaa* and *murabaha* financing for infrastructure projects. Bahrain also teamed up in November 1999 with the IDB and Labuan, the offshore financial centre in Malaysia, in an initiative to develop an Islamic International Money Market, covering all of the 53 member countries of the IDB. The money market will give Islamic banks in these countries direct access to a wide range of money market instruments such as unit trusts, asset-based bonds and insurance-linked products.

Yet, Bahrain has its competitors. Dubai has aspirations for this role, and some are already speaking of Malaysia as an international Islamic financial centre (Babai, 1996). Whether, and to what extent, Malaysia may have dented its chances by the imposition of capital controls in response to the Asian financial crisis remains to be seen. What is important, however, is that if one or a number of international Islamic financial centres develop, their creation and expansion should not be hampered by government-led initiatives at the international level, but instead meet the market test. They should be allowed to evolve more or less naturally, as a result of market forces based on locational strengths and real needs which can be met.

NOTES

1. The major contributors are Muslehuddin (1982) and Siddiqi (1985). Anwar (1994) provides a later commentary (and critique) while Wahib (1999) gives a practitioner's guide. A recent directory published by the Institute of Islamic Banking and Insurance (1999) examines the operational issues.
2. The critiques are long-standing, dating back to Ibn Abidin (1784–1836), see Kilingmulier (1969).
3. Although a *Takaful* life company could conceivably be a proprietary life office, which is wholly owned either by shareholders or by another company, the company's main purpose and the way it operates and distributes its excess or profits makes it more similar to a mutual life office.
4. Of course, if the term were long enough (for example 120 years) it would effectively approximate a whole-of-life policy!
5. This is as stated in The Holy Qur'an: 'And no person can ever die except by Allah's Leave and at an appointed term ...' (3: 145).
6. The International Investor is a Kuwaiti Closed Shareholding Company, engaged in investment and related financial services permissible under the *shari'a*. Share capital consists of 170 million authorised, issued and fully paid up shares of 100 fils each. IIC has its main office in Kuwait, with The International Investor Advisory Group Limited being based in London. In 1998, TII had KD797 million funds under management as fiduciary and advisory assets. The three main sources of income were management fees, placement fees and gains on trading sales.
7. This example is provided by Mahmoud A. El-Gamal on his website.
8. *The Jakarta Post*, February 25, 2000 (on line).
9. *The Wall Street Journal Europe*, 30 November, 1999, p. 26.
10. These factors were those identified in a survey undertaken in 1996 of 100 banks, financiers and government officials in Bahrain. Details are reported in Algaoud and Lewis (1997).

10. Conclusion

OUR APPROACH

The aim of this book has been to analyse the nature and role of Islamic banks from what we hope is a distinctive East–West perspective. In doing so, the analysis has been based on three cornerstones.

Religion

First, there was a detailed examination of the philosophical and religious underpinnings of Islamic finance and economics; that is, of the economic and financial environment in which adherents to Islam are allowed to operate. Banking business must be conducted on principles expressed in Islamic law, the *shari'a*, revolving around the use of productive (real) investment rather than monetary investment that attracts interest and usury (*riba*).

Our approach to these religious requirements has been from two directions. From one side, we have looked at the sources of Islamic law, and the definition of *riba,* along with the reasons given by Islamic scholars for its prohibition. From the other angle, we have analysed Mosaic Law and Christian doctrine on the question of usury. As the third of the great monotheist religions, Islam shares a common heritage with Judaism and Christianity.

Not surprisingly, we found there to be very close parallels between the Christian attitude to usury and the Islamic stand. The sticking point for both is the inequity of the lender demanding, and enforcing by collateral, a fixed return from the entrepreneur irrespective of the yield of the investment project. More unexpected, perhaps, was the finding of close parallels between the financing techniques used by Christians under the usury ban and those of Muslims, and that these techniques in fact included *mudaraba*-type bank deposits as well as the extensive use of partnership arrangements.

Theory

As the second cornerstone, traditional economic analysis was used to explain the function of banks in the financial system. In particular, the modern theory of financial intermediation emphasises the information asymmetries between banks and depositors, on one hand, and banks and borrowers-investors, on the other. These information problems shape the role of banks as 'delegated monitors', and the differences between the 'market-based' Anglo-Saxon model and the 'bank-based' German–Japanese model show that the information asymmetries inherent in financing can be handled in different ways. Another important issue in the literature is the design of financial contracts to ameliorate the incentive problems resulting from the delegation process of financial markets. These theoretical frameworks were then contrasted with the principles of Islamic banking so as to identify the informational, incentive and contracting issues which, at least to Western eyes, must be addressed in practice by Islamic banks.

Case Studies

The practical operations of Islamic banks formed the third cornerstone. Case studies were made of the activities of Islamic banks in three very different environments. One set of case studies was made of the three countries which have sought fully to Islamicise the financial and economic system, namely Iran, Sudan and Pakistan. Two distinctive models of how this Islamicisation process might be achieved, namely that of Chapra-Siddiqi and that of Ismail, prefaced the survey. Using Pakistan as an illustration, we also examined the intricate legal changes which need to be implemented to get the Islamicisation process under way and sustain its expansion. Finally, in view of Pakistan's aim of moving to a full Islamic economic system by 2001, we considered the issues that remain to be resolved.

The second group of case studies focused on the operations of Islamic banks in mixed systems, predominantly for local customers. Here the process of Islamicisation involves fewer legal difficulties, but the banks must operate in a more competitive and less controlled financial environment. This analysis proceeded in two stages. The first step was to look at deposit-raising and financing in the formative years of the 1980s, using Egypt and Malaysia for comparison. The next step considered more recent activities, using first aggregate balance sheets of 119 banks, supplemented then with an examination of Islamic banks in the DMI group, and finally case studies of Islamic banking in Malaysia, Bangladesh, Jordan and Australia.

The third group of case studies was of banking operations in Bahrain enabling, to our knowledge for the first time, an analysis of the activities of Islamic banks operating in an open, internationally-oriented, financial centre. This study was based around two sets of structured interviews with the banks concerned, and a targeted survey of leading bankers and financiers, reported in more detail elsewhere (Algaoud and Lewis, 1997, 1999) and summarised here. At one level, we provided details of deposits and investments for comparison with the other countries. At a second level, the focus was upon the system of corporate governance, especially the nature of *shari'a* supervision. At the third level, we considered the potential for Bahrain to develop as a catchment area for Islamic banking globally.

OUR CONCLUSIONS

This, then, is a summary of what was done. A number of conclusions are suggested.

1. There are now over 200 banks operating according to *shari'a* principles in five of the world's major continents, namely Asia, Africa, Australia, Europe and North America, along with other areas such as the Caribbean Islands. This geographical diversification shows both the flexibility and adaptability of the system of Islamic banking and the sizeable market which exists for the special products that Islamic banks have to offer.

2. Three countries, Pakistan, Iran and Sudan, have sought a complete transition of their financial systems to Islamic principles, but they differ markedly in the speed of the transition and the legal and social infrastructure fashioned to facilitate the process. Funding the government budget on a *riba*-free basis is a central problem, which has been skirted around in Iran and remains to be solved in Pakistan. We see public sector–private sector partnerships, and the financing of infrastructure using Islamically-acceptable project finance instruments, as one way around this impasse.

3. In other countries the introduction of Islamic financing has involved establishing Islamic banks which compete openly with conventional banks (and in some cases with other Islamic institutions). But, in all cases, Islamic banks have found a market niche. In many cases, they have diversified into *Takaful* insurance, investment banking, fund management and offshore activities.

4. While Islamic banking is clearly feasible, and can operate successfully, Islamic banks based in a modern economy face their own set of problems. Judged in terms of the modern theory of financial intermediation revolving around information asymmetries, delegated monitoring and incentive-compatible contracting, there is a central analytical dilemma. Islamic banks are unable to utilise *riba* contracts as an incentive device. They are also prohibited under profit-and-loss sharing partnerships from the exercise of covenants, collateral and other enforcement procedures that theory suggests are needed to reduce moral hazard and which form part of the standard lending methods employed by conventional banks.

5. In their formative years, most Islamic banks largely circumvented these difficulties by concentrating overwhelmingly on short-term *murabahas* and *ijara* financing which bear similarities to that of traditional banking in that the goods themselves can serve as collateral and there is a relatively certain rate of profit, albeit with some attendant risks. Nowadays, there is much greater diversity in the banks' Islamic investment portfolio, with some Islamic banks establishing systems for evaluation and monitoring under *musharaka* partnership financing and others engaging in direct real investments and longer-term investments. This monitoring effort is not necessarily a weakness of the system. Clearly, many Western banks over-relied on the protection afforded by collateral, which proved to be illusory during the downturn in real estate markets in the early 1990s (and late 1990s in Asia). It is no bad thing that Islamic banks are often forced to undertake the 'delegated monitoring' that economic theory says is the hallmark and productive role of financial intermediaries.

6. At the same time, this trend has not been universal and many Islamic banks have continued to downplay profit-and-loss-sharing techniques of financing in favour of mark-up methods. Nevertheless, many of the criticisms of their actions seem misplaced. Muslims are encouraged by the Holy Qur'an to pursue trade, and these instruments are the principal ones used for financing trade, both domestically and internationally. These financial techniques are also, to a degree, self-liquidating. It ought not to be forgotten that one of the traditional tenets of 'sound banking' was that banks should restrict their lending to the acquisition of self-liquidating claims, which in a sense describes the nature of a *murabaha* contract.

7. During the formative years of Islamic banking, another feature was that the institutions relied extensively upon the financial backing of prominent international luminaries in the Muslim world and the support of the local Muslim community for their establishment. They have continued to tap this source of support for subsequent growth. However, Islamic banks have probably now reached the stage – and this is supported by a number of marketing surveys – where the 'religious variable' alone is not enough. They operate in a market in which many conventional banks themselves have Islamic 'windows', and factors such as the quality of service, the availability and reliability of electronic networks, and the returns paid on investment accounts become the major conditioning factors.

8. If so, then it is increasingly likely that the preferences of depositors, rather than the preferences of the banks, will shape the Islamic investment portfolios of the banks. We have argued that it is a

characteristic of the PLS financing modes used by Islamic banks that they effectively convert those supplying loanable funds from being depositors, with guaranteed capital certainty, into being non-voting shareholders. That is, those depositors with investment accounts share the risk of loss with the banks, but cannot influence (at least directly) the selection of the investments. What they can do in a mixed system is not renew investment funds when they mature. In this way, they put pressure on the banks and thereby constrain and ultimately shape the risk–return characteristics of the banks' investments. Those Islamic scholars who criticise the Islamic banks for choosing a low-risk–stable return portfolio based around trade and asset financing ought perhaps to blame their fellow depositors. The bankers must be mindful of their fiduciary responsibilities to those entrusting them with their savings to invest, and the more so if they are to survive in a competitive marketplace.

9. One way out of this dilemma is for the portfolio decisions to be shifted more directly from the institutions, as *mudarib*, to those supplying the investment funds. This occurs already in terms of the restricted *mudaraba* investment accounts offered by the banks, but these services are confined to individuals with large funds to invest. The best way to extend this choice to those of moderate means is by virtue of the unit trust technique. Formally, at least, it would remain the case under the *mudaraba* principle that the institution or fund manager retains full discretion over the selection and the direction of investments of the fund. Nevertheless, the broad characteristics of the fund itself (for example, property, commodities, trade finance, global equities, venture capital, and so on) will indicate much about the inherent risk–return characteristics, thus effectively transferring the selection to the customer himself when choosing the type of fund. Islamic unit trusts have been a major growth area in recent years. We have also recommended that *Takaful* life insurance companies in terms of their family business could provide a range of switchable funds which would achieve the same result.

10. This brings out the point that product innovation within *shari'a* guidelines is perhaps the key element governing the future of Islamic banking and finance. Certainly it is one lesson of history. In our view, Islam has succeeded in sustaining the ban on usury, where Christianity failed, in large part because it invested resources in devising religiously acceptable financial techniques and showing Muslims how they could undertake banking and finance, while maintaining faith with religious convictions. In effect, Islam has systemised and fashioned strategies, which have allowed those wishing to avoid usury and engage in banking and finance in *shari'a* consistent ways to do so. Islamic unit trusts,

Islamic structured project finance and infrastructure financing, and *Takaful* insurance – all of which have been examined here – are illustrations of this systemisation and product development at work, although much can still be done to make some instruments flexible and responsive to changing market requirements.

11. We have also argued that this adaptation and innovation process would be aided by the formation – through the market – of an international centre for Islamic finance, and the further development of asset-based and equity-based financial instruments in line with *shari'a* principles. Much like London did for the Eurodollar market, we see that an Islamic financial centre could act as a 'magnet' for attracting *shari'a* acceptable investments from both Islamic and conventional banks, and become the main issuing centre for the equity- and asset-based instruments involved. It could provide a venue for the securitisation of these instruments and the facilities for trading the derivative securities so created. In this way, the centre would impart liquidity to the instruments while providing a market-place for the placement and investment of short-term funds and liquid balances. At the same time, it is important that the growth of the centres(s) be market-driven and be based on existing market strengths, rather than be the result of artificially-created features which have no foundation in terms of market behaviour.

12. A final comment concerns the importance of *shari'a* supervision, which is a central element in the Islamic system of corporate governance, ensuring that Islamic finance retains touch with the religious precepts that led to its birth. There is a valuable lesson here for Western economies. One trend that has emerged in the West over the past decade or so is a growth in 'ethical investments'. So far, however, this movement has had its major impact in terms of equity investments and various pooled funds. There has been little impact of the ethical investments movement on the banking sector other than the occasional picketing of banks for investing in the destruction of rainforests (or in South Africa in the past). The phenomenon of Islamic banking has demonstrated how a code of ethical investments can be built formally into institutional structures of corporate governance and be made to operate across the banking and financial system generally.

References

Abraham, J.P., N. Bervaes, and A. Guinotte (1994), 'The Competitiveness of European International Financial Centres', in J. Revell (ed.), *The Changing Face of European Banks and Securities Markets*, London: Macmillan, pp. 229-84.

Abu Zahra, Muhammad (1970), *Buhuth fi al-Riba*, Kuwait: Dar al-Buhuth al-'Ilmiyya.

ACLI (1999), *Life Insurance Fact Book, 1999*, Washington, DC: American Council of Life Insurance.

Ahmad, I. (1982), 'Islamic Social Thought', in W. Block and I. Hexham (eds), *Religion, Economics, and Social Thought: Proceedings of an International Symposium*, Vancouver, BC: The Fraser Institute, pp. 465-91.

Ahmad, K. (ed.) (1980), *Studies in Islamic Economics*, Leicester: The Islamic Foundation.

Ahmad, K. (1994), 'Elimination of *Riba*: Concept and Problems', in K. Ahmad (ed.), *Elimination of Riba from the Economy*, Islamabad: Institute of Policy Studies, pp. 33-63.

Ahmad, Sheikh M. (1952), *Economics of Islam*, Lahore: Institute of Islamic Culture.

Ahmed, Ausaf (1995), 'The Evolution of Islamic Banking', in *Encyclopedia of Islamic Banking and Insurance*, London: Institute of Islamic Banking and Insurance, pp. 15-30.

Ahmed, A.S. (1999), *Islam Today. A Short Introduction to the Muslim World*, London: I.B. Tauris.

Ahmed, N. (1997), 'Islamic banking and its mode of investments', *New Horizon*, **67**, September, 3-7.

Ahmed, Shaghil (1989), 'Islamic banking and finance. A review essay', *Journal of Monetary Economics*, **24**, 157-67.

Ahmed, Z., M. Iqbal and M.F. Khan (1983), *Money and Banking in Islam*, Jeddah: International Centre for Research in Islamic Economics, King Abdul Aziz University.

Alchian, A.A. and H. Demsetz (1972), 'Production, information costs, and economic organization', *American Economic Review*, **62** (December), 777-95.

Algaoud, L.M. and M.K. Lewis (1997), 'The Bahrain Financial Centre: its present and future role in Islamic financing', *Accounting, Commerce and*

Finance: The Islamic Perspective Journal, **1**(2), 43–66.

Algaoud, L.M. and M.K. Lewis (1999), 'Corporate governance in Islamic banking: the case of Bahrain', *International Journal of Business Studies*, **7**(1), 56–86.

Al-Harran, S.A.S. (1993), *Islamic Finance – Partnership Financing*, Selangor Darul Ehsan, Malaysia: Pelanduk Publications.

Ali, A.H. (1999), 'Islamic banking culture', *New Horizon*, **83**, January, 11–13.

Ali, Muhammad Moher (1997), *Sîrat Al-Nabi and the Orientalists*, Madinah: King Faud Complex for the Printing of the Holy Qur'an and Centre for the Service of Sunnah and Sîrah.

Ali, Mukarram (1996), 'Introduction. The Islamic Economic System – The Challenges Ahead', in D. Buckmaster (ed.), *Islamic Banking – an Overview*, London: Institute of Islamic Banking and Insurance, pp. iv–viii.

Al-Jarhi, Ma'bid Ali (1983), 'A Monetary and Financial Structure for an Interest Free Economy, Institutions, Mechanism and Policy', in Z. Ahmad, M. Iqbal and M.F. Khan (eds), *Money and Banking in Islam*, International Centre for Research in Islamic Economics, Jeddah, and Institute of Policy Studies, Islamabad, pp. 69–101.

Al-Kásáni, Abu Bakr ibn Mas'ud ([1910]1968), (d.587/1191), *Bada'i' al-Sana'i' fi Tartib al-Shara'i'*, 10 Vols, Cairo: Al-Galia Press.

Al-Quduri al-Baghdadi, Abu al-Husayn Ahmad ibn Muhammad (n.d.), *Kitab al-Mukhtasar*, Cairo.

Alrawi, Khalia Whayeb (1997), 'Evaluation of Jordan Islamic Bank Activities', *Proceedings of Accounting, Commerce & Finance: The Islamic Perspective International Conference 1*, Macarthur: University of West Sydney, 228–39.

Al-Rifai, Tariq (1999), 'Islamic equity funds. A brief industry analysis', *New Horizon*, Sha'ban, November, 1420.

Anwar, Muhammad (1987), *Modelling Interest-Free Economy: A Study in Macroeconomics and Development*, Herndon, Virginia: International Institute of Islamic Thought.

Anwar, Muhammad (1994), 'Comparative study of insurance and *Takafol* (Islamic insurance)', *The Pakistan Development Review*, **33**(4) Part II, Winter, 1315–30.

Aquinas, T., Trans. (1955), *Summa Theologica*, London: Oxford University Press.

Ariff, M. (1982), 'Monetary Policy in an Interest Free Islamic Economy: Nature and Scope', in M. Ariff (ed.), *Monetary and Fiscal Economics of Islam*, Jeddah: International Centre for Research in Islamic Economics, pp. 287–310.

Ariff, M. (1988), 'Islamic banking', *Asian-Pacific Economic Literature*, **2** (2),

University of Malaya, September, 48–64.

Arifin, Z. (1998), 'Islamic banking grows with Indonesian economy', *New Horizon*, 70/71, 19–21.

Armstrong, K. (1991), *Muhammad. A Biography of the Prophet*, London: Victor Gollanz.

Arrow, K.J. (1964), 'The role of securities in the optimal allocation of risk-bearing', *Review of Economic Studies*, **31**, 91–6.

Arrow, K.J. (1965), *Aspects of the Theory of Risk-Bearing*, Helsinki: Yrjo Jahnsson Foundation.

Arrow, K.J. (1974), *The Limits of Organization*, New York and London: W.W. Norton.

Ashley, W.J. ([1888, 1893]1913), *An Introduction to English Economic History and Theory*, 2 Vols, London.

Atiya, M.K. (1986), 'Muhasabat al-Zakat (Zakat Accounting)', in *Handbook of Islamic Banking*, Cairo and Mecca: International Association of Islamic Banks, **7**(3), 25–8.

Atiyah, E. (1955), *The Arabs*, Harmondsworth, Middlesex: Pelican.

Ayoub-Bey, N.E. (1999), 'Business Ethics – Implications for Islamic banking, *New Horizon*, 83, January, 14–15.

Babai, D. (1996), 'Malaysia as an Islamic Financial Centre: An International Perspective', International Islamic Capital Markets Conference, Kuala Lumpur, March 22.

Bagsiraj, M.I. (2000), 'Islamic Financial Institutions of India, Their Nature, Problems and Prospects: A Critical Evaluation of Selected Representative Units', in *Islamic Finance: Challenges and Opportunities in the Twenty-First Century*, Fourth International Conference on Islamic Economics and Banking, Loughborough University, pp. 527–56.

Baldick, J. (1998), 'Early Islam', in P. Clarke (ed.), *The World's Religions: Islam*, London: Routledge.

Baldwin, J.W. (1970), *Masters, Printers and Merchants*, 2 Vols, Princeton: Princeton University Press.

Banaga, A., G.H. Ray and C.R. Tomkins (1994), *External Audit and Corporate Governance in Islamic Banks*, Aldershot: Avebury.

Baster, A. (1934), 'The origins of British banking expansion in the Near East', *Economic History Review*, **5**(1), 76–86.

Benston, G.J. and C.W. Smith (1976), 'A transactions cost approach to the theory of financial intermediaries', *Journal of Finance*, **31**, 215–31, reprinted in M.K. Lewis (ed.), *Financial Intermediaries, The International Library of Critical Writings in Economics, 43*, Aldershot, UK and Brookfield, US: Edward Elgar, 1995.

Berle, A. and G. Means (1933), *The Modern Corporation and Private Property*, New York: Macmillan.

Billah, Mohd Ma'sum (1999), 'Life Insurance: An Islamic Paradigm', in *Directory of Islamic Insurance (Takaful) 2000*, London: Institute of Islamic Banking and Finance.

Blair, M.M. (1995), *Ownership and Control: Rethinking Corporate Governance for the Twenty-first Century*, Washington: Brookings Institution.

Boehm-Bawerk, E. (1922), *Capital and Interest*, translated by William Smart, London: Macmillan.

Born, K.E. (1983), *International Banking in the 19th and 20th Centuries*, Leamington Spa: Berg Publishers (English translation).

Brown, D.W. (1996), *Rethinking Tradition in Modern Islamic Thought*, Cambridge: Cambridge University Press.

Brown, N.J. (1997), *The Rule of Law in the Arab World*, Cambridge: Cambridge University Press.

Buchanan, J.M. (1958), *Public Principles of Public Debt*, Homewood, Ill: Irwin.

Buckmaster, D. (1996), *Islamic Banking – an Overview*, London: Institute of Islamic Banking and Insurance.

Cadbury Committee (1992), *Report of the Committee on The Financial Aspects of Corporate Governance*, London: Gee & Co.

Casson, M. (1982), *The Entrepreneur. An Economic Theory*, Oxford, Martin Robertson.

Chan, Y.S. (1983), 'On the positive role of financial intermediation in allocation of venture capital in a market with imperfect information', *The Journal of Finance*, **38** (5), 1543–68.

Chant, John (1992), 'The new theory of financial intermediation', in K. Dowd and M.K. Lewis (eds), *Current Issues in Financial and Monetary Economics*, London: Macmillan, pp. 42–65.

Chapra, M.U. (1982), 'Money and banking in an Islamic economy', in M. Ariff (ed.), *Monetary and Fiscal Economics of Islam*, Jeddah: International Centre for Research in Islamic Economics, pp. 145–86.

Chapra, M.U. (1985), *Towards a Just Monetary System*, Leicester: Islamic Foundation.

Chebel, M. (1997), *Symbols of Islam* (English Translation), Paris: Editions Assouline.

Cizaka, M. (1995), 'Historical Background', *Encyclopedia of Islamic Banking and Insurance*, London: Institute of Islamic Banking and Insurance, pp. 10–14.

Clarke, P. (1988), *The World's Religions, Islam*, London: Routledge.

Coase, R.H. (1937), 'The nature of the firm', *Economica* (N.S.) 4, 386–405.

Cobham, D. (1992), 'Islamic banking: perspectives from the theory of financial intermediation', Discussion Paper Series No. 9217, Department of Economics, University of St Andrews.

Cohn, H.H. (1971), S.v. 'Usury', *Encyclopedia Judaica*, Jerusalem: Keter Publishing House, pp. 17-33.

Cook, M. (1996), *Muhammad*, Oxford: Oxford University Press.

Council of Islamic Ideology (Pakistan) (1983), 'Elimination of interest from the economy', in Z. Ahmed, M. Iqbal and M.F. Khan (eds), *Money and Banking in Islam*, International Centre for Research in Islamic Economics, Jeddah, and Institute of Policy Studies, Islamabad, pp. 103-211.

Court, W.H.B. (1962), *A Concise Economic History of Britain, From 1750 to Recent Times*, Cambridge: Cambridge University Press.

Covick, O.E. and M.K. Lewis (1997), 'Insurance, Superannuation and Managed Funds', in M.K. Lewis and R.H. Wallace (eds), *The Australian Financial System: Evolution, Policy and Practice*, Melbourne: Addison, Wesley, Longman, pp. 221-93.

Crone, P. (1987), *Meccan Trade and the Rise of Islam*, Oxford: Basil Blackwell.

Dar, H.A. (1999), 'The Law and Practice of Mudaraba Companies in Pakistan', *New Horizon*, 83, January, 7-10.

Davidson, I.R. (1992), 'Unit Trusts', in P. Newman, M. Milgate and J. Eatwell (eds), *New Palgrave Dictionary of Money and Finance*, Vol. 1, London: Macmillan, pp. 730-31.

Davis, J.J., F.D. Schoorman and L. Donaldson (1997), 'Towards a stewardship theory of management', *The Academy of Management Review*, **22**(1), 20-39.

Davis, K.T. (1997), 'Public Sector Securities Markets', in M.K. Lewis and R.H. Wallace (eds), *The Australian Financial System: Evolution, Policy and Practice*, Melbourne: Addison, Wesley, Longman, pp. 431-76.

Davis, K.T. and M.K. Lewis (1982), 'Can monetary policy work in a deregulated environment?', *Australian Economic Review*, **1**, 9-21.

Davis, K.T. and M.K. Lewis (1992), 'Deregulation and Monetary Policy', in K. Dowd and M.K. Lewis (eds), *Current Issues in Financial and Monetary Economics*, London: Macmillan, pp. 128-54.

Dawn of Karachi (1981), '8.5 to 9 P.C. Profit on PLS Accounts', 40, July 20, 1-7.

Debreu, G. (1959), *Theory of Value: An Axiomatic Analysis of Economic Equilibrium*, New Haven: Yale University Press.

De Cecco, M. (1992), 'Genoese Exchange Fairs', in P. Newman, M. Milgate and J. Eatwell (eds), *The New Palgrave Dictionary of Money and Finance*, Vol. 3, London: Macmillan.

De Roover, Raymond (1948), *The Medici Bank: Its Organisation, Management, Operations, and Decline*, New York: New York University Press.

De Roover, Raymond (1954), 'New interpretations of the history of banking', *Journal of World History*, Paris: Librairie des Méridiens, 38-76.

De Roover, Raymond (1963), *The Rise and Decline of the Medici Bank, 1397–1494*, Cambridge, Mass: Harvard University Press.

De Roover, Raymond (1967), 'The Scholastics, Usury and Foreign Exchange', *Business History Review*, **43**, 257–71.

Dhareer, Al Siddiq Mohammad Al-Ameen (1997), *Al-Gharar in Contracts and its Effects on Contemporary Transactions*, Jeddah: Islamic Development Bank, Islamic Research and Training Institute.

Diamond, D. (1984), 'Financial Intermediation and Delegated Monitoring', *Review of Economic Studies*, **51**(166), 393–414. Reprinted in M.K. Lewis (ed.), *Financial Intermediaries. The International Library of Critical Writings in Economics, 43*, Aldershot, UK and Brookfield, US: Edward Elgar, 1995.

Diamond, D. and P. Dybvig (1983), 'Bank runs, deposit insurance and liquidity', *Journal of Political Economy*, **91** (3), 401–19. Reprinted in M.K. Lewis (ed.), *Financial Intermediaries. The International Library of Critical Writings in Economics, 43*, Aldershot, UK and Brookfield, US: Edward Elgar, 1995.

Divine, T.F. (1967), S.v. 'Usury', *New Catholic Encyclopedia*, New York: McGraw-Hill, pp. 498–500.

Doi, 'Abdur Rahman i (1989), *Shari'ah: The Islamic Law*, Kuala Lumpur: AS Noordeen.

Dowd, K. (1992), 'Optimal financial contracts', *Oxford Economic Papers*, **44**, October, 672–93.

Dowd, K. (1996), *Competition and Finance. A Reinterpretation of Financial and Monetary Economics*, London: Macmillan.

Downs, A. (1961), 'In defence of majority voting', *Journal of Political Economy*, **69**, April, 192–99.

Dresdner Bank (1996), 'Islamic banking – a promising market for conventional banks', *Trends*, April, Frankfurt, 11–15.

Dufey, G. and I. Giddy (1978), *The International Money Market*, Englewood Cliffs, NJ: Prentice-Hall Inc.

Dunning, J.H. (1981), *International Production and the Multinational Enterprise*, London: Allen and Unwin.

Ebrahim, Muhammed-Shahid (1999), 'Integrating Islamic and conventional project finance', *Thunderbird International Business Review*, **41**(4/5), July–October, 583–609.

Einzig, P. (1962), *The History of Foreign Exchange*, London: Macmillan.

El-Awa, M.S. (1983), *Punishment in Islamic Law: A Comparative Study*, Delhi: Marzi Maktaba Islami.

El-Gamal, M.A. (1999a), 'Involving Islamic banks in central bank open market operations, *Thunderbird International Business Review*, **41**(4/5), 501–21.

El-Gamal, M.A. (1999b), *There is nothing wrong with Murabaha*, Islamic Economics and Finance (www.ruf.rice.edu).

Erol, Cengiz and Radi El-Bdour (1989), 'Attitudes, behaviour and patronage factors of bank customers towards Islamic banks', *The International Journal of Bank Marketing*, **7**(6), 31–9.

Erol, Cengiz, Erdener Kaynak and Radi El-Bdour (1990), 'Conventional and Islamic banks: patronage behaviour of Jordanian customers', *The International Journal of Bank Marketing*, **8**(4), 25–38.

Errico, Luca and Mitra Farahbaksh (1998), 'Islamic banking: issues in prudential regulations and supervision', IMF Working Paper 30, Washington: International Monetary Fund.

Fama, E.F. (1980), 'Banking in the theory of finance', *Journal of Monetary Economics*, **6**, 39–57.

Fama, E.F. (1985), 'What's different about banks?', *Journal of Monetary Economics*, **15**, 23–39.

Forward, M. (1997), *Muhammad: A Short Biography*, Oxford: Oneworld Publications.

Freeland, R. (2000), 'The role of London law firms in Islamic finance', *New Horizon*, **104** (November), 5–6.

Frishman, Martin and Hasan-Uddin Khan (eds) (1994), *The Mosque. History, Architectural Development and Regional Diversity*, London: Thames and Hudson.

Gafoor, Abdul A.L.M. (1995), *Interest-free Commercial Banking*, Groningen, The Netherlands: Apptec Publications.

Galassi, F.L. (1992), 'Buying a passport to heaven: usury, restitution and the merchants of medieval Genoa', *Religion*, **22**, 313–26.

Gale, D. and M. Hellwig (1985), 'Incentive-compatible debt contracts: the one-period problem', *Review of Economic Studies*, **52**, 647–63.

Gätje, Helmut (1997), *The Qur'an and its Exegesis*, Oxford: Oneworld Publications.

Gelauff, G.M.M. and C. den Broeder (1997), *Governance of stakeholder relationships. The German and Dutch experience*, SUERF Studies No. 1, Amsterdam: Société Universitaire Européenne de Recherches Financières.

Gerrard, P. and J.B. Cunningham (1997), 'Islamic banking: a study in Singapore', *International Journal of Bank Marketing*, **15**(6), 204–16.

Ghazali, Abou Hamid Muhammad (nd), *Ihya' Ulum al-Din*, translated Maulana Fazul-ul Karim, Lahore: Sind Sagar Academy.

Giddy, I.H. (1986), 'Assetless Banking', in P. Savona and G. Sutija (eds), *Strategic Planning in International Banking*, London: Macmillan.

Glaeser, E.L. and J.A. Scheinkman (1998), 'Neither a borrower nor a lender be: an economic analysis of interest restrictions and usury laws', *Journal of Law and Economics*, **41**(1), 1–36.

Goodhart, C.A.E. (1988), *The Evolution of Central Banks*, Cambridge, Mass.: MIT Press.

Goodhart, C.A.E. (1995), *The Central Bank and the Financial System*, London: Macmillan.

Gopal, M.H. (1935), *Mauryan Public Finance*, London: George Allen & Unwin.

Gordon, B. (1982), 'Lending at interest: some Jewish, Greek and Christian approaches. 800 BC–AD100', *History of Political Economy*, **14**, 406–26.

Green, E.J. and P. Lin (2000), 'Diamond and Dybvig's classic theory of financial intermediation: what's missing', *Federal Reserve Bank of Minneapolis Quarterly Review*, **24**(1), 3–13.

Greenbaum, S.I. (1996), 'Twenty-five years of banking research', *Financial Management*, **25**(2), 86–92.

Grimsey, D. and M.K. Lewis (1999), 'Evaluating the Risks of Public Private Partnership for Infrastructure Projects', *The Third International Stockholm Seminar on Risk Behaviour and Risk Management, June 14–16*, School of Business, Stockholm: University of Stockholm.

Grossman, S.S. and O.P. Hart (1983), 'An analysis of the principal–agent problem', *Econometrica*, **51**, 7–45.

Gurley, J.G. and E.S. Shaw (1956), 'Financial intermediaries and the saving-investment process', *Journal of Finance*, **11**, 257–76, reprinted in M.K. Lewis (ed.), *Financial Intermediaries, The International Library of Critical Writings in Economics 43*, Aldershot, UK and Brookfield, US: Edward Elgar, 1995.

Gurley, J.G. and E.S. Shaw (1960), *Money in the Theory of Finance*, Washington D.C.: The Brookings Institution, 1995.

Hamid, A. (1992), 'Addendum on Recent Developments' in R.C. Effros (ed.), *Current Legal Issues Affecting Central Banking*, Vol. 1, Washington: International Monetary Fund.

Hamwi, B. and A. Aylward (1999), 'Islamic finance: a growing international market', *Thunderbird International Business Review*, **41**(4/5), July–October, 407–20.

Haque, Nadeem Ul and A. Mirakhor (1986), 'Optimal Profit-sharing Contracts and Investment in an Interest-Free Islamic Economy', IMF Working Paper, No.12, Washington DC: International Monetary Fund.

Haque, Z. (1985), *Islam and Feudalism: The Economics of Riba, Interest, and Profit*, Lahore: Vanguard.

Haron, S., N. Ahmad and S.L. Planisck (1994), 'Bank patronage factors of Muslim and non-Muslim customers', *International Journal of Bank Marketing*, **12**(1), 32–40.

Harris, M. and A. Raviv (1979), 'Optimal incentive contracts with imperfect information', *Journal of Economic Theory*, **21**, 231–59.

Hart, O. (1995), 'Corporate governance: some theory and implications', *Economic Journal*, **105** (May), 678-89.

Hasan, S.U. (1995), 'Islamic Unit Trusts', *Encyclopaedia of Islamic Banking*, London: Institute of Islamic Banking and Insurance, pp. 159-63.

Henry, C.M. (1999a), 'Islamic Banking Grows with Indonesian Economy, *New Horizon*, 70/71, 19-21.

Henry, C.M. (1999b), Introduction to special issue on Islamic banking, *Thunderbird International Business Review*, **41**(4,5), 357-68.

Hester, Donald D. (1994), 'On the theory of financial intermediation', *De Economist*, 142, 133-49.

Hirschman, A.O. (1970), *Exit, Voice and Loyalty*, Cambridge, Mass.: Harvard University Press.

Hodges, S.D. (1992), 'Financial Engineering: New Approaches to Managing Risk Exposure', in R. Kinsella (ed.), *New Issues in Financial Services*, Oxford: Basil Blackwell, pp. 142-61.

Hofstede, Geert (1994), *'Cultures and Organizations - Software of the Mind', Intercultural Cooperation and its Importance for Survival*, London: Harper Collins Business.

Hood, K.L. and R. Bucheery (1999), 'The interaction of religious (Islamic) auditors with reference to the audit expectation gap in Bahrain', *Accounting, Commerce and Finance: The Islamic Perspective Journal*, **3**(1 & 2), 25-58.

Hussain, Jamila (1999), *Islamic Law and Society. An Introduction*, Sydney: The Federation Press.

Hussan, Ali A. (1999), 'Islamic banking culture', *New Horizon*, 83, 11-13.

Iannaccone, L.R. (1998), 'Introduction to the economics of religion', *Journal of Economic Literature*, **36**(3), 1465-95.

Innes, R. (1993), 'Financial contracting under risk neutrality, limited liability and *ex ante* asymmetric information', *Economica*, **60**, 27-40.

Institute of Islamic Banking and Insurance (1999), *Directory of Islamic Insurance (Takaful) 2000*, London: Institute of Islamic Banking & Insurance.

International Association of Islamic Banks (1977-86), *Handbook of Islamic Banking*, published in Arabic, Cairo and Mecca: The International Association of Islamic Banks.

International Institute of Islamic Economics (1999), *IIIE's Blueprint of Islamic Financial System*, Islamabad: International Islamic University.

Iqbal, Z. (1997), 'Islamic Financial Systems', *Finance and Development*, **34**, June, 42-45.

Iqbal, Z. and A. Mirakhor (1987), 'Islamic Banking', International Monetary Fund, Occasional Paper 49, Washington, DC: IMF.

Iqbal, Z. and A. Mirakhor (1992), 'Comment on the Legal Framework', in

R.C. Effros (ed.), *Current Legal Issues Affecting Central Banking*, Vol. 1, Washington: International Monetary Fund.

Ismail, A.H. (1986), *Islamic Banking in Malaysia: Some Issues, Problems and Prospects*, Kuala Lumpur: Bank Islam Malaysia Berhard.

Janahi, A.L. (1995), *Islamic Banking, Concept, Practice and Future*, 2nd edition, Manama: Bahrain Islamic Bank.

Jaziri, 'Abd al-Rahman al (n.d.), *Kitab al-Fiqh 'ala al-Madhahib al-Arba's*, 6th edition, Cairo: al-Maktabat al-Tijariyya al-Kubra.

Jensen, M. and W. Meckling (1976), 'Theory of the firm: managerial behaviour, agency costs and ownership structure', *Journal of Financial Economics*, **3**, 305–60.

Jones, N. (1989), *God and the Moneylenders*, Oxford: Basil Blackwell.

Kareken, J.H. (1986), 'Federal Bank regulatory policy: a description and some observations', *The Journal of Business*, January, **59**(1), 3–48.

Karim, A.A. (2000), 'Incentive Compatible Constraints for Islamic Banking: Some Lessons from Bank Muamalat', in *Islamic Finance: Challenges and Opportunities in the Twenty-First Century*, Fourth International Conference on Islamic Economics and Banking, Loughborough University, pp. 579–616.

Karim, R.A.A. (1990), 'The independence of religious and external auditors: the case of Islamic banks', *Accounting, Auditing and Accountability*, **3**(3), 34–44.

Karsten, I. (1982), 'Islam and financial intermediation', *IMF Staff Papers*, **29**(1), March, 108–42.

Kazarian, E. (1991), *Finance and Economic Development, Islamic Banking in Egypt*, Lund Economic Studies Number 45, Lund: University of Lund.

Kazarian, E. and A. Kokko (1987), *Islamic Banking and Development*, Minor Field Study Series, No. 4, Nationalekonoimiska Institutionnen vid Lunds Universitet, Lund, Sweden.

Keen, S. (1997), 'From prohibition to depression: the western attitude to usury', *Accounting, Commerce and Finance: The Islamic Perspective Journal*, **1**(1), 26–55.

Khan, M.A. (1968), 'Theory of employment in Islam', *Islamic Literature*, Karachi, **14**(4), 516.

Khan, M.A. (1994), *Rural Development Through Islamic Banks*, Leicester: The Islamic Foundation.

Khan, M.F. (1995), *Essays in Islamic Economics*, Leicester: The Islamic Foundation.

Khan, M.S. (1986), 'Islamic interest-free banking: a theoretical analysis', *IMF Staff Papers*, **33**(1), 1–25.

Khan, M.S. and A. Mirakhor (1986), 'The framework and practice of Islamic banking', *Finance and Development*, **6**, March, 32–6.

Khan, M.S. and A. Mirakhor (eds) (1987), *Theoretical Studies in Islamic Banking and Finance*, Houston: Institute for Research and Islamic Studies.

Khan, M.S. and A. Mirakhor (1989), 'Islamic Banking: Experiences in the Islamic Republic of Iran and Pakistan', IMF Working Paper, WP/89/12, Washington: International Monetary Fund.

Khan, M.S. and A. Mirakhor (1990), 'Islamic banking: experiences in the Islamic Republic of Iran and Pakistan', *Economic Development and Cultural Change*, **38**(2), 353–75.

Khan, M.S. and A. Mirakhor (1992), 'Islamic Banking', in P. Newman, M. Milgate and J. Eatwell (eds), *New Palgrave Dictionary of Money and Finance*, Vol. 2, London: Macmillan, pp. 531–33.

Khan, W.M. (1985), *Towards an Interest-Free Islamic Economic System*, Leicester: The Islamic Foundation.

Khan, W.M. (1987), 'Towards an Interest-free Economic System' in M.S. Khan and A. Mirakhor (eds), *Theoretical Studies in Islamic Banking and Finance*, Houston: Institute for Research and Islamic Studies.

Kilingmulier, E. (1969), 'Concept and development of insurance in Islamic countries', *Islamic Culture*, January, 27–37.

Kindleberger, C.P. (1974), *The Formation of Financial Centres: a Study in Comparative Economic History*, Princeton Studies in International Finance, No. 36, and Princeton, NJ: Princeton University Press.

Kindleberger, C.P. (1984), *A Financial History of Western Europe*, London: George Allen & Unwin.

Kuran, T. (1995), 'Islamic economics and the Islamic subeconomy', *Journal of Economic Perspectives*, **9**(4), 155–73.

Landes, D.S. (1958), *Bankers and Pashas: International Finance and Economic Imperialism in Egypt*, New York: Harper and Row.

Langholm, O. (1984), *The Aristotelian Analysis of Usury*, Bergen: Bergen Universitetsforiaget; distributed in the USA by Columbia University Press, New York.

Lannoo, K. (1995), 'Corporate Governance in Europe', CEPS Working Party Report No. 12, Centre for European Policy Studies, Brussels.

Le Goff, Jacques (1979), 'The Usurer and Purgatory', *The Dawn of Modern Banking*, Los Angeles: Center for Medieval & Renaissance Studies, University of California, pp. 25–52.

Le Goff, Jacques (1984), *The Birth of Purgatory*, Trans. A. Goldhammer, Chicago: University of Chicago Press.

Leland, H.E. and D.H. Pyle (1977), 'Information asymmetries, financial structure and financial intermediation', *Journal of Finance*, **32**, 371–87, reprinted in M.K. Lewis (ed.), *Financial Intermediaries, The International Library of Critical Writings in Economics, 43*, Aldershot, UK and Brookfield, US: Edward Elgar, 1995.

Lerrick, A. and Q.J. Mian (1982), *Saudi Business and Labor Law*, London: Graham and Trotman.

Levine, Aaron (1987), *Economics and Jewish Law: Halakhic Perspective*, Hoboken: Ktav and Yeshiva University Press.

Lewis, A. (1991), *Law of Banking Services*, Wirral: Tudor Business Publishing Ltd.

Lewis, M.K. (1988), 'Off Balance Sheet Activities and Financial Innovation in Banking', *Banca Nazionale del Lavoro Quarterly Review*, 167, December, 387–410.

Lewis, M.K. (1990), 'Liquidity', in J. Creedy (ed.), *Foundations of Economic Thought*, Oxford: Basil Blackwell, pp. 290–330.

Lewis, M.K. (1991), 'Theory and practice of the Banking Firm', in C.J. Green and D.T. Llewellyn (eds), *Surveys in Monetary Economics, Volume 2: Financial Markets and Institutions*, Oxford: Blackwell, pp. 116–65.

Lewis, M.K. (1992a), 'Asset and Liability Management', in P. Newman, M. Milgate and J Eatwell (eds), *New Palgrave Dictionary of Money and Finance*, Vol. 1, London: Macmillan, pp. 70–74.

Lewis, M.K. (1992b), 'Balance Sheets of Financial Intermediaries,' in P. Newman, M. Milgate and J. Eatwell (eds), *New Palgrave Dictionary of Money and Finance*, Vol. 1, London: Macmillan, pp. 120–22.

Lewis, M.K. (1992c), 'Modern Banking in Theory and Practice, *Revue Economique*, **43**(2), 203–77.

Lewis, M.K. (1992d), 'Market-making and liquidity', in R. Kinsella (ed.), *New Issues in Financial Services*, Oxford: Blackwell, pp. 9–39.

Lewis, M.K. (1994), 'Banking on Real Estate', in D.E. Fair and Robert Raymond (eds), *The Competitiveness of Financial Institutions and Centres in Europe*, Dordrecht: Kluwer Academic Publishers, pp. 47–71.

Lewis, M.K. (1995a), 'Financial services location and competition amongst financial centres in Europe', *Review of Policy Issues*, **1**(4), Spring, 3–30.

Lewis, M.K. (ed.) (1995b), *Financial Intermediaries*, *The International Library of Critical Writings in Economics, 43*, Aldershot, UK and Brookfield, US: Edward Elgar.

Lewis, M.K. (1996), 'Financial Services', in Bijit Bora and Christopher Finlay (eds), *Regional Integration and the Asia-Pacific*, Melbourne: Oxford University Press, pp. 99–127.

Lewis, M.K. (1997), 'Derivative Markets', in M.K. Lewis and R.H. Wallace (eds), *The Australian Financial System: Evolution, Policy and Practice*, Melbourne: Addison, Wesley, Longman, pp. 503–57.

Lewis, M.K. (1999a), 'The Globalization of Financial Services: An Overview', *The Globalization of Financial Services, The Globalization of the World Economy, Volume 7*, Cheltenham UK and Northampton, MA, US: Edward Elgar, pp. xiii–xxxiv.

Lewis, M.K. (1999b), 'International Banking and Offshore Finance: London and the Major Centres', in M.P. Hampton and J.P. Abbot (eds), *Offshore Finance Centres and Tax Havens: The Rise of Global Finance*, London: Macmillan Press, pp. 80–116.

Lewis, M.K. (1999c), 'The cross and the crescent: comparing Islamic and Christian attitudes to usury', *AL-IQTISHAD, Journal of Islamic Economics*, **1**(1), Muharram, 1420H/April, 1–23.

Lewis, M.K. (1999d), 'Corporate Governance in Six Cultures: an Exploratory Study', *Keynote Address, The Third International Stockholm Seminar on Risk Behaviour and Risk Management*, School of Business, University of Stockholm, June.

Lewis, M.K. (2000), 'The next property cycle: a survival kit for banks', in Bo Green (ed.), *Risk Behaviour and Risk Management in Business Life*, Dordrecht: Kluwer Academic Publishers.

Lewis, M.K. and K.T. Davis (1987), *Domestic and International Banking*, Oxford: Philip Allan and Cambridge, Mass.: MIT Press.

Lewis, M.K. and P.D. Mizen (2000), *Monetary Economics*, Oxford: Oxford University Press.

Lewis, M.K. and P. Morton (1996), 'Asset and Liability Management in Retail Banking', in F. Bruni, D.E. Fair and R. O'Brien (eds), *Risk Management in Volatile Financial Markets*, Dordrecht: Kluwer Academic Publishers, pp. 225–51.

Lindholm, C. (1996), *The Islamic Middle East. An Historical Anthropology*, Oxford: Basil Blackwell.

Llewellyn, D.T. (1999), *The New Economics of Banking*, Société Universitaire Européenne de Recherches Financières Studies No. 5, Amsterdam: Société Universitaire Européenne de Recherches Financières.

Lopez, Robert Sabatino (1979), 'The Dawn of Medieval Banking', *The Dawn of Modern Banking*, Los Angeles Center for Medieval & Renaissance Studies, University of California, pp. 1–24.

Mahdavi, H. (1995), 'Islamic Banking in Iran', *Encyclopedia of Islamic Banking and Insurance*, London: Institute of Islamic Banking and Insurance, pp. 221–30.

Maimonides, Moses (1956), *The Guide for the Perplexed*, New York: Dover Publications.

Mannan, M.A. ([1970]1986), *Islamic Economics: Theories and Practice*, (originally Lahore: Islamic Publications, 1970), Kent: Hodder and Stoughton.

Mastura, Michael O. (1988), 'Islamic banking: the Philippine experience', in M. Ariff (ed.), *Islamic Banking in Southeast Asia*, Singapore: Institute of Southeast Asian Studies.

Mawdudi, Sayyed Abul A'la ([1950]1961), *Sud* (Interest), Lahore: Islamic

Publications.

Mayer, C. (1988), 'New issues in corporate finance', *European Economic Review*, **32**, 1167–89.

McCulloch, J.H. (1986), 'Bank regulation and deposit insurance', *The Journal of Business*, **59**(1), 79–85.

Mints, L.W. (1945), *A History of Banking Theory in Great Britain and the United States*, Chicago: University of Chicago Press.

Mirakhor, A. (1987), 'Analysis of Short-Term Asset Concentration in Islamic Banking', IMF Working Paper No. 67, Washington, DC: IMF.

Mirakhor, A. (1995), 'Theory of an Islamic Financial System', in *Encyclopedia of Islamic Banking and Insurance*, London: Institute of Islamic Banking and Insurance.

Mirrlees, J. (1974), 'Notes on Welfare Economies, Information, and Uncertainty', in M.S. Balch, D.L. McFadden and S.Y. Wu (eds), *Contributions to Economic Analysis*, Amsterdam: North-Holland.

Mirrlees, J. (1976), 'The optimal structure of incentives and authority within an organisation', *Bell Journal of Economics*, **7**(1), Spring, 105–31.

'Modaraba Companies and Modaraba (Flotation and Control) Ordinance, 1980 (Ordinance No. XXXI of 1980)', *Gazette of Pakistan*, June 26, 388–400.

'The Modaraba Companies and Modaraba Rules, 1981', *Gazette of Pakistan*, January 26, 171–217.

Modigliani, F. and M.H. Miller (1958), 'The cost of capital, corporation finance and the theory of investment', *American Economic Review*, **48**, 261–97.

'MOFNE Financial Markets ("FM") Unit' (1994), International Islamic Finance – The Key Strategic Vision for Bahrain International Financial Centre. A Scenario-Building Discussion Paper, Ministry of Finance and National Economy, Bahrain.

Mudawi, A.B.Y. (1995), 'The Experience of Islamic Banks in the Sudan', *Encyclopedia of Islamic Banking and Insurance*, London: Institute of Islamic Banking and Insurance, pp. 246–50.

Munn, G.G., F.L. Garcia, and C.J. Woelfel (1991), *Encyclopedia of Banking and Finance*, ninth edition, London: McGraw-Hill.

Murvat, S.K. (1992), 'The Legal Framework for Islamic Banking: Pakistan's Experience', in R.C. Effros (ed.), *Current Legal Issues Affecting Central Banking*, Vol. 1, Washington: International Monetary Fund.

Muslehuddin, M. (1982), *Insurance and Islamic Law*, Delhi: Markazi Maktaba Islami.

Mustafa, Amira (1999), 'Public-private partnership: an alternative institutional model for implementing the private finance initiative in the provision of transport infrastructure', *Journal of Project Finance*, **5**(2), Summer, 64–79.

Naqvi, S.N.H. (1981), *Ethics and Economics. An Islamic Synthesis*, Leicester: The Islamic Foundation.

Naqvi, S.N.H., H.U. Beg, Rafiq Ahmed and Mian M. Nazeer (1980), *An Agenda for Islamic Economic Reform: The Report of the Committee on Islamization Appointed by the Finance Minister, Government of Pakistan*, Islamabad, Pakistan Institute of Development Economics.

Nelson, Benjamin (1949), *The Idea of Usury: From Tribal Brotherhood to Universal Otherhood*, Princeton: Princeton University Press.

Neusner, Jacob, Trans. (1990), *The Talmud of Babylonia: An American Translation*, Atlanta: Scholar's Press.

Nienhaus, V. (1983), 'Profitability of Islamic banks competing with interest banks: problems and prospects', *Journal of Research in Islamic Economics*, **1**, 37–47.

Nienhaus, V. (1988), 'The performance of Islamic banks: trends and cases', in C. Mallat (ed.), *Islamic Law and Finance*, London: Graham & Trotman.

Noonan, John T. (1957), *The Scholastic Analysis of Usury*, Cambridge, Mass.: Harvard University Press.

Nyazee, Imran Ahsan Khan (1994), *Theories of Islamic Law*, Islamabad: International Institute of Islamic Thought and Islamic Research Institute.

Nyazee, Imran Ahsan Khan (1995), *The Concept of Riba and Islamic Banking*, Islamabad: Niazi Publishing House.

Nyazee, Imran Ahsan Khan (1999), *Islamic Law of Business Organisation: Partnerships*, New Delhi: Kitab Bhamn.

Patinkin, D. (1968), 'Interest', *International Encyclopedia of the Social Sciences*, London: Macmillan.

Pemberton, Sir Robin Leigh (1984), 'A speech given by the Governor of the Bank of England to the Arab Bankers' Association', *Meed*, 5 October.

Presley, J.R. (1988), *Directory of Islamic Financial Institutions*, London: Croom Helm.

Presley, John and John Sessions (1994), 'Islamic Economics: The Emergence of a New Paradigm', *The Economic Journal*, **104**, May, 584–96.

al-Qaradawi, Yusuf (1989), *The Lawful and the Prohibited in Islam*, Kuwait, International Islamic Federation of Student Organisations.

Qadir, Ghulam (1994), 'Interest-free banking: a proposal', in K. Ahmad (ed.), *Elimination of Riba from the Economy*, Islamabad: Institute of Policy Studies, pp. 105–16.

Qureshi, Anwar Iqbal ([1946]1991), *Islam and the Theory of Interest*, Lahore: Sh. Md. Ashraf.

Rabinovich, L. (1993), 'Introduction to secured transactions in *Halakha* and common law', *Tradition*, **27**(3), 36–50.

Rahman, Fazlur G. (1958), 'A study of commercial interest in Islam', *Islamic Thought*, **5**(4, 5), July–October, 24–46.

Rahman, Fazlur G. (1964), 'Riba and interest', *Islamic Studies*, **3**(1), 1–43.

Rahman, Yahia Abdul (1999), 'Islamic instruments for managing liquidity', *International Journal of Islamic Financial Services*, **1**, April–June, 21–7.

Rangaswami, K. (1927), *Aspects of Ancient Indian Economic Thought*, Mylapore: Madras Law Journal Press.

Rayner, S.E. (1991), *The Theory of Contracts in Islamic Law*, London: Graham and Trotman.

Razi, Muhammad Fakr al-Din ([1872]1938), *Mafatih al-Ghayb* known as *al-Tafsir al-Kabir*, Bulaq Cairo: Dar Ibya al-Kutub al-Bahiyya.

Rida, Muhammad Rashid (1959), *al-Riba wa al-Mu'amalat fi al-Islam*, Cairo: Maktabat al-Qahira.

Rippin, A. (1993), *Muslims. Their Religious Beliefs and Practices, Volume 2: The Contemporary Period*, London: Routledge.

Roll, E. (1953), *A History of Economic Thought*, London: George Allen & Unwin.

Rosly, Saiful Azhar (1999), '*Al-Bay' bithaman ajil* financing: impacts on Islamic banking performance', *Thunderbird International Business Review*, **41**(4/5), July–October, 461–80.

Ross, S. (1973), 'The economic theory of agency: the principal's problem', *American Economic Review*, **63**(2), May, 134–9.

Russell, Bertrand (1946), *History of Western Philosophy*, London: George Allen & Unwin.

Saeed, A. (1995), 'Islamic banking in practice: the case of Faisal Islamic Bank of Egypt', *Journal of Arabic, Islamic and Middle Eastern Studies*, **2**(1), 28–46.

Saeed, A. (1996), *Islamic Banking and Interest*, Leiden: E.J. Brill.

Sahnun, 'Abd al-Salam ibn Sa'id ibn Habib al-Tanukhi (1905), *al-Mudawwanah al-Kubra*, Cairo: Matba'at al-Sa'adah.

Samad, Abdus and M. Kabir Hassan (1999), 'The performance of Malaysian Islamic banks during 1984–1997: an exploratory study', *International Journal of Islamic Financial Services*, **1**(3), Oct.–Dec., 1–14.

Sarker, M.A.A. (1999a), 'Agency problems, its nature, characteristics and relevance with the Islamic modes of contracts', *New Horizon*, 84, 9–13.

Sarker, M.A.A. (1999b), 'Islamic Banking in Bangladesh: Performance, Problems and Prospects', *International Journal of Islamic Financial Services*, **1**(3), Oct.–Dec., 15–36.

Schacht, J. (1964), *An Introduction to Islamic Law*, Oxford: Oxford University Press.

Schreyogg, Georg, Walter Oechsler and Harmut Wachter (1995), *Managing in a European Context, Human Resources – Corporate Culture – Industrial Relations, Text and Cases*, Wiesbaden: Gabler.

Schumpeter, J.A. (1951), *The Theory of Economic Development*, Cambridge,

Mass.: Harvard University Press.

Shah, Hazoor, A. (1981), 'Modaraba venture to be launched', *Dawn* of Karachi, 40, July 3.

Shah, Syed Yaqub (1967), *Chand Mu'ashi Masa'il aur Islam* (Islam and some Economic Problems), Lahore: Idara Thaqafat-e-Islamia.

Siddiqi, M.N. (1980), 'Muslim Economic Thinking: A Survey of Contemporary Literature', in K. Ahmad (ed.), *Studies in Islamic Economics*, Leicester: The Islamic Foundation, pp. 191–315.

Siddiqi, M.N. (1982), 'Islamic laws on riba and their economic implication', *International Journal of Middle East Studies*, **14**(11), 3–16.

Siddiqi, M.N. (1983), *Banking Without Interest*, Leicester: The Islamic Foundation.

Siddiqi, M.N. (1985), *Insurance in an Islamic Economy*, Leicester: The Islamic Foundation.

Siddiqi, M.N. (1986), *Islamic Banking: Theory and Practice*, Jeddah Center for Research in Islamic Economics, King Abdul Aziz University.

Siddiqi, Naiem (1948), 'Islami Usul par Banking' (Banking according to Islamic principles), Paper in the Urdu monthly *Chiragh-e-Rah* (Karachi), 1 (11 & 12), (Nov. & Dec.), 24–28 and 60–64.

Siddiqui, S.H. (1994), *Islamic Banking: Genesis, Rationale, Evaluation and Review, Prospects and Challenges*, Karachi: Royal Book Company.

Smircich, L. (1983), 'Concepts of culture and organizational analysis, *Administrative Science Quarterly*, **28**, 339–58.

Smith, C.W. Jr, and J. Warner (1979), 'On financial contracting: an analysis of bond covenants', *Journal of Financial Economics*, **7**, 117–61.

Spiegel, H.W. (1992), 'Usury', in P. Newman, M. Milgate and J. Eatwell (eds), *The New Palgrave Dictionary of Money and Finance*, Vol. 3, London: Macmillan.

Stigler, G.J. (1964), 'Public Regulation of the Securities Markets', *Journal of Business*, **37** (March), 117–32, reprinted in G.J. Stigler, *The Citizen and the State: Essays on Regulation*, Chicago: University of Chicago Press.

Stigler, G.J. (1971), 'The Theory of Economic Regulation', *Bell Journal of Economics and Management*, **2**(1), 1–21.

Stigler, G.J. and C. Friedland (1962), 'What can regulators regulate? The case of electricity', *Journal of Law and Economics*, October; reprinted in G.J. Stigler, *The Citizen and the State: Essays on Regulation*, Chicago: University of Chicago Press.

Stiglitz, J.E. (1974), 'Risk sharing and incentives in sharecropping', *Review of Economic Studies*, **61**, 219–55.

Stiglitz, J.E. (1975), 'Incentives, risk and information: notes towards a theory of hierarchy', *Bell Journal of Economics*, **6**(2), 552–79.

Stiglitz, J.E. and A. Weiss (1981), 'Credit rationing in markets with imperfect information', *The American Economic Review*, June, **71**(3), 393-410.

Stiglitz, J.E. and A. Weiss (1988), 'Banks as Social Accountants and Screening Devices for the Allocation of Credit', National Bureau of Economic Research Working Paper No. 2710, reprinted in M.K. Lewis (ed.), *Financial Intermediaries, The International Library of Critical Writings in Economics, 43*, Aldershot, UK and Brookfield, US: Edward Elgar, 1995.

Su'ud, M. Abu (1980), 'The economic order within the general conception of the Islamic way of life', *Islamic Review*, **55**(2), 2426 and (3), 1114.

Swank, Job (1996), 'Theories of the banking firm: a review of the literature', *Bulletin of Economic Research*, **48**(3), 173-207.

Tawney, R.H. (1926), *Religion and the Rise of Capitalism*, London and New York: Harcourt Brace.

Taylor, T.W. and J.W. Evans (1987), 'Islamic banking and the prohibition of usury in Western economic thought', *National Westminster Bank Quarterly Review*, November, 15-27.

Thomson, J.A.K. (1953), *The Ethics of Aristotle*, Harmondsworth, Middlesex: Penguin.

Trever, Albert (1916), *Greek Economic Thought*, Chicago: University of Chicago Press.

Usmani, Justice Muhammad Taqi (1999), 'Home purchase through Islamic financing', *New Horizon*, 87, May, Safar 1420, 6-7.

Uzair, M. ([1955]1978), *An Outline of Interest-Free Banking*, Karachi: Royal Book Company.

Vermaat, A.J. (1998), 'Insurance company ownership in the Netherlands: implications for corporate governance and competition' in M. Balling, E. Hennessy and R. O'Brien (eds), *Corporate Governance, Financial Markets and Global Convergence*, Dordrecht: Kluwer Academic Publishers.

Vogel, F.E. and S.L. Hayes II (1998), *Islamic Law and Finance: Religion, Risk and Return*, The Hague: Kluwer Law International.

Wahib, Rusil Bin (1999), 'Islamic Takafol Insurance', *New Horizon*, Part 1, 86,10-12; Part 2, 87, 16-17; Part 3, 88, 10-12.

Watt, M.W. (1996), *A Short History of Islam*, Oxford: Oneworld Publications.

Weber, Max (1930), *Die protestantische Ethik und der Geist des Kapitalismus*, in *Gesammelte Aufsäzte zur Religionssoziologic*, I. Originally appeared in the *Archiv für Sozialwissenschaft und Sozialpolitik*, xx-xxi, 1904-1905. English translation by Talcott Parsons with a Foreword by R.H. Tawney, *The Protestant Ethic and the Spirit of Capitalism*, London: Collins.

Williamson, O.E. (1980), 'The organization of work: a comparative institutional assessment', *Journal of Economic Behaviour and Organization*, **1** (March), 5-38.

Williamson, S.D. (1986), 'Costly monitoring, financial intermediation, and equilibrium credit rationing', *Journal of Monetary Economics*, **18**, 159–79.

Williamson, S.D. (1987), 'Recent developments in modeling financial intermediation', *Federal Reserve Bank of Minneapolis Quarterly Review*, Summer, 19–29, reprinted in M.K. Lewis (ed.), *Financial Intermediaries, The International Library of Critical Writings in Economics, 43*, Aldershot, UK and Brookfield, US: Edward Elgar, 1995.

Wilson, R. (1983), *Banking and Finance in the Arab Middle East*, London: Macmillan.

Wilson, R. (1987), 'Finance and development in the Arab Gulf: the Eastern Bank Experience, 1917–1950', *Business History*, **20**(2), 178–98.

Wilson, R. (1998), 'Markets without capitalism: an Islamic economic system', *New Horizon*, 82, December, 6–9.

Wilson, R. (1999), 'Challenges and opportunities for Islamic banking and finance in the West: the United Kingdom experience', *Thunderbird International Business Review*, **41**(4/5), July–October, 421–44.

Yasin, Norhashimah Mohd (1997), 'Shariah contracts used by Islamic banks', *Al-Nahdah*, 17, 5–11.

Yasseri, A. (2000), 'Islamic Banking Contracts as Enforced in Iran (Implications for the Iranian Banking Practices)' in *Islamic Finance: Challenges and Opportunities in the Twenty-First Century*, Fourth International Conference on Islamic Economics and Banking, Loughborough University, pp. 505–26.

Zaman, S.M. Hasanuz (1994), 'Practical Options for Central and Commercial Banking', in K. Ahmad (ed.), *Elimination of Riba from the Economy*, Islamabad: Institute of Policy Studies, pp. 197–216.

Zweigert, K. and H. Kötz (1998), *An Introduction to Comparative Law*, 3rd edition, Oxford: Clarendon Press.

Index

Abraham, J. P. 235
Abu Zahra, Muhammad 37
Accounting and Auditing Organisation
    for Islamic Financial Institutions
    (AAOIF) 171, 182
adverse selection 63, 78, 86, 130
agency theory, *see* principal-agent theory
Ahmad, I. 32, 35
Ahmad, K. 32, 93, 117, 154, 177
Ahmad, S. M. 3, 40, 117, 119
Ahmad, N. 150
Ahmed A. S. 32
Ahmed, Ausaf 47
Ahmed, N. 51, 52
Ahmed, S. 84,
Al-Arafah Islami Bank Limited 142
Al-Baraka Group 7, 12, 13, 14, 104, 121,
    126, 141, 142, 156, 157, 171, 172,
    174, 175, 177, 178, 181, 183, 222,
    224, 237
Alchian, A. A. 66,
Algaoud, L. M. 171, 183, 239, 241
Al-Harran, S. A. S. 59, 81, 105, 106, 118
Ali, A. H. 163
Ali, Muhammad Moher 32
Ali, Mukarram 118
Al-Jarhi, Ma'bid Ali 98
Al-Kásáni, Abu Bakr ibn Mas'ud 40
Al-Quduri al-Baghdadi, Abu al-Husayn
    Ahmad ibn Muhammad 42
Al Rajhi Banking and Investment
    Company of Saudi Arabia 14, 157,
    221, 222
Alrawi, Khalia Whajeb 143
Al-Rifai, Tariq 221
Al-Safa Investment Fund 220, 222
Anwar, Muhammad 210, 239
ANZ Bank 14, 236
Aquinas, St Thomas 190, 192
Ariff, M. 45, 131
Arifin, Z. 13
Armstrong, K. 32

Arrow, K. J. 66, 73, 168
Ashley, W. J. 204
Atiya, M. K. 91
Atiyah, E. 60
Australia 1, 121, 144–7
Aylward, A. 229
Ayoub-Bey, N. E. 170

Babai, D. 238
Bagsiraj, M. I. 13
Bahamas 1, 8, 12, 133, 214
Bahrain
    as financial centre 170, 171, 237-8
    institutions 8, 13, 120, 158, 171, 221,
        223, 227, 234
Bahrain Institute of Banking and
    Financial Studies 171
Bahrain Islamic Bank (BIB) 11, 126,
    171, 174, 175, 177, 178, 180, 183
bai-bi-thamin ajil (BBA) 55, 138–41,
    152, 229
bai' muajjal 55, 115, 142, 152, 154, 229
bai' salam 55–6, 103, 154
Baldick, J. 33
Baldwin, J. W. 193
Banaga, A. 179, 182
Bangladesh 23, 55, 126, 141–2
Bank Islam Malaysia Berhad (BIMB) 6,
    47, 126, 127, 128, 129, 135, 138,
    141, 147, 153, 156, 157
Bank Muamalat 13, 87, 232
Bank of Sudan 104, 105
Bank Raykat Indonesia 135, 232
Baster, A. 156
Benston, G. J. 87
Berle, A. 159
Bervaes, N. 234
Billah, Mohd Ma'sum 213
Blair, M. M. 159
Boehm-Bawerk, E. von 89
Born, K. E. 156
Brown, D. W. 60

Brown, N. J. 25, 26, 33, 39
Buchanan, J. M. 99
Bucheery, R. 184
Buckmaster, D. 49, 53, 229

Cadbury Committee 159
Canada 1, 8, 121
Casson, M. 69
Chan, Y. S. 87
Chant, John 86
Chapra, M. U. 3, 29, 88, 90, 95, 96, 97, 99, 117, 128
Chebel, M. 32
China 17, 232
Christianity
    general 16, 89, 185, 186-7, 191, 203, 204, 205
    relation to Islam 17-18, 186
    see also usury
Citi Islamic Investment Bank 171, 224, 237, 238,
Citibank (Citicorp) 14, 15, 82, 171, 224, 229, 236, 237
Cizaka, M. 4
Clarke, P. 32
Coase, R. H. 65, 66
Cobham, D. 86, 130
Cohn, H. H. 188, 189, 191, 202
conventional banking 5, 60, 62, 151, 152, 155, 177, 232, 236, 243
Cook, M. 32
corporate governance
    conventional banks 162-3
    defined 159-60
    Islamic banks 163-70
    role of culture 160, 163-6, 168
    shari'a supervision 104-5, 168-170, 179-82, 245
Council of Islamic Ideology 14, 37, 109
Court, W. H. B. 210
Covick, O. E. 211, 216
Crone, P. 4
Cunningham, J. B. 150

Dar al-Maal al-Islami (DMI) Group 7, 12, 13, 14, 120, 126, 127, 133, 135, 156, 157, 171, 174, 181, 183, 224, 241
Dar, H. A. 116
Davidson, I. R. 87

Davis, J. J. 160
Davis, K. T. 82, 94, 155, 210, 220, 233
De Cecco, M. 199
De Roover, Raymond 200, 202, 203, 209
Debreu, G. 66
delegated monitoring 70, 71, 82, 84, 105, 152, 162, 178, 243
demand deposits (current accounts) 46-7, 127, 128, 129, 138, 143, 145, 167, 173
Demsetz, H. 66
Den Broeder, C. 159
deposit insurance 70, 87, 162
development banks 7, 11, 96, 126, 228-9, 238
Dhareer, Al Siddiq Mohammad Al-Ameen 31, 32
Diamond, D. 68, 70, 71, 79, 87, 162
Divine, T. F. 2, 190, 205
Doi, 'Abdur Rahman i 21
Donaldson, L. 160
Dow Jones Islamic Market Index Fund 222, 223
Dowd, K. 74, 76, 86
Downs, A. 210
Dresdener Kleinwort Benson 15, 236, 237
Dubai Islamic Bank 11, 126, 183
Dufey, G. 236
Dunning, J. H. 235
Dybvig, P. 79, 87, 162

Ebrahim Muhammed-Shahid 230
Egypt 5-6, 26, 120, 127, 128-30, 135, 227
Einzig, P. 199
El-Awa, M. S. 197
El-Bdour, Radi 150
El-Gamal, M. A. 117, 157, 239
Erol, Cengiz 150
Errico, Luca 81
ethical investments 30, 165, 179-82, 223-4, 245
Evans, J. W. 210

Faisal Islamic Bank of Bahrain (FIBB) 142, 171, 172, 174, 175, 177, 178, 181, 183, 237
Faisal Islamic Bank of Egypt (FIBE) 11, 127, 128, 129, 133, 135, 149, 168

Faisal Islamic Bank of Sudan (FIBS) 104, 136
Fama, E. F. 67, 87
Farahbaksh, Mitra 81
Federal Shariat Court of Pakistan 3, 114
financial intermediation
  and direct financing 62-5
  incentive-compatible contracts 45, 63, 71-6, 131
  information asymmetries and costs 63, 67, 68, 69-71, 130, 167
  transactions costs 63, 65-6, 168
fiqh 21, 32, 47, 52, 53, 55, 60-61
foreign currency transactions 60, 111, 127, 156, 175
Forward, M. 32
Freeland, R. 236
Friedland, C. 210
Frishman, Martin 32
futures contracts 31

Gafoor, Abdul A. L. M. 40, 156, 208
Galassi, F. L. 200
Gale, D. 72
Garcia, F. L. 2
Gätje, Helmut 209
Gelauff, G. M. M. 159
Gerrard, P. 150
gharar 28, 30-32, 99, 211, 215
Ghazali Abou Hamid Muhammad 89, 117
Giddy, I. H. 87, 236
Glacser, E. L. 189, 193
Goldman Sachs 14, 15
Goodhart, C. A. E. 87, 118
Gopal, M. H. 185
Gordon, B. 187
Green, E. J. 87
Greenbaum, S. I. 65
Grimsey, D. 100, 227
Grossman, S. S. 84
Guinotte, A. 235
Gulf states 25, 26, 171, 175, 233, 234, 237, 238
Gurley, J. G. 65

hadith 16, 20, 21, 24, 29, 35-6, 91, 189
halal bank 6, 91
Hamid, A. 3
Hamwi, B. 229

Handbook of Islamic Banking (HIB) 30, 31, 46, 52
Haque, Nadeem Ul 85, 170
Haque, Z. 46
haram 28, 30, 37, 168, 222-3
Haron, S. 150
Harris, M. 73
Hart, O. P. 84, 159
Hasan, S. U. 222
Hassan, M. Kabir 138
Hayes, S. L. II 33
Hellwig, M. 72
Henry, C. M. 6
Hester, Donald D. 86
Hirschman, A. O. 81
hiyal 118, 200-201, 209
Hodges, S. D. 99
Hofstede, Geert 163
Holy Qur'an 17, 18, 19, 20, 21-2, 23, 24, 28, 29, 34, 35, 38, 39, 41, 89, 91, 109, 155, 186, 187, 189, 195, 208, 239, 243
Hood, K. L. 184
housing finance 58, 109, 145-6
Hussain, Jamila 26, 33, 194

Iannaccone, L. R. 207
ijara (leasing/hire purchase) 27, 28, 56-8, 91, 111, 134, 137, 138, 142, 143, 151-2, 153, 174, 175, 221, 228-9, 230
ijtihad 21, 22-3
India 13, 16, 17, 121
Indonesia 6, 13, 87, 231, 232
infrastructure financing 100, 114, 151, 227-31, 237, 238, 242
Innes, R. 74
Institute of Islamic Banking and Insurance 15, 239
Interest
  definition 77, 186
  exploitation 3, 37, 91, 189, 192, 194, 207
  prohibition in Islam 2, 34-8, 89
  relation to *interesse* 186, 198, 209
  relation to usury 2, 186-7, 193, 205-6, 207, 209-10
  views of Aristotle 190, 192, 195, 205, 209
International Association of Islamic

Banks (IAIB) 7, 13, 15, 22, 61, 132, 133, 138, 157
International Institute of Islamic Economics 100
international Islamic financial centre 233-9, 245
investment accounts 46, 48, 127, 128, 129, 135, 139, 142, 143, 147, 157, 166, 172, 220, 244
investment banking
  by conventional banks 63, 64, 68, 224-6
  by Islamic banks 140, 224, 226-7, 228-9
Iqbal, Z. 80, 101, 108, 151
Iran, 1, 14, 39, 88, 101-4, 120, 131, 133, 242
Iraq 6, 23
Ireland 1, 236
Islam
  essence 16-20, 166, 194
  ethical principles 24-6, 29, 30, 34, 39, 85, 116, 131, 165-6, 170, 194
  financing principles 28-32, 34-9, 211, 212, 222-4
  relation to Christianity 17-18, 185, 194-5, 208
  relation to Judaism 18, 194
  shias 23, 33
  sunnis 23-24, 33
Islamic Bank of Bangladesh Ltd (IBBL) 141, 142, 147
Islamic Bank of Western Sudan 104, 126
Islamic banking
  agricultural financing 5, 51-2, 55-6, 82, 105-7, 132, 153, 157
  bank runs 79-80, 83, 87, 94, 117
  deposits 46-8, 81, 90-91, 117, 119, 127, 128, 129, 135, 138, 143, 149-50, 172
  incentive and information issues 45-6, 66, 76-9, 81-5, 107, 116, 142, 143, 144, 151, 167-70, 178
  interest rate risk 141, 152, 157
  investments 48-59, 83-4, 102, 114, 129-32, 135, 137, 140, 143, 144, 151-2, 174, 177, 243
  practical problems 45-6, 115-17, 130-32, 142, 144, 150-52, 178
  principles 2-5, 22, 39-40, 43-5,

  80-88, 83-4, 90-92, 119-20, 244
  syndication 53, 175, 229, 237
Islamic banks
  development 7-13, 119-20
  early experience 101, 104, 114, 126-32
  geographical activities 12, 133, 134, 174-5, 231-2, 242
  government role 6, 105, 119, 120, 126, 127, 128, 148
  marketing 120, 127, 149-50, 175-7, 233, 243
  operations 46-60, 101-17, 127-32, 132-3, 138-47, 149, 170-79
  shareholders 46, 60, 79, 80-81, 121, 126, 127, 133
  see also Islamic financial institutions
Islamic Cooperative Development Bank 104, 126
Islamic Development Bank 7, 11, 121, 126, 141, 228, 229, 238
Islamic financial institutions
  assets 7, 12, 13, 133, 134, 137
  early origins 4-7, 119-20
  location of operations 7-11, 12, 132-3, 171, 212-13, 221-2, 235-9
  numbers operating 7, 121-6, 132-3, 134, 211, 221
Islamic financial systems
  ideal structure 94-100, 128
  objectives 88-94, 128
Islamic insurance *(takaful)*
  basis 214-15
  companies 133, 136, 138, 211, 212-13
  compared to unit-linked 216-19
  objections to conventional insurance 31-2, 211, 213, 219
  types of policies 214, 217, 219
Islamic Investment Company of the Gulf 14, 133, 171, 183, 229, 238
Islamic law
  commercial aspects 27-8, 197
  hadith 20, 22, 24, 29, 35-6, 91, 189
  ijma 22, 23, 24
  obligations on Muslims 21, 24-6, 30, 163
  qiyas 22-3
  relation to secular law 22, 24-5, 38-9
  rulings on banking 47, 57, 58, 89, 154, 197

sources 3, 16, 20–24
  see also shari'a
Islamic securities 59–60, 97–9, 138, 178,
    221, 230
Islamic 'windows' 12, 14, 15, 135,
    149–50, 237, 243
Islamisation
  Iran 14, 101–4
  Pakistan 6, 14, 108–17
  Sudan 14, 104–7
Ismail, A. H. 95, 96, 99, 128
istisnaa 56, 103, 229, 238

Janahi, A. L. 165
Jaziri, 'Abd al-Rahman al 47
Jensen, M. 84
Jersey 1, 13, 236
Jones, N. 193, 209
Jordan 120, 142–4, 227
Jordan Islamic Bank for Finance and
    Investment (JIB) 143, 144, 147, 168
ju'alah 56
Judaism 17, 18, 19, 29, 185, 187–9, 191,
    195, 202, 204, 209

Kareken, J. H. 87
Karim, A. A. 13
Karim, R. A. A. 182
Karsten, I. 77
Kaynak, Erdener 150
Kazarian, E. 4, 5, 93, 120, 129
Keen, S. 209
Khan, H. U. 32
Khan, M. A. 3, 82, 84, 105,
Khan, M. F. 32, 93
Khan, M. S. 3, 40, 46, 80, 81, 83, 90, 91,
    94, 101, 114, 131,
Khan, W. M. 80, 83, 90, 117
Kilingmulier, E. 239
Kindleberger, C. P. 199, 236
Kokko, A. 93, 120, 129
Kotz, H. 24, 33
Kuran, T. 177
Kuwait 11, 15, 121, 126, 221, 223, 226,
    227, 229, 239
Kuwait Finance House 11, 121, 126,
    221, 229

Labuan 13, 238
Landes, D. S. 156

Langholm, O. 209
Lannoo, K. 159
Le Goff, Jacques 193, 209
Leland, H. E. 87
Lerrick, A. 39
Levine, Aaron 209
Lewis, A. 87
Lewis, M K. 64, 82, 86, 87, 94, 99, 100,
    118, 155, 157, 159, 163, 171, 183,
    209, 210, 211, 213, 216, 220, 227,
    233, 235, 236, 239, 241
Lin, P. 87
Lindholm, C. 60, 209
Llewellyn, D. T. 86
Lopez, Robert Sabatino 196, 202
Luxembourg 1, 13, 14, 236

Mahdavi, H. 103
Maimonides, Moses 192
Malaysia 6, 17, 55, 126, 138–41, 150,
    214, 223, 229, 238
Mannan, M. A. 3, 31, 99
Margoliouth, D. S. 32
mark-up *see murabaha*
Mastura, Michael O. 12
Mawdudi, Sayyed Abul A'la 40, 119
Mayer, C. 64
maysir 28, 30, 211
McCulloch, J. H. 87
Means, G. 159
Mecca 19, 32
Meckling, W. 84
Mian, Q. J. 39
Miller, M. H. 66
Ministry of Finance and National
    Economy (MOFNE), Bahrain 233
Mints, L. W. 155
Mirakhor, A. 3, 46, 80, 85, 90, 94, 98,
    101, 108, 114, 115, 117, 131, 151,
    170
Mirrlees, J. 87
Mit Ghamr Savings Banks 5–6
Mizen, P. D. 118
Modigliani, F. 66
moral hazard 73, 78–9, 86, 151, 162,
    167, 242
Morton, P. 157
mudaraba
  basic features 27, 40–42, 44–5,
    76–8

certificates and companies 110–11,
116
defined 3–4, 27, 40–41, 42, 110
examples in medieval banking 202–3,
207
guarantees 44, 77
importance in Islamic banking 45,
102, 111, 133–4, 135, 142, 143,
146, 177, 229
in Islamic insurance 214, 215, 217–19
origins 4, 40, 41, 91–2
problems 78–9, 82, 116, 142, 166
profit and loss sharing 41, 42, 44–5,
48, 61, 77–8, 90–91, 166, 172
restricted and unrestricted 41, 44, 172,
220, 244
two-tiered arrangement 43–5, 48–9,
78, 90, 98, 166
mudarib 4, 41, 42, 44, 45, 219, 244
Mudawi, A. B. Y. 105, 118
Muir, Sir William 32
Munn, G. G. 2
muqarada 59-60, 118
murabaha
basic features 52–5, 139
collateral 86, 153
criticisms by Islamic scholars 114,
153–5, 177
deferred payment 52, 53, 139, 146
importance in Islamic financing 91,
102–3, 114, 130, 133–4, 135,
142, 146, 156, 174, 177
legality 53, 55, 139, 154
mark-up and profit 52–3, 114,
140–41, 157
trade finance 52, 141, 142, 143, 155,
243
Murvat, S. K. 108
musharaka
basic features 4, 27, 42–3, 49–51, 107
diminishing participation 43, 51, 58,
146, 230
in Islamic financing 49–51, 58, 105–7,
111, 134, 135, 142, 143, 151,
153, 177, 230
management 82, 84, 107, 166
profit and loss sharing 4, 43, 49, 61,
105–7, 166, 177, 230
termination 49, 51
Muslehuddin, M. 213, 239

Muslim 17, 18, 19–20, 119, 163–6,
231–2
Muslim Community Cooperative (Aust)
(MCCA) 144, 145, 146, 149
Mustafa Amira 100
mutual funds
general 80–81, 87, 220–21
Islamic 59, 98, 110, 220–24, 244
muzarah/musaqah 51–2, 103

Naqvi, S. N. H. 91, 109
Nasser Social Bank 5, 6
Nelson, Benjamin 186, 188, 204, 205,
209, 210
Neusner, Jacob 185
Nienhaus, V. 131
Noonan, John T. 209
Nyazee, Imran Ahsan Khan 27, 42

Oechsler, Walter 163
oil wealth 7, 12
Organization of Islamic Countries (OIC)
Islamic Fiqh Academy 7, 32, 238

Pakistan 1, 6, 14, 16, 23, 39, 55, 88,
107–17, 120, 131–2, 133, 157, 171,
229
Partnerships
in Islamic law 27, 40, 60–61, 201
types of 4, 27–8, 33, 102, 107, 166
Patinkin, D. 186
Pemberton, Sir Robin Leigh 148
Philippine Amanah Bank (PAB) 12
Pilgrims Management and Fund Board
(Tabung Haji) 6, 126, 128, 138
Planisek, S. L. 150
Presidency of Islamic Researches 35
Presley, J. R. 32, 39, 46
Prime Bank Limited (PBL) 141, 142
principal–agent theory 73, 86, 87,
159–60, 162–3, 167–8
profit and loss sharing 1, 3, 4, 14, 39, 40,
60–61, 77–8, 79, 81, 83, 94, 105–7,
108, 114, 115, 116, 128, 152, 156,
163, 166, 173–4, 215, 217, 219,
231, 244
project finance 58, 152, 227–31
property rights 90, 108, 192, 194
Prophet Muhammad (pbuh) 3, 4, 16, 17,
19, 20, 21, 22, 24, 25, 28, 35, 36, 38

public finance 99–100, 103, 115, 118, 132, 150–51, 242
Pyle, D. H. 87

Qadir, Ghulam 153, 177
qard hasan 59, 111, 146, 150
Qatar 25, 227
Qur'an *see* Holy Qur'an
Qureshi, Anwar Iqbal 40, 119

Rabinovich, L. 191
Rahman, Fazlur G. 36, 60, 206
Rahman, Yahia Abdul 53
Rangaswami, K. 185
Raviv, A. 73
Ray, G H. 179, 182
Rayner, S. E. 60
Razi, Muhammad Fakr al-Din 37
religious supervisory board, *see shari'a* adviser/supervisory board
riba
  and usury 2–3, 29, 35, 37, 194
  defined 2–3, 29, 34–5, 103, 115
  distinguished from mark-up 52–3, 57, 114, 154, 157, 178
  prohibition 28–9, 34–7, 89–91, 109, 194, 196–7
  reasons for prohibition 37–8, 89, 194
  revisionist views 2, 36–7
  risk-taking 39, 40, 108, 154
Rida, Muhammad Rashid 37
Rippin, A. 60
Roll, E. 189
Rosly, Saiful Azhar 140, 157
Ross, S. 87
Russell, Bertrand 190

Saeed, A. 34, 60, 61, 149, 183
Sahnun, 'Abd al-Salam ibn Sa'id ibn Habib al-Tanukhi 61
Samad, Abdus 138
Sarker, M. A. A. 141, 142, 167
Saudi Arabia 6, 7, 11, 12, 14, 24, 39, 120, 127, 133, 157, 214
savings accounts 5–6, 47–8, 127, 128, 129, 143
Schacht, J. 33, 34, 197, 200
Scheinkman, J. A. 189, 193
Schoorman, F. D. 160
Schreyogg, Georg 163

Schumpeter, J. A. 90
Sessions, J. 32, 46
Shah, Hazoor A. 109
Shah, Syed Yaqub 206
Shamil Bank of Bahrain 11, 171
shari'a 16, 22, 24–6, 38–9
  see also Islamic law
shari'a adviser/supervisory board
  auditing 181, 182, 184
  composition 30, 133, 147, 168
  duties 158, 179–80
  for *takaful* insurance 211
  for unit trusts 223–4
  importance for Islamic banks 105, 168, 170, 183, 245
Shaw, E. S. 65
Shi'ism 23, 33
Siddiqi, M. N. 30, 90, 91, 95, 117, 128, 156, 239
Siddiqi, Naiem 40, 119
Siddiqui, S. H. 40
Smircich, L. 163
Smith, C. W. Jr 87, 162,
Social Investment Bank Limited (SIBL) 142
Spiegel, H. W. 208
State Bank of Pakistan 111, 113, 153, 154
Stigler, G. J. 210
Stiglitz, J. E. 67, 84, 87
Su'ud, M Abu 3, 117
Sudan 1, 14, 39, 82, 88, 104–7, 126, 131, 133, 214
Sudanese Islamic Bank 104, 105, 107
sunna 3, 20, 22, 24, 29, 36, 41, 109
Sunni Muslims 23–4, 33
Swank, Job 65
Switzerland 1, 12, 133, 227
Syria 6, 23

takaful see Islamic insurance
Tawney, R. H. 32, 190, 193, 203, 207
Taylor, T. W. 210
The International Investor (TII) 222, 224, 226–7, 239
Thomson, J. A. K. 192
Tomkins, C. R. 179, 182
Trever, Albert 209
Turkey 6, 23, 231, 232

UBS Switzerland 224, 237
umma 17, 166, 170
unit trusts *see* mutual funds
United Arab Emirates (UAE) 11, 120,
    227, 238
United Kingdom 1, 14, 121, 220, 226,
    228, 233, 236, 239, 245
United States 1, 121, 222, 226, 227
Usmani, Justice Muhammad Taqi 58
usury laws 2, 39, 185, 205, 206, 210
usury
    Christian prohibition 89, 187–90,
        190–93, 203, 204, 207
    lifting of prohibition 203–6, 207–8,
        210, 244
    meaning 2, 35, 185, 186–7, 188, 193
    methods of avoidance 197–203, 207,
        209
    treatment of usurers 189, 193, 195–6,
        208
Uzair, M. 40, 90

Vermaat, A. J. 161

Vogel, F. E. 33

Wachter, H. 163
Wahib, R. B. 213, 219, 239
Warner, J. 162
Watt, M. W. 32
Weber, Max 204, 207
Weiss, A. 67
Williamson, O. E. 66
Williamson, S. D. 73, 75
Wilson, R. 5, 53, 118, 156, 233, 236
Woelfel, C. J. 2

Yasin, Norhashimah Mohd 49, 55, 139
Yasseri, A. 102

zakat
    collection by Islamic banks 29–30,
        147, 179, 181
    religious duty 19–20, 29–30, 93
Zaman, S. M. Hasanuz 154, 156, 177
Zweigert, K. 24, 33